Defenses Against
the Dark Arts

Politics, Literature, and Film

Series Editor: Lee Trepanier, Samford University

The Politics, Literature Film series is an interdisciplinary examination of the intersection of politics with literature and/or film. The series is receptive to works that use a variety of methodological approaches, focus on any period from antiquity to the present, and situate their analysis in national, comparative, or global contexts. Politics, Literature, & Film seeks to be truly interdisciplinary by including authors from all the social sciences and humanities, such as political science, sociology, psychology, literature, philosophy, history, religious studies, and law. The series is open to both American and non-American literature and film. By putting forth bold and innovative ideas that appeal to a broad range of interests, the series aims to enrich our conversations about literature, film, and their relationship to politics.

Advisory Board
Richard Avaramenko, University of Wisconsin-Madison
Linda Beail, Point Loma Nazarene University
Claudia Franziska Brühwiler, University of St. Gallen
Timothy Burns, Baylor University
Paul A. Cantor, University of Virginia
Joshua Foa Dienstag, University of California at Los Angeles
Lilly Goren, Carroll University
Natalie Taylor, Skidmore College
Ann Ward, University of Regina
Catherine Heldt Zuckert, University of Notre Dame

Recent Titles
Defenses Against the Dark Arts: The Political Education of Harry Potter and His Friends by John S. Nelson
Between Science and Society: Charting the Space of Science Fiction by Douglas A. Van Belle
Pedagogic Encounters: Mastre and Disciple in the American Novel after the 1980s by Aristi Trendel
The Politics of Twin Peaks edited by Amanda DiPaolo and James Clark Gillies
AIDS-Trauma and Politics: American Literature and the Search for a Witness by Aimee Pozorski
The American Road Trip and Political Thought by Susan McWilliams Barndt
Baudelaire Contra Benjamin: A Critique of Politicized Aesthetics and Cultural Marxism by Beibei Guan and Wayne Cristaudo
Updike and Politics: New Considerations, edited by Matthew Shipe and Scott Dill
Lights, Camera, Execution! Cinematic Portrayals of Capital Punishment by Helen J. Knowles, Bruce E. Altschuler, and Jaclyn Schildkraut
Possibility's Parents: Stories at the End of Liberalism by Margaret Seyford Hrezo and Nicolas Pappas

Defenses Against the Dark Arts

The Political Education of Harry Potter and His Friends

John S. Nelson

LEXINGTON BOOKS

Lanham • Boulder • New York • London

Published by Lexington Books
An imprint of The Rowman & Littlefield Publishing Group, Inc.
4501 Forbes Boulevard, Suite 200, Lanham, Maryland 20706
www.rowman.com

6 Tinworth Street, London SE11 5AL, United Kingdom

British Library Cataloguing in Publication Information Available

Library of Congress Control Number: 2020949548

ISBN: 978-1-4985-9260-4 (cloth : alk. paper)
ISBN: 978-1-4985-9261-1 (electronic)

*For Anna and Aaron
and Samantha and Josie:
Are there greater privileges or pleasures
than sharing again the great books of childhood?*

Contents

List of Tables

Introduction

Political Education for Dark Times

For decades, books and films on Harry Potter and his friends have dominated our early education in politics.[1] Harry Potter's friends include tweens, teens, and adults the world over. At this writing, Harry's books have sold more than half-a-billion copies. These rival or exceed the sales for Dr. Seuss, Stephen King, and Louis L'Amour—among my favorites, because all brim with implicit political theory.[2] In its first quarter-century, the Potter franchise of books, films, toys, parks, regalia, and such has enjoyed tens of billions of dollars in sales. Hence, Potter books position themselves well to teach politics to people at early stages in life, when lessons can be highly influential and enduring. This seems intended by author J. K. Rowling, for politics are central also to her later novels for adults. But make no mistake: many of Harry's readers *are* adults, and the Potter books mark Rowling as one of the few writers whose signal works appeal greatly to children *and* adults.

This political education is more historical and institutional than might be implied by the existentialist politics of death, identity, and maturation that also permeate the Potter series. It's more diverse and detailed than fantasy's generic politics of power. It's also more personal and practical than many theories of politics aspire to be. The book at hand highlights some of what we can join Harry and his friends in learning about politics and personal action in our times.

In the Potter series, Rowling uses the flexibility of ingenious fantasy inventions to weave engaging episodes full of provocative politics. These are politics that a reader can expect to face in coming years, because they are persistent politics already with us. Especially impressive are the specific, practical defenses against debilitating politics that the Potter books explore. Often these defenses appear as spells, potions, and other magical devices. They get suggestive names, instructive explanations, and enticing demonstrations.

1

Together they provide smart, memorable introductions to many of the politics that we currently practice.

PLACES FOR POLITICS

What precisely are the politics in the Potter series? Answering in a single sentence is a hazardous exercise. Potter politics are so varied that the whole of this book manages only initial characterizations, which surely remain partial and debatable. As a political theorist, I've learned from the likes of Ludwig Wittgenstein and John Gunnell not to essentialize or homogenize our politics into "the political" as a singular, timeless, universal sector of action.[3] Nonetheless, we need a good place to start. Let it be the overarching form of the Potter books as a popular genre.

Taken in parts, the Potter series includes two epic quests, one epic odyssey, several detective tales, a war story, the sort of political horror story we call a dystopia, several other horror stories, and a time-travel tale. But overall, it's a fantasy that features magic and many turns into horror. Thus we may read it as "dark fantasy." This attunes Potter politics to the generic fascination of popular fantasy with power and performance. In general, we may say, Potter *politics* are *projects of power and performance* as *arts of community*. The Potter books portray ours as dark times in important part because fascist and authoritarian-unto-totalitarian politics corrupt defensible practices of power and community. To resist these perversions, Harry and his friends learn potent politics of care, ecology, liberation, love, joy, perfection, and folly.

So where exactly are these politics in the Potter saga? Often they keep company with its literary virtues. By the standards of best sellers, the Potter characters, creatures, and settings are vivid, inventive, and teeming symbolically with politics. They evoke developments and choices that shape our situations for action. Potter scenes and plots contribute too. Even Potter naming and wordplay snap with political implications. Overall the Potter saga pursues four main angles on our politics—exploring them as ideologies, movements, philosophies, and especially styles.

Political ideologies appear primarily in details about Potter institutions. These include the many offices in the Ministry of Magic, Gringotts Bank, Azkaban Prison, international codes and conventions, St. Mungo's Hospital for Magical Maladies and Injuries, the *Daily Prophet* and *The Quibbler*, as well as wizard games and schools, especially the Hogwarts School of Witchcraft and Wizardry. Thus the liberal regime of Hogwarts School under Albus Dumbledore interacts with the conservative unto authoritarian regimes of the Ministry of Magic under Cornelius Fudge and Rufus Scrimgeour. Then fascist Death Eaters under Lord Voldemort puppeteer the

Ministry, turning it toward totalitarianism resisted by the republican Order of the Phoenix, Dumbledore's Army of rebellious students at Hogwarts, and *Potterwatch* as a pirate-radio station. The Potter series can be read to recommend "republican" and "liberal" politics, yet in European, lower-case senses rather than American meanings associated with the Republican and Democratic Parties.

Among fantasies accessible to children, Potter novels are nearly unique in giving specific attention to an imaginary national government that closely resembles current state institutions in advanced industrial societies. This Ministry of Magic is crucial for Potter events and politics. Yet politics beyond the Ministry are ideological too. Hogwarts enacts liberalism. St. Mungo's Hospital and the Knight Bus provide socialist services. Azkaban Prison is an authoritarian jail. Even so, the Potter saga decenters state institutions to highlight cultural and personal politics in everyday lives. Accordingly it attends most to our political movements, styles, and philosophies.

In Pottery, political movements appear more in characters and creatures than institutions. Potter books show Hermione Granger as a feminist and house-elves as housewives to dramatize tensions between movements for women's liberation and some of their would-be beneficiaries. The magical animals and animated plants embody several variants of environmentalism. These enable Potter books to personalize green politics without stripping nonhuman creatures of radical otherness. Acromantulas, centaurs, dementors, giants, goblins, leprechauns, merpeople, trolls, veela, and the like spotlight our specism. Muggles (non-magical humans), squibs (non-magical offsprings of mages), pure-bloods, half-bloods, plus such staples of horror as ghosts, ghouls, vampires, and zombies help the Potter books examine nativism and racism. (On the other hand, Potter takes on nationalism rely more on such institutions as sports, schools, and newspapers.) Populism gets satirized and theorized through the self-celebration of Gilderoy Lockhart in Book 2, the cleansing of doxies from a virulently elitist Black House in the fifth volume, and the momentary removal of garden gnomes from an eminently populist Burrow of Weasleys in Book 6. Likewise anarchism receives a smart spin from "foolish" agents of chaos such as the Weasley twins, Fred and George, as well as Peeves, the poltergeist at Hogwarts School.

A signal strength of the Potter books is discerning attention to personal styles of political action. Modern ideologies and postmodern movements typically appear partly in conventions of individual performance: postures, gestures, habits, phrases, standards, choices, assumptions, associates, manners, demeanors, tastes, questions, sensibilities, and so forth. There are distinctive styles of liberal action, socialist behavior, and conservative conduct. Nationalist and populist styles have been prominent in election campaigns even when nationalist and populist policies have not. At times, environmentalists and feminists promote changes in laws less vigorously than changes in lifestyles: recycle, share childcare, curb litter, trade house-hold chores, eat local food, and so on. Thus politics that readily form ideolo-gies or movements for us also form personal styles of performance as well, and these styles are frequently where politics surface in our ordinary lives. *Harry Potter* is particularly attuned to politics in our characteristic modes of everyday conduct.

Since the onset of the modern state, political theory has neglected most styles in favor of ideologies and movements. Nor has it shown much inter-est in other forms of political action, such as stances and stands, utopias and dystopias, or epics and satires.[4] This is unhappy because many kinds of politics prominent in our times have yet to be ideologized effectively, if at all. Current styles such as bureaucratism, conformism, elitism, idealism, ironism, patronism, perfectionism, existentialism, realism, and republicanism evidence little drive or aptitude for ideological formulations, and seldom do these styles seek to inform self-conscious movements. Yet citizens in elec-tronic democracies have far more opportunities to observe and participate in personal styles than in public policies, government elections, international organizations, or the other forms of politics that dominate political science and political theory.[5] A glory of the Potter novels is their examination of the properties and possibilities of political styles neglected by our news and scholarship, especially political styles in the everyday lives of teens and young adults.

Engaging these many aspects of current politics, the Potter novels nonethe-less manage as well to engage many philosophical topics important for poli-tics. The first two books contribute to epistemic debates of naturalism versus conventionalism and objectivism versus perspectivism. Later books ponder dynamics of time and tradition. The Potter novels address complications of violence, remorse, and forgiveness. Issues of identity, memory, prediction, and truth suffuse the Potter saga. So do long-standing perplexities of death, freedom, love, and responsibility.

Regular readers, let alone litterateurs and theorists, might assume that there are general, in-principle, almost automatic advantages of novels over movie versions when probing politics. This isn't my experience. Plenty of novels far surpass the movies made from them, but the reverse is true too.[6] With *Harry Potter*, the novels are the key resources for political analysis. Politics in the Potter books are enormously more developed, diverse, and instructive than politics in the Potter films, skillful as those might be in comparison to other films mainly for children and teens. Even at two-plus hours a film, along with an extra film to include plot convolutions of the last novel, the movies (must) omit so many scenes and subplots that the politics suffer markedly.

SYMBOLS FOR POLITICS

It's easy for even the best of commentators to skate past political intricacies of the Potter volumes. Reading more for characters and stories, Harry's fans are apt to pick up only at times on the myriad institutions, principles, styles, strategies, and symbols that give the Potter saga a political drive categorically beyond most other fantasies, especially for young people. Critics of cinema and literature are more schooled in assessing aspects other than politics. Thus books and essays to date target aesthetic, moral, and mythic dimensions of *Harry Potter*.[7] Their specific political analysis is peripheral, and they translate into other registers most of the political details.

The many other projects of the Potter series are plenty adventurous in themselves. They justify comparing Potter themes to similar concerns in longer-standing classics for people young and old. These moves can be highly instructive, and so they get ample attention from scholars. I enjoy such works just as much as the next Potter enthusiast. What sets the Potter volumes apart, though, is their intense scrutiny of politics in our world. Potter books emphasize the government institutions, political styles, campaign strategies, public policies, media machinations, tactical gambits, world-historical events, and everyday complications that comprise political practices in our lives. These topics and motifs merit careful consideration to see what Harry and his friends can be learning about politics that keep emerging in our times, dark and difficult as they may be.

Some of the Potter politics are overt, literal, and eminently historical. For example, the Potter books allude several times to the Salem witch trials at the end of the seventeenth century in North America. Lately the Pottermore website and the film prequels on *Fantastic Beasts* that begin with Newt Scamander in the United States are developing aspects of this link in detail.

More of the Potter politics are allegorical. They provide simple, somewhat regimented, but still figural links between Potter particulars and historical specifics. By allegory, a Potter detail signals an individual event, person, institution, invention, or other element familiar from politics recently in the headlines or from politics in an earlier period. Thus the Potter backstory invites us to see Gellert Grindelwald—who's eventually defeated by his former friend Albus Dumbledore in a Continental confrontation in 1945—as a riff on Hitler and Nazi Germany. The Potter prequels on *Fantastic Beasts* elaborate on this, casting Johnny Depp as a trickster version of *der Führer*. Such allegorical politics of historical characters and occurrences inform some commentaries on how the Potter books teach history, international relations, and the like.

To be specific or potent, however, political symbolism need not be "allegorical" in this strict sense, with the one-to-one equations of George Orwell's

Animal Farm.[8] There Napoleon the pig just *is* Josef Stalin, and him only. Snowball the pig simply *is* Leon Trotsky, exclusively. And their uprising on the Animal Farm symbolically *is* the Russian Revolution that begets the Union of Soviet Socialist Republics. J. R. R. Tolkien's political connections are seldom like that, and neither are Rowling's. Their ties to historical politics are looser but also richer: not the one-to-one of strict allegory but the many-to-many links of symbolism in a larger sense.[9]

Multiple, flexible connections let each symbolic particular ramify in many directions. In the Potter series, Rowling pursues far more detailed politics of pressing importance in the present than do any works of literature I know aimed principally at children, tweens, or teens. (I say a little more on this in the conclusion.) Rowling uses the flexibility of ingenious fantasy inventions to weave an engaging story full of diverse and provocative politics. These are politics that her readers can expect to face in coming years, because they are politics already with us.

Among the many earlier books on Pottery, Bethany Barratt's about *The Politics of Harry Potter* is the most salient for this one. Barratt predicates her analysis on a primacy of authority for politics, treating authority as legitimate power in a general sense not differentiated by kinds of politics or theories.[10] On this basis, she considers what Potter events and institutions suggest for several concerns of current politics. Prominent among these are justice and punishment; racism, resistance, tolerance, and human rights; plus war, terrorism, intelligence, and the garrison state. For college instruction, the Barratt book fits a topical course that introduces students to headline politics, and it helps a lot. Here I've been writing to complement the Barratt approach by examining the overarching arguments and theories that emerge for politics in *Harry Potter*.

Some Potter commentaries focus on treatments of historical events such as witch trials or world wars.[11] Here the interest is less in the methods of historical investigation or explanation by Harry and his friends—let alone the acuity of any historical allegories in Pottery—than in the kinds and accounts of politics that take shape for situations relevant to Harry and company in action. Other analyses address philosophical issues of ontology, epistemology, language, or meta-ethics in *Harry Potter*.[12] Such questions arise at times in this book, but the concerns here are mainly practical, more directed to political action. Still other works assess how *Harry Potter* relates to individual fields in the social and natural sciences, with specific kinds of Potter politics making good platforms for scholarly collections.[13] I've learned from these varied reflections on *Harry Potter*, and I hope that there come to be many more. Nonetheless the sheer wealth of politics in Pottery helps explain the surprisingly scant overlap of earlier takes on the Potter saga with this present sketch of its political education for Harry and his friends.

The concern here is for politics of the Potter series rather than politics of J. K. Rowling. As a global celebrity, sometime activist, and subject of many interviews, Rowling as a political figure attracts lots of controversy.[14] Fairness to Rowling, her critics, and her supporters requires more than occasional comments to address the resulting debates—let alone relate them to Potter texts. But detailed attention to Rowling's personal politics would hijack or at least distract from the current project of spotting politics in the Potter books themselves. Much the same holds for the fascinating dynamics of Potter fandom, which are generating their own body of scholarship.[15] Instead the analysis at hand features the politics taught in Potter books to Harry and his friends.

STORIES FOR POLITICS

Yet to appreciate Potter politics adequately is not just to notice or analyze them; it's to learn from them—for action in politics. At times, this means reading as though Rowling were theorizing politics. But more often, it means treating Pottery as a political mythos: a network of recurrent characters, settings, and events. Myths are symbolic stories, where the details mean more than they say literally. Why take myths as theories, or treat stories as politics? Why not study political realities directly, in themselves? Aside from histories and documentaries, some people dismiss stories, films, and fiction as not-fact, with politics imaginary rather than real. If Rowling knows about politics, shouldn't we prefer reports or interviews to fantasies from her? And isn't it especially dubious to learn politics from fantasies in important part for children?[16]

Both theorists and storytellers describe and pattern our world. Political theorists advance reasons and evidence to explain political patterns, while storytellers use settings and characters to evoke political actions. Of course, stories could offer ideas and evidence that combine logically into theories, and some children's literature can address "adult politics" in detail. Published for children by L. Frank Baum, *The Wizard of Oz* is a fantasy take on American populism late in the nineteenth century.[17] Unlike Rowling, Baum wrote in the *Animal Farm* mode of allegory, with one-to-one mapping of story elements to historical figures. And Baum's take on populist politics suits satirical sniping better than theoretical insight. Rowling's evocation of our politics yields both. The insight stems mainly from her inventive attention to complicated characters. They act impressively in diverse situations, to reach beyond policy to ideology and other kinds of politics.

Yet most important, I argue, are the many specific, practical defenses against debilitating politics that Rowling has her characters explore in the

Potter books. Often advanced as spells, potions, and further magical artifacts, the defenses come with playful, suggestive names plus instructive demonstrations or explanations. To assess their complicated symbolism for politics can fill a book like this one, and its purpose is to spark an initial appreciation of their insight. Most Potter politics emerge in extensive networks of symbols that evoke political ideologies, movements, styles, and philosophies. My argument is that these politics contest and complement each other to provide a political education for action in our times of darkness and difficulty. That's why the pages at hand sketch several overarching patterns of Potter politics.

Pottery focuses the argument's first part. Its chapters evoke how Harry's world is ours and suffers dark times. They explain how our times are dark in urgently political ways. They explore how Potter magic features dark arts and defenses against them. Then they introduce the Potter confrontation between two branches of perfectionist politics that stem from Potter magic, with Harry's politics successfully opposing the politics of Voldemort and the Death Eaters.

Polity organizes the argument's second part. Each of its chapters analyzes three kinds of politics prominent in the Potter books. The ideologies are fascism, authoritarianism, liberalism, conservatism, and socialism. The movements include populism, nationalism, environmentalism, feminism, totalitarianism, and anarchism. And the styles are idealism, realism, conventionalism, conformism, existentialism, perspectivism, and republicanism. Chapters in this second set end with detailed attention to dark challenges and magical performances. Then the conclusion briefly addresses how exploring Pottery encourages personal platforms for political action in dark times.

I advance this argument through analysis of narrative and political structures of the Potter books, through exploration of their symbolism, and through attention to many examples. There's no way for the current examination or evidence to be exhaustive. Often I demonstrate patterns across several Potter books, and whenever possible, I probe Potter characters, creatures, devices, and performances in detail. Always the hope is to draw readers into their own considerations of Pottery implications for politics. Please feel encouraged to explore further cases and questions.

Many books on Potter politics differ in priorities from this one. They use Potter episodes to teach vividly what the authors take us to know already. Sometimes they test Potter elements against the current consensus in an academic field. What's the twentieth-century history behind what Rowling says about Gellert Grindelwald and Albus Dumbledore? (Of course, the *Fantastic Beasts* films offer more on this.) What's the psychology in how the Dursleys raise Harry with hostility and deprivation? How do hoary myths surface in the Potter story? How do Hermione's efforts to free house-elves compare to antislavery campaigns? The idea is that the Potter works are student-friendly resources for instruction, because they're age-appropriate fiction that puts important facts, concepts, and such into engaging characters, witty dialogue, and memorable events. So they do, and that's fine as far as it goes, but Potter politics develop our theories too.

From Potter books, we can learn politics that we don't already know. Thus we can *do* political theory by parsing Potter books, just as we can by analyzing Shakespeare plays, Homer poems, Dickens novels, or Locke treatises. What we learn can sometimes surpass anything that the author intended to include. Making good novels (or movies) focuses on creating characters, settings, and events more than articulating politics. Hence the overriding dynamics of narrative, drama, cinema, or poesis provide many particulars apart from any intended politics; then these details can evoke political implications beyond any plans or previous knowledge of the author.

Can, not *must*. To tell if Potter details actually do make patterns that augment our takes on politics, we need to probe them. Here I explain how the Potter series contributes in five ways. It enriches our accounts of ideologies and movements by detailing how they surface in everyday action of individuals. It clarifies some prominent politics better than before. It shows the current significance of some movements and styles neglected in recent theorizing. It spotlights several forms of political action neglected in recent theorizing. And it attunes our ideas about politics to our needs to face dark times.[18] So I sketch some contributions of each kind, hoping to spur more exploration of Potter insights for political action. As Albus Dumbledore urges Harry—and us as his friends, "let us step out into the night and pursue that flighty temptress, adventure" (VI.56).[19]

THANKS FOR HELP

But before we proceed, many blessings need many thanks. The stellar books by J. K. Rowling make her a great benefactor, for me and innumerable others, and I thank her for this.

Enormous gratitude goes to my family and students too. This book would not, *could* not, have happened without Connie Nelson; and it's hers as much as mine. Many students, too, have played with me in the fascinating fields of Pottery. I hope I've enriched their reading of Potter books and viewing of Potter films; I know they've enriched mine.

Thanks extend also to the wide range of Potter commentators, who've taught avid readers like me more than we might have imagined about the Potter saga. I thank the diverse theorists of politics who've reacted helpfully to preliminary versions of these Potter arguments for Lexington Books and several professional panels. And I thank the editors at Lexington

Books who've encouraged this project: Lee Trepanier, series editor for Politics, Literature, & Film; Assistant Editors Madhumitha Koduvalli and Bryndee Ryan; and especially Joseph C. Parry, senior acquisitions editor for Economics, International Relations, and Political Science. May we all whistle while we work!

NOTES

1. See Anthony Gierzynski with Kathryn Eddy, *Harry Potter and the Millennials* (Baltimore: Johns Hopkins University Press, 2013), 1–2.
2. On Stephen King, see John S. Nelson, "Horror, Crisis, and Control: Tales of Facing Evils," *The Politics of Horror*, ed. Damien K. Picariello (New York: Palgrave Macmillan, 2020), 17–31. On Louis L'Amour, see John S. Nelson, *Cowboy Politics* (Lanham, MD: Lexington Books, 2018), 13–203.
3. See Ludwig Wittgenstein, *Philosophical Investigations*, trans. G. E. M. Anscombe (New York: Macmillan, third edition, 1958). Also see John G. Gunnell, *Political Theory* (Cambridge, MA: Winthrop, 1979); John G. Gunnell, *Between Philosophy and Politics* (Amherst: University of Massachusetts Press, 1986); John G. Gunnell, *The Descent of Political Theory* (Chicago: University of Chicago Press, 1993); John G. Gunnell, *The Orders of Discourse* (Lanham, MD: Rowman and Littlefield, 1998). And see John S. Nelson, ed., *Tradition, Interpretation, and Science* (Albany: State University of New York Press, 1986).
4. See John S. Nelson, *Tropes of Politics* (Madison: University of Wisconsin Press, 1998), 205–30; John S. Nelson, *Politics in Popular Movies* (Boulder: Paradigm, 2015), 18–104.
5. See John S. Nelson, *Popular Cinema as Political Theory* (New York: Palgrave Macmillan, 2013), 1–16; Nelson, *Politics in Popular Movies*, 173–88.
6. *Contact* (1997), *Fight Club* (1999), *Forrest Gump* (1994), *Interview with the Vampire* (1994), *The Milagro Beanfield War* (1988), *The Prestige* (2006), *Wag the Dog* (1997), and many other movies are more potent and intelligent in their politics than are their literary inspirations, notwithstanding the literary and political merits of the novels. A different kind of comparison is clear in *Charlie Wilson's War* (2007): the focused politics of the film are subtler and smarter than the greater scope and complexity of politics in the long tome (of investigative journalism) that informs it. See Carl Sagan, *Contact* (New York: Pocket, 1985); Chuck Palahniuk, *Fight Club* (New York: Henry Holt, 1996); Winston Groom, *Forrest Gump* (New York: Simon and Schuster, 1986); Anne Rice, *Interview with the Vampire* (New York: Ballantine, 1976); John Nichols, *The Milagro Beanfield War* (New York: Ballantine, 1974); Christopher Priest, *The Prestige* (New York: Tom Doherty Associates, 1995); Larry Beinhart, *American Hero* (New York: Ballantine, 1993); George Crile, *Charlie Wilson's War* (New York: Grove Press, 2003).
7. See Giselle Liza Anatol, ed., *Reading Harry Potter* (Westport, CT: Praeger, 2003); Giselle Liza Anatol, ed., *Reading Harry Potter Again* (Santa Barbara: ABC-CLIO, 2009); Christopher E. Bell, ed., *Wizards vs. Muggles* (Jefferson, NC:

McFarland, 2016); John Granger, *Unlocking Harry Potter* (Wayne, PA: Zossima Press, 2007); Suman Gupta, *Re-Reading Harry Potter* (New York: Palgrave Macmillan, second edition, 2009); Elizabeth E. Heilman, ed., *Harry Potter's World* (New York: RoutledgeFalmer, 2003); Travis Prinzi, *Harry Potter & Imagination* (Hamden, CT: Winged Lion Press, 2008); Lana A. Whited, ed., *The Ivory Tower and Harry Potter* (Columbia: University of Missouri Press, 2002, 2004).

8. See George Orwell, *Animal Farm* (New York: New American Library, 1946).

9. Unfortunately some literary commentators confuse the matter by equating *allegory* with any sort of *symbolism*. Then there need not be a strict regimen of each literal detail corresponding to one and only one figure as referent. This is akin to the confusions introduced by literary theorists who equate *representation* with any old kind of *figuration* or *symbolism*—rather than respect it as *re-presentation*: one specific trope among many with other dynamics.

10. See Bethany Barratt, *The Politics of Harry Potter* (New York: Palgrave Macmillan, 2012), 5 and 9–25.

11. See Daniel H. Nexon and Iver B. Neumann, eds., *Harry Potter and International Relations* (Lanham, MD: Rowman and Littlefield, 2006); Nancy R. Reagin, ed., *Harry Potter and History* (New York: Wiley, 2011).

12. See John Granger, *Harry Potter's Bookshelf* (New York: Berkley Books, 2009); Travis Prinzi, ed., *Hog's Head Conversations* (Hamden, CT: Winged Lion Press, 2009); Colin Manlove, *The Order of Harry Potter* (Hamden, CT: Winged Lion Press, 2010).

13. See Neil Mulholland, *The Psychology of Harry Potter* (Dallas: BenBella Books, 2006); Jean Sims, ed., *The Sociology of Harry Potter* (Hamden, CT: Zossima Press, 2012); Mark Brake, *Science of Harry Potter* (New York: Racehorse Publishing, 2017).

14. See Cynthia Hallett and Peggy J. Huey, eds., *J. K. Rowling* (New York: Palgrave Macmillan, 2012).

15. See Melissa Anelli, *Harry, A History* (New York: Simon and Schuster, 2008); Valerie Estelle Frankel, *Harry Potter, Still Recruiting* (Hamden, CT: Zossima Press, 2012); Lisa Brenner, ed., *Playing Harry Potter* (Jefferson, NC: McFarland, 2015); Christopher E. Bell, ed., *From Here to Hogwarts* (Jefferson, NC: McFarland, 2016); Amanda Firestone and Leisa A. Clark, eds., *Harry Potter and Convergence Culture* (Jefferson, NC: McFarland, 2018); Valerie Estelle Frankel, *Fan Phenomena: Harry Potter* (Chicago: University of Chicago Press, 2019).

16. On learning politics from myths, literary fictions, and popular entertainments, see Nelson, *Popular Cinema as Political Theory*, 164–66.

17. See L. Frank Baum, *The Wizard of Oz* (New York: HarperCollins, 1899); *The Wizard of Oz* (1939); Henry M. Littlefield, *"The Wizard of Oz"* (n.d.): http://www .amphigory.com/oz.htm.

18. See Hannah Arendt, *Men in Dark Times* (New York: Harcourt, Brace and World, 1968); Roberto Vacca, *The Coming Dark Age*, trans. J. S. Whale (Garden City, NY: Doubleday, 1973); Robert L. Heilbroner, *An Inquiry into the Human Prospect* (New York: Norton, 1975); Jean Kellogg, *Dark Prophets of Hope* (Chicago: Loyola University Press, 1975); L. S. Stavrianos, *The Promise of the Coming Dark*

Age (San Francisco: W. H. Freeman, 1976); Jane Jacobs, *Dark Age Ahead* (New York: Random House, 2004); Elizabeth Kolbert, *The Sixth Extinction* (New York: Henry Holt, 2014); Naomi Oreskes and Erik M. Conway, *The Collapse of Western Civilization* (New York: Columbia University Press, 2014).

19. See J. K. Rowling, *Harry Potter* (New York: Scholastic Press, in seven volumes). I reference these parenthetically in the text, with Roman numerals for each book and Arabic numerals for pages: I. *Harry Potter and the Sorcerer's Stone*, 1997; II. *Harry Potter and the Chamber of Secrets*, 1999; III. *Harry Potter and the Prisoner of Azkaban*, 1999; IV. *Harry Potter and the Goblet of Fire*, 2000; V. *Harry Potter and the Order of the Phoenix*, 2003; VI. *Harry Potter and the Half-Blood Prince*, 2005; VII. *Harry Potter and the Deathly Hallows*, 2007. But let me use hereafter the British title of the first book (*Harry Potter and the Philosopher's Stone*), while allowing me American rather than British spellings (*defense* rather than *defence*) and words (*specialty*, not *speciality*).

Part 1

POTTERY

Chapter 1

Political Theories for Dark Times

In *Harry Potter and the Deathly Hallows*, J. K. Rowling suggests that children's stories should amuse but might also instruct. In the most lasting, we can find lessons for life. These can even include the adult challenges of politics. Rowling's dark, epic fantasy of *Harry Potter* excels at this. "If teaching life-lessons is one of the jobs books do," says Stephen King, "then the *Potter* novels teach some fine ones about how to behave under pressure."[1] In Potter books, the pressure comes from what Max Weber, a progenitor of political science, called "times of icy darkness and hardness."[2] Those were Weber's times, they are Harry's times, and they are ours. To Harry and his friends, both within the books and beyond, the Potter troubles and responses are educations in politics. They clarify what we should do in our times of darkness and difficulty.

POLITICS IS A PLURAL NOUN

There are many sorts of politics, so we treat the word as a plural noun. Our project is to learn about politics faced by Harry Potter. Politics make (and break) our homes in the world.[3] So politics are our community arrangements, particularly as pursued through communications. In the ancient Greek polis, which invented western politics, their first self-conscious practice and systematic study was rhetoric. Its (eventually republican) attention to speech-in-action-in-public is the well-spring for several sorts of politics prominent in the Potter books. Modern ideologies such as liberalism, socialism, and conservatism develop from republicanism. So do postmodern movements such as nationalism, populism, and feminism. Thus beginning with a definition from the republican-rhetorical tradition seems fitting. Yet Harry faces many other politics too.

Especially Harry and his friends face the darker takes on politics as *arts of excellence and power*. Many politics, including in republics, seek to direct or surpass other people, whether for their good or yours. In some politics, like authoritarianism and fascism, these aims predominate; in others, such as liberalism and socialism, they are merely prominent. Our crafts of community and communication often involve endeavors of excellence and power. These need not be wrong or evil, although they have been at times. But in success as well as failure, politics can harm as well as heal. To many people, therefore, politics seem risky and dark, if indispensable. In fact, this is the primary political lesson for Harry Potter and his friends:

POLITICS *ARE* THE DARK ARTS *AND* OUR DEFENSES AGAINST THEM

So suggest the ancient Sophists, modern Machiavellians, postmodern Nietzscheans, and more.[4] Friends and followers of Harry Potter join this company. As Rowling writes of Harry's cohort at Hogwarts, "The class everyone had really been looking forward to was Defense Against the Dark Arts" (I.134). In Potter parlance, dark arts are crafts for inflicting effects on others. These are "arts" in requiring advanced knowledge and practice to succeed at all, even as they repay refinement with reliability and experiment with discovery. They are "dark" because they "do unto others" without the others' initial awareness, or at least agreement, let alone direct benefit. The temptation is to say that dark arts are complicated, powerful ways to do wrong or impose harm. But we do well to realize that "wrongs" can be debatable, educational, justifiable, or redeemable. Especially Harry and his friends must learn that we need dark arts at times to do good. For *Harry Potter* and for politics, *dark* need not mean *evil*, although it can come close.

For a young witch or wizard, the dark arts signal adult power and respect. The damage they can do and the skill they can require mark an ascension to mature responsibility as a mage. For student mages, the dark arts sound mysterious, dangerous, and sexy. For good or ill, their effects can reach beyond family and friends to the larger world: just like the headline politics of offices, elections, movements, or revolutions. To face these responsibilities is to come of age.

In *Harry Potter*, of course, the dark arts are magical. In some literatures at the moment, magic alone is enough to mark deeds or powers as "dark." In DC Comics, the "Justice League Dark" features supernatural heroes such as John Constantine, Deadman, Madame Xanadu, and Zatanna Zatara. All have magical powers by contrast with the (merely) superhuman powers of Justice League members such as the Flash and Superman. Most Potter magic, however, is *not* exclusively or even distinctively "dark," in character or in use. Hence most Potter magic gets studied in courses like Charms, Runes, Arithmancy, Divination, and Transfiguration. Few of the magical animals or plants in Potter's world are categorically "dark" either. Boggarts, dementors, werewolves, and other horror creatures do get studied in Defense Against the Dark Arts (DADA). Still it's easy to imagine objections from Hermione Granger and Rubeus Hagrid—even Remus Lupin.

The Potter books themselves include good uses, aspects, and examples of almost every kind of magical creature, and they spot threats nearly everywhere too. Hogwarts's Herbology studies dangerous plants like Mandrakes, Devil's Snare, Venomous Tentacula, and Whomping Willows, while Care of Magical Creatures addresses dicey animals such as doxies, dragons, nifflers, and skrewts. Each *can* be good, but consider the havoc wreaked by a cute, affectionate niffler in Book 5 or in *Fantastic Beasts and Where to Find Them* (2017). Yes, "dark wizards" and "dark magic" mostly (try to) do evil in the Potter world, and this matters more for calling them "dark" than do any magical capacities to inflict awful harms. Yet defending against dark magic often necessitates knowing how dark creatures, spells, potions, or other contrivances can work. Then mages can stop harmful measures, turn them against their sources, or even redirect them for good. This justifies teaching some dark arts in a course on DADA, despite the title's hint that dark arts undo good, civilized magic. Then we can imagine Potter magic sometimes leaping—for good *and* ill—beyond the modern resources and "enlightened" sciences of the last several centuries.

For Potter magic and for politics, a better meaning of "dark" than "evil" or "harmful" is "complicated, troubled, and perilous," for the mage as well as the target. Potter magic solves problems that are fairly pat by means that are relatively tame. But it also tackles troubles that are horribly vexed by measures that are highly dangerous. DADA faces these troubles with moves that range from the ridiculous (III.123–40) to the drastic (II.101; VI.177–81). And so do politics.

Taught in Harry's fourth year of DADA, the Unforgivable Curses (IV.211–17, 659–63) are good examples. They overflow with persistent issues and current debates within politics. The Cruciatus Curse engages political concerns of violence and pain; it also puts Americans in mind of Bush-Cheney "rendition" to "black sites" for torture to elicit "actionable intelligence" or punish intractable enemies (IV.531; V.515, 544). Even Harry uses it to retaliate against Bellatrix Lestrange (V.810). The Imperius Curse enables the two Barty Crouches to dominate each other in turn as well as Mad-Eye Moody (IV.681–9). It lets Death Eaters puppeteer Pius Thicknesse as Minister of

Magic (VII.5, 208). Yet it helps Harry manipulate a Death Eater and a goblin
to take a Voldemort horcrux from Gringotts Bank (VII.528–32). These dark
dynamics of collaboration and coercion appear recurrently in our headlines,
while their Potter cases raise enduring concerns of freedom, identity, and
will. Of course, the Killing Curse (*Avada Kedavra!*) implicates a range of
controversies that attend troubles of assassinations, executions, weapons,
war, and vigilantism. In *Harry Potter*, even the worst, the vilest of dark arts
are significantly political.

Likewise in Harry's world and ours, even the best, the noblest of politics are significantly dark. For all their soaring idealism, Potter books are
insistently down-to-earth in their realist and other recognitions of darkness
in people's interactions. This is partly, but not only, because good defenses
against the dark arts depend on good knowledge of resources and techniques
for attack. So coming chapters probe both the idealism and the darkness for
diverse politics in *Harry Potter*.

At Hogwarts, therefore, DADA melds the allures of maturity, mystery, and
power. Still the student clamor for DADA comes also from a sense that the
survival of the students and their civilization might well depend on it. For
Harry and his friends, the Dark Lord Voldemort and his Death Eaters loom
malignantly over their lives. Just as their grandparents had learned firsthand
about Gellert Grindelwald's reign of terror in Europe, their parents had almost
succumbed to the Dark Lord's persecution and domination. Was Voldemort's
abrupt disappearance for good? Or even as Harry's cohort enters Hogwarts, is
the Dark Lord's unspeakable return already at hand? The signs are mounting,
and many symbolize horrendous developments all too evident for us.

DARK TIMES ARE ENDURING CONDITIONS
OF TERRIBLE TROUBLES

At the *Potter* mid-point, Dumbledore tells the international assembly at
Hogwarts for the Triwizard Tournament that "we are all facing dark and
difficult times" (IV.724).[5] Potter movies have Dumbledore declare dark
times a bit differently, but twice. *Harry Potter and the Goblet of Fire*
(2005) cuts directly from Triwizard people memorializing Cedric Diggory to
Dumbledore speaking privately to Harry in his dormitory. "Dark and difficult
times lie ahead. Soon we must all face the choice between what is right and
what is easy. Remember this," says Dumbledore to Harry, "you have friends
here; you are not alone."[6] Almost two years earlier, in *Harry Potter and
the Prisoner of Azkaban* (2004), Dumbledore welcomes Hogwarts students
to a new year at the school but warns of gathering darkness. After a choral
performance by students of the witches' warning of approaching trouble in

Macbeth, Dumbledore explains that dementors are guarding the grounds to intercept Azkaban escapee, Sirius Black. Dumbledore sees those dark creatures as harbingers of terrible troubles. "Dementors are vicious creatures. They will not distinguish between the one they hunt and the one who gets in their way. Therefore I must warn each and every one of you, give them no reason to harm you. It is not in the nature of a Dementor to be forgiving. But you know," he adds, "happiness can be found even in the darkest of times, if one only remembers to turn on the light."[7] Then he ignites a candle with a wave of his magical hand.[8]

Dark times challenge our survival politically, morally, culturally, even biologically. By themselves, the hard times of recession or even depression can feel less apocalyptic, except that economic troubles usually compound our darkest times. Many Potter troubles are specifically political: bureaucracy, ecological catastrophe, elitism, exploitation, nationalism, sexism, slavery, terrorism, torture, totalitarianism, and war. Some alternate histories and dystopias try to show how a hell we see or imagine someplace else (alien invasion, anarchy, degeneracy, depopulation, enemy victory, genocide, plague, or political nightmare) could happen *here*. Often the injunction is to see how it *is* happening here, *right now*, in all too many ways that we might try to ignore but *must* face. Add *Harry Potter* to this literary list.

In striking ways, Harry's dark times are ours. No pandemic, but as Shira Wolosky says, Harry's saga links to World War II, Nazism, and racism. It has "party hacks" who preside over "fraudulent courts" and an increasingly authoritarian government falling to a totalitarian regime. That includes a prisoner who "looks like a concentration camp victim," "an eye of surveillance," Gestapo-like abduction, hostage-taking of children and parents, training akin to "the Hitler youth [when] Voldemort takes over Hogwarts," confiscating private properties, plus "appeasement" of totalitarians.[9] Resistance faces official nonsense, government scapegoating, and citizen despair.

Harry and his supporters also face classism, nativism, specism, and corrupt institutions. The inept and debased Ministry of Magic (MOM) botches challenges big and small. The magical press makes these worse while succumbing to commercial interests and Ministry pressures. Even the education at Hogwarts School bows before Dolores Umbridge, Severus Snape, and the Carrows. Eventually the troubles reach from climate change to totalitarianism. But long before the climax, Rowling has exposed Harry's magical world *as* our political world, and Harry acts in recognition of this. By Book 5, Harry monitors "our" TV news, more than the *Daily Prophet*, for signs of Voldemort's machinations. Harry even discusses them with his magic-denying uncle. Then dementors attack Harry and his cousin in Little Whinging. Earlier barriers are breaking (V.37).

Persistent problems and recurrent crises mark dark times but do not suffice to make them. Dark times involve dreadful, intractable *troubles* that feed pervasive senses of imminent danger, awful injustice, and intense anxiety about what (if anything) we ordinary people should be doing. Such dread and anxiety are akin to terror more than fear, especially fear in its instrumental use by groups and governments. All modern governments rely on fear of punishments, as well as hope of rewards, to inform individual decisions on obeying laws. Modern markets depend on similar incentives, negative and positive. Fears put humanly apprehensible and actionable faces on our situations. Accordingly fears move us to coherent deeds. Terrors resist this. Often they present themselves as faceless, unfathomable, and disconcerting. Terrors freeze or make us frenetic. As *Harry Potter* shows with Voldemort, terrors may not even be (directly, readily, safely) nameable.

Dumbledore doesn't speak of Voldemort in the usual ways as "He-Who-Must-Not-Be-Named," "You-Know-Who," or even "the Dark Lord." Intending to terrorize, Voldemort wants it the usual way. Instead of mystifying this boogeyman, Dumbledore names Voldemort clearly, plainly, without bogus honorifics. Harry does the same, repeatedly resisting pressures of social conformity and intimidation. Dumbledore knew "Voldemort" as a Hogwarts student, and sometimes uses his boyhood name of Tom Riddle to demystify him further. To face Voldemort still more adequately, Dumbledore collects people's memories of Riddle then uses a Pensieve to share them vividly with Harry. This is a key part of Harry's political education in dark times.

To complete this training for the mythic hero to turn and face his longtime nemesis, the books have Harry confront one version of Voldemort after another. Before the last showdowns in Book 7, when Harry goes one-on-one against Voldemort at the height of his power, Harry gets lots of (dangerous) practice. It enables Harry to face and defeat fully that terrifying wizard. The earlier confrontations give Harry help, or they supply a warped and weakened Voldemort for Harry to resist. As an infant, Harry has his mother's love to defend him. Hidden under Quirinus Quirrell's turban in the first book, Voldemort is barely a shadow of his full self, so that Harry's touch burns unbearably into Quirrell and his lord's dark remnant. In Book 2, Riddle is still reforming from his diary when Harry's impulsive stab with a basilisk fang kills that horcrux and its rematerializing piece of Riddle's torn and perverted soul.

From Book 3 onward, Harry faces Voldemort indirectly in many nightmares and visions. These join the Pensieve memories in specifying Harry's understanding of Voldemort as a human foe. Books 3 and 6 offer many of these important moments but keep the two mages from facing off fully, bodily, in person. In the graveyard duel at the climax of Book 4, Harry fends off a newly resurrecting Voldemort, not yet at his most powerful, and Harry gets decisive help from his wand. This happens again when the wand disarms the Dark Lord early in Book 7, just as Voldemort has Harry dead-to-rights in flying (with decoys) from his boyhood home. And when Voldemort casts a curse to kill Harry during the Book 5's culmination in the MOM, Dumbledore arrives just in time to protect Harry and take over that duel.

STOPPING TERRIBLE TROUBLES
STARTS WITH FACING THEM

To act effectively in the face of even a sharp fear calls mainly for courage and rationality. Harry has plenty of both. So do friends of his such as the Weasleys, Hermione Granger, Neville Longbottom, Luna Lovegood, Rubeus Hagrid, Minerva McGonagall, Dumbledore, Sirius Black, Remus Lupin, and many others. If a fear isn't overwhelming, what can be done about it is often clear, even if the cost would be prohibitively high. This is because a fear presents to us a known nature and source. It gives us a humanly comprehensible face, since its source wants us to act in some ways rather than others. The fear aims exactly at steering our rational capacities for action.

But to act effectively in response to a terror is categorically more demanding. We cannot respond rationally to the terror without discerning a humanly actionable face for it. To do so, we must summon a courage that reaches beyond any risk assessment. This is the kind of surpassing courage often needed to turn our faces toward the terror as (initially) We-Know-Not-What. It's also the great bravery required to maintain our attention there, until we can figure out what the terror is as well as what we can do to defeat or diminish it. In Harry's world, this often involves DADA skills, to keep terrors at bay long enough to figure out how to face and defeat them. With loads of grit and practice, Harry and his magical friends also turn out to be effective on this front. Since *their* dark times of terrible troubles are largely *ours* too, we do well to learn from them as many of the dark arts of politics as we can. Enter instruction in DADA.

At Hogwarts, DADA instruction begins by acquainting students with dark creatures and spells. To defend against dangerous attacks and terrible troubles begins with discerning specific threats. It involves recognizing their natures and sources. Then it requires acting appropriately, accurately, and quickly. The mythic formula prominent in popular fantasy teaches the threatened figures to *turn-and-face* their troubles. In other words, to resist a terror is first to recognize it.

Professors at Hogwarts teach DADA in different ways, some (much!) better than others. In Harry's first year, the timid Quirrell attempts to rely mainly on hesitant, tedious lectures that seem to avoid any creature which terrifies him. In Harry's fifth year, Dolores Umbridge limits students to reading and copying a theory textbook in class. As with Quirrell, this seems mostly to involve dry descriptions and stilted illustrations, with questions and discussions discouraged. There might be a little more life in DADA during Harry's second year, but not much. Gilderoy Lockhart narrates, and uses students to enact, his (stolen) celebrity adventures in facing horror figures like banshees and vampires. "Wands away" seems to be the usual rule for students in these classes. This bores most students, and it keeps the young mages from practicing defensive responses to dark arts and creatures. Still the words, pictures, stories, and gestures can tell how to recognize some of the terrors and troubles that might await many students in the wider world. This might enable students to pass DADA examinations at the Ordinary Wizarding Levels, but it fails to ready young mages for defending themselves, let alone others, in dark and difficult times.

Fortunately student wands are "out" and active for practicing spells in Harry's other three years of DADA at Hogwarts. Thus Harry's third year of DADA is graced by Remus John Lupin. Before he's "outed" as a werewolf, to force his resignation from Hogwarts, Lupin makes DADA more informative, exciting, and thus effective for students. He even teaches Harry the patronus charm to repel dementors (III.233–51). In Harry's fourth year, DADA is taught in disguise by Barty Crouch Jr., a fanatical Death Eater who's thought to have died in Azkaban Prison. Junior impersonates Alastor "Mad-Eye" Moody, notorious as a gruff but all-time-great hunter of Death Eaters, who has seen better days before his recent retirement as an auror for the Department of Magical Law Enforcement. With Dumbledore's approval, "Moody" teaches Harry's class such advanced dark magic as the three Unforgivable Curses and how to defend against them (IV.209–27). And in Harry's sixth year, Severus Snape finally gets to teach DADA, his favorite subject. Snape's DADA enthusiasm and expertise might be lost on Harry, as his least favorite student, yet Harry learns DADA equivalents by the boatload from what turn out to be Snape's marginalia in the Potions textbook taught this year by Horace Slughorn. (More on such complications in a bit.)

For all their troubles, though, Harry's dark times are not some simple, undeniable fact. (Nor are ours.) We learn why Cornelius Fudge is motivated as Minister of Magic to stay blind to the insistent signs of Voldemort's return (V.93–4). But even without such personal cowardice or calculation, many wizards, witches, and muggles largely miss *years* of the country's descent into darkness—as Harry and his friends experience it. Some people take children's fantasies to be simple unto simplistic: showing the heroic triumph of pure Good over sheer Evil. Likewise talk of dark times might seem simple and strictly objective, yet Potter politics are more sophisticated. In part, this is because they attend acutely and empathetically to differences in perspective.

Thus the Potter books teach us that our perspectives help constitute our situations for political action. This holds for times of routine or crisis, and it reaches from ages of gold to periods of darkness.

DARK TIMES ARE WHEN WE FACE THEM

In Potter politics, perspectives matter. For Harry, family is empowering; for Ron, it's stifling. For Harry, celebrity is annoying; for Ron, it's thrilling. Hermione wants authoritative truths; Luna Lovegood is comfortable with daring dissents. Potter episodes show the validities, advantages, and downsides of these contrasting perspectives (and many others). Potter novels show how these points of view interact to shape various conditions and experiences in the world that Potter characters mostly share with each other (and us too). Failing (let alone refusing) to face constellations of troubles does not keep them from powerful, pervasive effects, and it might even compound them. Still the specific dynamics of dark times operate only when we face them.

Even the most terrible of troubles depend in important part on *how* people face them. For Dumbledore, Grindelwald's fascism is a perversion of their youthful philosophizing on wizard domination for the Greater Good; and Dumbledore sees this face shadowed further by guilt over their roles in the death of Dumbledore's sister, Ariana (VII.357–9). Together Dumbledore and Harry also face Voldemort in Pensieve memories of Tom Riddle going beyond bad, in Snape's spying on the Dark Lord, and in Harry's encounters with Voldemort in person or vision. Yet a sense of strong similarities between Grindelwald's fascist regime and Voldemort's initial reign of terror encourages Dumbledore, as a defender of liberal democracy, to face Voldemort as a totalitarian leader. Harry, on the other hand, acts more as a hardboiled detective who faces a serial killer obsessed with young Harry himself. And Snape faces Voldemort as the charismatic Master of Dark Magic who could not be bothered to spare Snape's beloved, even though Snape had been a most loyal and talented lieutenant.

As we'll soon be seeing, these and other faces for Voldemort converge on a perversion of perfectionist politics similar to the Nazi caricature of Friedrich Nietzsche's *Übermensch*. This is not an accident. As the Potter books suggest, a sophisticated appreciation of perspectives is not a bar to truth, agreement, or action; instead it's a way to face and learn from individual differences. Moreover it's a way to understand how individuals can act as though their times differ radically.

Dark times are perspectival too. Conditions for Cornelius Fudge can differ from settings for Albus Dumbledore, and their perspectives are important aspects of this. So Fudge can run a MOM for normal times, with no Dark

Lord on the horizon, even as Dumbledore can run a school of magic for dark times, when Voldemort has begun his comeback. Measured by ciock or calendar, these different political times can be simultaneous. Measured by Rowling's storytelling, they can clash, and readers can find it better (as well as easier) to take Dumbledore's perspective. Yet Books 4 and 5 give readers decent platforms for perceiving normal times as presented by Fudge, the *Daily Prophet*, Seamus Finnigan, and others.

Even in fantasies, dark times are not simply, unarguably given. Rather they are when we face them. The Potter saga works hard to provide the multiple perspectives nearly definitional for politics. This enables us readers to explore how perceiving action situations typically matter even more than conceiving action strategies. As Norman O. Brown explained, the key question for politics can be: "What time is it?"[10] For us, the Potter answer is: "A dark time, but far from hopeless." The Potter saga can help readers face their own times this way, and countenance their political resources accordingly.

NOTES

1. Stephen King, "Review of *Harry Potter and the Order of the Phoenix*," *Entertainment Weekly* (July 11, 2003): http://www.ew.com/ew/static/pdf/2007/03/stephenking.pdf.

2. Max Weber, "Politics as a Vocation," *From Max Weber*, eds. and trans. H. H. Gerth and C. Wright Mills (New York: Oxford University Press, 1946), 77–128 on 128.

3. See John G. Gunnell, *Political Philosophy and Time* (Middletown, CT: Wesleyan University Press, 1968), 40.

4. See John S. Nelson, "Political Theory as Political Rhetoric," *What Should Political Theory Be Now?* ed. John S. Nelson (Albany: State University of New York Press, 1983), 169–240.

5. Here "Dumbledore" names Albus, unless I specify his brother Aberforth. Later I argue that Dumbledore epitomizes liberal politics—as off-shoots that develop modern individuality and rationality in the pursuit of such republican priorities as liberty, respect, and civility.

6. *Harry Potter and the Goblet of Fire*, directed by Mike Newell (2005; Burbank, CA: Warner Home Video, 2006), DVD.

7. *Harry Potter and the Prisoner of Azkaban*, directed by Alfonso Cuarón (2004; Burbank, CA: Warner Home Video, 2004), DVD.

8. Nevertheless in a ruefully humorous touch missing from the book, the third film's seasonal bluebirds of happiness at Hogwarts suffer terminal troubles throughout.

9. Shira Wolosky, *The Riddles of Harry Potter* (New York: Palgrave Macmillan, 2010), 34–37.

10. See Norman O. Brown, *Closing Time* (New York: Random House, 1973).

Chapter 2

Dark Arts for Dark Times

By genre, fantasies expect dark times to come from dark arts, at least in important part. And by convention, fantasies are fascinated with the possibility that dark times return the favor by making dark arts more than welcome, if only to fight fire with fire. All this helps explain the genre's abiding problematics of *power* in the singular. Fantasies generically configure power as the source, process, or product of dark arts. Fantasies thus define most kinds of power, and so defend most sorts of politics, by the principle that dark times demand dark arts. This disposition is especially strong in fantasies for children, tweens, and teens, which usually caution that power corrupts—save with the wisest of rulers. Before the present century, this also characterized most "science fantasies," as we might term the science fictions that (used to) idolize science—and so try to "cut the politics."[1] Fortunately this has not kept the genre from lots of political theorizing.

DARK ARTS ARE HOW WE USE THEM

The Potter difference is to develop the usual warning against absolutized or singularized power within diverse contexts of authoritarian, bureaucratic, fascist, nationalist, totalitarian, and other politics taken in these democratic days to be notably perverse. Particularly in fantasies, to pluralize the politics is to pluralize the powers. The Potter saga sometimes pits these against one another. It also mobilizes resources for action from further politics available at present: realism, feminism, environmentalism, liberalism, republicanism, patronism, populism, and more. Liberal power lies in objective mechanical leverage. Realist power is in subjective manipulation of the beliefs that resource materials will be used. Green power emerges in intersubjective sharing of paths to community healing, grace, and play. Potter sophistication in politics arises in important part from this cornucopia of political perspectives. Because dark times are when we face them, and politics as dark arts help us face them, the Potter series is widely relevant. But as the early books underscore, even before Dumbledore heralds the arrival of dark times, we need politics—as dark arts and their defenses—in and for *all* times.

Potter arts and creatures of magic are "dark" from uses of them and perspectives on them as much as any other features arguably more intrinsic or inherent. In the world of Harry Potter, dark deeds of magic are done by many of the same spells, potions, and devices as other magical deeds used to defend against them. Potter politics are in the symbolism of disarming charms, polyjuice potions, and flying broomsticks as these are used in Harry's world and experienced by us readers. In like manner, the magical creatures in Potter's world participate in its vast political symbolism, as do the personalities and histories of its mages and muggles alike. Potter politics emerge from the saga events that resonate with events in our recent and ongoing history. They surface also in Potter institutions and practices. These include Potter businesses, entertainments, holidays, services, schools, and sports. The series names and characteristics tell us symbolically about Potter politics, yet the Potter actions and uses say even more. Attending to Potter politics as dark arts means emphasizing the Hogwarts course in DADA.

DADA IS A USEFUL FOCUS FOR
POLITICAL EDUCATION

The Hogwarts curriculum might have included DADA since the school's inception in the middle ages. Yet DADA teachers change with each of Harry's years at Hogwarts (II.115), and each book treats DADA differently. Dumbledore hints to Harry that the turnover might result from Voldemort cursing the Hogwarts job that he wanted but was denied (VI.442–6). Whatever the instability sources, the DADA changes combine with other details to focus each Potter book on a distinctive antinomy of two political styles. And book by book, we also do well to notice the Potter treatment of a third political movement or philosophy. Thus the DADA teachers help Harry and his friends, including us, face dark arts in dark times.

I'm *not* claiming that the seven books divide their politics into neat clumps by book. The Potter saga is beautifully integrated, and many of its diverse politics are clear throughout. Even so, some are much more prominent in the whole, and each gets featured by another book or two in addition to the one I target for it. For example, most Potter books include republican versions of idealist *and* realist politics, often pitting them against one another. Here I discuss them mainly in regard to *The Prisoner of Azkaban*, but another focus for realism-versus-idealism is the sixth book on *The Half-Blood Prince*, as its title suggests. And thanks mainly to the Weasley twins, Fred and George, all Potter books explore politics of folly and irony. Still, staying flexible, the DADA pattern from one book to the next can give us a good overall guide to Potter politics.

The same goes for the main sites of Potter magic as performances of politics. The Potter books distribute their distinct resources and practices of magic across several prominent places, and the books develop these separate sites to strikingly different extents. We learn more about Diagon Alley than Knockturn Alley, for instance, and more about the Black House than the Weasley Burrow. This is similar to how the U.S. Constitution distributes aspects of its distinct executive, judicial, and legislative powers across and among its three branches of government, rather than effecting a strict "separation" of those powers branch by branch. Neither DADA, Slytherin House, nor the MOM is the main site for the darkest arts or creatures of magic—any more than healing magic happens only or at times mainly, in St. Mungo's Hospital.

What *is* the DADA pattern? It's easy to notice that Hogwarts gets a new DADA teacher for each Potter book, that is, each of Harry's (projected) seven years there. (On the run from Death Eaters, the heroic trio of Harry, Ron, and Hermione doesn't attend Hogwarts for a seventh year.) Less formally, though, the pattern in this period is arguably *two* different DADA teachers a year. In two Potter books, early departures by appointed teachers necessitate late replacements. In two others, the teacher who takes up the DADA assignment turns out not to be the person pretended. And in three Potter books, perversions of this teaching assignment spur unofficial substitutes to attempt at least some of the DADA tasks. All these teachers pursue somewhat distinctive spells and strategies of teaching. But mainly, these characters also enact different kinds of politics.

Structures for the whole series inflect DADA arrangements too. The Rowling plan was to write initially for young boys, especially. Year by year for Harry and his friends at Hogwarts, the Potter books would address progressively older, more sophisticated readers. (Along the way, the author surely noticed that the books were attracting a huge, highly inclusive readership.) As a result, the first three books are much younger in sensibility than the last four. Hence in several ways, the series more or less starts over with Book 4. It repeats the first book's epic form and ending challenges, but with increasing danger and darkness. By Book 7, the epic form has metamorphosed from heroic quests to a long and winding odyssey of troubles on the way back to a home in terrible jeopardy. Thus the first three books are (much) shorter, simpler, and more idealist than the final four. Book by book, the situations and events turn ever darker. Even before Dumbledore calls for colleagues to face dark times, DADA endeavors have been growing more and more complex. Charting Hogwarts DADA teachers and their politics can show this (table 2.1).

In this table (2.2), DA stands for Dumbledore's Army, and HBP for Half-Blood Prince, aka Snape. The far-right column is especially telling. Each book covers a year of Hogwarts education slated for Harry Potter. This enables every Potter book to tie each of its two pivotal politics to one of its two teachers of DADA for that Hogwarts year. Still this organization arises from rough generalizations that bring out only some aspects of the series structures. Most of these sorts of politics weave throughout the Potter saga, and those relations are instructive too.

In Harry's first year, the recognized DADA professor is Quirrell. But he turns out to be a virtual puppet of the Voldemort revenant, which hides behind Quirrell's headwrap. Who is the actual DADA teacher? We do well to take both into account. Quirrell seems mostly to conform to usual conduct, in order to keep his secret unsuspected, whereas Voldemort epitomizes the horror genre's perversions of perfectionist politics. (Fortunately, those get resisted by the more admirable kinds of perfectionism developing in Harry and some friends at Hogwarts.) Similar DADA doubling is a complication in every one of the seven Hogwarts years for Harry's cohort.

The next year, there's no DADA replacement when Lockhart loses his memory, because the last term is almost over. But Lockhart does so little as DADA teacher that the year's most vivid DADA instruction comes from Severus Snape helping introduce students to the institution of the wizard's duel. Lockhart's celebrity and prominence in popular culture link him to

Table 2.1   DADA Teachers and Politics

Potter Books	DADA Teachers	DADA Roles	Potter Politics
Philosopher's	Quirinus Quirrell	DADA Professor	Conformism
Stone	Lord Voldemort	Quirrell Puppeteer	Perfectionism
Chamber of	Gilderoy Lockhart	DADA Professor	Populism
Secrets	Severus Snape	Wizard Duel Teacher	Fascism
Prisoner of	Remus Lupin	DADA Professor	Idealism
Azkaban	Severus Snape	DADA Substitute	Realism
Goblet of Fire	Mad-Eye Moody	DADA Professor	Republicanism
	Barty Crouch Jr.	Moody Impersonator	Fascism
Order of the	Dolores Umbridge	DADA Professor	Bureaucratism
Phoenix	Harry Potter	DA Leader	Republicanism
Half-Blood	Snape under Dumbledore	DADA Professor	(Realist) liberalism
Prince	HBP under Slughorn	Potions Marginalia	(Realist) patronism
Deathly	Amycus Carrow	DADA Professor	totalitarianism
Hallows	Neville Longbottom	DA Leader	Democratism

Source: Table developed by author.

populist politics. These lately get accused of becoming fascist in the encompassing modes of Mussolini, Hitler, white supremacists, and others. Such fascism is all too clear in *The Chamber of Secrets*. The muggle and "mud-blood" persecutions by Voldemort's Death Eaters start to emerge in the taunts of the Malfoys, the predations of the basilisk, the myth of the Heir of Slytherin, and indeed in the defining spirit of the House of Slytherin as headed by Snape.

Lupin proves to be a fine DADA teacher for the third year. But Snape pressures Lupin as a werewolf to resign then finishes the course for him. These two evoke a virtual duel of idealism versus realism. Lupin becomes the model for Harry's dedication to Dumbledore's ideals. Snape enters adulthood as a Death Eater, but he actually renounces this fascist allegiance to Voldemort. In penance for his role in the murder of Harry's parents, Snape spies for the resistance led by Dumbledore. So clever and talented that he becomes a top acolyte of Voldemort, Snape lives spy-versus-spy convolutions minute-by-minute for many years, and these epitomize realist politics.

In *The Goblet of Fire*, the younger Crouch uses polyjuice potion to take Mad-Eye's place as DADA teacher. So we have to wonder when that Death Eater is doing what the auror would, in order to impersonate him plausibly, and when students get Voldemort's disciple instead. It's no surprise that the politics of these adversaries are entangled as well as antithetical, for fascism intentionally twists early republicanism from ancient Rome. Still the prominence of those two politics throughout the series lets us link them to other Potter books, clearing the way to address movements also important to this fourth book: nationalism, environmentalism, and feminism. And by this point, DADA complications echo narratival and political complications in the series.

To suppress practical instruction in DADA, the MOM then imposes Dolores Umbridge on Hogwarts, where she enacts a vicious version of bureaucratic politics. In response, the heroic trio forms Dumbledore's Army, the DA, to have Harry lead DADA practice in secret. The DA parallels the Order of the Phoenix led by Dumbledore himself. Both armies and orders are specifically republican institutions. They spotlight the authority, discipline, militarism, and personal responsibility promoted by republican politics—especially in resistance to Umbridge as a tyrannical ruler of Hogwarts and to Fudge as an increasingly authoritarian Minister of Magic.

In Harry's sixth year, Dumbledore finally lets Snape teach DADA. Snape has lobbied for years for this assignment. He reveres and romances the subject, but we get few details of his work for this year. Snape's antagonism to Harry (and vice versa) inhibits Harry's learning in the course, so his instruction shifts sites. Starting late in the previous year, Snape's private lessons in Occlumency teach Harry some valuable things—but *not* how to block his intrusive visions of Voldemort. Dumbledore's individual sessions with Harry provide crucial collaboration, context, and practice in DADA. So let's treat (the realist) Snape working under (the liberal) Dumbledore as one major nexus of DADA instruction for Harry in his sixth year. The other nexus arises from Dumbledore (re)hiring Horace Slughorn to replace Snape as Potions professor. Slughorn focuses Harry's education in the dark arts of patronist politics, and Slughorn's course is Harry's platform for learning DADA from notes by the "Half-Blood Prince" (Snape) in Harry's Potions textbook.

Harry, Ron, and Hermione skip what would have been their seventh years at Hogwarts. As the three evade a MOM dominated by Death Eaters, the heroic trio works to undo Voldemort's dark forces and defenses. At Hogwarts, Dark Arts replaces DADA, and Amycus Carrow, a Death Eater, has students practice dark spells on others who misbehave (VII.573). All this makes Amycus an emblem of Voldemort turning Hogwarts into a leading edge of the fascist society he seeks for all of Britain. With Harry a fugitive from this incipient totalitarian regime, Neville leads the resisting Hogwarts students into hiding. Their renewed Dumbledore's Army operates from the Room of Requirement, lately linked by a secret underground passage to the Hog's Head pub run by Aberforth Dumbledore in Hogsmeade. Maybe Neville *could* have become "the Chosen One," instead of Harry, as Sibyll Trelawney's first prophecy on Voldemort allows (V.839–43; VI.510–12). And Neville *does* become the DA leader in Harry's absence. But as a gentler version of the primary hero, Neville is less magically talented (more ordinary) than Harry. Neville is still heroic: make no mistake about that. Even so, Neville is less a glorious republican hero in the mode of Harry (or Ron) than Neville is an effective democratic hero.

As a hero, Neville is more like the rest of us could be. (Yes, I *might* think this because I'm a workaday professor and Neville becomes one—rather than a dashing auror like Harry or a lofty Minister of Magic like Hermione.[2]) In *The Lord of the Rings*, hobbits are salt-of-the-earth foils for the totalitarian Sauron and his Nazguls. Likewise Neville is admirable, tenacious, and effective (if unspectacular) as an obstacle to the totalitarian ambitions of Voldemort and his Death Eaters, such as the Carrows. Thus Neville is less a (republican) leader than a (democratic) doer, but his opposition to the totalitarians is no less heroic for that. He epitomizes democrats as egalitarian defenders of us ordinary people, especially when enacting this style in everyday life.

IN EVERYDAY LIFE, POLITICS MOSTLY ARE STYLISTIC

For popular fantasy accessible to children, the Potter series pays extraordinary attention to the high, portentous politics of states, institutions, and leaders. Yet it excels in linking these to the low, humbler politics of every-day life. The implication is that these connections are what we need—and make—in facing the terrible troubles of dark and difficult times.

As we've already started to see, the Potter books tap lots of symbolism to present their politics. Often these are readily recognizable. In talking Potter politics, however, the book at hand still is apt to use some unfamiliar terms or even familiar terms in unfamiliar ways. Most of the labels evoked here for kinds of politics appear in the current speech of politicians, press, and public. Yet the meanings here are those of political theorists, who try to be especially clear and consistent in political analysis. Theirs can be a political discourse of -isms, and the Potter books don't read that way. The hope is that the theory "translations" can help show how distinct kinds of politics cohere and relate to others—in the Potter books and in our lives. Many politics can be pursued as creeds or ideologies. Many can be practiced as looser move-ments. But many times, especially in everyday life, these -isms name even less formal styles of action and experience. Rowling has Harry Potter and company mainly practice their politics as everyday styles.

As the name implies, ideologies are idea-logics.[3] Ideologies keep politics consistent by defining concepts clearly and detailing firm relationships among the principles that combine concepts into directives for action. Movements are much less regimented in reasoning or action. They cohere through the shared motion and emotion of members who hold somewhat disparate ideolo-gies—or none at all. As a movement, feminism has included intersectional feminists, difference feminists, eco-feminists, radical feminists, liberal feminists, socialist feminists, and others of various stripes. As a movement, environmentalism (what some call "ecologism") has encompassed agrarians, anarchists, conservationists, deep ecologists, naturalists, eco-feminists, eco-liberals, eco-socialists, and so on. Thus women's liberation and green politics might seem inchoate in their proposals and their reasons for policies, institu-tions, and lifestyles. On the other hand, their coalitions can be more inclusive and resilient across changing conditions.

By contrast, political styles are recurrent demeanors, roles, and sensibilities that inform action. They cohere by cultural convention more than political creed, and elective resemblance more than logical rigor. Political styles are flexible and personalizable. Yet they typically are unmistakable in practice. Styles feature familiar characters, scenes, sounds, looks, and deeds. Thus republican heroes lead disciplined orders or adventurous bands to rid their communities of corruption and re-found constitutive virtues. Following such leaders, republican citizens enact personal responsibility for specific tasks, local knowledge of particular situations, and continual vigilance against abuses of power. Such heroes and citizens are staples of thrillers and action-adventure films. Perfectionist superheroes leap beyond what ordinary people see as good, evil, or even possible. They blaze trails that acolytes cultivate for others to imitate. The "purity" of perfectionist looks is standard for vampire films (with stark black, pale white, and blood red) and early superhero movies (with bright primary colors). Vampire aesthetics typically express the perversions of (Nietzschean) perfectionism enacted by various supervillains, Voldemort, and Death Eaters. In recent movies, the color schemes for superheroes as constructive perfectionists often darken their clothes and settings. The Potter films do much the same.

The fascism of Voldemort and the Death Eaters is perhaps the fullest Potter presentation as an ideology. Fascist doctrines of blood purity and superiority, cults of leadership and action, plus persecutions of enemies-within mark the dark times denounced by Dumbledore. (Similarly we may be chilled by the recent upsurge for one country after another in warnings about fascist politics—sometimes assimilated to populism.) Such fascist projects function as the ideology that joins the atomization, bureaucratization, death squads, secret police, surveillance, terrorism, and other elements of the Dark Lord's totalitarian movement and regime in the last two Potter books. This fits Hannah Arendt's theory that totalitarianism originates in the bureaucracy, imperialism, and racism pioneered in the nineteenth century, while ideology, surveillance, and terror become abiding aspects of totalitarian movements and regimes, respectively, in the twentieth century.[4]

Also treated as movements are some politics that arguably loom largest in *Goblet of Fire*. These are nationalism, environmentalism, and feminism. All three get sympathetic but notably critical treatment in the Potter saga. It compares nationalism to the dynamics of student Houses at Hogwarts, supporting (or opposing) Quidditch teams, and the incorrigibly destructive conduct of blast-ended skrewts bred by Hagrid. Hermione Granger's Society for the Promotion of Elfish Welfare (SPEW) seeks a green movement (IV.224), perhaps an Elf Liberation Front (IV.363–84). Since house-elves seem at times to be stand-ins for housewives, however, feminism and women's liberation are also at stake. Hermione is their fierce champion, but there are critics too.

Most politics in the Potter series appear as styles. They take shape symbolically in the names, features, deeds, and words of Potter figures, major and minor. These include characters, creatures, spells, potions, places, institutions, songs, tools, and such. The Potter saga starts with conformism as a political style evident in patterns and principles of personal conduct, especially by the Dursleys who shelter Harry after the death of his parents. To that style, it counter-poses the constructive perfectionism of Harry and (eventually) many of his magical friends. They leap beyond the ordinary or standard, and they Just Do It for the excellence or exhilaration in itself. They don't seek acceptance (conformism), approval (populism), or admiration (republicanism). Harry leaps unaware to a school roof in avoiding

Dudley's gang (I.25), and even more to the point, Harry finds pure exultation in the discovery of his flying talent on a broomstick (I.148). But lest we or Harry be intoxicated by such power trips, Rowling has Quirrell and Voldemort show vividly how similar but perverse perfectionism can corrupt and destroy (I.290–5).

The Potter series begins with the antagonism between conformist and perfectionist styles, and it's not coy in condemning conformism while promoting Harry's kind of perfectionism. The series develops this recommendation throughout. Yet it warns clearly against the (per)version of perfectionism evident in (the fascist totalitarianism of) Voldemort, Death Eaters, and Quirrell. The series attends almost as much to the political debate between idealism and realism, which is as old as western civilization, mostly stylistic, and strongly substantive. Neither idealism nor realism has functioned much as an ideology or a movement. Although authoritarian and liberal politics have been amply ideologized, their Potter appearances are stylistic and governmental. Potter books treat (movement politics of) populism stylistically, and other Potter politics also appear mainly as styles. This helps Harry and his friends engage these politics in everyday life.

DADA FEATURES DEFENSES AGAINST DARK TIMES

Telling the intertwined stories of Harry Potter, his friends, and his enemies positions the Potter series to emphasize the stylistic politics in the characters' lives. In turn, this brings to the fore aspects of community action and arrangements important for our dark times but not always prominent in our political theories. At least at the moment, these are mainly politics in everyday life and popular culture. DADA and the Potter books overall are especially helpful with these.

The first book pits different inflections of perfectionist politics against conformism. We meet Harry Potter as a rule-breaker. This focus on conforming to rules or surpassing them serves to situate Potter accounts of politics in the philosophical tradition of conventionalism. It stresses human making, interpreting, enforcing, and violating rules, roles, and meanings. Rather than evoking a time without communities or politics, in order to see how they arise, conventionalism locates us in the midst of ongoing politics to make sense of them.

The second book compares the populism linked to Gilderoy Lockhart with the fascism of the Malfoys and the Heir (plus the House) of Slytherin. In this context, we see Hagrid as a half-giant repeatedly scapegoated by fascists. In response, Hagrid's philosophy of perspectivism can shine in his conduct. Hagrid shows how an amazing aptitude for the care of all magical creatures stems from his appreciation of their different characteristics and experiences. A magically tough hide and a socially marginal status also position him to assess others with fine attunement to their distinctive relations with the world. This earns him respect, even affection, from an astonishing range of creatures (or enmity from others). Harry and Hermione grow into his greatest students.

The third book is a good platform for seeing how a Hogwarts education for Harry and his friends has them learn from both idealism and realism, rather than treat the two as implacably opposed or mutually exclusive. The name is realist: the whole hog, warts, and all. The gates are idealist: winged boars, for when pigs can fly (III.87). Starting in Book 3, Lupin the idealist and Snape the realist struggle to cooperate in supporting Dumbledore's resistance to Voldemort. Along the way, Lupin shows realist skills too, while Snape also reveals idealist values. Both are leavened by the restless and disordering Sirius. He is a rebel, with existentialist impulses wary of undue discipline. These can make him winningly playful, dashingly heroic, and ready to take stands against dark forces in dark times. Yet Sirius resists self-discipline too, even when it might be needed most. As much as anyone, Sirius teaches Harry about politics of time, life, and death.

The fourth book turns decisively into dark times. It's much longer than any predecessor, and it restarts the series with significant attention to many politics. Here let me spotlight three political movements prominent in our times. The book opens with the Quidditch World Cup and organizes the later events around the Triwizard Tournament. To foreground competitions among countries is to evoke the politics of nationalism. These lurk in other templates too: competitions among Hogwarts Houses, team sports, even the blast-ended skrewts bred by Hagrid. Presiding is Ludovic Bagman, a former Quidditch star and Minister for Magical Games and Sports (IV.61). The macho dynamics of nationalism get feminist responses in gender equality demonstrated day by day in Hogwarts classes, sports, and traditions. These trace to the founders, two witches and two wizards, while a current exemplar is the strikingly autonomous and capable Ginny Weasley. Hermione Granger is another, and her campaign to liberate house-elves from slavery to mages is simultaneously a provocative (but vexed) symbol of environmentalism as well as feminism.

The fifth book introduces Dolores Umbridge to personify evils of bureaucracy. In league with Cornelius Fudge as an increasingly authoritarian Minister of Magic, Umbridge arrives at Hogwarts as DADA professor, has herself made High Inquisitor, and then supplants Dumbledore as Head of the whole school. To resist her regime, Harry leads Dumbledore's Army in the secret practice of defenses against dark arts. This republican institution echoes the equally republican Order of the Phoenix led by Dumbledore against Voldemort's fascist movement of Death Eaters. Therefore analysis of the fifth book features Potter takes on authoritarian and bureaucratic styles of action as aspects of dark times—plus Potter takes on republican styles of action in resistance.

The sixth book links Harry's dark times to ours, then it brings Horace Slughorn back to Hogwarts as Potions professor. Slughorn practices patronism. The politics of patrons, protégés, and advancement networks operate throughout the series; but they reach a peak in the sixth book. It encourages Harry to contrast Slughorn's patronism with Dumbledore's liberalism, bringing out stylistic aspects of liberal politics that we otherwise might underplay. Dumbledore's liberalism also offers good comparisons for clarifying the largely conservative politics of Cornelius Fudge.

The seventh book explores the political contrast central for the twentieth century—and all too salient for the twenty-first. Since ancient Greece and Rome, western civilization had mostly taken tyranny (as illegitimate rule by one individual) to be the worst possible polity: Political Hell on Earth. The best possible polity, Political Heaven on Earth, had been a republic—for melding the peak features of monarchy, aristocracy, and democracy as legitimate forms of rule. Then the twentieth century revved these into totalitarianism (as full control and domination of a populace) in contrast to democracy (as full participation and power for the people). In *Deathly Hallows*, Voldemort and sadistic Death Eaters such as the Carrows seek totalitarian rule, while Neville Longbottom becomes their main opposite as a democratic model for political action. Attention to democratic socialism can articulate aspects of Neville's alternative, while focus on anarchism can underscore the radical resistance that arises to totalizing order. This gives us a good way to appreciate Rowling's appropriation of traditional folly into a chaotic anarchism that contrasts strikingly with the kinds usually addressed by political theorists. Inventive humor is a hallmark of the Potter saga, yet its uses go well beyond comic relief. The politics of the Weasley twins, Peeves the poltergeist, and others are unmistakably dark arts. For example, their pranks can hurt badly in body, mind, self-esteem, and social standing. Yet their resources of folly are still among the principal devices recommended by Rowling to resist dark uses of dark arts in dark times.

Symbolically situated in our dark times, Potter politics are many and complicated. Most have some redeeming moments or features. The exceptions are fascism and totalitarianism. But authoritarian and bureaucratic politics can be close behind in villainy. The other politics in the Potter series are more mixed in character and use, yet all are dark arts. Even so, the Potter series identifies several politics as especially effective in defending against the dark arts of fascism and totalitarianism. The Potter defenses feature liberal democracy, republicanism, folly as chaotic anarchism, and especially Harry's sort of perfectionism. Their attunements and leaps, friends and mentors, rights and strategies, tricks and traps all help Harry and his friends defeat the Dark Lord and the Death

Eaters. By implication, these can help us defend against other troubles too: eco-cide, genocide, gaslighting, slavery, torture, treachery, and so on. Also highly helpful in the Potter saga are politics linked to philosophies of conventionalism, perspectivism, existentialism, and ironism. The Potter saga is long, and even the basic patterns of Potter politics are extensive (table 2.2).

Table 2.2 Potter Politics and Epitomes

	Potter Politics	A Few Defining Aspects	Potter Epitomes	Some Potter Symbols
1	Conformism	Bullies, gangs, and routines	Dursleys	Invisibility Cloak
	Perfectionism	Self-referential excellence	Harry Potter	Deluminator and wands
	Conventionalism	Rules, roles, and meanings	Luna Lovegood	Philosopher's Stone
2	Fascism	Classism, racism, and specism	Lucius Malfoy	Death Eaters and fountains
	Populism	Celebrities and uprisings	Gilderoy Lockhart	Mandrake and acromantula
	Perspectivism	Care and kind-ness	Rubeus Hagrid	Centaurs, goblins, and elves
3	Idealism	Deeply principled doing	Remus John Lupin	Boar wings and flying car
	Realism	Deeply practical doing	Severus Snape	Marauder's Map and wizard chess
	Existentialism	Resistance communities	Sirius Black	Department of Mysteries
4	Nationalism	Showy pride in country	Ludovic Bagman	Hogwarts Houses, sports, and skrewts
	Ecologism	Eco-centrism and wilding	Hermione Granger	hippogriff, thestral, and ELF
	Feminism	Full equality for females	Ginny Weasley	cauldrons and Nagini
5	Authoritarianism	Top-down regimentation	Rufus Scrimgeour	Azkaban Prison
	Bureaucratism	Rationalize and specialize	Dolores Umbridge	Decrees and High Inquisitor
	Republicanism	Respect and responsibility	Ron Weasley	Gryffindor House
6	Patronism	Patrons and networks	Horace Slughorn	Slug Club and spiders
	Liberalism	Diversity, merit, and rights	Albus Dumbledore	Hogwarts and the Sorting Hat
	Conservatism	Law and social order	Cornelius Fudge	Ministry of Magic
7	Totalitarianism	Surveil, control, and terrorize	Lord Voldemort	Unforgivable Curses
	Socialism	Equalize and empower	Neville Longbottom	St. Mungo's Hospital
	Anarchism	Freedom, folly, and laughter	Weasley Twins	Peeves and *Riddikulus!*

Source: Table developed by author.

Book by book, the Potter series doesn't turn away from any of these politics, but carries them into ensuing volumes. Thus the Dursleys enact and enforce conformism from the first book to the fifth and again in the seventh. Harry develops his constructive perfectionism throughout the series, and Voldemort directly displays his destructive perfectionism in every volume but the third. As these examples suggest, the Potter series epitomizes each of its many politics in at least one person. Moreover it symbolizes each in particular spells, creatures, artifacts, or institutions. Such symbolism helps diversify and specify Potter politics.

DARK TIMES NEED NEGLECTED POLITICS

Here the project is not to provide good, basic characterizations for each kind of politics in the Potter books. For that purpose, there are fine textbooks on political ideologies and political philosophies. (To introduce students to political theory, I often teach such books along with the Potter series.) Nor is the present endeavor to compare Potter accounts overall with the contents of such textbooks, let alone the larger literatures that they distill. Instead the effort at hand is to analyze Potter takes on politics significant for everyday lives in our dark times. Some of these politics are featured in recent theories, and some are neglected in them. This book concentrates on what the Potter series says about recent politics that seem neglected but especially important.

Attention to the everyday-life levels of political style is the biggest Potter contribution to current theories of politics. How well can we understand liberal politics without a good sense of daily conduct by liberals? How well have we analyzed conservative politics without accounts of their life-styles and life-worlds? This takes us into cultural dynamics of politics, which lately surface more in theories of political movements such as feminism and environmentalism than in accounts of ideologies like socialism or authoritarianism. The Potter series takes us farther than usual into everyday styles of action and experience, and these are forms of politics ignored lately in the field of political theory. In our times, bureaucratic and republican politics get theorized as government structures, but they operate principally as political styles. The lesson is that recent theories can learn from these neglected *forms* of politics.

Pottery also spotlights neglected *kinds* of politics. This begins with the first Potter book. Political theorists lately say more about mass society than conformism. The two differ in telling ways. Masses supposedly are atomized, for example, whereas conformists seldom are. Nor are Potter characters, for the most part. Nor are we. So the Potter emphasis on conformism speaks more adequately to the experiences of Harry and his friends. Furthermore the Potter antidote for conformism is Harry's kind of perfectionism. Treating it in sympathetic detail is truly unusual in recent political theory, and situating it in everyday life is another move mostly missing from the few recent accounts of such politics. For a political theorist, consequently, the Potter series can start with a bone-shaking bang—like Weasley fireworks as an examination surprise.

Chamber of Secrets appeared as the second Potter book in 1999. Toward the end of the twentieth century, political theory had been slighting populist politics for decades. At that time, in fact, little had been done in the hundred-plus years of populism to provide general accounts of it.[5] Looking back from the twenty-first century, though, Rowling's book can seem prescient in its recognition of intersections for populist and fascist politics.[6] The same goes for its attention to populist dynamics of adventure, charisma, culture, memory, and especially celebrity. Even at *this* writing, only charisma has gained theoretical respect as a major element of populist politics.

Particularly in connection with the Weasley twins and Peeves, the Hogwarts poltergeist, Potter books revel in the politics of folly, irony, humor, satire, and laughter. From the inception of western civilization, these have been recognized as dark arts, in part because their destructive power can be erosive or explosive. Still these arts of folly have shown themselves to be crucial defenses against dark arts in dark times. Do recent theories of politics respect them? Not that I can tell, though I've looked hard and long. At stylistic levels, the Potter books draw instead on what anthropologists, sociologists, and historians have reconstructed as a political tradition of folly—which is to say, purposeful, inventive foolishness. The Potter books work through its resources and logics at everyday-life levels, and they give us great fun in doing so!

Another preoccupation of the Potter books could be called the politics of *patronage*, except that American Progressives have taught people to treat this term as synonymous with *corruption*. These are highly personalized politics of helping others survive and advance when you can, in their careers or otherwise. Full-fledged, the strategy is to create a network of people who stay in touch and return these favors in various ways. Personal ties become one of the main considerations in allocating resources and making other decisions. Modern merit treats personal characteristics and connections as irrelevant and tainting. Recent theories of politics follow suit, giving patronage little attention and no respect. Yet every Potter book features dynamics of what we can term *patronism*. Book 6 even has Dumbledore analyze several of them for Harry.

Why? One reason is that most walks of life include patronist politics—whether they are welcome, suspect, or otherwise. Acknowledging this helps the Potter series situate Harry and his magical friends plausibly in our world. Another reason is that patronist politics *might* be more effective, efficient, and just than their supposedly impersonal alternatives such as meritocracy and bureaucracy. Patronist politics are not intrinsically corrupt, and the Potter series presents several variants. But the clinching reason is that the Potter series recommends patronist politics as mainstays of community. The series portrays patronism as projects of friendship and loyalty. Then it makes them central to the politics of personal assistance celebrated throughout the series.

These are the politics of help, especially from friends. The second book concludes with Dumbledore explaining to Harry and others that "help will always be given at Hogwarts to those who ask for it" (II.263–6). The third book introduces the patronus charm, which proves to be the single most significant spell in the series. Not only does it help with dementors, by chasing away their deadly doom and gloom, but it accurately and instantly transports messages and spans the great distances needed at times to connect communities and protect friends. The fourth book gives Harry one helper after another to get safely through the Triwizard Tournament then out of the graveyard ambush by Voldemort. The fifth volume institutionalizes such help into the Order of the Phoenix and Dumbledore's Army. Then the sixth book shows how the patrons, protégés, and networks of patronism can go beautifully right, but also badly wrong, in helping. When we speak of "patron saints," of course, we recognize how patrons are helpers. Indeed the "hallows" in the title of the seventh book are exactly such helpers, bringing acutely needed (but dangerous) powers beyond those ordinarily available to us humans. (More of Harry's perfectionism here!) An emphasis on the politics of personal help suits our dark times, as it does Harry Potter's.

To begin that last volume, Rowling quotes the invocation by Aeschylus in *The Libation Bearers*: "Now hear, you blissful powers underground — / answer the call, send help. / Bless the children, give them triumph now" (VII .xi). Calling on the dark arts of politics for help is *the* Potter recourse for our dark times. At a familiar intersection of the neglected politics of personal help (patronism) and of playful trickery (folly) is *the* Potter holiday of Halloween: All Hallows' Eve. Its motifs suffuse the series. Perhaps like you, I saw this in my first reading of the books, and its horror symbolism made sense for a saga about dark arts in dark times. But I was puzzled by the many casual, seemingly disconnected images of beetles: finding them in buttons, eyes, a reporter, and more.[7] What might they mean politically, and how might they link to Halloween? Well, when the idea hits, it's hard to resist: Didn't the Beatles sing insistently about "Help?"

NOTES

1. See Greg Bear, *Heads* (New York: Tom Doherty Associates, 1990).

2. See Jack Thorne (script with story by J. K. Rowling, John Tiffany, and Jack Thorne), *The Cursed Child* (New York: Scholastic Press, 2016).

3. This take on ideology links to that of Hannah Arendt, as referenced in the next note, whose political theory informs the present study. See John S. Nelson, "The Ideological Connection: Or, Smuggling in the Goods, Parts I-II," *Theory and Society* 4, nos. 3–4 (Fall-Winter 1977): 421–48 and 573–90. Attention here to political styles in everyday life learns from Antonio Gramsci's view of ideology as cultural hegemony: *The Antonio Gramsci Reader*, ed. David Forgacs (New York: New York University Press, 2000). It also develops aspects of Clifford Geertz's analysis of ideology as a cultural system: "Ideology as a Cultural System," *Ideology and Discontent*, ed. David Apter (New York: Free Press, 1964), 47–76.

4. See Hannah Arendt, *The Origins of Totalitarianism* (New York: Harcourt Brace Jovanovich, 1958, fourth edition, 1973).

5. Exceptional are Ernest Gellner and Ghiţa Ionescu, eds., *Populism* (New York: Macmillan, 1969); Margaret Canovan, *Populism* (New York: Harcourt Brace Jovanovich, 1981). Historians paid populist politics much better attention.

6. But see Robert Penn Warren, *All the King's Men* (New York: Random House, 1946, second edition, 1953).

7. On Hagrid's beetle-black eyes, see I.46; 2.54; 4.544 and 718. For Rita Skeeter as animagus beetle, see IV.427, 504–5, 513, 576, 714, 727–28, 738; V.543–69. For other beetle invocations, see I.81; II.94–95; III.10; IV.515–16; V.103–4, 258; VII.14.

Chapter 3

Defenses Against Dark Arts

Throughout the seven books, Harry and his friends learn by leaps and bounds about dark arts and defenses against them. To learn DADA is to learn forms and principles for politics. It's to learn them within and with regard to governments, movements, and policies—but also media, families, schools, businesses, games, and more. This is because DADA involves experiencing an elaborate field of resources, uses, methods, settings, performances, and consequences of politics. Far from all DADA education for Harry and his friends is in school—let alone in formal courses of study. They consult several books on dark arts, with research taking Harry and Hermione into the Restricted Section of the Hogwarts Library to access a few.[1] When instructing Dumbledore's Army, Harry begins to tap books on defenses against dark arts.[2] In addition, there are defensive pamphlets from the Ministry of Magic (MOM) (VI.42–3), defensive cautions from Dumbledore (VI.168), defensive spells for wizard's duels, and defensive drills from Harry for the DA. Especially there are encounters with dark arts directed against Harry and his friends. Episode after episode, these take us readers vicariously through many "learning experiences" and "teachable moments."[3]

Nonetheless the Hogwarts curriculum is meant to be a good early step for young mages-in-the-making, and it can serve us in this way. That holds beyond courses officially on DADA. Thus becoming an auror, to arrest dark wizards for the MOM, requires strong work in a wide range of courses (IV.161; V.662–5). In fact, since all Hogwarts courses teach magic—which is to say, arts of action with dark and anti-dark uses—the entire curriculum can be taken to advance the political education of Harry and his friends, including us.

Potter books provide most attention to the teaching topics, materials, methods, and class meetings of four courses: DADA, Divination, Potions, and Care of Magical Creatures. This can be a surprising roster, because auror preparation could be said to replace Divination and Care of Magical Creatures with Charms and Transfiguration. We learn more about several courses from homework for Gryffindor students and books named throughout the saga. Of course, all aurors and most mages learn how to apparate; so Hogwarts offers a short course on it in the sixth year of study.[4] (And we specify apparating's instructive politics of realism and perfectionism in chapter 8.) Yet we do well to start with political principles apparent in Harry's six years of courses that focus on defending against the dark arts.

DADA PRINCIPLES

For most of Harry's time at Hogwarts, the DADA textbook is *The Dark Forces: A Guide to Self-Protection* by Quentin Trimble (I.67, IV.210). The subtitle is introduced as a quick joke in connection with the trembling Quirinus Quirrell. Still it articulates the school's rationale for DADA: to develop skills needed by students to protect themselves against dark uses of the dark arts. The book shows readers how to recognize and counter dark creatures and spells. Potions are so many, material, intricate, and important (to dark magic especially?) that they get a book and a course sequence of their own. (Snape's approach to the two disciplines suggests their affinity.) Possibly dark devices such as vanishing cabinets and animated brooms—think *Fantasia* (1940) as well as Quidditch— seem to be addressed mainly in Charms, if at all.[5]

We learn little further of the DADA contents from Harry's first year with Quirrell, his fifth year with Dolores Umbridge, or his sixth year with Severus Snape. The other three DADA professors seem to agree that the most urgent challenge is to teach students to face their disabling "fears" (II.101; III.132–3, 155; IV.211–2). The textbook author's last name of Trimble reinforces this, by sounding like *tremble*. Here is the focus for defending against dark creatures and mages. "Fears" is Rowling's word, but as chapter 1 explains, "terrors" or "dreads" might be more appropriate. For the darkest dangers are faceless, overwhelming, and thus especially difficult to withstand. Declining to name Voldemort is refusing to face him as a threat, which magnifies his menace. Therefore the books on defensive magic include *Confronting the Faceless* (VI.177).[6]

A further DADA principle is for the teacher to make this inherently scary instruction as safe and individual as possible (II.101; III. 134–9; IV.212–9). After an incompetent initial lesson with Cornish pixies, which disrupt every-body in the classroom, Gilderoy Lockhart bails on this balance. He puts safety first, defanging and deindividualizing the lessons by merely rehearsing "his" fabricated confrontations with supposedly dark creatures. Confining courses to *Defensive Magical Theory*, by Wilbert Slinkhard, Dolores Umbridge prevents any danger to students (and especially the MOM), any personalization for students, and any practice by students. Everyone hears the lie in Umbridge saying that this will suffice for students to handle the Ordinary Wizarding Level exams, since they include practical components for actually performing magic (I.262; V.243–4).

To offset that, DA coaching by Harry personalizes practical instruction in the Room of Requirement. It's a safe space where cushions, teams, and pointers limit damages. All too soon, several DA members are facing actual enemies in the Umbridge office and the Department of Mysteries. In the midst of action, let alone combat, sophisticated magic needs composure, focus, and quick wit to recognize threats and respond effectively. When inventing new artifacts, mages may experiment with more safety, with less urgency, even with less intense concentration. Still there can be danger in magical experiments, as the death of Luna Lovegood's mother shows (V.863), as the Weasley twins risk (V.252–4, 292–4, 368), and as the MOM tries to regulate (IV.86). Is there decently safe practical instruction for us muggles in political action? It's easy to think of civics classes, youth groups, student councils, and student clubs in these terms. Yet it's more discerning to appreciate how we practice and even experiment in myriad settings of everyday life. As with Harry at the Dursleys', sometimes we don't know we're doing this, but sometimes we do.

An advantage of acknowledging lots of early and mundane action as practically political is that it can work against hyping or romanticizing political action.[7] Treating politics as a major marker of adulthood and a venue of advanced power does something similar to treating dark arts and their defenses that way in *Harry Potter*. Most young people are induced to be overeager for DADA at Hogwarts. Then most become disillusioned when they encounter unexciting examples of DADA experts, as Harry and classmates do in their initial courses with Quirrell and Lockhart. Lupin finally manages to show Harry's cohort how intriguing DADA can be. Yet he begins with comedic ridicule (*Riddikulus!*) to disperse boggarts, and this probably helps tether the attraction to what's familiar and sometimes silly rather than mysterious and exalted (III.123–40). Harry is not wrong to worry that DADA, let alone dark arts, can dominate ambitions and imaginations so as to motivate dark mages (VI.180–1). As *the* place for power-hungry mages-in-the-making, Slytherin House even seems to cultivate those ambitions (IV.176–7). To the contrary, though, still another DADA principle is not to romanticize the dark arts more than the defenses.

DADA is about being prepared to face dark arts, dark acts, and dark times (V.244, 325). In addition to skills for recognizing and countering dark perils, DADA sensitizes mages to stay alert for threats. This is Mad-Eye Moody's (republican) principle of constant vigilance.[8] To do this and to take advantage of whatever warning signs arise can require staying informed. First Hermione then Harry must learn to give careful, critical attention to the news media (IV.540; V.2–8). This is for spotting events, spins, and views—but gaps and silences too. Gossip, rumor, and even speculation help at times.[9] (Nothing is fool-proof.) Staying informed extends to historical investigation, although Hermione's efforts and results put Harry and Ron to shame until late in the saga. It includes cultural information, where rearing in a magical family gives Ron a notable advantage over Hermione and Harry. This holds until, ironically, Ron's knowledge of *The Tales of Beedle the Bard* as children's stories seems to impede his recognition of their relevance to the trio's quest—although Ron *is* the first of the three to grasp the significance of Harry's Invisibility Cloak (VII.414–7).[10] Especially vigilance involves the series attention to spying, to penetrating the information defenses of others. So "be prepared" means "be vigilant" means "be informed."

Yet the DADA principle emphasized by Hogwarts students is to "know" it—through and through, in your blood and bones, nerve and sinew. You're truly prepared to defend against the dark arts when your knowledge is not just informational but experiential. That's why they reject the Umbridge ban on practical instruction. Still they realize that even making the spells second nature under the tutelage of a Lupin, a Moody, or a Potter is insufficient. The consensus is that you're ready when your defenses against the dark arts aren't merely practiced but performed in the clutch, when the chips are down, especially with lives on the line. Stringent but safe practice under Lupin's supervision is a big advance for his Hogwarts students, but it's not clear to the students whether Lupin has distinguished himself in dire, life-or-death situations—and *knows* these firsthand (III.130–41). The heroic three are exceptions, witnessing Lupin's defense of them against a dementor (III.81–6). The degree to which Lockhart's DADA books and lessons engage students is the extent to which he's good at relating as his own deeds the firsthand details taken from others (II.161). The gush of enthusiasm for "Moody's" DADA teaching traces to his ethos as a veteran auror: "He *knows* . . . what it's like to be out there *doing* it" (IV.208). It also stems from his method of students learning by full-fledged experience to fight the dark arts: straining personally to overcome the imperius curse, for example (IV.212–9). Harry, too, *knows* DADA (V.327–8), and his reputation for *knowing* is crucial to recruiting Dumbledore's Army (V.341–2).

DADA COGNATES

The rest of the Hogwarts curriculum can be seen as ingredients for dark arts and defenses against them. Several of these courses in magic remain mostly mysterious to us readers of the Potter books. Courtesy of Dumbledore's bequest to Hermione, the Study of Ancient Runes helps focus the heroic threesome on the potential importance of "The Tale the Three Brothers" in his copy of *The Tales of Beedle the Bard* (III.57; VII.405–23). Beyond that, we can guess that runes could be useful for DADA in recovering spells and potions from ancient texts.[11] All we learn of Arithmancy is that it's Hermione's favorite subject (II.251–2). From the name, we might guess that it shares the link of arithmetic to logic—hence to Snape's logic puzzle about potions, solved by Hermione on the path to the Sorcerer's Stone (I.284–6). If so, its pertinence to DADA and to politics can include plans and strategies (I.284–6). Or Arithmancy might implicate numerology, leading into astrology as Divination or number symbolism as principles of rhythm and timing for political action and community.[12] About Astronomy, we learn only that it's taught by Professor Sinistra; the heroic trio sits for OWLs in it; and it deploys telescopes to chart stars, planets, and moons (II.204; V.717–22). The uses seem astrological, so it relates to DADA principally through Divination (I.253–9).

Aside from exceedingly rare powers of seers and admittedly limited talents of centaurs, divination gets treated by Potter books as mostly baloney. Yet the books give Divination courses as much attention as any at Hogwarts, and more than most. Why? Especially from the political perspectives of dark arts and defenses against them? Part of it is Pottery humor for comic relief, and part is Pottery satire for resisting disciplinary regimes. We examine both as kinds of politics in chapters to come.[13] Another part is narrative presaging of events, often found in fantasies and connected to their power politics.[14] Potter books also detail modes of divination for their varied political symbolism. Divination devices of *fortune-telling* evoke prominent aspects of realist politics, even though Hermione uses that term to dismiss the whole subject as fraudulent and foolish (I.260). Divination interest in *omens*, *portents*, and *signs* figure into the perspectivist dynamics of "spotting" that boost Harry, Hermione, Hagrid, and Dumbledore to excellence in political action.[15] Divination modes of *dream interpretation* help parse the perfectionist politics of Harry's visions of Voldemort plus his existentialist dreams of desire and of detection (V.236–8). *Prophecy* attention to seers and centaurs surfaces significantly in forthcoming discussions of Pottery takes on liberal politics of freedom, perfectionist politics of attunement, and realist limits on political planning and action. With all divination methods, there's enormous room for playful laughter, often at Trelawney's expense. As the realist assessment of prognostications by Sybill and her students suggests, though, their possible accuracy is another of J. K. Rowling's sly jokes.

Three fields of study at Hogwarts target what most mages have seen as beings different in kind from mages: plants, animals, and muggles.

Respectively these courses address Herbology, Care of Magical Creatures, and Muggle Studies. Under Dumbledore, these courses implicitly or explicitly resist turning the differences they teach into judgments of inferiority or subordination. Mainly they teach respect for the differences. On the other hand, all three sequences teach their subjects instrumentally: What are the uses and dangers to mages of plants, animals, or muggles? All three fields are mage-centric. (In terms of green politics, none of the fields is eco-centric.)

Herbology teaches the magical uses of plants, specifically magical plants and otherwise. The uses include specialized food for magical animals, ingredients for magical potions, resources for magical healers, and powers for magical effects. An example of a magical effect that doesn't fit well into the other sorts of uses is how gillyweed webs Harry's feet and gives him gills to take oxygen from water for the second task in the Triwizard Tournament (IV.491–4). All the uses are highly relevant to DADA. The same holds for dealing with dangers from magical plants such as devil's snare, mandrake, and venomous tentacula.[16] At Hogwarts, Professor Pomona Sprout is a matter-of-fact teacher of Herbology, and her no-nonsense respect for plants follows her inclusive and egalitarian (unto democratic) politics in heading Hufflepuff House (I.133; IV.693; VI.479). This does amplify the politics of environmentalism examined in chapter 9.

Care of Magical Creatures claims great attention when and because it's taught by Rubeus Hagrid in books three through five. A beautiful emblem of Hagrid's courses is his textbook on *The Monster Book of Monsters*: fierce, dangerous, but tamed by a simple stroke to its spine that no one else thinks to try (III.13, 52–3, 112–3). When Wilhelmina Grubbly-Plank substitutes for Hagrid as professor, the presentation of magical animals is safer, organized better, and often more engaging to students, yet sometimes less helpful for defending against dark arts and creatures. This is because some of the creatures are less "monstrous" (IV.435; VI.359). As the Hogwarts keeper of keys, grounds, and game, Hagrid enlarges the education of Harry and others through spurring ventures into the Forbidden Forest, dark lake, and other places with magical creatures seldom met otherwise.[17]

It's not clear that Care of Magical Creatures attends much to domesticated animals like magical owls or mage familiars such as cats and rats. It could be said to focus on wild creatures, although individuals sometimes get tamed as pets (Fawkes the phoenix) and whole species such as acromantulas speak with "intelligence." Its discipline of magizoology covers the distinctive behaviors, habitats, and powers of fantastic creatures like bowtruckles, hippogriffs, and thestrals. Courses probably teach the properties and uses of parts of magical animals. These presumably include wand animators such as unicorn hairs, phoenix feathers, and dragon heartstrings (I.84). They likely encompass healing and protection by unicorn blood and horns, phoenix tears, and dragon hides (I.250, 258; II.207, 321–2; V.430). So Care of Magical Creatures serves the environmental politics in chapter 9. As taught by Hagrid, it also develops the perspectivist politics of "kindness" and "spotting" evoked in chapter 7, plus the perfectionist politics pitted against conformism in chapter 6. The Potter series treats all these politics as DADA mainstays.

DADA is the province of supposedly "dark creatures." Those include a standard list of supernatural horrors and some less familiar to many readers.[18] As dark fantasy, Pottery treats its witches, warlocks, goblins, ghosts, and poltergeists more as magical movers and shakers than as horrors. It does this for wizards, dwarfs, and elves, too, but its DADA creatures do cover many mythic figures.[19] Magizoology addresses a few of these, but Care of Magical Creatures doesn't.

A scandal lurking in this field is its classification of centaurs and merpeople (plus other intelligent speakers?) as magical beasts. Newt Scamander reports that the two species asked for this categorization from the MOM.[20] Perhaps this suggests their desires to be left apart, hints at their possible senses of superiority to humans of all kinds, and implies their likely distrust or disgust for mages. Thus the Potter series and its magizoology symbolically impeach mage specism just as the saga and its Muggle Studies indict mage racism—and ours as humans, of course. Hogwarts seems to reserve most of its lessons on centaurs, elves, giants, goblins, and merpeople to History of Magic, where they're not practical lessons or even apt to be memorable.

Muggle Studies can reflect structurally the prejudice among many mages that humans who aren't magical are inferior and dangerous to humans who are. The prejudice is diffuse or unconscious in many cases but focused, even vicious in others. The long history of antagonism between magical and non-magical people plays into this. At Hogwarts in Harry's time, however, the courses in Muggle Studies seem to be premised on equality and respect, even fascination, for humans who lack magic—notwithstanding the field's disparaging name.[21] Hagrid, of all people, repeatedly belittles Harry's Uncle Vernon by calling him a "great Muggle" (I.52, 58). The term has become so normalized in magical Britain that Harry and Hermione use it casually, although it's easy to imagine Hermione turning against it later in life. Harry and Ron never take Muggle Studies, since their family backgrounds mean they enter Hogwarts knowing much more about non-magical people than many Hogwarts students would. Born and raised as non-magical, Hermione nonetheless wants to take every course in her third year (II.252). It's telling that, when she drops Divination mid-year, it's because she's affronted by it (III.296–9); yet when she stops Muggle Studies, it's instead because she lacks time for it (III.430). Apparently the course respect for equality and marriage with non-mages spurs an opinion piece that goads Voldemort to abduct and murder Charity Burbage as the Hogwarts teacher of Muggle Studies (VII.3–16).

Another three fields of study and instruction tie so pervasively to dark arts and defenses against them that major reasons to pursue the disciplines separately include their vast scopes and exceptional complexities. These fields are Potions, Charms, and Transfiguration. Potions could be treated as DADA that emphasizes cauldrons rather than wands. Charms could be regarded as DADA that features spells not often cast for the generally "dark" uses of curses, hexes, jinxes, and maledictions (V.317). Transfiguration could be respected as DADA that works many of the most difficult and fundamental changes done with spells. Since politics are the dark arts and our defenses against them, courses on potions, charms, and transfiguration teach important politics.

Potions can amount to magical chemistry (alchemy). Potions can change elements into magical substances, just as cooking (especially baking) can change ingredients into palatable foods.[22] Both pursue substances that require the (specified) interaction of the ingredients in order to come into existence, and both use fire (or other heat) in many cases to help produce emergent properties. For Hogwarts students, the aim of instruction in Potions is to learn basic moves: find and read recipes, get and prep ingredients, measure and mix and heat them, age or distill or decanter the products, assess and apply them, and so forth. Like cooking, potion-making means peeling, chopping, shredding, or mashing some ingredients or intermediate products. It means timing the selections and additions just right. Politically the temptation is to compare this with the legislative slicing and dicing of policy provisions in order to make sausage—er, law. Yet *most* deliberation or other community (political) interaction resembles this in important ways.

The usual results are liquids (draughts and lotions), but the craft also makes solids (often powders) and gases or aerosols such as Garroting Gas (V.737). Some coat or penetrate surfaces, but many get ingested. Sometimes partly or temporarily, the swallowed or inhaled concoctions usually change a body through and through—chemically, as it were; so potion effects are often more profound than magical effects of easily learned spells. Prominent examples are aging and love potions, poisons, the Draught of Living Death, the Elixir of Life, Felix Felicis, Veritaserum, and Polyjuice Potion. In this respect, Potions is more like Transfiguration than (early years of) Charms. To judge from potions in the seven Potter books, the main kinds of uses are poisoning, healing (e.g., antidotes), cleaning, and enhancing performance or impeding it (often by mistake). The PEDs include the Invigoration Draught (Pepperup Potion) and the Wit-Sharpening Potion, but Hogwarts students investigate many other candidates as OWLs draw near (V.706–8).

Spells seem mostly to come in two parts, words and gestures; but potions usually get made with many ingredients in many steps. In this sense, potions are more complicated than spells. As an aspect of DADA, potion-making mainly involves practicing basic moves, then following recipes for specific draughts, perhaps learning also some principles of substitution or other adjustments in ingredients. It's unclear if Hogwarts students are expected to remember many potion formulas, but it's likely that they're taught principles of potion-making along with the names, properties, and uses of important potions—rather than memorizing recipes for them. The contrast with spell-casting is stark. In class and beyond, spells get practiced until effective, if not perfected. In the short term, this is so that they can be performed more or less instantly and automatically on request in exams. In the long term, it's so that mages can do spells on the spur of the moment, as needed to be effective in action. This would not hold for all spells, by a long shot; yet it would include many. Potions, to repeat, generally require planning and preparation.

During Quidditch tryouts, Hermione simultaneously sees the usefulness and achieves the effect of the Confundus Charm on Cormac McLaggen's goal-keeping; she thinks to say the spell *Confundo!* and direct it gesturally at him, so she just does it (VI.225–32; VII.529). It's so fleeting that McLaggen doesn't know what's hit him. A Confusing Concoction would take lead time to plan, make, and administer (III.318). How could it go unnoticed by McLaggen prior to the key moment, and how could it pass soon enough to spark no inquiry? The partial exceptions to this DADA contrast in learning and doing potions versus charms would be the specialists in potions such as Slughorn and Snape. Annotations in the text of the Half-Blood Prince show that, even as a student, Snape practiced and experimented with many potions (as well as possible spells) until perfecting (or at least improving) them *and* memorizing them, if mainly by repetition. Still the notes also argue against any specialist ambition to recall all details for all potions at all times.[23]

Charms is the principal curriculum on spell-casting with wands. At Hogwarts, courses in Charms seem to teach important spells and techniques not covered by courses in the other fields. As the name implies, the emphasis is on empowering—rather than defensive or offensive—uses. These contrasts in uses are perspectival, of course: who's doing what to whom, how, why, and with which effects? Accordingly DADA as a field encompasses Charms completely, if only by implication at Hogwarts.[24] The one key aspect of spell-casting that Hogwarts seems to teach in DADA rather than Charms is the value and method of what Rowling has Snape call "nonverbal" spells (VI.178–80, 603). The epithet is a misnomer, because these spells are silent, unvoiced, or unspoken; yet they mostly (still) involve mentally specified words. So these spells are nonvocal rather than nonverbal. Snape stresses the offensive and defensive advantages of any enemies not being able to hear what you're (on the verge of) doing—as (or just before) you do it. Is this *why* the topic goes to sixth-year DADA rather than Charms? To complicate matters, there might be spells (like *Liberacorpus!*) with incantations for names but which need silent casting (VI.238–9).

Transfiguration goes to the soul of Potter magic as constructively perfectionist politics.[25] This is because it knows how form can be content, style can be substance, figure can be essence. In Pottery, to transfigure is not merely to transform but to transubstantiate. Polyjuice potions and disillusionment spells change appearances or surfaces; transfigurations change beings, depths, or identities. Harry, juiced to look through-and-through like Goyle, is still Harry (II.212–25). Barty Crouch Jr. continually drinking from his flask to appear as Alastor Moody is still a Death Eater rather than the famous auror: not only does each sip make only a temporary change in his looks, but the younger Crouch is still operating under the guise of Mad-Eye (IV.670–91). In Minerva McGonagall's courses, to transfigure a wood and phosphorous match into a needle yields a bone or metal tool sharpened for stitching—*not* a slim wood stick with its phosphorous tip replaced by an "eye" for thread. To transfigure a teapot into a tortoise produces a shelled animal rather than a ceramic figurine. In Potter magic, to transfigure anything is to re(con)figure it. Potter realities are figural, arguably like ours. Hence Potter magic treats figures as intrinsic to the very stuff of things. To redo the figures is to remake the things: from vinegars into wines or from owls into opera glasses. Transfiguration emphasizes how Potter magic works with figures, with tropes.[26]

Potter charms join figures of speech (as plays with words) to figures of deed (as gestures with wands). Potter potions meld figures of stuff (e.g., Goyle's hair or fingernail clippings to help inform Harry's body with Goyle's physique) with figures of deed (e.g., knives cutting, wands stirring, and fires heating). And transfigurations use similarities of form (hedgehogs into pincushions) or name (guinea fowl into guinea pigs) or setting (air into yellow birds) or source (vinegars into wines) or the like to help spells refigure specific realities.[27] Chapters 4 and 6 evoke how Potter magic shares this focus on tropes with philosophers of perfectionist politics from the ancient Sophists to Ralph Waldo Emerson and eventually to Stanley Cavell.[28]

Limits on transfiguration are telling. It's easy for things to differ too much *figurally* for transfiguration to succeed, and presumably a talent for magical transfiguration features spotting figural similarities and focusing them powerfully in spells and gestures. Presumably this is how Hermione can transfigure air into yellow birds, even though Gamp's Law of Transfiguration is that neither thin air nor any other version of nothing can be transfigured into (nourishing) food (VII.292–3). Yet it's also possible for things to share so much figurally that transfiguration spells accomplish little. Hagrid thinks that this is how Dudley Dursley merely got a pig's tail, when Hagrid tried to make him fully into a pig: Harry's cousin was already so much like a pig that Hagrid's spell couldn't do much (I.59). Hogwarts students (are supposed to) learn as another limit that transfiguration across species requires adaptations in usual spells (I.385). Surely they do learn that, in transfiguration, size matters.[29] As beginners, students keep size pretty constant across objects. Matches and needles, mice and snuffboxes, rabbits and slippers are similar in respective sizes. Desks can be transfigured into pigs, and rats into teacups, because their similar sizes help, although the further figural platforms might be harder to identify (I.53, 134). Yet the masterly McGonagall overcomes the size limit in magnifying ordinary chess pieces to life-size and giving them life in order to produce a participant version of wizard chess (I.281–4). In short, it's hard to see how a mage can get really good at DADA without excellence at transfiguration.

If DADA is initially the featured attraction among Hogwarts courses, History of Magic is the consensual dud. The contents might promise excitement, with goblin rebellions and sources of current troubles capable (in principle) of keeping students interested.[30] But its delivery by the ghostly Professor Binns is dry as dust (II.148). He doesn't offer events as vicarious experiences for students, thus engaging their energy and educating their political judgment as a realist might in teaching history as DADA.[31] As the consummate student, Hermione nonetheless brings to the trio's quests key facts and contexts from her study of history in class and books, notably Bathilda Bagshott's *A History of Magic* and *Hogwarts: A History* (I.66, 117). By field of study, histories and biographies double the number of books that any other field offers as DADA resources for the trio's political adventures.[32] Republican politics teach (and monumentalize) the "lessons of history" for us in the here and now, but Binns seems reluctant to connect his courses to current concerns (II.149–52). Lacking a sense of personal relevance is a problem for Harry. He's better at recalling history from chocolate frog cards and newspaper obituaries than History of Magic.[33]

DADA ADVANCES

Missing from the curriculum is the DADA principle to get organized. This is not merely another way of saying in general to be prepared; instead it's a directive to recognize the skill and strength in well-coordinated cooperation among defenders. Arguably this principle is the most overtly political (and specifically republican) because it's the most clearly communal. None of the DADA lessons in Hogwarts books or classes available to us readers teach modes and needs (or powers and flaws) of organizing people for concerted action, whether offensive or defensive. Of course, the relevant kinds of organization can range in scope from countries and empires to families and friendships. Hogwarts as a school and its houses are relevant too. But for Hogwarts students of DADA, getting organized mainly turns out to feature clubs, teams, orders, and maybe militias. From a few talkative members of the Order of the Phoenix, the heroic team learns a bit about reasons and devices for getting organized. But then Umbridge inadvertently spurs some of the most determined DADA students into learning organization by starting to do it with the DA.

Advanced magic important to DADA surely includes Legilimency to sense and interpret the mentation of others plus Occlumency to block that mental detection (V.382, 519–24, 530–53). Evidently there are several ways to deflect Legilimency as a learned skill, just as there often are several ways to defend against any other "dark" act.[34] Dark arts not taught at Hogwarts seem to involve complicated, multi-step magic to create horcruxes, modify memories, implant false ones, possess other beings, or do further dark deeds (VI.367–81; VII.105). This is comparable to the skillful combination of several sorts of enchantments to make magical artifacts such as flying broomsticks, Pensieves, the Weasley family clock, photographs that move or even speak, stairs that shift position at Hogwarts, living portraits, the Hand of Glory, the Mirror of Erised, and others. Even Dumbledore's Deluminator seems to link basic spells. It might well join the wand magic of *Lumos*, *Nox*, and their projection at a distance with the incantatory magic of marking spoken names, the magical "trace," and the pre-programmed apparating of portkeys. Similarly Hagrid figures out how to breed manticores with fire-crabs to make blast-ended skrewts (IV.196, 438).

Implicit in the whole Hogwarts curriculum is the DADA principle that most magic gets generated, recognized, or resisted by combining the basics. Hogwarts teaches the basics. As Hagrid reassures Harry, Hogwarts must begin with basics because it includes students who've known nothing of mages and little-or-nothing of magic, until invited to the school (I.86). But it either leaves most creative and practical combinations to advanced courses that we readers don't sample, or it expects these to come with adult endeavors after graduation. At any rate, Hogwarts doesn't aspire to be a "research school," similar to a research university in muggle Britain or no-maj USA. This doesn't even seem to characterize Hogwarts instruction to prepare for Nastily Exhausting Wizarding Tests (III.314). Neither teachers nor students routinely venture basic inquiries or do the applied-unto-professional work of inventing magical artifacts. To establish further principles for a branch of magic adds to the basics. Fundaments of magic would include Golpalott's Third Law (VI.374) and Gramp's Law of Elemental Transfiguration, with its five exceptions (VII.578). To identify properties of magical ingredients, such as Dumbledore contributes for uses of dragon's blood, also augments the basics. Therefore Dumbledore *might* be an exception, but Hogwarts is for teaching and studying—not discovering—the basics about dark arts and their defenses.

Does this tame an otherwise unduly dangerous education? Hogwarts is meant to develop emerging magical abilities safely. This is meant to help harness the powers of young mages for the wizarding world—rather than against it, by intent or accident. Yet it's also to protect young mages from themselves. And of course, it's to make them safe for magical *and* muggle Britain, plus the rest of the world, particularly as governed by the International Statute of Secrecy, which is to protect mages from persecution by keeping magic under wraps (V.21, 44, 74–5). The films on *Fantastic Beasts* put even more emphasis on this than do the *Harry Potter* books and movies.

In Pottery, advanced—let alone innovative—magic arises through skills, experiences, and experiments in melding basic spells, potions, even creatures. The most successful combinations manifest emergent properties that yield distinctive uses and powers. In the next chapter, we see how some of this fits the perfectionist politics of troping as inventive leaping. Later we see how other aspects suit the republican-rhetorical tradition of treating political actions and institutions as conventional-unto-creative performances that join words, gestures, characters, and settings to do familiar or new (free, unforced) things.[35] Politics of these (and other) kinds are promoted in the Potter books, as ensuing chapters explain.

In Harry's time at Hogwarts, the champions of magical experiments and inventions are the Weasley twins, Fred and George. Their genius is to see what's magically possible and useful while thinking creatively and acting with little regard for others' rules. The twins also have lots and lots of fun, even when pressured by Hermione to experiment mostly on themselves. Their Canary Creams briefly transfigure people into big birds and back again: no mean feat (IV.367). Their Headless Hats hide the body parts beneath those enchanted toppers (V.540). Their Skiving Snackboxes match poisons or other potions to antidotes, to get visibly "sick" students excused from classes then let them recover for the "free periods" which result (V.102–5).

Like computer whizzes of late, the twins find their formal schooling to be more hindrance than help. So they leave Hogwarts earlier than their siblings to focus on innovation and business. This "foolish" move seems to enlarge their magical creativity. Soon Weasleys' Wizard Wheezes is selling Pygmy Puff(skein)s as cute new pets. It offers intriguing Daydream Charms, a line of WonderWitch products, and another of dark arts defenses. These appear in a vast array of clever amusements: some useful, some silly, some subversive, and several at Voldemort's expense (VI.116–21). Nearly all involve advanced magic, which is impressive to mages well-positioned to assess the spells and potions deployed. As the saga proceeds, even the twins are surprised by the DADA uses that develop for various of their innovations. Hence the twelfth chapter attends in detail to the Weasley politics of folly. It treats these as a kind of chaotic anarchism that resists the authoritarianism, fascism, and other oppressive politics that Harry faces—and we do too.

NOTES

1. On dark arts, see *The Rise and Fall of the Dark Arts* (I.106); *Moste Potente Potions* (II.160); *Basic Hexes for the Busy and Vexed* (IV.339); *Magick Moste Evile* (VI.381); and *Secrets of the Darkest Art* (VII.102). Also consider *Aids for Magical Mischief-Makers* (III.190) and *Saucy Tricks for Tricky Sorts* (IV.486).

2. On defenses against dark arts, see *Asiatic Anti-Venoms* (V.331), *A Compendium of Common Curses and Their Counter-Actions* (V.390), *The Dark Arts Outsmarted* (V.390), *Self-Defensive Spellwork* (V.390), *Jinxes for the Jinxed* (V.390), *Practical Defensive Magic and Its Use Against the Dark Arts* (V.501). Also relevant is *The Healer's Helpmate* (VI.100).

3. On mediated, vicarious, virtual, and symbolic modes of experience, see John S. Nelson and G. R. Boynton, *Video Rhetorics* (Urbana: University of Illinois Press, 1997), 195–232.

4. On the Apparation course, see VI.354–56. Also see *Common Apparition Mistakes and How to Avoid Them* (VI.369).

5. On vanishing cabinets, see V.626–27; VII.526, 586. On brooms and charms, see III.232.

6. On facing, see Janice Hocker Rushing and Thomas S. Frentz, *Projecting the Shadow* (Chicago: University of Chicago Press, 1995); John S. Nelson and Barbara J. Hill, "Facing the Holocaust: Robert Arneson's Ceramic Myth of Postmodern Catastrophe," *Human Rights /Human Wrongs* eds. Robert Hobbs and Fredrick Woodard (Seattle: University of Washington Press, 1986), 189–209. Also see John S. Nelson, *Politics in Popular Movies* (Boulder: Paradigm Publishers, 2015), 24–30 and 154–58; John S. Nelson, *Cowboy Politics* (Lanham, MD: Lexington Books, 2018), 179–203 and 238–51.

7. See Murray Edelman, *Constructing the Political Spectacle* (Chicago: University of Chicago Press, 1988), 6–9, 90–102, and 120–30.

8. On constant vigilance, see IV.211–17, 407, 571; VII.95.

9. On gossip and rumor, see I.11; IV.226; VI.443, 528–29, 535; VII.620–21.

10. See J. K. Rowling, *The Tales of Beedle the Bard* (New York: Scholastic Press, 2007).

11. Pottery books on runes include *Ancient Runes Made Easy* (II.254), *Magical Hieroglyphs and Logograms* (V.574), *Spellman's Syllabary* (V.575; VII.94), and *Advanced Rune Translation* (VI.129).

12. Hermione has *Numerology and Grammatica* (III.315) and *New Theory of Numerology* (V.503). On politics of western number symbolism, see John S. Nelson, *Ironic Politics* (Chapel Hill: unpublished PhD Dissertation for the University of North Caroline Department of Political Science, 1976), 128–317.

13. Divination Books in Pottery include *Unfogging the Future* by Cassandra Vablatsky (III.53, 104), *Predicting the Unpredictable: Insulate Yourself against*

Shocks (III.53), *Broken Balls: When Fortunes Turn Foul* (III.53), *Death Omens: What to Do When You Know the Worst Is Coming* (III.54), and *The Dream Oracle* by Inigo Imago (V.237).

14. On presaging versus foreshadowing events, see John S. Nelson, *Cowboy Politics* (Lanham, MD: Lexington Books, 2018), 181–82.

15. On spotting the Grim as a portent of death, see III.34, 107, 178, 184, 298, 303, 334. On other omens, see I.2–6, 107, 253–59; IV.200. Sybill Trelawney teaches the interpretation of portents in astrological alignments, crystal balls, dreams, fire, palm lines, tarot cards, and tea leaves (III.53, 104). She also finds prophetic signs in Ornithomancy as the study of bird entrails, flight, flocking, and species plus Heptomology as the predictive decoding of snake innards, moves, sites, and species (V.237, 552).

16. On dangers of magical plants, see I.277–78; II.75–79, 91–94; III.182; IV.293; V.171; VI.189; VII.600. Pottery books on plants include *One Thousand Magical Herbs and Fungi* by Phyllida Spore (I.66, V.362, VI.539), *Encyclopedia of Toadstools* (II.63), *Magical Water Plants of the Mediterranean* (IV.220), and *Flesh-Eating Trees of the World* (VI.283).

17. On magical creatures, Pottery features *Fantastic Beasts and Where to Find Them* by Newt Scamander (I.67). The saga also mentions *Dragon Species of Great Britain and Ireland* (I.230), *From Egg to Inferno: A Dragon Keeper's Guide* (I.230), *The Handbook of Hippogriff Psychology* (III.300), *Fowl or Foul? A Study of Hippogriff Brutality* (III.300), and *Dreadful Denizens of the Deep* (IV.488).

18. In Pottery, supernatural creatures of horror include banshees, demons, ghouls, hags, harpies (veela), inferi, sprites, vampires, werewolves, and zombies.

19. In Pottery, dark figures of familiar myths and fantasies include basilisks, cerberuses, chimaeras, cockatrices, dragons, fairies, gnomes, griffins, leprechauns, mandrakes, manticores, ogres, pegasi, phoenixes, pixies, sphinxes, trolls, unicorns, and yetis.

20. See J. K. Rowling as Newt Scamander, *Fantastic Beasts and Where to Find Them* (New York: Scholastic Books, 2001), xii–xiii, 6, and 28–29.

21. Consider the saga's two works on muggles: *Home Life and Social Habits of British Muggles* (III.264) as a textbook for Muggle Studies plus *The Adventures of Martin Miggs, the Mad Muggle* as comics owned by Ron (II.40) in a family defamed as "muggle-lovers" (II.51; IV.729; VI.208).

22. See Michael Pollan, *Cooked* (New York: Penguin, 2013).

23. Available for consulting are a periodical—*The Practical Potioneer* (VII.17)— and books: *Magical Drafts and Potions* by Arsenius Jigger (I.66), *Moste Potente Potions* (II.160), *Asiatic Anti-Venoms* (V.331), and *Advanced Potion-Making* by Libatius Borage (VI.183–84).

24. The Pottery periodical is *Challenges in Charming* (VII.17). Miranda Goshawk offers *The Standard Book of Spells* grade by grade before OWLs (I.66; II.43; III.54; IV.152, 155; V.160). Also available are *Magical Theory* by Adalbert Waffling (I.66), *Basic Hexes for the Busy and Vexed* (IV.339), *Olde and Forgotten Bewitchments and Charmes* (IV.486), *An Anthology of Eighteenth-Century Charms* (IV.488), and *Achievements in Charming* (V.709).

25. Presumably we Pottery readers could learn more about this from analyzing *A Beginners' Guide to Transfiguration* by Emeric Switch (I.66), *Intermediate Transfiguration* (III.54; V.705), or the journal on *Transfiguration Today* (III.49).

26. See John S. Nelson, *Tropes of Politics* (Madison: University of Wisconsin Press, 1998); Nelson, *Politics in Popular Movies*, 105–72.

27. One spell used in some transfigurations is *Inanimatus Conjurus* (V.289).

28. See John S. Nelson, "Political Theory as Political Rhetoric," *What Should Political Theory Be Now?* ed. John S. Nelson (Albany: State University of New York Press, 1983), 169–240.

29. More generally, Snape points out to Harry that time and space count in magic (V.531).

30. On History of Magic in general and goblin rebellions in particular, see II.150–2; III.77; IV.234, 392, 449; V.725.

31. See John S. Nelson, "Prudence as Republican Politics in American Popular Culture," *Prudence*, ed. Robert Hariman (University Park: Pennsylvania State University Press, 2003), 229–57 on 245. Percy Weasley seems to read *Prefects Who Gained Power* (II.58) as Niccolò Machiavelli led realist republicans to read histories: for vicarious experience of events. And annotations by the Half-Blood Prince for recipes in Harry's potions textbook work somewhat like the action advice offered by Machiavelli for anecdotes in his handbook for princes. Also relevant, probably, is *Weird Wizarding Dilemmas and Their Solutions* (IV.487).

32. These include seven of the eight Lockhart books (save the one on household pests). Further Pottery books of history or biography are *Modern Magical History*, *The Rise and Fall of the Dark Arts*, *Great Wizarding Events of the Twentieth Century* (I.106); *Quidditch Through the Ages* (I.144), *Notable Magical Names of Our Time*, *Important Modern Magical Discoveries: A Study of Recent Developments in Wizardry* (I.197–98); *Sites of Historical Sorcery* (III.77); *An Appraisal of Magical Education in Europe* (IV.123); *Quidditch Teams of Britain and Ireland* (IV.410); *A Guide to Medieval Sorcery* (IV.488); *Nature's Nobility: A Wizarding Genealogy* (V.116); plus *The Life and Lies of Albus Dumbledore* (VII.22) and *Armando Dippet: Master or Moron?* (VII.252) by Rita Skeeter.

33. See I.103, 218; VII.21.

34. Can a natural-born Legilimens such as Queenie Goldstein in the films on *Fantastic Beasts* be completely blocked by anybody who's not a natural Occlumens? In *The Twilight Saga* (2008–2012), compare Edward Cullen as something like a vampirically born Legilimens with Bella Swann as (at least Edward's) naturally born Occlumens.

35. On republican actions as public performances, see Hannah Arendt, *The Human Condition* (Chicago: University of Chicago Press, 1958); Hannah Arendt, *On Revolution* (New York: Viking, 1963); Hannah Arendt, *Between Past and Future* (New York: Viking, 1963, 1968); Hannah Arendt, *Crises of the Republic* (New York: Harcourt Brace Jovanovich, 1972). On republican institutions as stitches in space and time, see John S. Nelson and Anna Lorien Nelson, "Institutions in Feminist and Republican Science Fiction," *Legal Forum* 22, no. 4 (1998): 641–53.

Chapter 4

Potter Magic as Perfectionist Politics

From the beginning, the Potter saga promotes perfectionism in Harry's conduct and ours. The best reason to recognize this Potter emphasis on perfectionist politics is that Potter magic is perfectionist in several, telling respects. In this sense, *perfectionism* is the pursuit of a truly, fully good life—with no limits given initially on how far this might go. Personal takes on what is good can differ. Indeed they're likely to be discovered, invented, and refined along the way. Still the commitment is to keep trying to exceed what we've done and who we are—in the best possible ways. The commitment is to excellence or, better, to excelling. It's about perfection not as an end-state but as a continual quest. Perfectionism is possible for various politics, but the versions of perfectionism prominent in Harry Potter's political action are illuminated by philosophers like Ralph Waldo Emerson, Friedrich Nietzsche, and Stanley Cavell.[1]

Philosophically these kinds of perfectionism are anti-foundational and anti-metaphysical. They treat realities as made by us and others—rather than given from above by God or below by Nature. They urge strength, vigor, individuality, and leaping the chasms in life. They appreciate genius and peak experiences; they also prize sharing, differences, and everyday conventions. Admittedly Nietzsche's accounts of perfectionism have been spun into myths of Aryan Overmen and defenses of fascism. There are no great adventures without dangers, after all, and the Dark Lord Voldemort epitomizes such awful possibilities. Yet perfectionisms also power American transcendentalism, the Just-Do-It excellence in popular cultures, and the multicultural diversity in personal styles. These strenuous perfectionisms feature exertions and experiments in daily lives attuned to community and biology. They pursue daring that *could* turn predatory, and sometimes does, but that *should* stay responsive to the many others and opportunities in our lives. Potter books

57

promote this response-ability by inflecting their strenuous perfectionisms with the contrapuntal perfectionisms of Buddhist mindfulness and Christian love. Mindfulness makes Harry, Ron, and Hermione great spotters; love makes them great friends; and daring to Just Do It makes them great heroes.

The perfectionist politics in Harry Potter can operate on the "impulse power" of Just Do It because they can Let It Go, turning away from aims of control or even manipulation.[2] It's to leap beyond vengeance, possession, obsession, and maybe even memory. Hence it's also to resist the despair that can come from failing for now to bring about what's good, just, helpful, or otherwise sought. Don't brood on failure, don't contest water under the bridge, rather accept emergent situations and keep trying to excel. The heroic three suffer setbacks, but their persistence is remarkable as well as magical.

The saga offers five early templates for Potter magic. All fit perfectionist politics, and all develop as the series unfolds. Together they meld (symbols of) masculine and feminine powers. They also heal antagonisms between Apollonian enlightenment and Dionysian projects of going dark. First is the Deluminator invented by Albus Dumbledore. Second is spell-casting through playful words and mimetic gestures as taught at Hogwarts School. Third is Diagon Alley as the main street for magical London. Fourth is Harry's talent and delight in flying on a broomstick. And fifth is Knockturn Alley as London's place for dark objects, dark creatures, and dark arts.

THE DELUMINATOR FOR GOING DARK

Initially called the Put-Outer, the Deluminator is more or less literally Dumbledore's way of Going Dark, and this is a major paradigm of Potter magic. It looks like a humble lighter for cigarettes, yet it sucks in nearby lights one at a time for storage and later replacement: not light bulbs, lamps, or the like, mind you, but somehow the discrete illuminations themselves. We may mistake this for merely turning lights off or on, albeit at a distance and without switches—except the last book has the Deluminator putting lights into places they weren't before. However clever the magic that makes this device, though, isn't it mainly testimony to Dumbledore's whimsy? A magical wand can light (*Lumos*) or extinguish (*Nox*) its tip, if illumination is needed or not: easy spells for young mages to do. Why see the Deluminator as a big deal, politically or otherwise?

Unlike wands, cauldrons, and other magical equipment, the (one-of-a-kind?) Deluminator is specifically for Going Dark. This perfectionist mode is not acting when depressed or unhappy. Nor need it turn to evil. Instead it turns away from the west's primary reliance on sight. Thus it enables effective action in dark times. Figurally these dim, distort, or defeat the light needed for most western politics to serve people well. Thus, to take just one example, republican pru-dence would have us act with fore-sight, but it must falter when conditions keep even keen vision from making good sense of our situations. Going dark informs action with sensoria other than sight and resources other than light. It taps further human senses—of sound, smell, touch, and taste. It also cultivates attunement to inquiries and inferences not based on sight. Perfectionists have company in feminists in reaching beyond epistemologies of sight almost alone. Christians can get there, too, through the Epistle to the Hebrews, which used to be attributed to Paul and which celebrates faith paradoxically as "the evidence of things unseen." Similarly the environmentalist Wendell Berry points out that knowing the dark *as* the dark means setting aside light to go dark.[3] To recognize Potter magic as often going dark can make it much easier to recognize politics as the dark arts and our defenses against them. The Deluminator is especially helpful for doing this.

The Deluminator is the first magical device presented in the Potter series, appearing even earlier than cauldrons and wands (I.9). Thereafter it gets only a few, cursory mentions until the last book reveals its further, related powers. One helps by bringing lights to dark, wandless, and otherwise desperate set-tings: in the Malfoy dungeon where Harry and Ron join Luna, Griphook, and Ollivander. The other, more drastic and romantic power helps by bringing friends—loved ones—back together. Hermione's distant utterance of Ron's name sounds from the Deluminator, leading him to click it. This not only darkens the local lights but generates a pulsing blue light that moves near his heart then lets him apparate to Harry and Hermione, even though he doesn't otherwise know his destination. He goes by sound, goes without sight into the darkness, then goes out to the light, and the light goes into him. The Put-Outer begins by bestowing darkness, but going dark can eventually bring light. This puts together the Apollonian and the Dionysian.

It also ironizes one of the worst curses from Voldemort. Avoidance of the Dark Lord's self-given name long provides a sign of fearing and respecting him. Followers use his self-styled title, but others speak of "He-Who-Must-Not-Be-Named" or "You-Know-Who." Only unusually careless fools or extraordinarily courageous foes say "Voldemort." Once the MOM falls to his minions, general disuse of that name lets him turn its utterance into an instant locator of such, shall we say, insufficient supporters (VII.389). Death Eaters then apparate to capture, interrogate, or kill the offenders. When Ron deserts Harry and Hermione, Hermione's anger and Harry's deference to it have them not speaking Ron's name for all too long. But the Deluminator lets Ron hear his name's eventual enunciation, then the blue light helps him apparate (as often as needed) to rejoin the two, despite Ron having no sense of destination beyond going back to them. It's as though the blue, Portkey-like light directs his personal determination to reunite with them. The Deluminator could be said to charm the speaking of Ron's name, at least by his best friends.

SPELL-CASTING FOR GOING FIGURAL

In magical Britain, avoiding Voldemort's name might make more sense than we readily imagine, even before its utterance gets cursed. This is because Potter magic also is spell-casting magic. It's what probably comes to mind as wizards waving wands just so, while saying special words exactly right, whether aloud or silently. In Pottery, words—with gestures—can summon and direct magic; so a mage must learn to take care with them. (In politics, including politics in our everyday lives, words and gestures can be powerful too; hence we also do well to learn such care.) Spell-casting melds the incantatory magic of verbal formulas with the mimetic (imitative) magic of bodily motions. Spell-casting looms especially large in Hogwarts courses for Charms, DADA, and Transfiguration.

In political terms, spell-casting magic connects to the republican-rhetorical tradition that cultivates speech-in-action-in-public.[4] These are politics that originate in ancient Rome, possibly even ancient Greece, as the first systematic study and practice of memorable deeds and words in community affairs. As an academic and political discipline, rhetoric analyzes speech into words and action into gestures. Yet it's loathe to do either without the other, because it knows that raw behavior becomes meaningful deeds mostly when refined by words, just as visual marks or vocal sounds become intelligible words mainly when tied to deeds. Hogwarts educates mages in these arts of words-with-motions and gestures-with-incantations. Harry finds some spells easy, as with the disarming charm (*Expelliarmus*), for expelling wands from mages' hands. Harry finds others hard, needing help from Hermione with the summoning charm (*Accio*), for accessing objects at a distance. Later he gets taunted by Bellatrix Lestrange for his weak version of the torture curse (*Cruciatus*), meant to produce excruciating pain (V.810). Yet it tells us great things about Harry that he soon becomes a prodigy with the patronus charm (*Expecto patronum*), for expecting the helper. Chapters 6 and 11 say more on this last, particularly important spell.

Politics associated with republics prove highly important to the Potter series, so they get detailed attention in pages to come. But for now, we need only acknowledge that spell-casting magic is rife in the popular genre of fantasy and that it can feature republican-rhetorical politics. This provides a platform for appreciating how Rowling twists the magic of words-and-gestures in perfectionist ways with clever, insistent wordplay and its gestural counterpart. Perfectionist politics frequently seem to spring from republican politics as the main western roots for modern ideologies and postmodern movements. In particular, perfectionism in the Emerson-Nietzsche-Cavell mode characteristically revs or leaps beyond republican politics. Thus it doesn't (try to) fit nicely into western civilization. (Several sorts of feminism and environmentalism also can be postwestern in their efforts to get past many, many major projects of the modern west—such as patriarchy and industrialism.) Potter politics make spell-casting perfectionist by Going Figural.[5]

Perfectionists akin to Harry Potter emphasize the conventionality of languages, let alone politics, as community constructions of *tropes*. In ancient Greece, these were the *turns* we take together in words, deeds, and events to change meanings or outcomes. We usually limit tropes to figures of speech, which we contrast to literal language, when words say just what they mean ordinarily—and no more. Perfectionists also acknowledge figures of thinking, doing, and being. Further, perfectionists appreciate words and other figures as always already altering themselves, however slowly, in use. Thus truth, for Nietzsche and other perfectionists, is "a mobile army of metaphors, metonymies, anthropomorphisms," and other "human relations" that can seem fixed yet we can still shift.[6] With Emerson, perfectionists perceive that "we are symbols, and inhabit symbols," while "language is fossil poetry." As turns, tropes are dynamic, even transformative. So figures are flows. Think of skaters etching figures onto ice. For perfectionists, everything is in action, in motion, in play. Change is not the rarity but the rule. Forms of humanity, speech, even nature "flow," which is exactly what the Potter play with words and deeds helps us to sense in politics. For perfectionists, the change can become a "perfecting" leap—so that, in Emerson's words, "within the form of every creature is a force impelling it to ascend into a higher form."[7]

Like the names of magical characters and creatures, the Potter words for magical spells, potions, and devices play with linguistic roots, often from Latin. The humor in Rowling's puns and other figures of speech is ample. Much of it is accessible on the surface, so that readers can smile often at her verbal inventiveness. For unlocking doors, to open and close them, *Alohomora* evokes *Aloha* to say *hello* and *goodbye* in Hawaiian. Yet her little jokes and wry comments turn eventually into political keys, because the wordplay and the associated gestures open into whole networks of implications for actions and institutions. Here let's leave the symbolism of character names largely to other analysts, who've delved already into many such insights, while letting one early example suffice. At Flourish and Blotts— note the perfectionist embrace of exuberance and messiness in this—Harry spots a book on *Curses and Counter-curses (Bewitch Your Friends and Befuddle Your Enemies with the Latest Revenges: Hair Loss, Jelly-Legs, Tongue-Tying and Much, Much More)*. It's by Professor Vindictus Viridian (I.80). The author's name plainly (but figurally) reinforces the idea that

curses are vicious instruments of revenge and envy: *Vindictus* comes from
Latin for *vindictive* or *vengeful*, and *Viridian* similarly denotes a blue-green
color associated with greed or envy. These links get developed when the specific curses occur in later books, with the implicated politics turning out to
be vengeance and envy as republican vices plus greed as a liberal-capitalist
motive.

The Potter strategy in Going Figural is seldom to seek profundity in
individual tropes but instead to proliferate symbolic associations in mythic
complexes for politics. In the same verbal neighborhood as the curse-book's
author is the earliest spell we find to get sustained attention from Professor
Flitwick in Charms. Again from Latin, *Wingardium Leviosa* suggests a *winning or victorious enclosure or limitation of levitation*—as a modest kind of
soaring controlled from a distance. Precisely spoken, which Ron has trouble
doing, it's a spell to lift an object and make it hover. It also requires an exact
swish-and-flick of the wand, which Seamus Finnigan struggles to master.[8]
Performed correctly, the incantation-and-gesture lowers the object gently
back to where it started, as Hermione (of course) excels in demonstrating.
The spell isn't for full-fledged flying or forceful throwing. Yet Ron soon uses
this spell in haste to save Hermione from a mountain troll, by levitating its
club to fall (accidentally?) on the troll's head, hard enough to knock it out.
And in the last book, the spell helps keep Harry's sidecar airborne (briefly
but sufficiently) with the enchanted motorcycle that Hagrid uses to fly Harry
away from Death Eaters and Voldemort. Effective magic is inventive; and
Going Figural evokes—possibly even supplies—some of the flexible, creative, perfectionist potential of Potter magic, which flows beyond its initial
uses.

Spell-casting in Potter magic twists beyond straightforwardly republican
empowerment into perfectionist leaping—in lots of directions we don't
always anticipate. Thus *Expelliarmus* turns out to deflect even the deadliest
of curses—not only away from Harry but sometimes back at Voldemort.
Imperius turns out to subdue others less by projecting force and inflicting
pain, as we typically take imperialism to do in imposing foreign rule, than by
soothing any will to resist. This tropal take on the cultural politics of colonialism and dominion is intriguing by itself. Add only one letter, though, and
produce the repelling charm (*Impervius*)—likewise suggestive in this political context. For all the precision needed in enunciating words and moving
wands, magical spells in the Potter saga aren't limited to singular meanings
and effects. Fantasy spell-casting is typically literalist in word and deed:
one rigorous incantation plus one exact gesture produces one specific result.
By Going Figural, Potter spells implicate families of meanings and effects.
We might say that Potter spells flow beyond their literal limits and initial
uses. Perfectionists recognize that this holds also for our words, deeds, and

identities. Rather than end, contain, or defy this, perfectionists often would go with the flow.

DIAGON ALLEY FOR GOING SLANT

A further perfectionist aspect of Potter magic is signaled by Diagon Alley as *the* London locale for mages to meet and equip themselves. It seldom takes readers long to realize that this name amounts, by a different spelling, to *diagonally*. What's diagonal is "at a slant." In relation to mundane (or muggle) London, even the fully respectable magic on Diagon Alley is at a slant. So we may say that magic in the Potter series involves Going Slant, which is a strange staple of perfectionist politics. In fact, Diagon Alley is where Potter witches and wizards shop for slant.

Slant is the trajectory and territory of contrarians, tricksters, sacred clowns, and agents of chaos.[9] It fits the perfectionist bent for creativity, non-conformity, and turning every which way but loose.[10] It cuts across the grain (in nature or convention), the right (in angle or morality), the regular (in procedure or timing), and the square (in spirit or truth). Slant can be direct or evasive; it can seem naïve or sophisticated. Slant excels by deviating in direction rather than outpacing in speed or exceeding in distance. Accordingly it often leaves behind the Apollonian civilization of the west. In environmentalist terms, slant is wilding but not exactly savaging, as when the flying car deposits Ron and Harry near Hogwarts then drives itself into the dark and forbidden forest. It returns to rescue the two from acromantulas, but then it resumes roaming alone. Having turned into a magical, autonomous being in its own right, the car leaps past the paved paths of the west. Dumbledore writes aslant (VII.134) and, with sharp peripheral vision, looks aslant too (V.610–1).

Harry's personal affinity for perfectionist magic as Going Slant becomes clear early. In the life-sized game of wizard chess that Professor McGonagall contrives to protect the Hogwarts path to the Philosopher's Stone, Ron casts Harry as a bishop. Thus Harry moves on the diagonal, at a slant. Hermione as a castle or rook moves vertically and horizontally, on the square, to suit symbolically who she is and how she acts. Ron becomes the most strategically powerful piece, the queen, for going far in any direction, and he calls moves for the black pieces. The trio's side is black because McGonagall has made the white pieces into obstacles for pursuing the Stone. The need, figurally, is to show magical prowess by going dark; and this reinforces further symbolism in the obstacle course to the Stone. For example, Snape's logic problem with potions blocks the way forward with a curtain of black fire. The chess match ends in similar territory. Ron figures out that sacrificing himself as the strongest piece can win by going beyond the usual moves; and he does this hard, heroically republican deed despite pleas from Harry and Hermione. Still Ron knows what he's doing, and his sacrifice lets Harry checkmate the opposing king—on the slant.

BROOMSTICK FLIGHT FOR GOING HIGH AND FAR

Magical spells, potions, and devices are to fantasy what wild talents are to science fiction, and superhuman powers are to the superhero genre. Probably the easiest way to recognize Potter magic as perfectionist is to appreciate how Hogwarts education helps budding mages refine hosts of superpowers or wild talents: to move objects without contact (telekenesis), make fires without kindling (pyrokinesis), read minds (telepathy), or jump instantly to distant places (teleportation). We associate super-speed, super-strength, super-vision, super-hearing, and such with Superman; and many know that the comic-book invention of this first superhero reacted in 1938 to the Nazi vision of a New Aryan Race of *Übermenschen*. This was adapted (perversely) from Nietzsche's perfectionist *Übermensch*. He's a figure who leaps creatively beyond herds of ordinary humans. The term transliterates as *Overman* or *Superman*, as the recent incorporation of *uber* into English readily suggests. But to make Superman's practices of perfectionism "safe for democracy," this super-powered alien gets raised from infancy by Ma and Pa Kent in Smallville to pursue "Truth, Justice, and the American Way." Voldemort follows the Nazi perversion of perfectionist powers by trying to leave behind his humanity and become "much, much more than a man" (IV.15). It's up to Harry and his friends to approach super-heroism more than super-villainy—by turning their magical, symbolically perfectionist powers toward better politics.

Superman's signature superpower is flying. (Initially he "leaps tall buildings at a single bound," but soon this turns into outright flying.) Harry is surprised and thrilled to discover early in the first book that he's "a natural" at broomstick flying. (Adding to this is Harry's exceptional skill as a spotter, with more on that perspectivist talent to come later; and together these abilities make him a superb seeker in the wizard game of Quidditch.) There are magical substitutes. Floo travel requires advance linking of floos and involves soot. Apparating teleports a mage instantly to a destination, while flying moves through space and takes time. Yet apparating faces distance limits (VII.473), while offering no pleasures of soaring or steering through the sky. (Nor could apparating serve Quidditch.) Riding thestrals seems too strange (V.766). Harry prefers to fly.

Until the series is starting to end, no wizards fly on their own; all need magical creatures or devices to fly high or far. Harry flies on a hippogriff in book three, a thestral in Book 5, and a dragon in Book 7. He's glad for each but not eager to go again. Better than broomsticks, flying carpets can carry families or other small groups. Still the MOM has banned their import, presumably because carpets too easily come to the attention of muggles. Yes, other muggle objects can be magicked to fly people: Arthur Weasley enchants the flying car for Book 2, and Sirius Black the motorcycle that Hagrid flies in Books 1 and 7. The point, even so, is that Harry Potter first stands out on his own at Hogwarts for prowess at flying. Harry flies broomsticks, and the political symbolism in this is perfectionist in ways similar to Superman.

The talent is in Harry, the magic is in the broomsticks. His magical broomsticks seem to be craft items—but hand-assembled on a sizable scale, like Lamborghini cars. There have been several makes, with new models over the years. If medieval witches enchanted ordinary brooms to fly, leading muggles to mistake them for sweepers, Harry's flying equipment doesn't risk this. His broomsticks look a little like stylized jet skis, streamlined much further for parting currents of air instead of water. Each model seems to get swifter, steadier, more responsive, quicker to turn and stop. For Harry, flying them is exhilarating! But beyond flying as a premier figure of perfectionist politics, because it's a power that exceeds what's been possible for humans, Potter broomsticks stand out symbolically for uniting the Potter motifs of male and female magic.

By standard cultural associations, witches fly on brooms and mix potions in cauldrons, which mimic wombs. These female figures are balanced by the broomstick (or handle), which evokes a wand or penis as male. So the flying broomstick combines classically feminine with classically masculine figures. Harry's first fully conscious encounter with magic has Hagrid wield his pink umbrella, which likewise melds a masculine wand for its pole with a cauldron-shaped canopy for its feminine camouflage. (In stereotypical terms, Hagrid serves Harry as a foster mother.) From Harry's initial trip to Ollivander's for a wand, to Harry's healing of that wand with his last use of the Elder Wand, wands are Pottery's most overt metonyms of magical power. (Presumably Harry's last job for the Elder Wand was inspired by his realization that it must have been deployed by Dumbledore to repair Hagrid's wand, snapped by the MOM.) Yet Harry enters Diagon Alley through the Leaky Cauldron, and the saga's attention to cauldrons ranges from subtle to jokey, but stays persistent. Nietzsche's writing is notorious for its misogyny; but Potter perfectionism leaves that behind in many ways, including the telling parallels between Harry and Hermione. So in this respect, the flying broomstick becomes the saga's emblem of perfectionist politics to transcend the west's privileging of men over women.

Harry *loves* to fly: usually high, often far, sometimes alone. This fits the perfectionist profile for excelling. It also fits the magical powers of broomstick flight. What's up in the sky might be a bird or a plane; in Pottery, it might even be a car or a carpet. But we readers of *Harry Potter* might imagine most vividly someone soaring high and far—on a broomstick.

KNOCKTURN ALLEY FOR GOING HARD WITH ART

A fifth paradigm for Potter magic as perfectionist politics is the foreboding place called Knockturn Alley, which branches from Diagon Alley. Harry finds himself in Knockturn Alley by (fortunate) accident in Book 2, then he returns with Ron and Hermione when tailing Draco in Book 6. This side street is the site of Borgin and Burkes, a shop for what we might call the darkest arts. (Voldemort and the Malfoys concur.) If nothing else, Knockturn Alley is a stone-cold reminder that Pottery magic as dark arts *can* go as evil as super-powered humans are able, and sometimes does. That's why Harry and his friends need effective defenses. Yet horrifying hints and demonic demonstrations of these evils, magical and otherwise, are plentiful in further parts of Harry's saga. Knockturn Alley is not merely or mainly an evocation of the Voldemort perversions of perfectionism, although it should keep us mindful of them. As with Diagon Alley, the punning is particularly important. Knockturn Alley tells us that Potter magic is perfectionist in facing hard facts and acts (*knocks*), in order to trope (*turn*) them, by going dark (*nocturnally*) with art (*nocturne-ally* as musically, aesthetically, mythically—with myths as musical words).[11]

Realists pride themselves on facing hard facts then on hardening themselves to do what's necessary for turning bad situations into maximum good with minimum harm. Sentiment and hesitation must be short-circuited. Calibration of plans must yield to audacity of actions. The Potter saga respects and contributes to realist politics, as chapter 8 explains. Yet the Potter perfectionism can be hard-headed and hard-nosed. Furthermore it cultivates artistic attunement to the many myths and perspectives in the making of facts, as chapter 7 probes. Then it has the attunement spur bold, creative deeds worthy in artistry as well as artifacts. Magical devices of attunement to dark times in the Potter saga include dark detectors: foe glass, probity probes, secrecy sensors, and sneakoscopes. Apparently these work well—even the pocket sneakoscope purchased by the Weasleys in Egypt for Harry (III.10). Yet Rowling's little joke for us readers is that their alarms get sidelined, simply ignored, or foolishly explained away as malfunctions. Of course, Harry's scar can be said to work as a powerful dark detector of Voldemort misdeeds; and this extends to Harry's dreams and visions of Voldemort as well.

Results are what count for realists. Nietzscheans sometimes sound the same in learning from Darwinian evolution that their success is measured by succession, that is, their survival into subsequent generations. The Overman Just Does it, heedless of imitators or other followers; but we assess the attunement of each deed to the times by its resonance for others. These others may merely be onlookers; or they may fully be "cult followers," who turn the perfectionist leaper into a "charismatic leader" as a "cult figure" who informs a lasting culture. Yet the resonance is not in the results, the products, the artifacts alone; it's also in the doing, the performance, and the artistry. Potter perfectionists practice and appreciate style as substantive. After Dumbledore "confesses" his responsibility for Dumbledore's Army to Fudge and Umbridge, a flash of phoenix fire takes the great mage instantly away from aurors ready to imprison him in Azkaban. Even the living portrait of Phineas Nigellus is impressed, telling the Minister that he can't deny Dumbledore's "got style" (V.623). (The film features this punch line, but gives it to Kingsley Shacklebolt.)

For perfectionists, the attuning *and* the doing are premier arts of politics; and they are dark in eluding the Enlightenment literalism, methodism, foundationalism, metaphysics, and other disciplinary devices used to certify rational results and stomp on coloring outside the lines. Perfectionists reject the *asceticism* in these straightjackets for feeling, thinking, and acting. To them, such discipline is authoritarian. Instead Potter perfectionists embrace the *aestheticism* of mythic culture. They celebrate the art in the dark arts. Snape rhapsodizes potions and other dark arts for going with the flow, flexibility, and invention within their magic (I.137; VI.177–8); and when Harry condemns this as romancing evil, Hermione points out how Harry echoes Snape in presenting defenses against the dark arts (VI.180–1). This is Going Hard with Art. It's doing art in politics responsive to hard realities in dark times. Such aestheticism is exactly what the Potter series does in its self-conscious political mythmaking for our times, and this can be perfectionist.

The usual accusation is that aestheticism lacks substance, responsibility, and morality. It's that the political artist, who does aesthetics rather than strategy, policy, or even propaganda, merely plays with politics by ignoring the hard, cold, crucial realities whenever it's convenient. Especially when the political arts are fantasy and mythmaking, critics take this to be a recipe for distortion and disaster. Yet Potter books immerse us in the political troubles of our times. Some who "do aesthetics" get called *aesthetes*, rhymes with *elites;* and some aesthetes get caricatured as *dandies*. Their artful, stylish, at least stylized clothes and conduct call attention to themselves. Dandies are routinely regarded as sophisticated fools, since their attire and action are (mis)taken to show (merest) style without substance or significance. Gilderoy Lockhart is the Potter case in point. But Albus Dumbledore and Horace Slughorn are equally vivid as dandies; and they offer Potter counter-cases for aesthetes as potentially serious, substantive, even superlative mages.

Worries about aestheticism have general relevance to the Potter project. One concern is that art-for-art's-sake is apt to slight reality and lose referentiality. Another is that it turns into an avant-gardism which seeks excess, novelty, and trendiness for their own sake. For perfectionists, however, action is art because art makes meaning. Yet "meaning" without any reference to us—and thus to our world—is not meaning (for us) at all. In Darwinian terms, it has no (capacity for) fit; and it gets selected out. In perfectionist terms, it finds no (place in) culture; it doesn't work as myth. This is how the political mythmaking of the Potter series is a kind of political action, entering our culture to shape our meanings. It's how our myths are meaningful, musical words.

Myths aren't just widely held beliefs, let alone false ones; rather myths are stories. They are tales that might be true, false, tropal, or otherwise. In ancient Greek, *mythos* is a story uttered by mouth. Oral narratives sound rhythms among characters, settings, events, and symbols. Such rhythms are sometimes called styles, especially when they're repeated with different particulars. Hence *mythos* suggests a chanted, musical, or poetic tale—recited or sung aloud. Myth is story music. The political power of poetry, myth, music, drama, dance, and related arts was conceded by Plato when he wrote that these arts should be banned by an ideal commonwealth. Plato saw their tropal power as daunting; and this fed his distrust of the dramatists, musicians, and sophists who treated such perfectionist figuration and flow as intrinsic to rhetoric and thus fit for politics. By contrast, Hannah Arendt argued (as an existentialist republican) that western civilization fails to promote public action as political freedom because the west has no name for "doing beauty."[12] A perfectionist word for beauty-in-action is *style*, and political myth is a perfectionist place for it.

As a kind of music, the nocturne evokes nighttime with mystery as well as melancholy, with quiet darkness as well as subtle lyricism. As musical words, political myths of dark times can do comparable beauties. Nietzsche hinted at this in tracing *The Birth of Tragedy* and myth as "eternal return."[13] In the Potter books, rumors, prophecies, and newspapers put Harry into the midst of myths as "the Boy Who Lived" and "the Chosen One." These characterizations place him mythically in dark times, yet they make him a bearer of hope. Occasionally he resists some aspects of these identities, for neither celebrity nor glory is his game. Mostly, though, Harry has the self-effacing style to inhabit but enlarge his heroic archetype. As a friend, he defends others yet brings them effectively to the front lines of action. As a foe, he resists writing off Draco yet lets the remorseless Voldemort fall. As a victim, Harry still manages to wrap his heart (as well as his mind) around the terrible heroism of Snape. And as a human, Harry then leaps from self-sacrificial lamb to living lion. This is the perfectionist magic that Rowling has Harry Potter do.

NOTES

1. See Ralph Waldo Emerson, *Essays and Lectures*, ed. Joel Porte (New York: Library of America, 1983); Friedrich Nietzsche, *The Will to Power*, ed. Walter Kaufmann, ed. and trans. Walter Kaufman and R. J. Hollingdale (New York: Random House, 1967); Friedrich Nietzsche, *On the Advantage and Disadvantage of History for Life* trans. Peter Preuss (Indianapolis: Hackett, 1982); Stanley Cavell, *Conditions Handsome and Unhandsome* (Chicago: University of Chicago Press, 1990); Stanley Cavell, *Cities of Words* (Cambridge, MA: Harvard University Press, 2004).

2. Yes, this riffs on *Frozen* as well as the Force in *Star Wars* and the Beatles' advice from Mother Mary to "Let It Be." Compare "Make It So" as Captain Jean-Luc Picard directs in *Star Trek*.

3. See Wendell Berry, "To Know the Dark," *Collected Poems, 1957–1982* (San Francisco: North Point Press, 1985), 107.

4. See John S. Nelson, Allan Megill, and D. N. McCloskey, eds., *The Rhetoric of the Human Sciences* (Madison: University of Wisconsin Press, 1987); John S. Nelson and G. R. Boynton, *Video Rhetorics* (Urbana: University of Illinois Press, 1997); John S. Nelson, *Politics in Popular Movies* (Boulder: Paradigm Publishers, 2015).

5. See John S. Nelson, "Political Theory as Political Rhetoric," *What Should Political Theory Be Now?* ed. John S. Nelson (Albany: State University of New York Press, 1983), 169–240; John S. Nelson, *Tropes of Politics* (Madison: University of Wisconsin Press, 1998); John S. Nelson, *Cowboy Politics* (Lanham, MD: Lexington Books, 2018).

6. Friedrich Nietzsche, "On Truth and Falsity in Their Extramoral Sense," *Essays on Metaphor*, ed. Warren Shibles (Whitewater, WI: Language Press, 1972), 1–13 on 5.

7. Emerson, "The Poet," *Essays*, Second Series, 1844.

8. Later Ron's the student with gestural trouble for the silencing charm (*Silencio!*), because he waves loosely rather than jabs sharply with his wand (V.375).

9. See Norman Spinrad, *Agent of Chaos* (New York: Popular Library, 1967); Wendell Berry, "The Contrariness of the Mad Farmer" and "Manifesto: The Mad Farmer Liberation Front," *Collected Poems, 1957–1982*, 121–22 and 151–52; Greg Bear, *Slant* (New York: Tom Doherty Associates, 1997); *Longmire*, "Tell It Slant," season 2, episode 6, 2013. I say more about Potter versions of such "folly" in the twelfth chapter.

10. See *Every Which Way but Loose* (1978); Nelson, *Tropes of Politics*, 150–79.

11. See Claude Lévi-Strauss, *Myth and Meaning* (New York: Schocken Books, 1978), 44–54.

12. See Hannah Arendt, "Thinking and Moral Considerations," *Social Research* 38, no. 3 (Autumn 1971): 417–46; J. Glenn Gray, "The Winds of Thought," *Social Research* 44, no. 1 (Spring 1977): 44–62.

13. See Friedrich Nietzsche, *The Birth of Tragedy* and *The Genealogy of Morals*, trans. Francis Golffing (Garden City, NY: Doubleday, 1956). Also see Joan Stambaugh, *Nietzsche's Thought of Eternal Return* (Baltimore: Johns Hopkins University Press, 1972); Alex Ross, "The Eternal Return: Why Thinkers of Every Political Persuasion Keep Finding Inspiration in Nietzsche," *New Yorker* 95, no. 31 (October 14, 2019): 34–39.

Chapter 5

Perversions of Perfectionist Politics

Some Potter spells and devices substitute for human (muggle) technologies familiar to us, such as antibiotics and telecommunications. But other Potter magic outreaches what we already do or readily imagine. This makes most Potter magic, not just broomstick flying, similar to the superhuman powers in superhero stories and the wild talents in science fiction. All three genres acknowledge that pursuing perfectionist politics can be "playing with fire," as we muggles say in an old cliché. Humans being who they are so far, perfectionist politics *can* go disastrously bad, *can* be viciously perverted. The Potter saga concurs with these genres in basing defenses against perversions of perfectionist politics on better sorts of perfectionism. This involves three moves.

First, the Potter saga is careful *not* to condemn perfectionist powers as intrinsically evil. Instead Pottery treats its magic as inherently dangerous. This is to say that magical powers in Pottery are political. In other words, ironically, magical powers are "human." Let me repeat, accordingly, that magical arts in Pottery are dark more by use than by nature. Some magic and politics might lend themselves more than others to evil, yet the use styles and situations matter immensely.

Second, people often need special, specifically magical powers to defend against the dark arts of magic. It might not take dark arts to know them, to recognize them in action. Yet it *does* take dark arts, in the plural, to counter them. It takes politics to defend against them. Magically and politically, we often face more than one dark art or political act at a time. Typically the dark acts come at Harry and his friends in tandem, in teams, even in droves. The Battle of Hogwarts is an extreme example. The shootouts in the Department of Mysteries and the Hogwarts tower are more usual. But even the restroom duel of Draco and Harry or the serial poisons besetting Ron in Book 6 are what magic and politics generally portend. These are not so much matters of "fighting fire with fire" as they are challenges of "fighting fires with fires."

Third, therefore, Potter magic makes clear that not all fires are the same. Part of Snape's fascination with the dark arts is due to their multitudes, flexibilities, and subtleties. We start to learn this with the Quidditch confrontation where Hermione saves Harry from what she thinks is a Snape curse (I.191). As for the Devil's Snare to come, Hermione generates blue flames that are waterproof and portable. This arguably makes them safer than "normal," muggle fires; and blue flames become a go-to charm for Hermione (II.181–3). As a waterproof horror show loosed by Vincent Crabbe in the Room of Requirement during the Battle of Hogwarts, fiendfyre is by contrast so devastating that it destroys a horcrux (VII.631–5). On a different plane, Gubraithian fire is everlasting (V.428). And then there's the fire of the phoenix, Fawkes, who defends Harry from the basilisk and Dumbledore from Fudge's aurors. Effective defenses against the dark arts depend on quick selections among dark arts for deeds tailored precisely to specific uses. For good or ill, perfectionists seek such speed and flexibility.

To comprehend what the Potter series does with perfectionist politics is to appreciate how they go dark for good *and* ill. To sell athletic gear, Nike goes benignly perfectionist with "Just Do It," to evoke leaping brilliantly into action. Superheroes earn that moniker by doing good, often great good. But of course, they're also defined by seeking to stymie supervillains, whose deeds are horrific. Yet even appalling uses of superpowers can prove attractive sometimes to some people—possibly including us, at least momentarily. Thus Nike's perfectionist advertising also sounds totalitarian at times: "Become One. Dominate All." The previous chapter identifies in Potter magic as perfectionist politics the impulses for adventure, invention, and impossibility that can make them defensible paradigms of the dark arts. We do well at times to leap beyond familiar ends, means, and sensibilities. Nonetheless the present chapter examines Pottery motifs of dark creatures and characters. These evoke vividly the dire dangers that can turn perfectionist politics into evil arts. The Potter saga shows how we do ill to indulge them.

To repeat: dark arts sometimes need to go perfectionist to defend against perfectionist politics gone perverse. The Dark Lord and the Death Eaters enact perversions of Nietzschean perfectionism familiar historically from the evil politics preached by Adolf Hitler, practiced by his Nazis, and parroted since. Related perfectionism can—and has—gone bad in other political directions too, as chapter 12 considers in connection with totalitarianism. An intractable foe of conformism, perfectionism nevertheless suits several other versions of noxious politics: communism (in the East Bloc sense), fascism, imperialism, nationalism, racism, and more.

Six (arguably seven) motifs of perfectionist figures loom largest in the Potter series. Four (or five) appear at the start and continue to the end. One is directly present in just the first book, while initial mention of another is not until the second. Only dementors and Voldemort seem fully, irredeemably evil from start to finish. But all have evil variants. (Please keep in mind that even good variants have evil uses, and every benign use has some malign potential.) Thus the Potter books show perfectionism to be dangerous, but they also show it to be needed in the dark times defined in part by its dangers. To learn how Harry and his friends can make perfectionism safe for their civilization, which is ours, the need is to learn in detail what we're up against.

VAMPIRES

At first glance, vampires might seem too peripheral to analyze. Like zombies and several other creatures of horror, vampires are kept almost completely off-stage in the Potter saga. The only literal vampire we meet is Sanguini. He comes to the Christmas party thrown by Potions Professor Horace Slughorn (VI.315). Like Harry, we lose sight of Sanguini in the next moment. But look again, and we can register many more references to vampires than we might remember: more by far, for example, than to banshees or zombies.

Accounts of Nietzschean perfectionism in popular culture do well to include vampires. The popular genre of horror conventionally configures vampires as Nietzschean Overmen. As the narrating vampire puts it in *The World on Blood*, "like most literate vampires, I had read my Nietzsche—the philosopher of choice among those of us who become *Übermenschen* when we drink blood."[1] Such a vampire is a species above and apart from the humans who are its prey. Many dark fantasists would have made Voldemort a vampire outright, because he seeks exactly to become that kind of Overman. Visually Rowling comes close to doing so. Yet the Pottery interest in our cultural, historical, and institutional politics might argue against overt use of a generic character from popular horror. (The successful counter-cases aren't at all for children.) Before we attend in detail to Voldemort as a vampire perfectionist, however, let's notice that he has ample company—both literal and figural—in Potter's world.

In Potter books, the most literal allusions to vampires are slight and somewhat jokey. Even Sanguini is comic relief; and the same goes for his chaperon of sorts, Eldred Worple as the author of *Blood Brothers: My Life amongst the Vampires*. In *Prisoner of Azkaban*, Harry lies to Neville about going to the library to write a DADA essay on vampires (III.276). Percy, the prig among the Weasley boys, fumes that Rita Skeeter scolds his Ministry department for working on cauldron thickness when vampires need squelching, apparently in

Albania (IV.147). Traveling for Dumbledore to the giants, Hagrid shrugs off a pub dispute with a vampire in Minsk (V.426). Gilderoy Lockhart says that he tamed a vampire into a vegetarian (II.161), while Stan Shunpike flirts with veela by proclaiming himself a vampire hunter successful ninety times over (IV.126). And older readers might smile along with me when learning that the conspiracy-minded Xenophilius Lovegood is said by his daughter Luna to know that Minister of Magic Rufus Scrimgeour, who brings to mind Winston Churchill as an implacable opponent of the German Nazis, was actually a vampire (VI.314). Yet this is not to say that vampires are always laughing matters in Potter allusions. When Sirius Black as a posterized Azkaban escapee looks deadened but menacing to Harry, the image is likened to a vampire's (III.38).

DEMENTORS

Nevertheless there's more to vampires in the Potter series than meets the literal eye, and most figural vampires in Potter books are neither funny nor negligible. The DADA teacher who assigns Harry an essay on vampires is Remus John Lupin, who turns out to be a werewolf. His near-year at Hogwarts is arguably Harry's best in the subject (III.429). Likely implications are that Lupin knows how to defend against dark arts, how to teach this, and how to defend against dementors as "psychic vampires."[2] Classic vampires drink blood, preferably human, and ideally from healthy individuals. Psychic vampires ingest emotion, energy, even vitality, typically from people. In popular movies, *Immortality* (1998) portrays the first, *Snow White and the Huntsman* (2012) the second, and *Lifeforce* (1985) the third. Dementors are the horror creatures who guard Azkaban then Hogwarts, only to desert later to ally with Voldemort. Lupin is the train traveler who saves Harry from his first encounter with a dementor. Lupin knows to ward off dementors with a patronus and to cure close encounters with a chocolate bar (III.90). Lupin puts this strong practical sense to work in preparing Harry to face dementors, Voldemort, and other terrors.

Using boggarts to take the dementor form that Harry most dreads, Lupin tutors Harry in how to focus on the "happiest" of moments in order to banish dementors with his patronus. In Harry's case, this magical projection of personal vitality takes the silvery shape of a stag, in tribute to Harry's father. James Potter had made himself an animagus, turning into Prongs, an antlered deer, to keep Lupin company as a young werewolf who was dangerous to humans at Hogwarts. (Sirius Black had learned to become Padfoot, a large black dog; and Peter Pettigrew had become Wormtail, all too aptly the rat who'd betrayed Harry and his parents to Voldemort then hid as Scabbers, the magical pet passed down to Ron from Percy.)

Even more than their moldering, graveyard appearance, it's what dementors do to their prey that qualifies them as psychic vampires. As an authoritarian unto totalitarian oppressor, a dementor absorbs a victim's energies and emotions. Then its "kiss" sucks out the victim's soul (III.247). Dementors leave victims like inmates of concentration camps and laborers in gulags, as little more than empty bodies, barely living. This is exactly what psychic vampires do. By horror convention, of course, all vampires are undead, lack souls, and so are damned for all time. Whether biologically with blood or psychologically with passion, the twilight persistence of vampires depends on taking vitality from humans. Harry's traumas attract dementors to him. His "extreme experiences," as an existentialist might term them, are exactly the psychological charge that dementors tap. But as I'll explain in the next chapter, Harry's capacity for strong feeling can also power his patronus to disperse those terrifying creatures.

Like Dumbledore, Lupin regards dementors as creatures "too dark" to serve decent magic or civilization. The Dark Lord shares this assessment. At his vile "rebirthing party," Voldemort predicts that dementors and giants are bound to ally with his Death Eaters (IV.651–2). We learn in the end that many giants do go with Voldemort; but as Grawp suggests, the giants might not altogether be lost causes where civilization is concerned. Not even the early service as Azkaban guards for the MOM holds out significant hope, though, that dementors can become constructive. As psychic vampires, they seem to be creatures of horror from beginning to end. Retaining only an eighth of his soul, Voldemort nears the vampire's fragile, damnable condition.

DRAGONS

In the Potter series, such vampire figures point insistently at Voldemort and the Death Eaters. They are the most significant set of perverse perfectionists in Harry's world. But before we focus on Voldemort and his crew, let's recognize further vampire links. The saga reinforces another kind of connection to vampire perfectionism in its several references to Transylvania as the liminal homeland for Dracula, the preeminent vampire in fiction and film. Some mentions of Transylvania are pedestrian: at Quidditch, England loses 390–10 to Transylvania (IV.63). Some are laughable: Ron Weasley's fake identity for robbing Gringotts Bank is Dragomir Despard . . . from Transylvania (VII.528). These days, Transylvania is part of Romania, which is in the same neighborhood as Bulgaria, whence hail Viktor Krum and his Quidditch team. Nearby is Albania, where Bertha Jorkins from the MOM goes missing, gets trapped by Pettigrew, and gets tortured to death by Voldemort as he's trying to bootstrap his way back to fully vampirical form (VI.61). Albania is also where Voldemort recovers Rowena Ravenclaw's lost diadem and makes it into a horcrux. And so on. In Harry's world, the Transylvania neighborhood remains a hub of "vampirical" activity.

Especially Transylvania remains the ancestral home of the vampire to begin all vampires: Dracula. Dracula by name and other vampires by heritage are the horror equivalents of dragons in fantasy. Even little, dragons can be deadly. Trying to "worm" information from Hagrid about Fluffy, his giant, three-head dog for guarding the Philosopher's Stone, a hooded stranger who's surely Quirinus Quirrell conveys a dragon egg that hatches into Norbert, a horrendously vicious Norwegian Ridgeback. Hagrid's too enamored of monsters to notice how he's being tricked into telling how music puts Fluffy to sleep; and as a half-giant, Hagrid's too tough to recognize the danger that even the baby dragon poses to Harry and other Hogwarts students. Eventually the heroic trio prevails on Hagrid to send the dragon to Ron's brother: Charlie Weasley in Romania, of course, where he's studying dragons (I.228–41; II.46; VII.120). Dragons aren't thick on the ground in Europe. Compensating figurally for an informal concentration of vampires in the east, though, dragons are said to be scattered more widely. Ron explains to Harry and Hermione, who were raised by muggles, that mages often must use memory charms to make people forget seeing dragons (I.231). Yet in the more-or-less human forms of perverse perfectionists, dragons might be emerging as more of a menace in Harry's world.

Literal dragons are big deals in the fourth and seventh books as well as the first. In *Goblet of Fire*, dragons provide the initial test for champions in the Triwizard Tournament. Viktor overcomes a red Chinese Fireball, Fleur Delacour outwits a Common Welsh Green, Cedric Diggory subdues a blue-gray Swedish Short-Snout, and Harry outflies a Hungarian Horntail (IV.327). Yes, there's a lot of political symbolism in the colors and countries. But the key point is that the primary test for a champion mage is to defeat another kind of perfectionist, all females to boot. In *Deathly Hallows*, the Gringotts robbery reverses the task into something of a rescue. A gigantic but blind dragon has been chained and tortured by Gringotts goblins to guard the deepest, most valuable vaults in the bank (VII.531–6). This casual cruelty appalls us readers as much as the three, who nonetheless retrieve Helga Hufflepuff's cup as a Voldemort horcrux. When Griphook outsmarts (or double-crosses) the trio (depending on your perspective) to claim the Sword of Gryffindor, the three leap onto the old dragon, unchain it, and hang on for dear life as it flies up and out of the bank. Much later, once free of pursuit, they slide safely from the dragon into a North Country lake. Mages who would defend themselves and others against dark arts must ally themselves, occasionally or momentarily, with other kinds of perfectionists. (Fantasy usually treats dragons as perfectionists, but it often portrays them as so old individually or by species as to pre-date our contrasts between "constructive" and "perverse" perfectionisms.)

Yet figural dragons in Harry Potter's world are not limited to vampires. To suggest the susceptibility of people to perfectionist appeals, *Chamber of Secrets* has Professor Sprout work with students all year on Mandrake, that is, *Mandragora*. It can be a restorative cure for curses and transfigurations, but it seems more person than plant. The name says man-dragon, hinting that there might be some of each in the State of Nature for humans (II.92). This Potter book uses life-stage characteristics of the mandrake to crack wise about humanity. A seedling looks like an "extremely ugly baby;" and its cries knock out people for several hours (II.93), as though they'd been worn out by a human infant crying. Older mandrakes can suffer acne, become moody and secretive, then throw loud parties like teens. Left unarticulated, but still available symbolically, is the suggestion that a mature mandrake is restorative because it *is* a man-dragon. This indicates it's capable of "perfecting" (i.e., making whole—which is to say, healing) humans who have been harmed grievously. In particular, they've been "petrified" by the indirect gaze of a basilisk. The image invites us to compare (implicit politics of) such a living corpse to an undead vampire.

SNAKES

By fantasy tradition, dragons are "worms"—in another word, "snakes." By face, as vividly, chillingly depicted in the Potter movies, Voldemort has pale white skin (like a Byronic vampire) but air holes without a nose (like a snake). He also has snake eyes that are red like a vampire's. Voldemort can speak Parseltongue, the language of snakes. When his killing curse rebounded from Lily Potter's beloved toddler, saving Harry but disembodying Voldemort, that dark wizard had to inhabit some animals to survive; but of course, he preferred snakes (IV.654). The argument is that (perverse) perfectionist politics permeate this family of figures. The more prominent these figures are in the Potter series, the more predominant perverse perfectionisms are the Potter world. (Of course, Jews and Christians routinely treat the snake in the Garden of Eden as evil in corrupting Eve and Adam.)

The only hint of affection that Voldemort shows is to his pet snake, Nagini. (*Fantastic Beasts* shows that she's a maledictus, whose maturation means that she can no longer transform between woman and snake, but must remain in her "animal" form.) As a huge snake with a taste for humans such as Charity Burbage (VII.11–12), Nagini also becomes a horcrux for Voldemort then an occasional vessel for his possession, his conscious direction. This is how Harry, who sometimes can't help but share the awareness of Voldemort, can see at times through Nagini's eyes. We have to wonder whether the horcrux magic or some other dark act by Voldemort has turned Nagini undead. For it's hard to see Voldemort entrusting a piece of his soul to any vessel that could die and decay. That holds all the more because Voldemort sends Nagini on dangerous missions. He has the snake disappear Frank Bryce, the Riddle gardener (IV.7). He has Nagini seek the Trelawney prophecy in the Department of Mysteries, where she nearly kills Arthur Weasley as that night's guard for the Order of the Phoenix (V.465). He has her inhabit the body of Bathilda Bagshott for attracting and attacking Harry in Godric's Hollow (VII.333–42). In the end, it takes the Sword of Godric Gryffindor, as wielded by Neville, to behead Nagini (VII.733). Of course, decapitation is one of the few classic ways to dispatch vampires as undead revenants.

The other snake featured by the Potter series also links to Voldemort. As the Heir of (Salazar) Slytherin, Voldemort—this time in horcrux form as Tom Riddle's diary—moves the deadly basilisk from the Chamber of Secrets into the water pipes and walls of Hogwarts Castle (II.291). Before learning that the rumored monster is a basilisk or Riddle is the Heir of Slytherin, Harry links the monster to Voldemort because not even other monsters like acromantulas want to say its name (II.281). (Does the extreme fluidity pursued by some perverse perfectionists defy even naming?) The venom in basilisk fangs is so fatal that it can kill even a horcrux, and a direct look at its gaze kills instantly (II.290). No living soul looks directly into the basilisk's eyes; yet even reflections of its stare petrify people, accounting for the earliest uses of Professor Sprout's *Mandragora*. Instead the basilisk dies, slain by Harry with the Sword of Godric Gryffindor that appears in the Sorting Hat flown to him by Fawkes, the phoenix. Soon Tom Riddle's diary dies, stabbed by Harry on impulse with a venomous fang of the basilisk. Then Gilderoy Lockhart's memory "dies," undone by the memory charm of *Obliviate* that backfires for Lockhart because of his selfish, foolish use of Ron's broken wand (II.303). In every instance, perfectionist powers seem needed to defend against or undo perfectionist assaults. Even Harry's impulsive act (in a Nietzschean mode) is defensive too, and effectively so, which holds throughout the Potter series.

QUIRRELL AND SNAPE

The one-book perfectionist in Harry's saga is his first DADA teacher of record: Quirinus Quirrell. Eventually we learn along with Harry that Quirrell has been controlled at Hogwarts by the little that's left of Voldemort after he fails in attempting to murder baby Harry. Yet the early introduction of Quirrell suggests that we recognize Quirrell as something of a vampire figure.

In the Leaky Cauldron, Quirrell stutters that he's getting a new book on vampires. Hagrid attributes Quirrell's nervous trembling to meeting vampires in the Black Forest (I.70–71). Quirrell, too, is comic relief. Yet in his case, like several others, this is a device to keep readers from suspecting Quirrell of anything dastardly—let alone of using his turban to conceal a remnant of Voldemort.

With Quirrell dead and gone, his DADA successor still stokes the first book's nexus of humor, vampirism, and perfectionism. Gilderoy Lockhart reads his books of stolen adventures and has Harry act out several of the menaces Lockhart claims to have mastered. Harry plays a "Transylvanian villager" beset by a babbling curse, plus a vampire left to eat only lettuce once Lockhart has come to the rescue (II.161). Again we get the Dracula homeland of Transylvania, a babbling villager reminiscent of the stuttering Quirrell, and a vampire unable to ingest what he needs for vitality. Here the first DADA teacher returns in symbol, but even more fully in farce.

Student excitement for DADA notwithstanding, Quirrell's own teaching extends the joke. His classroom stinks of garlic—by rumor, to ward away a vampire (from Romania!) who's taken to have threatened Quirrell (I.134). Gradually we readers infer that, in several senses, a vampire actually had taken Quirrell in Romania. The Dark Lord Voldemort turns out to be a figural and political vampire: a potent, pale, and "Dark Prince" in the mold of Dracula. (That Dark Prince of perverse perfectionism leaps beyond the original Prince of Machiavellian realism. So where does the Half-Blood Prince fit?)

For a time, the first book plays this gossip for little snickers rather than prophetic truths. The jokes are on Quirrell. Why does he wear a turban? Quirrell tells a silly lie about a zombie. Why does the turban, too, stink? The Weasley twins think it's full of garlic; and they bewitch snowballs to bounce off the back (I.134, 194): terrific intuition there! We readers share in the comic distraction of Hogwarts students and staff from Quirrell's peculiar character and sinister opportunities. It's true that the Potter series makes fun of other DADA teachers too: not just the self-important Lockhart but also the disheveled Lupin, the damaged "Moody," and the dangerous Umbridge. Rowling's comedic device of having Hogwarts students mock differences in light tones can be effective at hiding troubles that we might notice if we weren't smiling instead.

Still we should notice how the Weasley twins show an intuitive flair for detecting and defending against dark wizardry. Many students at Hogwarts start to suspect Harry of being the Heir of Slytherin who orchestrates monstrous attacks on the students. Ginny Weasley begins to realize that Tom Riddle's diary might be possessing her to instigate the attacks. A sense of guilt and a crush on Harry spur her to cry out against even satirical slanders of him: Fred asks Harry who he'll attack next, and George wields a clove of garlic to ward away Harry (II.210). Yet the ridiculous image of brandishing garlic to chase away the Heir of Slytherin, who turns out in the moment to be a Voldemort horcrux, again hints at the vampire perfectionism of Voldemort.

The other distraction from detecting Voldemort's puppetry of Quirrell is the suspicion of Snape that we readers share with the heroic trio of Harry, Ron, and Hermione. Outside the Slytherin House that Snape leads, almost everyone sees that he hates Harry; and save for trusting Dumbledore's faith in Snape, almost everyone fears that Snape might harm Harry. Like Salazar Slytherin, founder of his house at Hogwarts, Snape seems to be something of a perfectionist in his psychology and politics. Still he has turned away from the perversity evident in Voldemort and his faithful Death Eaters. Spoiler Alert: Snape turns out *not* to be a faithful Death Eater but Dumbledore's double agent. The persistent appearances to the contrary—as carefully contrived by Snape, Dumbledore, and Rowling—are detailed by Snape to Bellatrix Black Lestrange from the perspectives of Voldemort and the Death Eaters in *Half-Blood Prince* (VI.9–37). Through Quirrell, the duped Voldemort concedes the value of Snape as a distraction (I.288). By horror lore, we should remember, vampires sometimes transform into vermin: bats, rats, and snakes especially. Even as a boy running after the Evans sisters, Lily and Petunia, Snape already looks laughably like a bat (VII.665). And when he flees Hogwarts to join the Dark Lord's invading forces, Snape flies (on his own!) through the darkness like a bat (VII.599).

By his own account, Quirrell was ripe for recruitment by Voldemort because the dark wizard's perverse perfectionism entranced him. Quirrell presents it as a doctrine: "There is no good and evil, there is only power, and those too weak to seek it" (I.291). This mad fanaticism of domination is a familiar (mis)interpretation of Nietzsche's late notion of "the will to power." (More on that soon.) If it's better to be lucky than good, Harry and his friends fare much better in their first Hogwarts year than they easily might have. Surviving Quirrell's concealment of a radically weakened Voldemort is no small feat. Their radical mismatch can work for us readers because Rowling uses comedy to distract us. "Seeing" Snape try to crash Harry's broom in his first Quidditch match, Hermione uses her blue flames to distract Snape from eye contact with the flying seeker. Of course, we readers are the ones who get distracted. As Hermione scrambles to reach Snape, we don't notice Quirrell being bumped headlong into a lower row as anything but a moment of comedy (I.191). Only later do we learn that Hermione's bump broke the eye contact of Quirrell. At Voldemort's direction, Quirrell had been the teacher trying to kill Harry; Snape instead had been trying to keep Harry aloft (I.288–9).

VOLDEMORT

Voldemort's perfectionism is a perverse take on Nietzsche's. There are far more features of Nietzschean aphorisms-unto-philosophies than we can analyze here; and in any event, Pottery doesn't try to encompass them. (Rowling engages Nietzsche again in her first novel for adults.[3]) One way to inventory such features is to notice the networks of Nietzsche's "transvaluations" of values often taken to characterize a western civilization that begins with republican politics and Christian religion. By contrast with western politics and metaphysics, Nietzsche embraced blood over breath, feeling over thinking, volition over cognition, intuition over intellect, initiative over responsibility, and aesthetics over ethics. Nietzsche promoted vitality over honor, impulse over memory, biology over technology, charisma over authority, action over law, and life over justice. In short, Nietzschean perfectionism celebrates the superman over the common man. It's easy for westerners to revile *all* these figures as necessarily perverse, and Voldemort provides incentives to do so. The perfectionist challenge is to earn respect for versions of many such tropes, while opposing some others. The Rowling responses to this challenge are Harry Potter's takes on the dark arts and defenses against them. Yet there's a keen need to acknowledge Voldemort's evils.

To be sure, the perverse perfectionism of Voldemort has become a staple of popular horror. It's clear that generic horror helps perfectionist politics appear prominently in popular culture. Still the Potter series is not garden-variety horror, because it keeps peripheral most of the stock figures from horror. As dark fantasy, the Potter series is also an exercise in sword-and-sorcery. Even the powerful motif of vampire perfectionism has been transmuted into the several sets of figures considered here. Of these, the most striking remains the Dark Lord Voldemort.

We do well to notice that many of the other figures from popular horror that surface in the Potter stories get more benign roles by far than the figural vampires furnished by Voldemort and his Death Eaters. For example, Ron dreads spiders; while Hagrid has populated the Forbidden Forest with giant arachnids. Worse, these acromantulas are hungry for Hogwarts students and side with Voldemort in the Battle of Hogwarts. Yet their patriarch, Aragog, is one of Hagrid's best friends and provides crucial information for Harry and Ron. Hence the horror archetype of eight-legged menaces gets twisted fairly far. Likewise Peeves is the poltergeist in Hogwarts, and an agent of chaos if ever there were one. But usually, Peeves is a petty annoyance for provoking comic moments, until he allies with the Weasley twins to resist the bureaucratic regime imposed on Hogwarts by Dolores Umbridge. And the Hogwarts ghosts are like house mascots, helping students rather than haunting them. This goes too for the strangely living images of earlier heads of Hogwarts, who've been assisting the school's current leader for many generations. Politically and mythically, Voldemort is the main terror.

The first time Harry starts to become aware of seeing Voldemort himself in action, Harry still doesn't recognize quite who or what he's seeing. What Harry witnesses in the Forbidden Forest is a cloaked Quirrell-Voldemort vampirizing a unicorn through the vile act of drinking its blood (I.245). This initial appearance casts Voldemort simultaneously as a stalking snake which crawls over the ground and a hooded vampire which then defiles the unicorn—as the epitome of innocence and purity in fantasy magic.

The resurrection of Voldemort re-turns him from a disappeared revenant into a body that looks part-snake and part-vampire. In the process, Voldemort's residual soul drinks the blood of Harry Potter as it earlier ingests the blood of unicorns. The incantation is from Peter Pettigrew—called "Wormtail" to stress his craven character as an animagus rat who betrays both Potters and Weasleys. (With a squirmy rat's tail, Peter is a literal vermin and a figural snake unto dragon.) The magic is vampire perfectionism through and through. Into a giant stone cauldron goes the snaky excuse for Voldemort's fragment of body-and-soul. Peter adds a graveyard bone from the elder Tom Riddle to provide structure for the recreated son. At Voldemort's insistence, Wormtail amputates his own hand to flesh out the skeleton. (The Dark Lord soon replaces the sacrificed limb with a magical silver prosthesis that signifies how Wormtail is now the hand of Voldemort.) The magic also requires blood, of course. Once again in over his head, Voldemort makes Wormtail take the blood from Harry, which is one reason he's been brought by portkey to the graveyard in Godric's Hollow. Then Voldemort rises again in a new body that looks strongly like a perfectionist vampire (IV.640–3). (When Dumbledore learns about the blood from Harry, the old wizard is quietly delighted at the awful mistake that he guesses Voldemort to have made.)

As a vampire, of course, Voldemort is resurrected in a graveyard, is functionally undead, and is nearly soulless. He has divided his soul into horcruxes meant to make him immortal. Yet even with a remade body, this murderous process leaves Voldemort fragmented, insensitive, and vulnerable. As an Overman, he leaps beyond what is human, all too human, as Nietzsche put it. As the Dark Lord gloats to Frank Bryce, before siccing Nagini on the flinty gardener, Voldemort fancies himself a species apart (IV.15). By the start of the last book, Voldemort even surpasses other wizards by flying without a magical device (VII.78); and he soon teaches Death Eaters to do it. On Voldemort's view, his supreme power is conquering death. He's done this, he thinks, by dispersing parts of his soul to horcruxes hidden and otherwise protected from destruction. It has diminished his humanity to the vanishing point (VI.502), but he delights in that.

A little like a basilisk, a master vampire mesmerizes with his gaze. More generally, he attracts prey and disciples with charisma: a kind of animal magnetism, a personal energy that engages and directs others. As Max Weber suggested a century ago, charisma can be crucial for many Nietzschean versions of perfectionist politics.[4] Even as a boy, Tom Riddle generates such hyper-charm at the orphanage (VI.267–77). It's clear in his diary's hold over Ginny Weasley (II.309–10), his manipulation of Horace Slughorn (VI.494–9), and his attraction of an impressive range of talented, power-hungry wizards to be Death Eaters. The popular link for perfectionism is from charisma to a "will to power," suggesting sheer resolution so strong that it sweeps away all obstacles. This fits Voldemort, and it's symbolized by the vampire's gaze. Still the phrase is misappropriated from Nietzsche, who didn't treat will as a psychological faculty of individuals, let alone as the metaphysical power of choice evoked by Christian talk of "free will." Instead he was addressing cultural and communal empowerment.[5]

Fans and critics caricature Nietzsche's "will to power" as a perfectionism of resource, resolve, and violence. This version might miss Nietzsche's sense of community, but it hits Voldemort's perversion of perfectionism right between the eyes. Voldemort idolizes strength and reviles weakness. In their forest confrontation, Voldemort is outraged that Harry would defy him. Voldemort sees Harry as Dumbledore's acolyte, even pawn; and as his diary version had done in the Chamber of Secrets, Voldemort rails against the master as too weak of will to grab for the crown of total dominion (VII.738). Earlier Voldemort has sneered at Dumbledore as an envious and spiteful coward (VI.443). The Dark Lord's own grandiosity exceeds even Gilderoy Lockhart's; it inflates Voldemort's self-obsession and self-regard past arrogance or narcissism (VI.504; VII.290). Voldemort is determined to live beyond character, conscience, history, humility, judgment, morality, remorse . . . beyond whatever might leave him human (VII.741).

As conformists, the Dursleys dread departing from normality. As a humble hero, more eager for sacrifice than celebration, Harry is satisfied to be ordinary or not. But as a perverse perfectionist, Voldemort craves distinction, elevation, and exaltation. Dumbledore observes that even the young Tom Riddle held the ordinary in contempt and was desperate to leap above it. As conformists, the Dursleys are frantic to fit into society. As a humble hero, more attuned to what is good and true, Harry is happy for friends and help that doesn't endanger them. But as a perverse perfectionist, Voldemort is a loner who dispenses with friends as insufficiencies and impediments. Dumbledore says to Harry that young Tom tried for self-sufficiency and secrecy, and that Voldemort never wanted a friend—let alone had one (VI.277). Barty Crouch Jr. and Bellatrix Lestrange are rabid Voldemort fans, not friends: something almost altogether different.

Some perverse Nietzscheans, Voldemort among them, indulge in manias of blood and biology. The Death Eaters are fascist in their classism, racism, and specism, which camouflage their fears of others. Voldemort spurs these hatreds and probably shares them at some points, yet his terror is death (VI.566). At their showdown in the Department of Mysteries, Dumbledore chides Voldemort for this (V.814). Even at Hogwarts, Tom was trying to rise above mortality (VI.499). This helps explain how the Death Eaters get their name. In the graveyard, Voldemort reminds them that his goal is conquering death (IV.653)—but as he later muses, only for himself. In this aspect, especially, Voldemort's moral imagination can't keep up with his magical powers. When Dumbledore takes Harry to get the Slytherin locket that Voldemort makes into a horcrux and hides on a distant, dangerous island, an obstacle course awaits the two. Voldemort imposes vampirical prices for even entering: blood to come painfully from the intruding mage (VI.559). He mistakes death, pain, and all other feeling for weaknesses, and weaknesses for imperfections. The perverse perfectionist who would leave humanity behind (and below) typically seeks to stay himself insensitive. (Thus dementors and vampires seem to need strong feelings from others to sustain any vitality in themselves.) To be sure, pain is no fun; and susceptibility to it feels like a failing. Yet as Dumbledore tells Harry, his keen sense of pain is his greatest, most human power. It keeps him caring, and so it feeds his superior perfectionism (V.823–4). Nietzscheans not lost to Voldemort manias might see in this respect that what doesn't kill you can make you stronger.

Instead Voldemort parallels Vernon in trying to dispel any incipient sense of vulnerability by bullying others (VI.277). Looking ahead to the next chapter for a moment, we should notice that political contraries usually share some characteristics; and bullying is easy to find among (perverse) perfectionists and conformists. Dislike of questions also can be common to (perverse) perfectionists and conformists, even if the sources differ. Conformists dislike questions because they unsettle social orders, and questioners stand out. Conformists distrust ideas, imaginations, and impulses for similar reasons. Perverse perfectionists dislike questions because they dispel charisma and spur reflection. Ideas and imaginations might do this or not, leaving perfectionists mixed on them. But perverse perfectionists usually promote vital impulses *because* they short-circuit or chase out the analysis, reflection, and other intellection that can disrupt pure leaps into action. For Nietzsche, in fact, the "will" just is such a "vital impulse." It succeeds when attuned to each situation, but the perverse fear is that stopping to think what you're doing and why must disrupt (not inform) the attunement.[6] Conformists and vampire perfectionists share that fear.

It's hard to say for sure, since the Potter series rarely tracks Voldemort's paths into action; but a decent inference is that he plans more than he improvises. In other words, seldom does Voldemort "Just Do It." Instead it's Harry whose impulses prove golden, and therefore get trusted more and more as his experiences and responsibilities grow. Destroying a horcrux is next to impossible, and Dumbledore deals himself a slow death when he impulsively forgets to do this right with the Peverell ring. On the spur of the moment, though, Harry instinctively, impulsively kills the Riddle diary with a basilisk fang (II.322). Without "thinking it through," Harry simply retrieves the Philosopher's Stone—without revealing it to Voldemort in front of the Mirror of Erised. Book after book, Harry surmounts one challenge after another with good training, good luck, and brilliant invention on the spot. If the perfectionist take on genius is leaping creatively, impulsively to success, Harry is a genius-in-action. And Voldemort? Not exactly, not entirely.

NOTES

1. Jonathan Nasaw, *The World on Blood* (New York, Penguin, 1996), 164–65.

2. See Nina Auerbach, *Our Vampires, Ourselves* (Chicago: University of Chicago Press, 1995), 101–12; Laurence A. Rickels, *The Vampire Lectures* (Minneapolis: University of Minnesota Press, 1999), 326–34.

3. See J. K. Rowling, *The Casual Vacancy* (New York: Little, Brown, 2012).

4. See Max Weber, *On Charisma and Institution Building*, ed. S. N. Eisenstadt (Chicago: University of Chicago Press, 1968).

5. See Friedrich Nietzsche, *The Will to Power*, ed. Walter Kaufmann, trans. Walter Kaufmann and R. J. Hollingdale (New York: Random House, 1967). Also see Tracy B. Strong, *Friedrich Nietzsche and the Politics of Transformation* (Berkeley: University of California Press, 1975); Mark E. Warren, *Nietzsche and Political Thought* (Cambridge, MA: MIT Press, 1988).

6. See Hannah Arendt, "Thinking and Moral Considerations," *Social Research*, 38, no. 3 (Autumn 1971): 417–46.

Part 2

POLITY

Chapter 6

Rules and the Philosopher's Stone

The first book shows Harry Potter caught between the Dursley conformism that compels normality and the Dumbledore perfectionism that seeks to excel. On this axis, turn the politics of the Potter series. Blending in can be appropriate, even necessary, at times; and the same goes for striving to stand out. Yet both go readily awry. All the books, but especially the last on resisting Voldemort's totalitarian regime, display the perversities of making either into a policy, let alone an obsession or a system. Still the Potter embrace of magical powers and responsibilities signals how Harry's politics begin with perfectionist leaps beyond the ordinary, the familiar, the normal.

In a coy way, the first sentence announces this axis by introducing the Dursleys as proud to be "perfectly normal," a phrase repeated on page 4 then twisted later toward an appreciation of perfectionist magic (II.42). Harry is no Overman out of Friedrich Nietzsche or Superman from DC Comics. He's too relatable for that. But he does learn perfectionist leaps envisioned by the champions of human(e) excellence.[1] These reach from ancient Greece and Rome to Emerson, Nietzsche, and Cavell then on to some greens and feminists. Therefore "perfectly normal" says "not at all abnormal" but also "normality improved unto perfection." The Potter saga is far from the first fantasy to criticize conformity as a lifestyle or to explore perfectionist politics through magic. Yet its dedication to treating these as where to start—and return—in addressing recent politics in western civilization is unrivaled in specificity. This goes also for Potter attention to practical details of these politics in everyday action.

Thus *Philosopher's Stone* constructs a face-off between conformism and perfectionism that the rest of the Potter saga articulates. In the first Potter book, this culminates in Harry, Ron, and Hermione tackling the obstacle course that the Hogwarts staff constructs to defend the Stone from whatever remains of Voldemort and his minions. The Elixir of Life made with the Stone can return the Dark Lord to terrorizing Britain and beyond. Dumbledore knows already, we later read, what Harry won't learn for four more books: the Boy Who Lived is the magically ordained nemesis of Voldemort (V.839–42). To deploy him that way, Dumbledore helps educate and equip Harry to overcome the obstacles and defeat the Dark Lord. So we end this chapter as the first book ends: with the performative politics of Harry's magic before the Mirror of Erised.

CONFORMISM

The series starts by delivering Harry Potter as a newly orphaned infant to the care of his muggle relatives, the Dursleys. Aside from this magical prologue, though, the first Potter book begins and ends with conformist politics. It charts their dynamics, difficulties in resisting them, as well as needs and ways to do so. Harry spends his childhood with his maternal Aunt Petunia and Uncle Vernon plus their son, Dudley. The Dursleys are obsessed with conformity, with fitting into their social circles and their senses of normality. They're desperate to be accepted (by the right people) as prim and proper. But Harry is magical, "as not normal as it is possible to be" (II.3). Harry's abnormalities, even more than his powers, are what frighten the Dursleys.

For more than a century, political theorists have worried in various ways about crowds, mobs, blobs, masses, mass societies, peer pressures, majority tyrannies, and the like. All have been experienced as sources and results of conformism. The Potter books keep the focus more directly on ways that conformity systematizes itself. Thus they sidestep controversies about how literally to treat talk of group organisms or of individual alienation and anomie. Instead Potter books present conformism as a process and a product of pressures to act enough like others in your groups. Its aims are to stand out only in a few socially approved ways and to feel included completely in rituals of everyday life. Potter books also evoke feelings of envy and superiority that thread throughout conformism. They show individuals cleaving into little cliques and large fashions that can reassure each person of suiting a preferred (yet somewhat assigned) social mold better than some other people in view. This emphasis fits a major project of *On Liberty* by John Stuart Mill: promoting the independence of individuals from conformism as an everyday style.[2]

The Dursleys epitomize conformism as politics of normality. Even as conformists, the Dursleys applaud themselves as elite, and sneer at anybody or anything at all different. Yet the Dursleys are beset by anxiety. They worry, of course, that others sneer at them. Uncle Vernon monitors people at work, while Aunt Petunia looks over the fence to check the neighborhood. For conformists, normality is not a default or a least-effort option; it takes energy and ingenuity. It also takes bullying to enforce normality on outliers like Harry. But don't feel too sorry for the Dursleys because they must expend even more energy to push Harry toward normality. All of them, including Aunt Marge, get great senses of superiority and satisfaction from abusing him.

Conformist concerns of normality appear in every Potter book. Normality can be good on occasion (V.837), but mostly it's overdone and oppressive (I.1–7, 53, 307; II.3; III.21, 26; IV.31–40; V.39; VI.334–5; VII.669). Potter books portray conformism as rampant and related to current materialism and consumerism (I.22; II.10; III.3; IV.62). But rather than subordinate it to capitalism or mass society, as such ties are apt to do, the Potter books tackle conformism more in its own terms. In this case and others, a big advantage of the Potter books as political theory is that they start and stay with everyday politics as (even young) readers face them personally.

Not so incidentally, Potter books are much better than Potter movies at detailing their politics in everyday, personalized terms. Thus Potter films shrink their conformist politics to a little Dursley dialogue and a few glimpses of the exurban regimentation of Little Whinging and Privet Drive. The Dursleys live at Number Four, and Harry initially in its cupboard under the stairs. Similar houses, lawns, and cars link muggles at a glance to conformity; but not even the movie dialogue does much to specify dynamics of conformism as political style. This is notable because it's nothing like inevitable for books to outdo the political detail or sophistication of movies based on them. There are important cases to the contrary. To be sure, some innovations of the Potter films are worth analyzing; but we do well to keep the Potter books front and center.

In fact, the opening Potter movie has little on conformism: mainly an initial view of row houses on Privet Drive plus a late mention of rule-breaking. The first novel talks non-stop about rules, but the first film turns from rule-breaking to different dynamics. McGonagall punishes Hermione for "bad judgment" rather than rule breaking when she claims responsibility for the restroom confrontation with a mountain troll. Still the first movie retains the novel's "decisive" act by Neville Longbottom, who's eventually revealed to be a rough double of Harry (V.841–2). Neville stands up to his three friends to prevent another late-night, rule-violating mission beyond their dormitory. Hermione petrifies Neville, so the heroic trio can go to guard the Philosopher's Stone, and each of the three earns lots of extra points for their heroism. But Dumbledore awards *Neville* the key points that lift Gryffindor over Slytherin's total for the House Cup. These reward Neville's courage in facing his friends and refusing to conform to their peer pressure (I.306).

In the Potter books, conformist politics discourage departing from settled social places, whether in deed or idea. Conformism promotes mostly blind faith in some establishment that's supposed to keep everything (and every-body) normal. Any possibility that Harry—or anybody associated with the Dursleys—might act or think "outside the box" rattles Uncle Vernon. Acts or even thoughts of magic are more than he can take. For the conformist, though, even a magical establishment is better than no enduring or trustworthy nor-mality at all (VII.33). When deprived of a legitimate Ministry of Magic, even though he's hated and resisted it, Vernon is still in agony about stepping off the conformist line in order to seek safety. To move Vernon off the dime, at the last book's beginning, Harry has to turn to his hard-earned arsenal of horror images involving Voldemort: images which Vernon has been wishing away, at least for his nuclear family.

To conform is to keep the boat as quiet as possible, lest it suddenly takes on water or even turns over on you. So Vernon doesn't approve of ques-tions either (I.20). Questions can unsettle a social order; they can spotlight the questioners and the people near. Are they ignorant, unseemly in putting themselves forward, incompletely socialized, or mentally slow? Have they imagined possibilities out of bounds? Are they trying to rock or swamp the boat? What's "wrong" with *them*, in short, that they would question? No establishment would welcome them.

Even unconventional *talk* upsets Vernon and Petunia. Instead they engage in groupthink and speak primarily in terms of stereotypes (I.8). As conform-ists, they find dreams and fantasies especially unsettling (I.26). Ideas and imagination are dangerous—not only because they might undermine a good thing, but also because they might make somebody stand out. The Dursleys seem to have lots of company among muggles who work overtime to teach people to conform. The Potter books suggest that this is a principal opera-tion of neighborhoods, schools, businesses, media, and governments. For the Dursleys, Harry's magical inability to blend entirely into their society counts as a congenital bent toward crime. To avoid embarrassing questions on Hogwarts, they tell Aunt Marge that Harry goes to St. Brutus's Secure Center for Incurably Criminal Boys (III.19). For the Dursleys and many oth-ers, sadly, nonconformity at least feels like a crime.

Vernon, especially, fears that Harry will make his normal relatives into targets of gossip and sneering. So the Dursleys seek to conceal Harry, lodg-ing him in a cupboard under the stairs, where he keeps company with spiders. They try hard to suppress Harry's magic. Vernon leads Petunia and Dudley in bullying Harry toward conformity unto invisibility. Indeed we learn that the power trip of bullying others into line, so that they don't stand out, can be a major incentive for conformism. Seeing Vernon bully Harry is a favorite entertainment for Dudley (III.18); and Vernon enjoys bullying so much (I.4) that he goes to crazy lengths to keep Harry from boarding nearly year-round at the distant, secret Hogwarts School of Witchcraft and Wizardry (I.31–59).

When Harry goes anyway, Vernon is still loathe to let Harry absent himself further by visiting friends, the Weasleys, for much of a remaining summer (IV.31). In dread of public disgrace by the strange, magical likes of Harry, Vernon still likes having Harry under his enforcing thumb.

Dursley bullying seeks to shame, shun, and abjectify Harry. To keep him beneath notice by others, it tries to teach him that he has no place in normal society. Thus the Dursleys mostly exclude Harry from ordinary rituals like family excursions, birthday celebrations, and Christmas gifts. Harry first gets a birthday card only at age thirteen, and it isn't from the Dursleys (III.5–8). For his second year at Hogwarts, where he stays at Christmas because he's unwelcome on Privet Drive, the Dursleys give Harry a Christmas toothpick and suggest that he stay at Hogwarts for the summer (II.212). For his fourth year, the Dursleys send a tissue (IV.410). Let the laughable exaggeration prove the point. Vernon and Petunia might think that Harry needs drastic measures to internalize the lesson; yet it's fair to notice that they want Harry to learn what they're trying to teach their own son, Dudley: There's safety in assimilation. So don't think for yourself, don't be different, don't be anybody. Don't step out of line, stay like others, stay correct. Conform.

Even so, there can be a strong contrast between wanting somebody to feel unwelcome or unworthy and wishing someone were dead. Kreature despises Harry as the leading threat to the pure-blood mania of perverse perfectionists like most of his beloved Blacks or the Dark Lord. For Christmas, the Blacks' house-elf gives Harry maggots (VI.339). As Dumbledore explains, there's residual love for Harry in the family ties and obligations to him observed by the Dursleys, almost despite themselves. Trying to make Harry insignificant, so that he doesn't stand out, is so contrary to his character and history that it has to feel hostile in the extreme. Yet the Dursley impetus comes mainly from an impersonal conformism all too evident in everyday life. To be sure, this gets magnified by Petunia's and Vernon's vaguely envious aversion to magic. Yet Dumbledore wants Harry to see even so that the Dursleys' mistreatment of him, while not defensible in the least, still doesn't arise principally from some personal animus against Harry.

But what the Dursleys intend as the conformist version of an invisibility cloak becomes for Harry a shield of humility. In placing the young Harry with his aunt and uncle, Dumbledore hoped for greater love than a begrudging act of family obligation, although this proves enough to complete the magical protection for Harry until he comes of age at seventeen. And Dumbledore foresees advantages in anonymity for a clever boy otherwise too renowned for his own good. As he says to Minerva McGonagall, Transfiguration teacher and Headmistress of Gryffindor House, early fame would swell Harry's head and warp his growth (I.13). Merlin implies the same when he takes Arthur as an infant from the court of Uther Pendragon, his father and king, to be raised as a son of Sir Ector. Harry's modest ego remains a great strength in combatting Voldemort.

We might fear that Harry would be riven by envy for the love and resources that go only to Dudley in the Dursley household. But Harry sees the harm in how Dudley is pampered into conformity. Harry's not free of envy, but it stays mostly mild and wistful. We might worry that Harry would be desperate for friends and their approval. Harry is happy enough to be included by others and to fit into society, but only to the point where people or principles are jeopardized. So the Potter books portray principled resistance to conformity as the signal virtue that Harry has learned (inadvertently) from the Dursleys. From the first, the Potter series shows that having the courage of your convictions, even in the face of disapproving friends, can be indispensable as a DADA of social interaction—as well as the depredations of Voldemort.

Conformism is herd behavior, and the human names for these herds range from gangs and groups to classes and cliques. Dudley is lead bully in a neighborhood gang that torments Harry when it can. Harry accrues his own little clique at Hogwarts, with several Gryffindors in addition to Hermione, Ron, and Neville. Draco Malfoy's clique, principally from Slytherin House, begins with Crabbe and Goyle. The clusters of students who walk the Hogwarts halls are often, like the cliques in schools the world over, that institution's everyday supports for people. Yet our individual needs for small-group supports leave all the more invidious the function of these sets of friends as organs of conformity and engines of mediocrity. The Potter books show how teamthink and making-alike, although good at times, can regress us to the mean. It's when Harry and his friends resist conforming, and strike out in distinctive directions, that they excel in magic, maturation, and making the future safe from Voldemort, the Death Eaters, and their ilk.

Dumbledore encourages Hogwarts students to resist herd behavior when he celebrates Neville for refusing conformity to his Gryffindor friends. In Book 5, Dumbledore does this too with Firenze, the centaur who often aids Harry and his friends. When Dolores Umbridge from the MOM sacks Sybill Trelawney from teaching Divination at Hogwarts, the response of Dumbledore is to hire Firenze for his centaur expertise in astrology. Yes, this is to keep Umbridge from appointing a Ministry stooge. But it's also to celebrate the independence and integrity of Firenze. And it gives Firenze a platform—initially reviled by the other centaurs, who seem later to repent—for contributing to the momentous events of his times. Firenze tells his Hogwarts students that he's been banished by his herd for helping Dumbledore as a wizard, which the herd takes to betray it (V.601–2). Even centaur conformity, which cites high principles worthy of respect for many reasons, seems misbegotten; and the Potter tales insistently teach that conformism is one of our worst temptations in the politics of everyday life. Even the Hogwarts song epitomizes anti-conformism. At Dumbledore's instruction, its words are to be sung more or less simultaneously and together to different, individual tunes, harmonics, and rhythms (I.127–8).

Conformist politics stay stylistic. Nobody theorizes them into a philosophy, marches for them in a movement, or scientizes them toward an ideology. Their significance stems from their prominence in schools such as Hogwarts and in neighborhoods like Little Whinging in Surrey, where the Dursleys live just outside Greater London. Conformism is important as the main foil for the vital perfectionism that Harry practices to resist the perverse perfectionism of Voldemort and the Death Eaters. Feeding diffusely into conformist politics in the Potter series are its further styles of authoritarian, bureaucratic, fascist, patronist, and totalitarian politics. In resisting those dark arts in our dark times, Harry and his friends enact everyday styles of perfectionist politics.

PERFECTIONISM

A Hogwarts education in Potter magic is an education in perfectionist politics. For such perfectionists as Nietzsche, this means leaving behind all-too-trenchant comparisons of human cliques to cattle herds. When Harry departs London for the first time on the Hogwarts Express, that train leaves behind clusters of cows and sheep as it takes students north (I.100–101). Harry and his friends even learn to dislike the paradoxical herds of elitists who flock to Voldemort. At Hogwarts, to be sure, Harry encounters diverse politics beyond the conformism he'd met at the Dursleys. The rest of this book addresses many kinds, more or less one at a time. He embraces several, opposes others, and learns from all. Still his main education is in (magically) excelling across and beyond the best of them, and that makes Harry's an education in perfectionist politics.

Yet there are diverse sorts of perfectionism, even in Potter politics; and Harry *isn't* adept at all of them, or drawn at all to some of them. In his first two years, Oliver Wood captains the Gryffindor Quidditch team; and he succumbs to a perfectionism, which can be called *compulsive* or *American*. This is enormously, sometimes frantically energetic in its unqualified dedication to practice-makes-perfect. Often it goes overboard to win-at-any-cost, even when what's won need not matter much beyond the moment. A cinematic example is *American Beauty* (1999), where the title roses offer brightly red petals but slight their scent. (Remember Shakespeare on roses?) Wood pushes his team to overdo every tiny thing, even obsesses over them. He takes too far the largely republican politics of winning at competitive sports. A glimpse of victory the previous year (I.216) returns Wood gung-ho for training to claim the glory (II.104–5; II.244–5). He tries to elevate the team from exerting to excelling. Instead he makes members tired and grumpy with each other. Then he tells Harry as seeker to grab the golden snitch or die trying, which comes all too close to happening (II.170). Similar situations arise in the fourth book, with competitions for the Quidditch World Cup and the Triwizard Cup. This can produce high quality, and Wood goes pro after he graduates. Yet it can prevent completing projects then letting them go, because they never seem good enough to satisfy impossible standards. Harry captains differently. Courtesy of Umbridge, he's had the benefit of a year away from playing Quidditch, to gain perspective on it.

Harry doesn't seem attracted in the least to the purely instinctual perfectionism of body over mind symbolized by the "golden beast" of Nietzsche and German Nazis.[3] (In Potter books, the "beast" is silver as the werewolf: more Fenrir Greyback than Remus Lupin.) Harry strongly opposes eugenic perfectionism and totalitarian perfectionism. The vigilante perfectionism of *The Dark Knight Trilogy* (2005–2012) might lure him momentarily—but not for long. The (somewhat) sunnier perfectionisms of Ralph Waldo Emerson and Stanley Cavell do suit Harry better, and we learn a lot about them in studying who Harry is and what he does. Nietzsche hated the Christian perfectionism of humility, remorse, forgiveness, love, mercy, and metaphysics. It's the obverse of his perfectionism of genius and leaping to leave behind justice and gods. Yet ironically, Harry excels at empathy, love, and joy—plus impulse, resolve, and invention. Hence his perfectionism escapes some Nietzschean troubles in order to resist Voldemort's predatory, vampirical version.

Early differences between Harry Potter and Tom Riddle aren't hard to identify or explain. Both are orphaned almost from the start, but Harry gets a year of parental love that Tom doesn't. In their first eleven years, both stand out as mages-in-the-making put into the midst of muggles who act as though there's no such thing as magic; and there's little way for either boy to discover who he is or could become. But Tom goes to an orphanage where his powers let him turn into a sneaky bully; whereas Harry goes to an upper-middle-class home of conformists who fear and bully him, while Harry mostly holds his own. Both boys are ecstatic to be claimed by Hogwarts. But Tom arrives as a loner who's arrogant, resentful, and manipulative; whereas Harry arrives as a surprised celebrity who's earnest, decently self-reliant, yet happy for friends. Oh yes, and Tom has a secret heritage-and-talent, which sorts him into Slytherin House; while Harry reacts against his early experiences of Draco Malfoy to choose Gryffindor House, where the Weasleys are.

The rest is . . . humility. As Dumbledore has hoped in placing him with the Dursleys, Harry isn't full of himself. Being bullied has stiffened his backbone while feeding his empathy and respect for underlings. (Dumbledore highlights more than once how Voldemort's contempt for those of lesser status leads him to underestimate them.) Celebrity doesn't get much chance to turn Harry's head before he learns its downsides. Moreover this dampens any ardor he otherwise might have felt for the (republican) glory that Ron craves so acutely, from measuring himself by older brothers who distinguish themselves at school and afterward. Harry sees that "his" success owes much to help and luck (V.327; VII.379). Harry's able to acknowledge the talents of others, even when greater than his, without disparaging them or needlessly making them rivals. Yes, he enjoys scoring above Hermione by using the Half-Blood Prince's book in Potions. Yet they're both happier by far to stay friends, and Harry's not jealous of her superior grades in most courses. Perhaps more important, Harry neither soaks in self-pity nor delights in learning that he's "the Chosen One," let alone lords it over others. In a word, Harry is humble.

Along with humility, Harry appreciates and practices several other attributes of Christian perfectionism. These surface in Emerson and Cavell too. In the Potter books, as commentators spotlight, remorse is the key precondition for forgiveness. Whether Christian forgiveness is less conditional can be debated. But remorse confesses as well as feels guilt, which gets recognized and promoted—if not exactly recommended—by several skeins of Christianity. Nietzsche hated the "moralized memory" of guilt, justice, and (most) history. He treated them as woeful western, human disabilities. They tangle us in briar patches of bad faith, bad feeling, and bad reflection. These snag people short of any leaping at all. Like shame, they feed the miasma of anxiety that enforces conformism. Potter perfectionism melds leaping, regretting, and forgiving. The realist maxim is that it's better to ask forgiveness than permission; the perfectionist precept is Just Do It. Potter perfectionism recognizes that forgiving yourself as well as others can clear your way for leaping far indeed.[4]

Leaping might not come easily to people most of the time, but remorse and forgiving can be horrendously hard. The pain of remorse is apt to be terrible, and it might be unbearable. This is what Hermione tells Harry and Ron about healing a soul riven into horcruxes (VII.103). Harry is beset by stabbing remorse at his role in the death of his godfather, Sirius Black. Dumbledore persuasively takes enough of the blame to help Harry let go of his sharp sense of guilt (V.820–44; VII.215). Yet forgiving himself remains hard for Harry, and forgiving others is hard for most of us too. When Percy rejoins the rest of the Weasleys for the Battle of Hogwarts, he can't seem to find enough ways to denounce his craven deeds and self for siding with the corrupted MOM; and only when Percy affirms Fred's vehement additions can Fred forgive him. When he leaves Harry and Hermione, Ron is immediately remorseful. Once the Deluminator helps him return, Ron earns forgiveness with a lengthy and romantic apology. He also saves Harry's life, retrieves the Gryffindor

Sword, and suffers horcrux torments that vivify his sense of his failings. Even after all that, Hermione needs him to sustain a chastened demeanor for weeks (VII.370–88), though Ron's croaked request for her worked faster after he'd been poisoned (VI.399–423). Ron needs Hermione's expression of remorse to forgive her for Crookshanks's harassment of Scabbers (III.292). But the great case of remorse is Snape living a torturous life to atone for his part in the murder of his beloved Lily Evans Potter. This sacrifice helps Dumbledore then Harry to forgive Snape at last (V.851; VII.672–83, 758).

Mercy is in the family of forgiveness. Three times, Draco tries to kill Dumbledore, and gets others grievously hurt in the process of never quite pulling the trigger. Dumbledore tries to get Draco to recognize the mercy in the headmaster's refraining from response, hoping that the experience of mercy might eventually teach Draco how to turn away from Voldemort (VI.592). Mercy, even more than fear, restrains Draco from identifying Harry, who's been disfigured by a stinging hex from Hermione, ere snatchers bring him to the Malfoy mansion (VII.457–9). Later Harry mercifully saves Draco from fiendfyre in the Room of Hidden Things. Harry mercifully can't bring himself to have Pettigrew killed for the murder of Harry's parents (III.375–6, 381–2, 426–7). Later the brief pause by Peter's silver hand in killing Harry is fatal—to Peter (VII.470).

Like forgiveness, mercy is a form of love for offenders; and it extends even to enemies. Neither Christian love of this kind nor republican friendship of the sort practiced by Harry, Ron, and Hermione is merely or principally an emotion. Rather each is a deed, at the least, and more likely an entire course of conduct. This perfectionist love is similar to the greatest republican friendship—or perhaps surpasses it, leaps beyond it. Dumbledore attributes Harry's seemingly impossible defiance and eventual defeat of Voldemort to such love. First it's Lily's love for Harry, shown by sacrificing herself for him to thwart Voldemort's killing curse. Next it's Aunt Petunia's love for her feared and envied sister, done by taking in Lily's orphaned son (V.835–6). Then, time and again, it's Harry's love for many whom he will not see destroyed by Voldemort or others (VI.509–11). He knows that this "old magic" of love is celebrated by Dumbledore, yet Voldemort insistently denigrates and disregards it (IV.653; VI.444). Harry, however, enacts it.

Harry's capacity for love is evident in his talent for joy, and this is especially clear in his early power to cast a corporeal patronus. DADA Professor Lupin gives Harry private lessons in the patronus charm, so that he can chase away dementors drawn by his extraordinary intensity. Lupin specifies no gesture to go with the spell's words: *Expecto Patronum!* (Expect the helper!) Instead he stresses that the caster must focus exclusively on a single, supremely happy memory. Harry's initial efforts flounder: his first broomstick flight, Gryffindor winning the House Cup, and finding that he's a wizard bound for Hogwarts. Lupin and Harry infer that the focal thoughts might not be happy enough (III.237–42). But Harry's starting to recognize that he's desperate for the previously inaccessible memories (even of the murder) of his parents that the boggart in the form of a dementor elicits. His concentration is divided, and he doesn't whole-heartedly *want* to banish the boggart-dementor. Still the diagnosis of deficiencies in his happy thoughts has merit too. These three efforts imply that the perfectionist exhilaration of flight, the republican glory of victory, and the existential thrill of a better identity and condition do not suffice for Harry. His first fully formed patronus instead comes at Quidditch, when Draco's fake dementors spur Harry to Just Do It, without stopping to think (III.262). Harry leaps. His patronus does not come from a focused, willful pursuit of happiness as glee (let alone contentment or property). It flows from a surge of keenest attunement to the vitality of life, which some Christians call *joy*.[5] Joy leaps the abyss that lured Nietzsche, and it counters the nihilism of absurdity that he longed to resist.

Perhaps Rowling has her characters talk instead of *happiness* because it's the everyday word that's nearest to *joy*. In *Philosopher's Stone*, Dumbledore claims that the Mirror of Erised would show "the happiest man on earth" just as he is (I.213). Completely attuned to all aspects of his life, that man's deepest desire would fully reflect his present reality. His would be a joyful condition, but it needn't be a moral condition. In stripping muggle-born mages of their wands, lives, and identities, Umbridge is perversely "so happy," so much "in her element," so joyful that her patronus glows brightly (VII.259). By contrast, Neville never musters a corporeal patronus, because even the fiercest focus (V.606) is no substitute for the joy that powers most Potter magic in general. Harry actually speaks of joy as this full attunement when he commiserates with Ron for failing his first apparating test by leaving half-an-eyebrow behind. "No joy," says Harry to console Ron; yet it could be to teach him too (VI.476). Teleporting himself whole necessitates that Ron overcome anxieties (like Neville's) that can disrupt his complete attunement to mind-body and deed. (Yes, I may be punning on Harry's idiomatic phrase; but consider that its grace arguably comes from the greater, significantly Christian meaning of *joy*.)

In Tom Riddle and Gellert Grindelwald, this magical, energetic joy appears early as their "wild" happiness and *merriment* (VI.499; VII.28.3). Gellert Grindelwald, the prodigious wizard who goes from Dumbledore's teenage friend to the scourge of Europe, becomes in Harry's mind the merry thief because his image glows with joyful energy (VII.281–3; 291). Professor Galatea Merrythought, Riddle's DADA teacher, has a synonym for *joy* as her last name (VI.369, 432). When Nagini seizes Harry and Voldemort flies to Godric's Hollow, Harry senses Voldemort's "leap of joy" (VII.339). When Harry figures out his relation to the Deathly Hallows, joy propels Harry's leaps of inference (VII.430). But when a fierce longing for those hallows distracts Harry from his quest for the horcruxes, it saps his joy—specifically (VII.435). And when Harry must conjure his patronus to scatter the Umbridge dementors at the MOM, it's the joy of his friendship with Ron and Hermione that breaks through the dementor despair (VII.556). In the Lovegood house, Harry sees how Luna has painted her bedroom ceiling to shine with the joy of her friendships with Harry, Hermione, Ron, Neville, and Ginny. The dust tells Harry that Luna's been away; the joy reminds us that Luna's magic, like her mother's, is strong (VII.417). The super-magic of Felix Felicis as liquid luck keeps Harry almost impossibly joyful, persuasive, and productive for hours (VI.477–93).

Quasi-Nietzschean *charisma* has some features of Christian joy. Early Christians adapted the word from ancient Greeks to name the Holy Spirit as divine *grace*. People who are joyful or charismatic can seem to radiate a sort of energy; they can seem to overflow with a kind of power. Both are species of *enthusiasm* (*inspired by a god*), and this can engage or infuse others. Charm projects interest rather than enthusiasm; it impresses others by letting them impress the charmer. Gilderoy Lockhart tries for charm, and he succeeds with some fans like Molly Weasley, although his narcissism and self-interest offend others (II.59). Bathilda Bagshott might have had plenty of company in finding young Gellert Grindelwald to be charming (VII.356). Dumbledore charms many, and Voldemort can be charming when he wants (II.310; VI.433–9, 495). As Tom Riddle and even after his bodily rebirth, Voldemort manifests a vampirical kind of charisma (IV.643–4; VI.361–2). Dumbledore's aura of energy and power can be awesome (III.91; IV.706–8; V.64).

Charisma is like charm in extending to others while depending on others. This is to say that audiences help make charisma—sometimes as much as the charismatics do. Clear cases can include Barack Obama and Donald Trump: both became charismatic speakers in important part because of their enthusiastic audiences, which leaves others to wonder what makes the fans and followers so excited. Joy, by contrast, isn't in the experiences or responses of beholders; nor is joy made directly by audiences, no matter how much their expressions of support might lift an actor. Joy surges from doers into their deeds, from Potter mages into their magics; and it's the deeds or spells—not any energy, power, or magnetism—that others shape as well as experience. Thus Harry and Hermione are formidable mages in the making, powered by joy (as we may say). But they aren't awesome presences like Grindelwald, Dumbledore, or Voldemort. At best and worst, Harry and Hermione become celebrities. (There's more on celebrity in the next chapter.)

Further aspects of perfectionist politics in Harry and his magic are still more Nietzschean. Earlier chapters have addressed several but not others.

Hence leaping, going dark, and turning can benefit from more focus on Harry in particular. Strengthening, diverging, and creating need further attention to Pottery in general.

Perfectionist *leaping* is acting on vital impulse—*not* calculation, control, cultivation, planning, reflection, research, tradition, or any other western ground. Perfectionists who leap Just Do It. For Harry, impulsive action in the first book stays unidentified as such. This seems to be because it's his magical action. Before Hogwarts, Harry literally doesn't know what he's doing when leaping to the schoolhouse chimney (I.25) or vanishing the boa constrictor's glass (I.26–9). At the time, arguably, he doesn't even know what he's done. Hence it's not so much that Harry Just Does It as that it Just Happens to him.[6] At Hogwarts, the emphasis is on Harry learning magical spells and portions by thinking carefully about what he's doing. The signal exception, of course, is Harry's flare for broomstick flying. But after book one finishes with Harry fending off Quirrell-Voldemort through several impulsive moves (I.288–95), Harry leaps repeatedly, acting specifically on impulse.[7]

This usually contrasts with apparating, where the "leaper" changes instantaneously from one place to another (distant) one. The act of apparating, analyzed later as mainly realist in its political symbolism, is not exactly impulsive. Instead it involves prefiguring a "destination," purposefully summoning the "determination" to move there, then monitoring the process with "deliberation" along the way. There are hybrid cases, as when Hermione apparates the heroic trio from the Weasley wedding to Tottenham Court Road in order to escape Death Eaters who crash the reception. This can count as an impulsive, perfectionist leap because the destination, determination, and deliberation arise for Hermione only in the act of leaping and not in advance (VII.162). Impulse by Hermione also apparates the three from the Black House doorstep to the Quidditch World Cup woods (VII.268–71), which doesn't go well because Ron gets splinched. Of course, the more that specific apparations get repeated to the point of routine, the more that perfectionist impulses can be cultivated into republican habit, instinct, or "second nature." The twins do this in apparating between floors of Number Twelve Grimmauld Place (V.68, 160).

The key contrast for Harry is between (perfectionist) leaping and (modern) planning of the kinds connected with realist strategies and tactics or the sorts linked to political ideologies of liberalism and socialism. The "bigger" the realist plan, the more it should be for organizing and using resources into the near future than for sufficing to secure results. (This is what the step of "deliberation" adds to apparating.) Liberal plans are usually meant to "solve" relatively limited "problems." Socialist plans are more for larger-scale regulation or control of societies. In these terms, Gellert Grindelwald and Albus Dumbledore propound early plans (dreams might be more like it), which could count as socialist, at least according to Aberforth Dumbledore (VII.561). The plans by Ron are mostly realist, while plans by Harry and Hermione are mainly liberal in style. In their own ways, Ron and Hermione both are better planners than Harry. Ron regularly beats Harry (and Hermione) at the realist planning called chess, while thinking ahead lets Hermione preempt troubles that go unanticipated by Harry's impulses (VII.263).

All come from rational planning meant to be calm, cool, and dispassionate. It's to identify all ends and means. Ideally it works out every detail in advance: step by step. In our time, the model has become a computer program that uses if-then statements to specify responses to all contingencies in the order of their possible appearances. The existentialist criticism, of course, is that this can't be done (even in principle, let alone in fact) for many matters important to human communities. This is because they're communities (not computers) of humans (not gods). Even plans involve leaps, in epistemic senses. Remember this, stay ready to adjust and improvise, and plans can help. Forget this, cling to initial ideas about conditions and consequences, then plans often fail. Worse, they readily mismanage resources, misdirect efforts, even miscarry in effects.

Eventually Dumbledore *might* become a master planner in the realist style. But "better to be lucky than good," even so, because his grand strategy for Snape and the Elder Wand doesn't work as planned. Yet it still helps others attain the intended results (VII.721). Plans by Harry, Ron, and Hermione frequently go awry; whereas their perfectionist leaps, especially Harry's, do better. Yet their plans work as signs of modern rationality to reassure them, especially Hermione (IV.351; VII.307, 320, 351, 464). And it's as though their plans serve often as wrackspurt siphons, to eradicate distractions (VII.404). Then on the spur of the moment, with the plan of the moment falling apart, they can Just Do It. Perfectionists might wish that the three could discard planning as happy talk that occasionally makes their situations more dire (VII.534). *Harry's* perfectionist point, though, is that plans can't replace deeds (VII.230–1, 552). The need can be to Just Do It.

Because perfectionist leapers aren't prudent and don't look carefully ahead to see where they might be bound, we could conceive leaping as *going dark*—and vice versa. This is worth appreciating, even as earlier chapters show how the two tropes help articulate different aspects of perfectionist politics. Potter books tell often of Harry leaping, but even more of him going dark. In books about "dark arts" in "dark times," it's no wonder that *dark* is a word that appears often. Like leaping, going dark is a figure that emerges clearly in the second book. Until Fawkes pecks out the basilisk's eyes, Harry must fight with his own eyes shut tight (II.318–22). For Harry, at least, going dark is an aspect or moment of entering a Pensieve to engage the thoughts of others

(VI.199, 363, 433). This holds also for apparating, including by portkey, at least for Harry.[8]

The Potter saga distinguishes (but connects) four main takes on going dark. It can be *going in secret* (III.397, V.58), although Harry more often uses the school's hidden passages or his own Invisibility Cloak. Going dark can be *going without sight*. This means acting with eyes disabled or disregarded, by relying on other senses; or it uses magical substitutes for human vision. These include the Marauder's Map and Moody's magical eye, for both foil invisibility charms and cloaks.[9] Going dark can be *going without information*, while acting instead on trust, impulse, impetus, or luck.[10] And it can be *going without hope*, by letting go of plans for control, drives for success, even thoughts of survival.[11] Frequently we readers find Harry going dark.

Nonetheless the foremost feature of Harry's perfectionist politics is *turning*. As troping or going figural, turning constructs all Potter spell-casting. There the tropes are not only figures of language in the words spoken but also figures of action in the gestures performed to complete the charms, curses, enchantments, hexes, jinxes, vows, and other incantations. As the chapter on Potter magic explains, the figures—the turns—are behavioral as well as verbal. They also can be perceptual and communal.[12] Turning is arguably the primary project of perfectionist excelling.

Like *dark*, *turn* is toward the very top of Potter words in frequency; and it links to Potter magic and perfectionist politics in important ways beyond spells. As a template of Potter magic, Diagon Alley is said to "twist" and "turn . . . out of sight" (I.71). As a branch of Potter magic, Transfiguration is specifically about "turning something into something else" (I.125). Perhaps because its magic is especially difficult and dangerous, Hermione claims it as her focus (I.134). At Hogwarts, Transfiguration is taught by Minerva McGonagall (and Dumbledore before her). Its tasks include turning matches into needles (I.126, 134), mice into snuffboxes (I.262), beetles into buttons (II.94), white rabbits into slippers (II.284), teapots into tortoises (III.317), hedgehogs into pincushions (IV.233), raccoons into something not named (IV.238), guinea fowl into guinea pigs (IV.385), owls into opera glasses (V.705), air into yellow birds (VI.284), and vinegars into wines (VI.515). Hermione excels at these; by mistake, Ron turns a dinner plate into a mushroom (V.713). Notice the figural links in names, shapes, sources, and more: wordplay, yes; but truly perfectionist, figural logic too. Similarly there is transfigural humor and justice in the human to animal transformations: McGonagall to a bespectacled cat, Sirius to a large black dog, Lupin to a wolf, Pettigrew to a rat with a wormtail, James Potter to a stag, Draco Malfoy to a white ferret, and Rita Skeeter to a beetle (mosquito as no transformation at all?). Figural logic also holds for the patronus cast by each character. And the series starts with the most famous transfigurational totem in alchemical magic: the Philosopher's Stone is for turning base metals into gold, and for transforming ingredients into the Elixir of Life, which Flamel consumes and Voldemort covets.

In politics, other kinds of turns can be significant too. The ancient Greek word identifies events that change the fates of individuals, the outcomes of battles, the futures of communities: "for want of a nail" begins the proverb. Elphias Doge memorializes Dumbledore in these terms, noting that his defeat of Grindelwald is widely seen as a major "turning point in magical history" (VII.20). The Potter saga sometimes gives a perfectionist spin to these turning-point events. In the third book, the name for the Time-Turner is not just a figural pun on its shape and operation as an hourglass (III.395). It also suggests how the device does its magic, enabling Hermione and Harry to turn events toward different outcomes and meanings. Because the events are entangled and already have been experienced by many people, turns must be made with great imagination and precision to keep the results from unraveling. Better than the horror of a witch seeing herself in duplicate, this explains why turning back time to tinker with events can so readily go awry.

It can also explain how Harry's ingesting of Felix Felicis, the luck potion, does help him persuade Slughorn to share the unaltered memory of Voldemort asking many years before about horcrux*es*—in the plural (VI.477–93, 514–6). Magically the potion turns more than twenty-five intersecting events in Harry's favor. (I've counted.) Yes, some are minor (getting back into the Gryffindor common room). And some lack salience for retrieving the memory (splitting Ron and Lavender Brown as well as Ginny and Dean Thomas). But most seem crucial: heading to the vegetable patch, inviting Slughorn to Aragog's burial, Slughorn proposing a wake, making available rarities for Slughorn to pad his pocket, Hagrid turning the talk to reminiscence of Lily, and so on. For a rhetorician, the story shows how persuasion is complicated and usually exceeds words. For a perfectionist, the episode traces how leaping from turn to turn can succeed at what otherwise would be impossible. On a civilizational scale, Hannah Arendt analyzed the "turning operations" that found polities or end cultures. Turning-the-corner is a related figure, one which links these perfectionist politics of turns to the cusps, thresholds, and tipping points of the "chaos mathematics" for nonlinear systems such as hydraulic flows or political movements. And on a personal level, Søren Kierkegaard examined the "rotations" that remake us individually. From the outset, Pottery shows such turns redoing individual characters and conduct (I.13, 113, 159).

Strengthening is a perfectionist twist on the life-and-death stakes in excelling. Perverse perfectionists such Death Eaters and fascists make cult figures of "strong men," and so do some authoritarians. But they miss the Nietzschean shading of strength toward resilience and learning. (Those take flexibility and humility, of course, while "strong men" are almost defined by rigidity and arrogance.) This is because the Nietzschean sense of "strength" is evolutionary. It's about survival more than domination or force. Nietzsche's well-known aphorism is, "What does not kill me makes me stronger." This is the figure of strengthening in Potter perfectionism.

Voldemort's killing curse fails to murder young Harry, but it does mark his forehead with the famous lightning bolt that readily identifies and accredits Harry to friends and enemies alike.[13] From the start, Dumbledore holds that scars can be helpful (I.15; V.842). Harry's lightning scar seems to confer some of Voldemort's powers, including Parseltongue. As the saga progresses, this forehead scar serves Harry as a Voldemort alarm and vision conduit (IV.15–25, 706). It even sears or throbs as a dark detector for other foes and dangers (V.275). After the fifth book, it's a major resource for Harry and his friends; yet it's also a vulnerability, because Voldemort can use it to mislead Harry, and its pain can threatens to overwhelm him. The scars from the Umbridge inscriptions on the back of Harry's hand likewise warn him about her (V.275; VI.347; VII.91, 131, 249). Voldemort burns the Dark Mark as a scar into the forearm of every Death Eater, so that he can touch only one of them to summon all of them. Fleur Delacour takes pride in the facial scars inflicted by Fenrir Greyback on her beloved Bill Weasley, seeing them as badges of his bravery (VI.623). After Ron tangles with brains in the Department of Mysteries, Rowling jokingly has Madam Pomfrey warn that his healing can take a while because thoughts scar deeply (V.847). Yet the deeper joke is that Ron could be said thereafter to become more effectively reflective.

What doesn't destroy can strengthen even when it doesn't scar. Dumbledore tells Harry that his ability to feel pain acutely and persistently, in part because it's been cultivated by all too much painful experience, still should be respected as one of his signal strengths in comparison to the formidable Voldemort (V.823–4). Similarly the Sword of Gryffindor only takes into itself what can make it stronger. This explains it imbibing the venom of the basilisk which Harry used the sword to kill. In turn, Ron and Neville can use the sword's venom to destroy the Voldemort locket and snake horcruxes, as Dumbledore has used it to destroy the ring horcrux. Dumbledore (imagined by Harry to speak in King's Cross Station) even guesses that Harry's wand has acted independently of Harry to defend him from Voldemort because Harry's wand has absorbed some identifying powers and qualities of Voldemort's wand (VII.61, 711). Some of these examples even fit the twisted precept voiced by the perfectionist Joker in *The Dark Knight* (2008): "What doesn't kill you simply makes you stranger."[14] Nevertheless Harry's own perfectionism doesn't exactly embrace such a flamboyant defiance of Dursley conformism.

Diverging is committing fully and definitively to *one* among mutually exclusive courses of action. It faces such a choice without hesitation or trepidation, and it sees the commitment all the way through. Especially it turns away from mundane advice for "moderation in all things" or "splitting the difference." Yogi Berra, Hall of Fame catcher and manager for the New York Yankees, waxed perfectionist when he said, "If you come to a fork in the road, take it."[15] This gets a laugh because it seems to miss the choice. What else are you going to do? Isn't the real question which tine to take? Yet a usual response to the biggest, hardest choices is to temporize, wish away the branching, and pretend that there can be routes with (at least some of) the best of both alternatives. Thus the key act, the most fateful choice, is to take the fork in the road. This entails turning one way *or* the other—rather than shying away from the divergence. We could say that it's an existential choice, because there's no way to know either path well until we take one, but then we can't know the other in a comparable way. Diverging approximates leaping; but it's not exactly impulsive, thus it's more like existentialist than perfectionist leaping. The two stay distinct as perfectionist tropes. Diverging involves a recognition of huge stakes and often some reflection on them, even though the main recognition is that no reflection can inform (or constrain) the choice enough to satisfy the demands of modern rationality.

The label comes from the familiar first line of the beloved poem by Robert Frost on "The Road Not Taken."[16] Diverging implicates the perfectionist precept that genius requires choosing between the life and the work: perfecting both is not (humanly) possible. This can clarify what Hermione learns from her third-year use of a Time-Turner to leave no Hogwarts course untaken. Through innumerable short jaunts of time travel and "burning the candle at both ends," she tries to "have it both ways," perfecting preparations for great work yet "getting a life" too (III.243–4). Brilliant though she is, Hermione manages to run herself ragged, make unforced errors, and bark at everybody—before learning better and turning in the Time-Turner (III.430). By contrast, the Weasley twins *face and take* their fork in the road by departing Hogwarts to elude Umbridge and especially to launch their "joke shop" (V.227). A year later, the heroic trio diverges from school and the ordinary pursuit of life plans to carry out their work against Voldemort (VI.650–2). Yet the choice that most agonizes Harry is leaving Ginny behind and unacknowledged as the love of his life. By the usual superhero convention, he must do so in order to protect her from retaliation against him. Nor do the two want her taken hostage to pressure him (VI.646–7). Likewise Harry asks the Dursleys to hide (VII.33), Ron supposedly gets kept home due to spattergroit that lets a ghoul impersonate him (VII.97–9), while Hermione obliviates and moves her parents (VII.95–7). These precautions are smart. Taking hostages turns out to be a standard operating procedure for Voldemort and the Death Eaters (VII.419, 574, 660).

For Nietzschean perfectionists, genius is not just intelligence but invention; it's not just knowing but discovering and especially *creating*. Slughorn is superb at making potions; yet his teaching is tethered to a textbook of recipes, and there's no indication that he deviates creatively from it in the manner of Snape's amendments as the Half-Blood Prince. More than that, Snape invents spells (*Sectum Sempra*) and possibly other dark arts; as Voldemort apparently does too. Dumbledore discovers (twelve?) uses of dragon blood (I.102–3; VII.26), and he evidently invents the Deluminator. Creating is the main mark of perfectionist genius.

In Harry's generation, therefore, the best candidates for genius are the Weasley twins. Fred and George experiment continually, and they invent successfully, as their "wizard wheezes" show. This bent seems inspired in part by their father, Arthur, who's an incorrigible tinkerer. In the tinkering is their intense and extensive curiosity about how things work, why, and with what susceptibility to alteration. In the incorrigibility is their disposition to keep rules from becoming obstacles. Of course, the twins take this further into glee, if not joy, in defying rules that they regard as oppressive. Hence their creativity seems inseparable from their rule-breaking. No less a judge than Hermione calls their magic "extraordinary" (VI.117). And what about Hermione, often proclaimed the brightest witch of her age? Yes, her intelligence and memory seem to be the best among her classmates at Hogwarts; still her creativity might be in question. To me, her most promising path for creativity turns out to be politics! Once she learns rule-breaking from Harry and Ron, her strong senses of justice and social finesse propel Hermione on truly creative paths for magical Britain: respect for females, freedom for house-elves, and power for goblins.

Harry's dash of genius is for action—or more exactly, for perfectionist leaping. Harry's creativity comes from combining respect for rules with terrifically attuned impulses for setting rules aside to Just Do It. Harry is a rule-breaker and a risk-taker. As with the Weasley twins, it's easy to see continuity between the talents of the father and the attainments of the son (III.424–5). And as with the twins, this can ready us to appreciate the perfectionist rejection of metaphysical and natural givens. Nietzschean and Potter perfectionists instead favor creative engagement in our construction of communities through their conventions.

CONVENTIONALISM

The Potter series introduces Harry—and features him throughout—as a rule-breaker. We might not expect this from stories for children, although it's far from unique to the Potter books. But it's highly unusual when a series that begins for children immerses readers from the first in the urgent politics of their times. Nothing even remotely as successful as the Potter works even attempts this. Still it's an implication of beginning with the importance of defying conformity. The political education for Harry and his friends begins in learning to bend and break rules.

Thus Pottery gives politics grounds of resistance and inversion attuned to our times. In political theory, grounds are beginnings. They are the premises and principles that generate or assess our accounts of politics. They need not be metaphysical or even nonpolitical. They need not be constructed strictly as axioms and definitions. Nor need they be stipulated as inarguable: as "plain to the least reflection" in the language of John Locke or as "self-evident truths" evoked by the American Declaration of Independence. By logic or rhetoric, grounds are where political theory starts. Their contents and treatments configure the political accounts we get.

Thomas Hobbes grounded his political theory in *nature*. Part I begins *Leviathan* with a psychology of human nature, and Part II with a sociology of the State of Nature as the human condition sans modern government.[17] Karl Marx sidelined *natural givens* to feature a dialectic of *historical inventions*, with people making themselves and their ways of life, but not in conditions of their own making; and Marxians ground their political theory in *history*.[18] Friedrich Nietzsche decentered *linear history* and *class analysis* in favor of *tropal genealogy and deconstruction*; while Martin Heidegger, Michel Foucault, and Jacques Derrida followed suit.[19] Then Ludwig Wittgenstein turned Nietzsche's *philological* and *poetical* takes on *language* toward probing the uses, coherence, and dispersion of *linguistic and practical conventions*.[20] Thus Wittgensteinians like Stanley Cavell, Richard Flathman, John Gunnell, Alasdair MacIntyre, Hanna Pitkin, Richard Rorty, and Michael Walzer ground their political theories in what we may call *culture*.[21] It treats normality as a network of conventions that enable us to act meaningfully, if we conform or not.

The Potter books twist all this. If a political theory treats communities as modes of rule, it says what rules are, then specifies and assesses many—showing how we make or unmake them, understand and follow them, enforce or violate them.[22] Hobbes unmade medieval rules and effected sovereign-state rules. To transcend those, Marx analyzed their sources and uses. To remake our senses and practices of rules, Nietzscheans repoeticize and repoliticize them; while Wittgensteinians assess the politics of rules for our practices inside *and* outside modern states or governments. By contrast, J. K. Rowling's character of Harry Potter breaks rules to thwart the threats that arise from forces entrenched or emerging. Rowling's and other accounts of politics that begin in resistance and rule-breaking can sometimes suit our situation and serve our action. They can sometimes do so better than accounts that start with existing rules to save or change those rules—or better than accounts that wish away existing rules to invent others.

The Rowling emphasis on rule-breaking stands out all the more because her Potter books also show playful awareness of prior grounds for political theories. The fifth book has "Hagrid's Tale" (5.420–40) introduce readers to Europe's remaining giants as struggling to survive in a Hobbesian State of Nature. All the Potter books, and especially the sixth, play with historical conditions to situate our troubles in other settings, to address in different ways.[23] Her wordplay provokes, even performs, refigurations of our politics.[24] And her attention to rules in diverse practices helps the Potter series read as a Wittgensteinian analysis of a world next-door to ours.

When menaced, however, Harry often defies conventional responses or crosses official lines. Thus he escapes threats, sidesteps restrictions, and redirects resources against the powers-that-be. In breaking rules, formal and informal, Harry repeatedly turns cultural canons around or turns established institutions upside-down. In the process, he often helps generate replacements. But especially, he helps ground accounts of politics on resistance and rule-breaking more than on previous platforms. Marx portrayed his dialectical materialism as turning the idealist G. W. F. Hegel from his philosophical head onto his practical feet. But Pottery's spins and inversions go further. They leave behind modern, philosophical dualisms of mind and body, analytical and empirical, voluntarist and determinist, idealist and materialist, or the like. They even sideline modern, ideological antinomies of freedom versus coercion, public versus private, individual versus social, ideal versus real, and such. Harry Potter and his friends generate many of their politics by bending, breaking, and otherwise resisting rules that seem outdated, oppressive, or arbitrary. Thus Harry and company seem to recognize that changing conditions and uses can make it acutely dangerous for us to accept many prior rules. And this can be a big challenge for political action in dark times like Harry's—and ours.

Beyond works for children, the rule-breaking hero is a familiar figure in teen and young adult works. Adult novels and movies have even made the rule-breaking hero into a political archetype. Make no mistake: this kind of rule-breaker is not a villain or an antihero, and next-to-nobody experiences Harry in either mode. Instead Harry and his ilk are definitely heroes or heroines, and full-fledged to boot. We might find this figure next door to—or sometimes in the same house as—the bad-ass. But Harry isn't "cool" enough stylistically for that brand. Even with his bent for rule-breaking and political inversion, Harry stays too respectful personally and too constructive institutionally for a badge of unbridled rebellion to fit. He's no James Dean.

Harry's figure can inform a good ground for theorizing our politics. It positions him to inflect the *maverick hero* as a mythic archetype. This figure is simultaneously an outsider and an insider who flouts rules from a resentment of regimentation. Yet the maverick hero learns larger responsibilities in time to save established orders, even if a personal style of prickly resistance to petty rules remains.[25] From the title figure in *Shane* (1953) to the Tom Cruise character in *Top Gun* (1986) to *The Girl with the Dragon Tattoo* (2011), this savior eventually settles into a happy home, rides into the sunset to take on other troubles, or at least steps to the sidelines. Harry turns the maverick into a hero who flouts rules out of personal resistance to terrible disorders that arise from what's established *and* who resists in ways that inform, even found, fresh politics and rules. Let's call this figure the *maverick founder*. To stymie terrors that arise from political styles and institutions long established, the maverick founder repeatedly bends and breaks rules. And *in the rule-breaking*, this figure provides grounds for further styles of action and rules of conduct—as foundations for later institutions and as patterns for emergent politics.

This is close to the template of political action evident in Erik Erikson's psychoanalytical studies of Martin Luther and Mahatma Gandhi.[26] In these cases, solving personal challenges that enact key troubles of the times can project forms of conduct that spread widely by responding effectively to people's needs and views. Personal demons propel these innovators to break away from strongly established and enforced ways of life. Yet the personal demons are emblems of perversities faced by a whole community. Thus the maverick founder's personal rebellions suit the situations of many contemporaries. This inspires followers to cultivate enthusiastically what the maverick ruler-breaker Just Does, sometimes on the spur of the moment. When Harry leaves Hogwarts, Neville leads the way in cultivating Dumbledore's Army as Harry-style resistance to the Death Eater regime that ensues (VII.582).

Harry and his friends face times dark with troubles arising from western politics. These include conformism, fascism, nationalism, authoritarianism, bureaucratism, and totalitarianism. To resist their troubles, Harry and his friends learn from republican politics, modern ideologies, and postmodern movements. They also learn to harmonize resources of idealism, realism, and perfectionism. Along the way, Harry and his colleagues ground their fresh, innovative politics in important part in rule-breaking. By the end of the book at hand, we can recognize these as the *politics of inversion*: turning institutions and styles at least momentarily sideways-unto-upside-down. Traditionally these are the politics of folly, of mythic fools. When might the politics of folly help humanity? The Potter answer is: in dark times, when we face Political Hell on Earth.

FACING THE MIRROR OF ERISED

Next to the Invisibility Cloak inherited by Harry, the most important magical artifacts in book one are the Philosopher's Stone and the Mirror of Erised. With great help from his friends, Harry comes at the climax to face Quirrell and Voldemort in front of the Mirror. Those perverse perfectionists want the Stone to fully revive the Dark Lord. They aren't sure what the Mirror is doing at the end of Dumbledore's obstacles, but they infer that Harry can use it to show them the Stone. An ordinary mirror brings people face-to-face with themselves. Will the dark mages look into the Mirror and see themselves as final obstacles and enemies? Will Harry use the Mirror to confront, criticize, correct, or even fully *become* himself, as we sometimes use reflection to do? All these mirror dynamics have intrigued theorists of politics, perhaps since Narcissus was said to contemplate his image in the still water of a pool. But the Potter dynamic differs significantly.

As Dumbledore has told Harry, this Mirror of Desire shows individuals enjoying what they most want. Whoever is trying to steal the Stone would see Voldemort re-embodied and the thief celebrated, because those are the kinds of desires that propel the theft. But as Dumbledore anticipates, what the Mirror shows Harry is Harry finding the Stone—and keeping it from theft. This is because Harry most wants to *find* the Stone—not *use* it for riches, longevity, or anything else (I.292–300). For Harry, the Stone and getting it are the ends, in themselves. They aren't just means to more important outcomes, products, results.

We could say that this shows Harry to be a hero from the beginning because he keeps his priorities straight. The Stone's lures of endless wealth and life don't corrupt him. This is true, as far as it goes; and it's a fine lesson for politics. Yet we mustn't miss *what* is his top priority, his heart's deepest desire: for Harry in this moment, it's the finding (and protecting). It's the *doing*, the deed—rather than a further act or effect. The first book culminates in a magical performance by Harry that demonstrates the political priority of . . . *performance*. *How* we do something can matter more than *what* we do, whether the *what* is a kind of act (helping or lying) or an outcome.

The *how* of performance is appreciated as *style* in the politics of republics. There it joins a person's causes, skills, resources, associates, results, and such to provide the characteristics that other actors use in constructing a memorable, public character for that individual.[27] This is the character to be displayed in republican busts and statues that memorialize the lessons of history.[28] In republican politics, it isn't entirely true that "style is the man." Other elements count too. But style does help form his public identity, which is the identity that matters most to the community. The republican sense is the one in which Dumbledore is colorfully said to have "style" (V.623).

Perfectionist politics also embrace performance as style, but less as styles of action in a classical public than as styles of life for an encompassing culture that includes diverse arenas of politics in endeavors from the everyday to the extraordinary. Perfectionist leaps do not measure means—in advance or on the way. In constructing cultures from the lifestyles that they sense in the leaps, followers *do* identify the leapers (more or less fully) with their distinctive styles. This holds for perfectionists who attract lifestyle imitators and cultivators. Yet striving for excellence can generate intriguing styles even without such followers.[29] For me, at least, an important part of the interest in following Harry Potter as a character is seeing his style in a perfectionist sense. His performance fascinates many of us readers from one situation to the next—across snubs and self-defenses on Privet Drive, routines and crises at Hogwarts, then confrontations beyond.

Talking about this sense of *performance* isn't easy for us, because we've learned to treat most politics (and everything else) in means/ends terms. If ends are destinations and means are paths to them, performances aren't which paths we take but specifically how we transit them. If all "roads" lead (from London, say) to Rome, I might take a ship, a train, a plane, a car, or a trek to get there. These are among the possible means to get to Rome at journey's end. But will I go "in style" by luxury class, in another style by economy fare, a third by hospitality work, a fourth by stowaway, or more inventively still—perhaps by hijacking or impersonation? Performance in this sense is not (mostly) about degrees of effectiveness or efficiency in reaching the end. Rather it's about aspects stressed or neglected, complications pursued or foregone, perspectives taken or possibilities emerging along the way. By "degrees," performance can be pathetic, perfunctory, exceptional, distinguished, idiosyncratic, and the like. But it's not capable of measurement on a common scale.[30] By "classes," performance can be patrician, plebeian, stellar, professional, retro, avant-garde, and such. Yet the order is strictly nominal, and these can't be arrayed in any stable figure. By "cultures," though, the possibilities of performance seem innumerable, inexhaustible.

To appreciate style or prize performance often seems beside the main project rather than an aspect of excelling at it. Surely it contravenes the modern, instrumental sense of rationality as calculation of effective and efficient means to specified ends. But it even goes against the grain of western wisdom about politics. From the ancients Greeks onward, western political practice and theory have been dominated by distinguishing ends from means.[31] Ends are *defined* as more valuable and consequential than means. That's because ends *are* consequences. They're results, conclusions, destinations: the ends of our journeys. By contrast, means are merely the way, on the way, sometimes unfortunately in the way. Thus ends must be worthy in themselves, means need not be, and ethics require that any means must serve an end (or more) that can justify them.

Yet since the nineteenth century, existentialists and perfectionists have been spotlighting troubles with this (as the sole) platform for political action and community.[32] Some try to present politics (in the proper or strictest sense) as entirely ends (in themselves), to appreciate politics as the highest and most fully human of activities.[33] Are politics then pure performance? At least a few conservatives, republicans, and perfectionists seem comfortable with this. But what about the reasons and results for doing? What of people's needs: material, social, and psychological? Other takes treat politics as the realm of means, with ends supplied from outside by morality, religion, tradition, or desire. A liberal focus on procedures or interests can look like this; so can a conservative stress on precedents or institutions. Pottery attends to all these politics and more. Throughout the saga, though, Potter magic emphasizes perfectionist politics. And from the first, Harry Potter as the lead figure makes room for the perfectionist senses of performance and style.

NOTES

1. See Hannah Arendt, *The Human Condition* (Chicago: University of Chicago Press, 1958), 47–49.

2. See John Stuart Mill, *On Liberty*, ed. David Spitz (New York: Norton, 1975).

3. See Philip K. Dick, "The Golden Man," *The Golden Man*, ed. Mark Hurst (New York: Berkley, 1980), 1–32.

4. See John S. Nelson, *Cowboy Politics* (Lanham, MD: Lexington Books, 2018), 205–306.

5. See C. S. Lewis, *Surprised by Joy* (New York: Harcourt, Brace, 1955).

6. See Joseph Heller, *Something Happened* (New York: Simon and Schuster, 1966); Peter Straub, *Ghost Story* (New York: Simon and Schuster, 1979).

7. See II.194, 322; III.25–30; IV.494, 632, 731, 755; V.327, 560; VI.478–79, 510, 533; VII.47.

8. See VI.58, 554; VII.236, 267, 322, 365, 423, 524.

9. See IV.125, 623–24, 641–42, 670–71, 698; VII.724–32. Also see III.347 and IV.322.

10. See III.393; IV.494–95; V.64, 327, 751; VI.478–79; VII.362.

11. See IV.662, 671–72; VII.698–704.

12. See John S. Nelson, *Politics in Popular Movies* (Boulder: Paradigm, 2015), 105–72.

13. See I.85; II.50, 91, 96; IV.100, 257–58; VII.399.

14. *The Dark Knight*, directed by Christopher Nolan (2008; Burbank, CA: Warner Home Video, 2008), DVD.

15. Yogi Berra with Tom Horton, *It Ain't Over . . . .* (New York: Harper and Row, 1989), 9.

16. Robert Frost, "The Road Not Taken," *The Poetry of Robert Frost*, ed. Edward Connery Lathem (New York: Henry Holt, 1969), 105.

17. See Thomas Hobbes, *Leviathan*, ed. C. B. Macpherson (New York: Penguin, 1651, 1968). For Hobbes, *nature* is modern, material, and mechanical by contrast with Aristotle's *nature* as classical, spiritual, and teleological. See Thomas A. Spragens, *The Politics of Motion* (Lexington: University of Kentucky Press, 1973). The ground of nature holds for Hobbes notwithstanding his respect for language, rhetoric, and powers of meaning: see Philip Pettit, *Made with Words* (Princeton, NJ: Princeton University Press, 2008).

18. See Karl Marx, *"The Eighteenth Brumaire of Louis Bonaparte,"* 1852, *Selected Writings*, ed. David McLellan (New York: Oxford University Press, 1977), 300–25.

19. See Friedrich Nietzsche, *Friedrich Nietzsche on Rhetoric and Language*, ed. and trans. Sander L. Gilman, Carole Blair, and David J. Parent (New York: Oxford University Press, 1979). Also see Martin Heidegger, *Being and Time*, trans. John Macquarrie and Edward Robinson (New York: Harper and Row, 1962); Michel Foucault, *The Order of Things* (New York: Random House, 1966, 1970); Michel Foucault, *The Archaeology of Knowledge* and *The Discourse on Language*, trans. A. M. Sheridan Smith (New York: Random House, 1969, 1971, 1972); Jacques Derrida, *Of Grammatology*, trans. Gayatri Chakravorty Spivak (Baltimore: Johns Hopkins University Press, 1967, 1974); Jacques Derrida, *Spurs* (Chicago: University of Chicago Press, 1978).

20. See Ludwig Wittgenstein, *Philosophical Investigations*, trans. G. E. M. Anscombe (New York: Macmillan, third edition, 1958).

21. See Stanley Cavell, *The Claim of Reason* (New York: Oxford University Press, 1979); Richard E. Flathman, *The Practice of Rights* (New York: Cambridge University Press, 1976); John G. Gunnell, *Political Philosophy and Time* (Middletown, CT: Wesleyan University Press, 1968); Alasdair C. MacIntyre, *Whose Justice? Which Rationality?* (Notre Dame, IN: University of Notre Dame Press, 1988); Hanna Fenichel Pitkin, *Wittgenstein and Justice* (Berkeley: University of California Press, 1972); Richard Rorty, *Achieving Our Country* (Cambridge, MA: Harvard University Press, 1998); Michael Walzer, *Spheres of Justice* (New York: Basic Books, 1983).

22. See Peter Winch, *The Idea of a Social Science, and Its Relation to Philosophy* (New York: Humanities Press, 1958); A. R. Louch, *Explanation and Human Action* (Berkeley: University of California Press, 1966).

23. See Shira Wolosky, *The Riddles of* Harry Potter (New York: Palgrave Macmillan, 2010), 3–6 and 34–44; Bethany Barratt, *The Politics of Harry Potter* (New York: Palgrave Macmillan, 2012), 157–61.

24. See Wolosky, *The Riddles of Harry Potter*, 1–2 and 9–16.

25. See Kiku Adatto, *Picture Perfect* (New York: Random House, 1993), 124–66.

26. See Erik H. Erikson, *Young Man Luther* (New York: Norton, 1958); Erik H. Erikson, *Gandhi's Truth* (New York, Norton, 1969). Also see Arthur Mitzman, *The Iron Cage* (New York: Grosset and Dunlap, 1969).

27. See Arendt, *The Human Condition*, 205–7; Hannah Arendt, *On Revolution* (New York: Viking, 1963); Hannah Arendt, *Between Past and Future* (New York: Viking, 1968); Robert Hariman, *Political Style* (Chicago: University of Chicago Press, 1995), 95–140.

28. See Judith N. Shklar, "Rethinking the Past," *Social Research* 44, no. 1 (Spring 1977): 80–90.

29. See Note 4.

30. See Derek L. Phillips, *Wittgenstein and Scientific Knowledge* (New York: Basic Books, 1975).

31. See Alasdair McIntyre, *After Virtue* (Notre Dame, IN: University of Notre Dame Press, 1984).

32. See Michael Oakeshott, *Rationalism in Politics* (London: Methuen, 1962).

33. See Note 1.

Chapter 7

Kinds and the Chamber of Secrets

The second Potter book, like the first, offers mystery and detection. Yet over-all it's a horror story, complete with deadly monsters and haunting ghosts. Through a strange diary, Book 2 reveals the Heir of Slytherin and how he framed Hagrid for murder fifty years earlier. Then it has Harry save Ginny Weasley by slaying the monster and its master in the Chamber of Secrets deep beneath Hogwarts Castle. It uses Polyjuice Potion for spying, plus a mandrake concoction to resuscitate Hogwarts victims from basilisk petrification. Along the way, it exposes the sham of new DADA teacher Gilderoy Lockhart in par-ticular and celebrity in general. And it ends with Harry freeing a faithful new friend, the house-elf Dobby, from cruel servitude to Lucius Malfoy.

Thus the main horror in Book 2, as in the whole Potter saga, turns out to be the racist, specist, pure-blood politics of fascism. This perversion of perfectionism is the master monster. And the main worry in Book 2 is that populism—the popular version of republican politics that takes itself to resist elitism, fascism, and other forms of dispossession—all too easily collapses in the face of fascism, or actually turns into it. Yet no one well-acquainted with Hagrid, even as a young mage, should have considered him a candidate for the pure-blood mania of the Slytherin Heir. Hagrid's defense of those (like him) who get feared, despised, and dispossessed is plainly perspectivist: to respect diverse angles of experience is to preempt manias of most kinds.

Likewise Dobby loves Harry for defending the different and downtrodden. This is part of what makes Harry the perfect nemesis for Salazar Slytherin's Heir and his monstrous snake. Book 2 explores how Hogwarts troubles reach to the foundations. It shows how oppressive politics promote inaction by most people as Others get victimized individually or a few at a time. And it emphasizes how sharing the Heir's perspectives enables Harry to act against the version of Voldemort who's leeching the life from Ginny. Hence the chapter at hand ends with the second book's climactic battles in the Chamber of Secrets, deep beneath the castle for Hogwarts School.

FASCISM

In constructive response to conformism, the Potter novels mostly recommend a humble perfectionism over a haughty elitism or a liberal freedom, let alone a libertarian autonomy. The argument implicit in the Potter books is that there can be "magic" in or from many of us, so we do better to leap for excellence than scramble to blend in. Better still, the Potter series not only concedes but insists that the historical burden of perfectionism has become its susceptibility to fascist, supremacist perversions. To present some perfectionist styles of action as plausible and palatable in our times is to defend against dangers of elitism, racism, irrationalism, and violence that we have reason to recognize in fascist and other politics inclined to totalitarianism. To face these dangers, the Potter series pits Harry against Lord Voldemort. The Potter novels carefully reckon similarities and differences between the two characters to investigate how Emersonian perfectionism can become Nietzschean, how Nietzschean perfectionism often goes horrifically wrong, yet how it can go urgently right instead.[1] Potter perfectionism assimilates dynamics of idealist, liberal, realist, and republican politics that turn it away from Death Eater fascism.

At the climax of Book 1, Harry glimpses the smudge that remains of Voldemort's face, as the revenant hiding on the back of Quirinus Quirrell's head. He hears Quirrell's sound bite on the fascist mania for power. And earlier in the Forbidden Forest, he's seen Voldemort drink the pure, innocent blood of a unicorn. Symbolically these are ingredients of fascist politics. But the Potter focus on fascism becomes direct and detailed with the pure-blood politics in *The Chamber of Secrets*. It builds into an indictment of fascism in several forms that menace our times. These include neo-Nazis, white supremacists, militia movements, some religious fundamentalists, and various demagogues for nationalist or populist movements scattered around the globe.

Examinations of twentieth-century fascism identify two paradigms then assimilate them. Nazi Germany under Adolf Hitler and fascist Italy under Benito Mussolini share enough figures, philosophies, and practices get viewed as kinds of fascism. The Potter series also acknowledges two candidates: Germany (or middle Europe) under Gellert Grindelwald and Britain under Lord Voldemort. (Britain's Oswald Mosley promoted Mussolini's fascism, and Oswald is the middle name of Minister of Magic Cornelius Fudge.) The Potter series leaves details of Grindelwald's rise and fall to the films on *Fantastic Beasts*. Yet stoking resentment of mages in hiding after the International Statute of Secrecy resonates with Nazi mobilization of Germans against oppression by the Treaty of Versailles after World War I (VII.193). Voldemort's initial violence, the uneasy lull after Lily's love repels his attack on Harry, then Voldemort's return get regarded by centaurs in terms similar to treating major conflicts of the twentieth century as episodes of one long world war (V.603). Even the main interlude feeds a frustrating sense of stasis that craves release in the political movement and violence offered by fascism *and* its resistance, while Harry goes through a similar period after dispersing dementors only to face possible expulsion from school (V.44). Thus the Potter portrait of fascist politics in movement and regime form includes many elements closely comparable to textbook accounts—but with some telling twists.

Fed by European Romanticism from the nineteenth century, fascism opposes the modern rationalism of directing all deeds by means-ends calculations. It mistakes Nietzsche's notion of a "will to power" as Quirrell does at the climax of Book 1 (I.291): anyone who doesn't want power above all else is a fool who fails to embrace the struggle that is life—and who isn't fit to survive it. (To eat and defeat death?) Good and evil give way to strength and weakness. Might makes right. Or for mages, "Magic Is Right" (VII.223–245). The ensuing cult of action finds freedom in overriding reasons with desires. Dumbledore and Harry master the Mirror of Erised, which tempts people to get (the priority of) desire backward, but Voldemort and Quirrell don't.

The rebuttal is that it *can* be destructive to override reasons with desires, but destruction can be creative when old orders dictate too much, as they seem to do. (Or so it feels to fascists.) If this seems to echo Joseph Schumpeter on the creative destruction accomplished by capitalism, it's because the sensibilities of Darwinian evolution loom large in both.[2] Whoever's on top of a competitive heap naturally deserves to be. Whatever is is good for now, and whatever becomes is better for then, so whatever we succeed at doing is justified by that success. For Darwinians, success is succession—as reproduction, as survival to further generations. At least until recently, though, most fascists have been anti-capitalist. This traces to collectivist or corporatist accounts of community. In fact, fascism is named for the ancient fasces that bundled sticks with an axe to evoke the power and jurisdiction of a magistrate, with the axe for strength and the bundling for community. Both skeins of fascism regard themselves as advances based on the Roman republic and empire in seeking strength and expansion. Both glom onto the earlier symbolism of stylized eagles and swastikas. Snakes and Dark Marks are the Death Eater equivalents.[3]

Some see the fascist celebration of official power as statist or authoritarian, as with the German Nazi mythologizing of the Third Reich. Yet it's usually coupled with official deference to a charismatic leader who's taken to epitomize evolution's next stage: Hitler is a leading edge of the New Aryan Race.

This cult of the leader is typically a cult of personality, and it can mean imitating the leader in taste, attire, activities, and talk—as well as taking the leader's orders and obeying the leader's urgings. The effect is that the leader, not the state, is the regime's center: the focus for fascist attention and authority. In Nazi Germany, Hitler claimed to be the only one who could restore glory, win the war, and so on. As Minister of Magic, Pius Thicknesse becomes the Head of State in the last Potter book, but Voldemort is acknowledged as the leader by everybody in the know. The fascist leader is the Number One Actor, and the fascist movement or regime is a cult of action. This action is said to serve the folk, the nation, the people—over the ordinary individual, who's portrayed as weak, lonely, anomic, and alienated. By contrast, the cultists are strong, supported, and empowered. Their ambition is to totalize the cult into a pervasive culture. In many fascist movements and regimes, the project is to mobilize the masses into spectacular demonstrations of adoration for leaders, solidarity with themselves as elect, and hatred for others.

In the Potter saga, Voldemort's new regime at Hogwarts might be preparing for that. In magical Britain as a whole, however, Voldemort's operatives rely more on mass *de*mobilization. By Book 7, the Death Eaters resemble Brownshirts in promoting a totalitarian regime puppeteered by Voldemort. In this reign of terror, Death Eaters and snatchers disappear people almost daily and arbitrarily: killing mages who resist, but random muggles too. They imperius Pius Thickness as Minister of Magic in order to turn citizens into bystanders by suppressing most information and activity available to them. The Death Eaters act as secret police (Nazi *Gestapo*) to surveil citizens and keep would-be resisters (like Harry, Ron, and Hermione) on the run. And the Death Eaters even act as paramilitary (Nazi *Sturmabteilung*) to liberate allies from prison or to assault organized resisters—like the Order of the Phoenix and Dumbledore's Army when they try to defend the Department of Mysteries. In Book 2, the Heir of Slytherin and the basilisk do the surveilling, terrorizing, and attacking; and in Book 3, the dementors do it. But by Book 4, the Death Eaters start to come out of hiding, and their leader returns to direct the mayhem.

The aim is to mobilize will (rather than reflection, deliberation, or calculation) for "the Greater Good." For Dumbledore, as a liberal and republican, this means the occasional heroism of sacrificing self for others; for Grindelwald, as a fascist, it means the daily sacrifice of personal and familial good to social good—but as embodied and enacted by the leader. Worse, it comes to mean the sacrifice of others such as muggles and centaurs to the good of mages: the true folk, especially the pure in blood, or perhaps in culture. Fascists often romanticize this as the struggle of elite heroes on the cutting edge of history to lead the rest of us in leaving behind the inferior individuals and institutions that have held back the genius of the true community. By the series' end, the Muggle-born Registration Commission enforces the Big Lie that first-generation mages must have stolen magical wands and secrets from real witches and wizards (VII.208–10, 246–67).

The romantic anti-rationalism in fascism often expresses itself in hostility to bureaucrats, experts, financiers, professors, scientists, and technologists. Fascists vilify the rationality of such figures as weakness of will and betrayal of solidarity. This might be surprising, because the two early paradigms of fascism boasted of state capability, scientific talent, and technical supremacy. What about the rocket scientists and pioneering technologists of the Third Reich, or the futurism and engineered cities of fascist Italy? These points of priority and pride for the regimes of Hitler and Mussolini were celebrated along with music, architecture, military strategy, and more as the marks of cultural creativity that elevate the Aryans and Italians as "races" of genius. Voldemort echoes this in claiming to have taken magic farther than ever before (VI.443), and the Karkaroff-directed Durmstrang ship evokes a German U-boat in surfacing near Hogwarts Castle (IV.246).

The scientific project that ideologizes some fascisms is the sociobiology of eugenics. It aspires to systematize the generation of one or more superior "races" of people as species above and beyond mere humans as *homo sapiens*. Diverse dehumanizing tortures in Nazi concentration camps justified themselves as scientific experiments to eliminate inferiors and produce superiors. Eugenics efforts in Britain and the United States sometimes share at least some of those politics, however incipiently. But most fascisms are not ideologized, and the Potter novels treat fascist politics mainly in movement terms. Biology of bloodlines is said to rule; but it doesn't, and it couldn't, because all but a few "pure-blood" families already have died out (II.116; V.113, 842). Inevitably the pure-blood politics of the Blacks and Malfoys work mainly by culture and politics. Voldemort is the right sort, regardless of a muggle father; while the Weasleys are pure in blood but wrong, disloyal, even traitorous in friends and sympathies. Voldemort's fascism weeds out, not breeds up; and recent fascisms lean more on genocide and ethnic cleansing than eugenics.

When Voldemort's forces start to take over the Ministry of Magic (MOM), they stay behind the scenes at the beginning. This helps mages who'd rather not be bothered by politics to look the other way. (Of course, this is contrary to the "constant vigilance" preached by Mad-Eye Moody as an auror experienced in the devious moves of "dark wizards.") The Death Eater regime hides itself behind false legalities and imperiused officials. It takes hostages, persecutes scapegoats, savages children, exiles classes, perverts histories and sciences, oppresses species, enslaves or eliminates "races," controls the media, propounds conspiracies, revs nationalism into nativism and xenophobia, pursues imperialism, atomizes then demoralizes the remaining populace, and so on. Such specifically political steps escalate toward the end of the Potter series, and they're typical of fascist movements trying to seize or expand power. Book 7 may not be as detailed and appalling as accounts by George Orwell and Aleksandr Solzhenitsyn for the totalitarian systems pursued by perverted perfectionisms: fascist, communist, and otherwise. But the Potter series is especially good at showing everyday entanglements of authoritarian and totalitarian devices in recent movements and regimes. (More on this in coming chapters.)

POPULISM

The Chamber of Secrets connects the heroic trio's detection of the Heir of Slytherin and his fascist project of pure-blood rule with its exposé of Gilderoy Lockhart's fraudulent celebrity. It links the celebrity of Lockhart and Harry Potter to populist politics developed subsequently in the series. And by intertwining these narratives, it gently suggests the sometime susceptibility of populism to shading over into fascism. Since the publication of this book, populist politics and their possible inclinations toward fascism have emerged as urgent issues of politics worldwide.[4]

As the Heir of Slytherin who arises from the horcrux diary, "Tom Riddle" enacts a fascist leadership principle to charm, deceive, and possess Ginny Weasley. (What might be suggested by Ginny interacting with the diary as though it were social media?) As an author and professor, Lockhart exploits the romance of (stolen) adventure stories to feed his celebrity and ego. Harry, Ron, and Hermione, on the other hand, champion the people who ordinarily inhabit Hogwarts. Until recently, political theories have paid little attention to populism and less to celebrity. Both emerge in the nineteenth century in the company of electronic communication and culture. Yet celebrity lifts politicians to office, publicizes various movements, and spurs this century's global burst of populist politics. Popular culture generally and celebrity culture specifically are pivotal for populist politics, especially in the United States and the United Kingdom.

A familiar, snarky definition says that a celebrity is someone famous for being famous. The implication is that celebrities are empty, insubstantial. Their main claim on our attention is merely that other people are noticing them—not that they signify some condition, deed, quality, or possibility of importance for us. Hence celebrity can seem to beg for exposés, to reveal depth that's missing or dirt that's not. By contrast, we're inclined to revere glory and fame as earned and substantive. Even so, *some* celebrity (like Lockhart's) is hard-won; and *some* (like Harry's) is merited or important for the community. With celebrity, granted, neither is necessarily so; and the two don't always (often?) come together. Still the sniping at celebrity seems aimed mainly at its links to style. The words and deeds—as well as the clothes and settings—of celebrities often seem stylized. Celebrity and stylishness can promote each other: note *Lifestyles of the Rich and Famous* (1984–95) and the hundreds of later "reality shows" that it helped inspire on television.

Pottery treats celebrity as a superficial sort of fame or a momentary, minor-league version of glory. Lockhart is arguably the purest example of celebrity—or at least the worst? He's a con man and a pretentious self-promoter who knows lots about how to cultivate his own prominence. Celebrity arises from "publicity" in the ordinary, social sense; and Lockhart is his own publicity machine, keeping his name and image in the news. Yes, his efforts eventually backfire (II.303); but even then, Lockhart continues to function as his own number-one fan (V.509–511). Harry's case is more complicated. Is he a celebrity at its best, or does he soar beyond it? As an epic hero who saves his community through personal sacrifice, Harry attains archetypal "depth." He does nothing (intended) to make or keep himself a celebrity. Rumor, reporting, and fan-talk do that for him. Lockhart's celebrity stays "superficial" as well as stolen; but Harry's celebrity deepens from the start, even as it arguably becomes eclipsed by his heroism and glory.

Many celebrities take care to stay stylish for the times. From hair and smiles to résumé and clothes, Lockhart is nothing if not stylish in this way (II.59, 99–100, 141–142, 236). Other celebrities stay stylized in personal brands, looks, sounds, and so on. As a dandy, Dumbledore displays colorful elegance in his clothes. (The books hint at this, the films show it.) Such a premium on style might mark celebrity as "superficial" in the sense of "focused on surfaces," but that mainly marks celebrity as postmodern rather than hollow or insignificant. Modern cultures make style (as surface or appearance) the antithesis of substance (as depth or reality). Electronic cultures sideline metaphysics in favor of aesthetics, and bracket ontologies in favor of phenomenologies. Our politics can be seen primarily as rhetorics or as aesthetics—which is to say, as styles. Hence postmodern publics are plural, partial, performative, sometimes spectacular, often intersectional. Thus postmodern politics feature fandoms and other "uncommon cultures," as Jim Collins calls them.[5] These readily spur postmodern movements and identity politics, along with the culture wars that insistently inform populism. Pottery needs political attention to celebrity.

The Potter series begins with the world-famous wizard Albus Dumbledore, celebrated on collectible cards sold with chocolate frogs for children (I.102–3). He acts to protect the orphaned Harry from the evil Voldemort. Just as crucially, he also acts to protect Harry from his own, all-too-early renown as the Boy Who Lived—and somehow stopped that Dark Lord's reign of terror

(I.13). Dumbledore wants to spare Harry some celebrity distortions that no child should endure. *The Chamber of Secrets* lets Lockhart tutor a resistant Harry in the arts of cultural publicity and precarious fame. Lockhart's a fraud and narcissist, not the adventurer and polymath he claims to be. But he's a shrewd student of celebrity, and he knows Harry's celebrity when he spots it.

The signal celebrity introduced by Book 3 is Harry's godfather, Sirius Black, as *The Prisoner of Azkaban*. Black supposedly murdered another wizard and many innocent muggles. A supposedly impossible escape from the wizard's prison posts his picture throughout Britain, while his name pops for months from news and lips. To be sure, this publicity is for dastardly, not admirable, deeds. But the Potter saga recognizes that such *notoriety* is a synonym, as much as an antonym, for *celebrity*. Accordingly the travails of Black amplify the education of Harry and his friends in the turbulent, largely populist politics of celebrity. Make no mistake, though, Harry's own celebrity continues to offer occasional advantages as well as sometime troubles.

In Book 4, Harry and Hermione Granger learn still more powers and perils of celebrity. Interviewing with a Quick-Quotes Quill and "bugging" them at every opportunity, Rita Skeeter's reporting for the *Daily Prophet* sketches several lessons in celebrity (IV.303–6, 726–8). Skeeter herself is a celebrity, and devoted to her public visibility. Former auror "Mad-Eye" Moody is a celebrity too, and hired to teach DADA at Hogwarts. But he gets imperiused and impersonated for most of the book by Death Eater Barty Crouch Jr., secretly escaped from the Azkaban Prison. This version of the renowned Moody dramatizes the substantive superficiality of celebrity, where post-modern surfaces decenter or disperse deeper identities and realities in public relations. We wonder, for instance, if Barty Jr. as "Moody" is even better than Moody himself at teaching the dark arts and their defenses. (Celebrity should be prominent in such curricula.) "Moody" and Skeeter join Black in showing how celebrity and notoriety come inextricably blended in one pot.

An international celebrity comes to Britain for the Quidditch World Cup and then returns for the Triwizard Tournament. A seeker in all the best senses, Viktor Krum becomes a model of celebrity deserved, many times over, while handled with poise and integrity (IV.83, 249). Krum is the best Quidditch player in Bulgaria and possibly in the world. He's excellent and admirable enough to earn Harry's respect and date Hermione. His fans even include Ron, despite the two competing for Hermione's favor. Starting with Ginny Weasley (I.97) and Colin Creevey (II.96–106), Harry's celebrity also draws fans. Tailing Harry for pictures, questions, and eavesdropping makes Creevey, Skeeter, and her photographer resemble paparazzi, which "bugs" Harry and his friends. Ambivalence about Harry as a celebrity shifts again into high gear after he returns from the graveyard to Hogwarts with Cedric Diggory's body and the personal report that Voldemort is back. When Fudge refuses to accept the news, the MOM moves its people and the *Daily Prophet* into relentless attacks on Harry and his supporters, especially Dumbledore. The ensuing controversy divides the wizarding community in Britain.

By Book 5, celebrity helps target Harry for personal attacks. An enemy of his, Dolores Umbridge, emerges as a celebrity herself. As trumpeted in the *Daily Prophet*, she rises swiftly from Hogwarts DADA teacher to Hogwarts High Inquisitor to Hogwarts Headmistress (V.211–4, 306–29, 624–50). On the other side, when she squelches practical education in DADA, Harry's celebrity and expertise attract several handfuls of students to resist her. He trains them secretly and effectively as "Dumbledore's Army." Moreover Harry's celebrity lures tons of readers to Rita Skeeter's tabloid presentation in *The Quibbler* of Harry's graveyard escape from Voldemort, and this Hermione idea helps greatly in rehabilitating Harry's reputation (V.564–9, 578–84).

In the final two books, the MOM, the *Daily Prophet*, and their followers hammer Harry and Dumbledore as perverse, pretentious celebrities. Once the Ministry has fallen to Voldemort and the Death Eaters, it posts Harry for punishment as "Undesirable Number One" (VII.252). By then, he, Ron, and Hermione all have had celebrity turns. If the Dark Lord is so visibly vile as to be notorious, he still seems "beyond celebrity" as a nightmare villain. After all, Voldemort is "He Who Must Not Be Named" in the media or everyday talk. Similarly Harry and Dumbledore start the series as celebrities, but by its end, they surely ascend to stardom as heroes. Celebrities, some major, some minor (not noted here), are persistent figures in the Potter saga.

By extension, celebrity culture is a major concern of Pottery because it's a major aspect of our politics. In cultures strongly oriented to celebrity, even small moments of celebrity make their marks. Dumbledore's worry is that celebrity inflates senses of attainment and worth (I.13). Yet Harry's zoo time allegorizes how Dumbledore's move to keep Harry away from other mages might shield him from them but makes him even more a curiosity (a celebrity) for them (I.26–30; II.23). Lest we miss the point, Molly Weasley echoes it, telling her daughter not to stare at Harry because he's not a creature in a zoo (I.97). Still Dumbledore keeps Harry out of the spotlight—if ignorant of his history, identity, and powers—until he can mature as a wizard. By Dursley, non-magical, middle-class standards, Harry suffers deprivation that humbles and toughens him. Later this helps stop him from being carried away by sudden celebrity or undone by some of its nastier permutations. No doubt the Dursleys often take this too far, scarring Harry in some lasting ways. But Dumbledore's philosophy is that scars can be helpful (I.15), and this holds for the signature lightning mark on Harry's forehead. The Dursleys lie that it comes from a car crash that killed Harry's parents. To learn that "facts" can be lies helps Harry handle celebrity, let alone heroism.

Both kinds of scars are (specifically populist) reminders to Harry of whence he comes, and this sense of origins serves him well in growing into a leader of mages. The lightning bolt marks Harry as sharing some of Voldemort's being and powers, and it might even bear them. It helps turn Harry into the nemesis that Voldemort feared (yet created) as prophesied (VI.509–12). In celebrity terms, the scar itself becomes Harry's brand: his mark of identity and his certificate of authenticity (another populist trope) as a cultural celebrity or political leader (II.96). As a sign of Harry's survival, the scar makes Harry sympathetic and admirable to mages who spot it; as a reminder of Voldemort's evil, the scar scares and unsettles them too. This is one among several versions of the telling (and distinctively populist) ambivalence about celebrities—whom liberals, socialists, and conservatives generally devalue while even postmodern republicans despise.

Tabloid sensationalism feeds a love-hate relation to celebrities; and Hogwarts students divide sharply at times over Harry, Lockhart, and others. Rita Skeeter's success testifies to the *Daily Prophet* reliance on the sensationalism of rumor, scandal, and celebrity (IV.147–54; V.73; VII.22–7); it's not reserved for *The Quibbler* (V.190–3). This typifies "the people" in populist politics. Celebrities and sensations fascinate us ordinary folks, who love the action and energy. In them, we see great hopes and great threats: greater sometimes than makes good sense, so that "we the people" sneer at celebrities as likely sources of disappointment, even disillusionment. Exposés and denunciations abound, as in the *Daily Prophet* when directed against Harry or Dumbledore by the MOM (V.72–4; VII.22, 207). Yet some of the same celebrities continue energetically and effectively to attract attention and invite investment by "the people."

In Book 2, sex appeal is surely an aspect of Lockhart's celebrity (II.59, 95); and that's not exactly unusual for celebrities (IV.296; VI.219). But the main lesson is that Lockhart self-consciously cultivates this and other resources for his celebrity. It depends on hard work and good timing. The hype(rbole) he supplies is more optional. Lockhart saves the news of his DADA post at Hogwarts for a book-signing at Flourish and Blotts (II.60). When Harry comes to buy his school books, Lockhart quickly incorporates Harry into a photo op for the *Daily Prophet* (II.60–1). When Lucius Malfoy goads Arthur Weasley into a scuffle that disrupts the occasion, Lockhart tries for more sensational treatment by including the fight in the coverage of his signing (II.63). He devotes hours and hours to autographing pictures and answering fan mail (II.119–21). Lockhart is careful to feed the fan appetite for personal, "private," supposedly behind-the-scenes information on himself (II.99–100). He senses, accepts, and even welcomes what Rowling elsewhere describes as "the assumption of intimacy fans felt with those they had never met."[6] On the other hand, he shows no sign of experiencing celebrity as falling prey to his fans or even the paparazzi; whereas Colin Creevey makes Harry feel hunted as a celebrity, and Rita Skeeter compounds that.

Pottery is also insightful in suggesting how celebrity and charisma are made in important part by fans and followers (II.91–9). Considering that they are a motley lot (V.525), this lesson seems missing or understated in most accounts of charisma; while many treatments of celebrity homogenize fandoms too much. Andy Warhol predicted a future with everybody getting fifteen minutes of global fame. Pottery doesn't explore this; but it does suggest that many fans crave at least a little celebrity, however temporary. Ron revels in a moment of celebrity (III.270), and his excitement soars near Krum as a celebrity (IV.249). Youngest brother Ron could be an odd case, but other student fans at Hogwarts also like to feel like celebrities in the presence of celebrities. As Dumbledore sees and Lockhart shows, celebrity can stoke self-importance into narcissism or egomania. Rowling says that it can be "very difficult to gauge the level of your own celebrity."[7] But this holds mainly for the uneasy celebrity. The eager celebrity, like Lockhart, shows a good sense of his public standing—despite his self-promotional hype (II.103, 163), incessant and false credit-claiming (II.93–4, 297–8), and denigration by others (II.91, 98, 163). It's easy to expect these from people seeking or sustaining celebrity; yet they help satirize celebrities with undue self-regard, preening like peacocks (II.163).

Harry Potter on celebrity points insistently to populist politics. Populism promotes "the people," and celebrities claim popular attention. Efforts to ideologize populism haven't made headway, so Pottery does well to treat it as a set of movements. Critics virtually define it as a kind of fascism by saying that its sense of the people is so exclusionary that it becomes nativist, racist, xenophobic, or otherwise anti-pluralist and anti-democratic. Some defenders distinguish among agrarian, campaign, cultural, democratic, economic, religious, urban, or other projects of populism; then they embrace one or more as the most safe, needed, or substantive kind(s). The Potter take on populism is more generally political: stressing celebrity and featuring resistance to elites (Malfoys and Blacks), experts (Lockhart and wrackspurts), bureaucrats (Umbridge and Mafalda Hopkirk), upstarts (dementors and goblins), institutions (Gringotts Bank and MOM), media (*Daily Prophet* and Wizarding Wireless Network), and politicians (Fudge and Scrimgeour). Across various populisms, such enemies of the people are legion. For Pottery as well as recent movements, a good synopsis is to say that populism rises to resist elite or upstart dispossession of the people, by taking back the powers and resources that are rightfully theirs.

All these are (Potter) figures or tropes of populist politics. There are more in the Potter saga, and together they offer an insightful take on recent populism. Analysts often emphasize that populist politics reach from Left to Right: for example, from socialism and liberalism to conservatism and reactionism. (More on this is in chapters to come.) In the United States, the populist Occupy Movement is to the Left, and the populist Tea Party is to the Right; just as in the United Kingdom, the Labour Party is to the Left, and the Conservative Party is to the Right. The rough equivalents tied to Lockhart as a popular celebrity are amusing and illuminating. Leftist populists often focus on everyday challenges for ordinary people, and Lockhart's version would be his book on household pests such as garden gnomes (II.29–37). Rightist populists address the social or civilizational scourges said to beset the people; and Lockhart's books about overcoming horror creatures like banshees, ghouls, vampires, and yetis fit that template (II.43–4, 161–2).

Populists portray the people as hard-working and productive. They take wisdom from experience. They act from common sense and moral (sometimes religious) fundamentalism that takes their cultural values to bind everybody, except people's champions who break the rules to benefit ordinary folks. (American southerners call these rule-breakers "rascals.") Harry (II.177–8, VII.488–9), Dumbledore (IV.648), and Godric Gryffindor (VII.507) are named specifically as populist "champions" of ordinary mages (not pure-bloods), muggles, and other magical species. Fascist leaders can become cult figures because most are charismatic, overflowing with a sense of energy and enthusiasm. Tom Riddle is strikingly handsome, able to draw eyes and ears from around any room. Yet some champions of the people are clearly charismatic, while others aren't. Harry's a celebrity and a hero, moreover Ginny has an early crush on him; but is he a magnetic personality whose aura fills and moves others? That's debatable. At a minimum, we'd need to talk about followers constructing Harry as charismatic, wouldn't we?

In populism, healers also are heroes of the people, especially for healing *them*. In Potter books, these include the healers at St. Mungo's Hospital for Magical Maladies and Injuries, who save ("muggle-lover") Arthur Weasley among many others. Madam Pomfrey qualifies too; yet the premier healer at Hogwarts might be Severus Snape (VI.523, 681), although this goes mostly unrecognized until the series ends. Among Harry's greatest acts is using the Elder Wand only to heal his own wand, helping Harry secretly return the series talisman of power to Dumbledore's tomb, to break its chain of possession (VII.748). Book 2 even evokes the people's power to heal their own community in the symbolism of Hogwarts mandrakes (men rising up as dragons) used to save Hermione and others from the fascist, nearly fatal put-down of basilisk petrification.

In the same neighborhood of symbolism, populists are reformers with brooms (magical or not) to sweep out corruption from the halls of established power, as Hercules cleans the Augean Stables or Jesus the temple. As magical brooms, Cleansweeps are mentioned in all three initial books as affordable and reliable, albeit less fleet and flexible than pricier models (I.152; II.111; III.254). Likewise cleaning out the elitist Black House is largely a populist endeavor too, with the mages at Number Twelve Grimmauld Place confronting one elitist corruption and fascist horror after another (V.83–177). *Some* populism is like fascism: some is nationalist or nativist, some racist, some conspiratorial, some cynical; some distracts, some surveils, some ostracizes "traitors" (Edgecombes versus Weasleys). Like fascists, populists often sensationalize and stage spectacles. Fascists idolize the fatherland or motherland, populists the heartland or homeland. Of course, both fascist and populist politics present themselves as purging corrupt systems. But fascist politics are vehemently anti-liberal and anti-pluralist; whereas many populisms embrace popular cultures where individuality, tolerance, and diversity are traditional or well on the way to becoming so. This seems to hold for most Hogwarts students educated by the liberal regime of Albus Dumbledore. (The signal exceptions, of course, are Slytherins.) When Harry and friends rise up in a populist rejection of the Umbridge regime, they're defending pluralism and tolerance.

Fascism is outright anti-rationalist, while populism wants its common sense informed by passion. Fascism features will (volition) and want (desire); while populism encourages emotion, feeling, sentiment, and empathy—not so much sympathy, which is more republican. From the perspectives of Enlightenment ideologies, populism is sentimentalist and sensationalist—as with tabloids like Xenophilius Lovegood's *Quibbler*. It's the flaky *Quibbler*, which publishes the interview with Harry that rescues his reputation and gives impetus in Book 5 to resisting the return of Voldemort. If perfectionists Just Do It, on impulse, populists Act Out. Angry and fed up, they lash out verbally and physically. They strike out at exploiters or oppressors or anything nearby that's symbolically associated. With Howard Beale, the Mad Prophet of the Airways in *Network* (1976), populists are "as mad as hell," and they're "not going to take this anymore!"[8] Throughout Book 5, Harry's teenager hormones magnify his resentments of unfair events and unfeeling "friends." Repeatedly he acts out to demonstrate his discontent. These "moments of madness," these jabs of rebellion and bouts of sulking, are typical of teenagers.[9] But they're characteristic of populists too, and we could do worse than liken teen behavior to populist action. Harry's godfather qualifies (V.377–83); and eventually this does him in, but it does considerable good before that. *Sometimes* acting out works *because* it's emotional and seemingly irrational.

Epistemically this emotionalism promotes a populist counterpart of perspectivism, which philosophers often acknowledge to sustain an elective affinity for perfectionist politics. As the word implies, political ideo*logies* of Enlightenment only respect epistemics of *logos*, of logic and rationality. Then what's *true* is what's *logical* or *factual*, that is, supported by *evidence*—as what's *seen*. Populist politics pursue epistemics of *pathos* too. Populists also recognize truths of feeling; they can treat as *true* what *feels right*, whether by common sense or by fervent passion. Even more often, populists disregard some reasons and data in distrusting what doesn't feel right. Populist distrust of experts sometimes works this way, and sometime it induces people to work at keeping possibly contrary information at bay. Thus many people practice the active ignorance of picking news sources that only reinforce what those people already feel.[10] In part, this is because many people get sick of the scorn they hear and see from elites who look down from on-high to smirk, sneer, and snicker at the pathetic behavior, information, and taste of ordinary individuals. Throughout the saga, the elitist Dursleys, Malfoys, Slytherins, and Snape inflict such expressions of scorn countless times on Harry, Ron, and Hermione. Now more on perspectivism is in order.

PERSPECTIVISM

Nietzsche qualified his own perfectionism with a separable style of perspectivism.[11] This usually gets analyzed as a philosophical doctrine of epistemology. But epistemology is often an extension of political theory, indeed of political action.[12] Accordingly it can be helpful to respect perspectivism as a style of political action. This spotlights a creative and humbling project of Potter politics, especially of its perfectionism. It highlights Dumbledore's liberal reach beyond toleration toward diversity and multiculturalism. And it illuminates the politics of a fascinating figure in the Potter saga: Rubeus Hagrid.

In doctrine, perspectivism embraces Dumbledore's take on "the truth . . . as a beautiful and terrible thing," to "be treated with great caution" (I.298). In method, as the name implies, perspectivism means appreciating truths in terms of the experiences and standpoints of different (kinds of) individuals, institutions, and interests. In action, perspectivism means troping truths to explore their figurality. Thus, as chapter 4 explains, Ralph Waldo Emerson regarded all language as "fossil poetry;" and he urged us to turn that awareness into relentless perfecting of our response-abilities. Such perspectivism in action is apparent throughout the Potter books.

One objection is that shifting perspectives are loose sands, which leave us no place to stand firm in making reliable judgments arbitrated by evidence. Another is that we need some access to singular, sometimes absolute Truth in order to reconcile our differences. A third is that poetic talk of tropes and play, figures and flow, is little more than the fancy dancing that cartoon characters do in mid-air before physics catches up to them. Then they plummet into the abyss of nihilism. It might be bottomless, or the fall and the characters might be broken by crashing into hard rocks of reality. But neither way will those figures find safety nets of substantive standards and testable truths. Hence there can be neither morality nor humanity. The political complaint, therefore, is that perspectivism paves a path to fascism, terrorism, totalitarianism, or some other fanaticism of destruction. The Potter response is to detail how its perspectivists don't go there.

Hagrid is the half-giant Keeper of Keys and Grounds at Hogwarts School. In his second year as a Hogwarts student, Hagrid was framed for murderous attacks by the Heir of Slytherin. Hagrid was expelled and his wand broken. But Hogwarts Professor Dumbledore got Hagrid kept as groundskeeper and seems to mentor him as a mage. Decades later, Headmaster Dumbledore asks Hagrid to bring the newly orphaned Harry to his relatives, the Dursleys; and another decade later, Hagrid delivers Harry to Hogwarts for magical education. Hagrid becomes Harry's friend.

More than that, Hagrid becomes something of a surrogate mother for Harry. In Harry's first year at Hogwarts, Hagrid actually describes himself as a baby dragon's mother (I.234–40). By Harry's third year, Hagrid gets appointed to teach the Care of Magical Creatures. Among his credentials is an erratically requited passion for strange and often dangerous "monsters" like dragons, acromantulas, hippogriffs, thestrals, blast-ended skrewts, even a cerberus—a giant and vicious three-headed dog whom Hagrid names "Fluffy." It matters politically that none of these is presented by the Potter books as a "dark creature," but everybody sees that some of Hagrid's enthusiasms can become almost insanely perilous. Who raises a fiery dragon in a wooden hut? Even Hagrid recognizes, with great reluctance, that baby Norbert(a) must go to Charlie Weasley as a dragon-keeper in Romania. And the dragon must go soon, before getting widely detected at Hogwarts and before getting too heavy to carry away, even with several flying broomsticks.

Perspectivism fits a fellow like this. As a gigantic outsider at Hogwarts, let alone in magical society more generally, he has lots of incentive to learn how others view things and respond. He tries to see from other's eyes, walk in other's shoes, and so on. Yet he plainly feels no (conformist) requirement to agree with others—or even to defer all that much to the power of others. Think of Hagrid's "Support Harry Potter" party in the face of Voldemort's fascist regime in Book 7 (VII.442). To be sure, that's not exactly prudent; but judgment for a perspectivist only begins in discernment then stretches to encompass experiment as well. A perspectivist can practice an ethic of care similar to feminists. For Hagrid, this combines enormous, if impulsive, empathy with mostly intentional insensitivity at key times.[13] Hagrid can harden when needed for action. These traits along with an open curiosity qualify him to teach Care of Magical Creatures. In contrast, Dumbledore cites Voldemort as lacking in care, empathy, and wide curiosity. And in consequence, Dumbledore says, Voldemort's perfectionism lacks not only humility but also the crucial resource for creativity that loves and learns from all creatures great and small.

As the series personification of perspectivism, Hagrid has several advantages: a giant's resistance to harmful magic by others; at least half a giant's size, strength, and toughness of skin and sinew; complete trust and support from the greatest wizard of his day, Albus Dumbledore; as well as some clever magic magnified by a semi-concealed wand apparently restored secretly to him by Dumbledore. Mostly this means that Hagrid is at least a little less vulnerable to harm than some colleagues and many students. This makes it easier and more plausible for Hagrid to open himself to appreciation of the experiences, interests, and virtues of radically other kinds of creatures than humans, mages, or giants. He readily takes their perspectives, even their sides.

Yet Hagrid's perspectivist style influences his friends, much to their moral and political improvement, especially as perfectionists of an Emersonian sort. For Hagrid's greatest resource by far is an incredible "kindness" that traces to his father and Dumbledore. This is *kindness* in the sense of *compassion, goodness*, and *benevolence*.[14] But it's also *kind-ness* in a classical unto postmodern sense, seldom articulated outside the Potter novels. It begins as a capacity to value even a vicious creature as a *good-of-its-kind*. It grows into a facility for appreciating almost any kind of creature for characteristic *goods-of-its-kind*.[15] Then it becomes an ability to learn from respecting distinctive *perspectives-of-its-kind*. Hagrid's nurturing compassion and benevolence loom so large because he's brilliant (and tough) at heeding each creature according to its kind. His perspectivism is insightful and influential because it just *is* his characteristic inclination and practice of kind-ness. Potter books feature kindness by Harry, his mother, and Hermione too.

Acting in terms of kinds can get rejected these days as stereotyping. That starts and ends with kinds, the kinds are drastic simplifications, and the simplifications are usually caricatures. As Hermione complains, mages in Britain stereotype giants as brutal, house-elves as happy, and werewolves as vicious even in human form. Muggles stereotype mages, mages muggles, and both stereotype themselves (I.8; VI.495, 616). Stereotyping feeds conformism (II.50; III.21). Worse it stokes versions of racism and specism.[16] Hence the contrary precept is that everybody, perhaps everything, deserves instead to be treated individually, completely apart from any types. But of course, humans aren't omniscient; so they can't know enough to individualize fully all the time. And their action is configured by language, which is to say: words, concepts, categories, kinds, and types (even of figures). Some typing is inevitable and—dare we say typically?—helpful. Thus stereotyping can have constructive places in human affairs, especially when it's self-aware, self-limiting, self-correcting, or playful. Nor is every type a stereotype. There are ideal types, archetypes, phenotypes, genotypes, allotypes, isotypes, endotypes, and such. There are many kinds of kinds. And this is to say that there are many modes and moves for perspectivism as kind-ness. Getting to particulars is crucial to the acuity and defensibility of typing, yet that's exactly the key to individualizing words and deeds. Thus perspectivism as kind-ness can help accomplish benevolence and consideration through informing and extending our empathy.

Are the kinds natural, conventional, inventional? Ah, more typing: in specific contexts, such distinctions can be (differently) illuminating; in others, they can be (variously) obfuscating; but as fundamental or philosophical contrasts, they can often be misleading and unsustainable.[17] This issue arises for efforts of the Sorting Hat to teach Hogwarts students about their "kinds" in teaching them about their houses (I.117–8; IV.176–7; V.204–7). As chapter 9 discusses, it arises when nationalist politics try to treat nations as given by nature. For Hagrid and his friends, kinds seem to begin as commonsensical, which need not be the same as stereotypical; but they get modified by experience and experimentation—which is to say, learning (IV.430). Courses on the Care of Magical Creatures can be good for this. So can courses on the History of Magic, when students like Harry and Ron can get past the dry-as-dust presentations of Professor Binns to see relevant angles in goblin rebellions and Slytherin heirs (IV.449; VII.517). This goes also for Herbology, DADA, even Divination—where centaur talk by Firenze on fortunes of "races," aka species, can teach a remarkable humility about wise action in terms of "kinds" (V.601–5).

The centaurs speak insistently of Mars reigning above them in the sky, and the sense that mages have been for most of the century in the midst of a long war about to rekindle into battle has a telling relation to Hagrid's lessons in kind-ness. He's gone from Hogwarts for half of Book 5, while trying to align the giants against Voldemort. Soon after he returns, Umbridge chases him away. Then passing OWLs means that Harry, Ron, and Hermione don't enroll in the Care of Magical Creatures for their sixth year (VI.170). Is their time for kindness passing for a while? If so, it's not because the increasing conflict should or does take the three to an opposite pole of "unkindness" (IV.265). There's no doubt that the series pranksters are often unkind, turning the acknowledgment of kinds against others who don't really deserve it. This includes the Weasley twins and Lee Jordan, of course, but also the Marauders: Sirius Black, Remus John Lupin, Peter Pettigrew, and James Potter (V.653). Yet speaking specifically of James, Lily Evans tells Snape that unkindness is *not* evil in the mode of his Hogwarts associates of Mulciber and Avery, both of whom join Snape in becoming Death Eaters (VII.674). Hermione cautions Harry that claims of *evil* should be made only with care (VI.638). But

Harry needs that word at times (VI.644–5). In Pottery, unkindness is more readily remedied than outright evil. Likewise unkind people are more readily redeemed than evil-doers. But in the case of Kreacher, Hermione might be right to insist that he isn't necessarily beyond redemption (V.831).

Sirius, Remus, and James develop kindness; and we notice that Ron, too, learns kindness. As late as the Book 6, Luna points out that Ron can be humorous but unkind (VI.310). By the Battle of Hogwarts, however, he's the one who thinks to protect the house-elves—even though they've been out-of-sight and out-of-mind for everybody else (VII.625). No doubt many of his experiences contribute, but one in particular stands out; and it seems to increase his emotional, intellectual, and political capacities in several ways. This is when Ron tangles with brains in the Department of Mysteries then Madam Pomfrey treats him for especially deep scarring (V.847). The coy joke seems to be that Ron's struggle with deep thoughts makes him more effectively reflective. He remembers better and acts more creatively (VII.396–7, 578). Thus Ron figures out that Draco has used his Hand of Glory to escape, after throwing Peruvian Instant Darkness Powder (VI.618). (This is when Draco almost gets stopped outside the Room of Requirement, whence he let other Death Eaters into Hogwarts to help him murder Dumbledore.) Ron's also the first of the three to recognize that Harry's Invisibility Cloak is a Deathly Hallow (VII.416). And Ron's the one who realizes that the basilisk fangs left in the Hogwarts Chamber of Secrets have venom for killing horcruxes. He even recalls Harry's Parseltongue sounds for opening the Slytherin locket and the chamber (VII.622–3).

Harry and Hermione, at least, learn perspectivism from Hagrid. Dumbledore seems to have become a perspectivist independently. But he recognizes Hagrid as a perspectivist, and he trusts Hagrid without reservation. This is a practical rebuttal of the familiar philosophical claims that perspectivists must be radical relativists or nihilists, who arguably lack defensible standards to contrast good and evil, right and wrong, justified and not. Not even Dumbledore's judgments are always correct; nobody's are. Still these perspectivists make and defend many good calls. In fact, such kind-ness is truly contrary to the nihilism that critics attribute to radical relativism and misattribute to Nietzschean perspectivism. Potter perspectivism does not annihilate differences or prevent reasoned choices. Instead it respects, learns, and selects among deeds, creatures, and friends as distinct kinds and as individuals. This perspectivist style of action as kind-ness seems to inform rather than impede judgments by Dumbledore, Hagrid, Harry, Hermione, and Ron—especially their perfectionist leaps. These often prove adventurous, quick, and effective (but not impossibly unerring).

Potter perspectivists seldom settle for saying that they can't understand what others are experiencing. Often they extend themselves to learn more.

Hagrid and Hermione learn about other kinds of creatures. Harry learns about Luna and her family, Hagrid's mother and his grief for Aragog, house-elf magic, and goblin property. Potter perspectivists seldom say categorically that nobody else can understand what they're experiencing. Hogwarts students who didn't live through Voldemort's first ascendance are sometimes excused from comprehending the terror of those times. But the main exception, and it's a flaming one, is Harry's teenage raging against a Dumbledore who's just saved Harry—but only after his godfather Sirius has died at the MOM (V.822–44). Still that's a case of Harry needing to vent his fury, and *not* be understood. The worries that perspectivism degrades knowledge and truth to opinion or meaninglessness, and that it disintegrates communities into melees or power plays, are rebutted by Potter politics. To be sure, Pottery is fiction, not philosophy; yet plausible politics and psychology can earn its perspectivism respect.

A distinctive Potter aspect of perspectivism is *spotting*. This is another favorite word in Pottery, one with many variants and uses. Versions of *spot* occur so often that American readers of a certain age might recall early reading instructions to "Run, Spot, run." The main meaning for Potter perspectivism is to see something not easily noticed and to realize that it's potentially important. In this sense, good spotters attune to situations well enough to stay alert to their most significant particulars. This holds almost no matter how hidden or unremarkable the details may seem to the rest of us. Superb spotting of the golden snitch helps makes Harry a great seeker in Quidditch (I.280). As he moves from one scene to another, moreover, Harry picks out one item or factor after another that develops his character, informs his action, or helps his friends. In Book 6, Harry spots the Peverell ring in several settings (VI.67–8, 207, 215). As early as Book 2, he spots a small piece of paper in the fist of the petrified Hermione (II.289). No spotters are infallible, and Harry's no exception. By Book 4, Ron's better attuned to Hermione, and he spots before Harry that her front teeth are shorter (IV.405). But Harry's so good at spotting, and it's so important to his success in action, that he might as well be named Harry Spotter.

Dumbledore and Hermione are superlative spotters too. Not all that far behind are Ron and other friends of Harry's. It's easy to see how acuity of visual recognition from one situation to the next demonstrates the importance of perspectives in Potter politics. Visual spotting occurs hundreds of times in the saga as a whole, and it'd happen more if Harry had no Invisibility Cloak (VII.416). What's striking politically, though, is the many further senses of *spot* that articulate Potter perspectivism into a network of figures. At times, to spot is to "see through" disguises to detect identities (IV.90, 333); or it's to recognize logical patterns (IV.597). Of course, spots are small, circular marks like polka-dots (VI.625). They're marks of character too (IV.472): to

be spotty is to be erratic or untrustworthy (VI.221); while to be spotless is to
be clean, unblemished (IV.268). Spots can be places (IV.145; V.39); and tight
spots are slim, threatening, or difficult to manage (VII.66). To spot something
can be to put it in a particular place, or to protect somebody by helping to get
something to its proper place—as in gymnastics or weight-lifting (V.39). To
be on the spot is to be present, even timely (IV.522). Spots can be quick, perhaps informal amounts of supper (VI.233), for example, or torture (IV.650).
All this spotting, visual and not, feeds into Potter perspectivism as a network
of standpoints and movements for political action that excels.

Yet the strongest connection between perspectivism and perfectionism in
Potter politics is "turning on the spot" to apparate. Once apparating takes off
in Book 6, turning on the spot is rampant. (In addition to an instant leap to a
distant destination, characters often turn on the spot to make a slow survey of
surroundings.) As the next chapter explains, apparating is a Potter paradigm
for revving the politics of realism and idealism into perfectionism. To turn
on the spot involves a flow of figurality so determined to reach a destination
that it overflows from here (on the spot) to there (turning into a distant spot).
For Potter mages, this means turning on the resources of perspectivism to do
better than before.

SLAYING THE SLYTHERIN BASILISK

The basilisk that lurks in the Chamber of Secrets is an emblem of the terrifying racism and fascism that erupt at Hogwarts School and beyond. The
monster and the chamber seem to date from fifty years before Harry's second
at Hogwarts. Yet what the monster and the chamber symbolize can reach all
the way back to the school's founding. Most of Book 2's storylines finally
intersect in the chamber, where Harry slays the monster and its magical master. So let's attend further to where the monster is found, what it is, what it
does, and how Harry destroys it.

Many metaphors might fit the chamber. A political staple is talk of scan-
dals as skeletons in the closet—shut away from view, discussion, and action.
Harry finds skeletons and shed skins in the chamber's passages and anteroom,
and Ron polishes Tom Riddle's recognition for helping to minimize the scandal of Myrtle's death earlier. There are more victims this time, though; and
parental clamor is closing the school, after suspending Dumbledore hasn't
ended the attacks. As chapter 9 details, the saga also shows Hogwarts Houses
struggling to stand together when divided against themselves by snake
attacks, sport contests, or other momentary provocations.

Yet the chamber is deep under the castle, and the monster's blood politics
trace to Salazar Slytherin as a school founder. Both evoke metaphors more

radical than closet skeletons and less transient than disconnected conflicts. The trouble for Hogwarts is a rot at the root, a fault in the foundation, a worm in the apple, a snake in the garden. Moreover it's a giant, magical, and poisonous snake. Returning intermittently to the halls of Hogwarts to feed, the basilisk can be said to haunt the school: it's a hungry ghost that enacts scenes of awful, long-standing injustice (II.137). In the basilisk or other forms such as Slytherin House, blood politics of racism poison and oppress mages at Hogwarts for generation upon generation (II.138).

In fascism and other forms, the divisive and venomous politics of blood are so often fatal to communities, let alone individuals, that we must consider if blood politics are original sins of western civilization. Indeed the basilisk almost becomes the castle by moving through its pipes, its plumbing, its infrastructure (II.291). Chapter 12 portrays the castle and the school as figures of western civilization. No matter how often defeated, repudiated, regretted, forgiven, or otherwise undone, do blood politics persistently reassert themselves in Hogwarts and the West? That countries wrestle for centuries with legacies of slavery, racism, and oppression should spur such questions. That the thousand years of Slytherin House extend after the Battle of Hogwarts should too. Accordingly the basilisk from the Chamber of Secrets embodies a foundational flaw of political community in the West.

The basilisk also enacts a fundamental trouble of political action in western civilization. Like the snake-haired Medusa of Greek myth, whose gaze kills by turning the seer to stone, the basilisk's gaze kills when seen directly. But Perseus could slay that mortal Gorgon because her image reflected in his shield provided an indirect view that let him lop off her head. Spotted by reflection or other indirection, the basilisk's eyes are more like the vampire's mesmerizing gaze: they seduce, disperse resistance, disable from action, and freeze in place. They pacify and petrify. A major trouble for political action in the West is that awareness of evil *arrests* many of us.[18] This is often because we feel that turning to face an evil could undo us, could end us altogether. (The monster wants us? The abyss is bottomless and borderless? We've met the enemy, and it's us?) In Tom's time, Myrtle looks the basilisk in the eyes, and dies. But in Harry's time, Tom can act only indirectly, as a demonic spirit who possesses Ginny; and nobody living views the basilisk's eyes directly. Mrs. Norris sees a watery reflection. Nearly Headless Nick is already dead, and Justin Finch-Fletchley sees a ghostly refraction. Colin Creevey sees darkly through a camera lens, while Penelope Clearwater and Hermione share a small mirror. All view through media that shield them from the worst that the basilisk's gaze can do (II.291). Yet they're immobilized, unable to act—against the basilisk or with others. Even the mediated gaze is arresting, disabling.

Resistance to official outlooks or popular opinions is particularly daunting as a challenge. The gaze of a disapproving public, like the venom of a hostile community, can be disabling (with conformism) or even deadly (with fascism). Political action in communities must surmount such hurdles. In Book 1, the cerberus room on the Hogwarts third floor is like the room off-limits in Bluebeard's Castle, because people have been told its location and been warned to leave it alone. The Chamber of Secrets is rumored to be hidden somehow in Hogwarts Castle. But since skilled searches haven't disclosed it, the place doesn't officially exist, its mysterious monster isn't much acknowledged, and rallying people to face the threat is difficult indeed. Even when the writing is on the wall and the attacks start, Hogwarts responses are sporadic, fearful, and merely defensive. Among students, only Harry, Hermione, and Ron seek to face the monster. Others are almost as passive as the petrified victims. Little hunted, let alone confronted, the basilisk is able to pick off further victims one or two at a time. Most of us know the formula, which at Hogwarts might go: "When it came for that pesky cat, I did nothing. When it came for a ghost, I worried. When it came for a classmate, I planned to leave. But when it came for me, was I too late with too little?"

Disabling action is a recurrent move in Potter politics. From the first, Voldemort shows the killing curse to be a horrifying possibility; and Hermione finds a humane alternative in the freezing spell (*Petrificus!*) that she uses on Neville Longbottom then later on Cornish pixies. By the middle of the series, when it turns more adult, the recourse is usually *Stupefy!* as the stunning spell (IV.326). Stunning is briefer and less drastic than freezing. (The disarming spell favored by Harry leaves wand recovery and other magic possible.) Draco's sixth-year plan for the cursed necklace misfires to petrify Katie Bell rather than kill Dumbledore. To keep Harry from heroism that could disrupt Dumbledore's Book 6 strategy of sacrificing himself as the most powerful player in the resistance to Voldemort, the old wizard freezes the cloaked Harry into bystanding. Then Harry can't move a muscle or say a word. In Book 2, with Hermione likewise petrified, however, Harry and Ron race into action to face the basilisk. After falling stones wall Ron away from the Chamber of Secrets, Harry proceeds like St. George to slay the Dragon and rescue the Damsel in Distress. In the saga, as in western civilization, decisive, full-fledged political action often is—and takes—heroism. Is that true all too often? And so is political action all too rare?

What's needed for effective political action is Gryffindor courage (or lucky recklessness), situational awareness and standing, relevant resources of various kinds, but also capacities of speech. Aragog tells Harry and Ron that basilisks are the worst enemies of spiders, even gigantic acromantulas. (What Ron dreads about spiders is *how they move*.) Basilisks, in turn, have deadly foes in roosters, which is why the diary Riddle has Ginny kill the roosters at Hogwarts. Here the symbolism is straightforward: basilisks kill or petrify and thus "put people to sleep," politically speaking, while roosters are known for their "wake-up calls"—crowing at the break of dawn, to rouse us to action (II.115). In political terms, the petrified are not just motionless but voiceless, silent. Political action, like Potter magic, depends on voice as well as gesture. Our speech gives precise, distinct meanings to our bodily motions in making them into political deeds. To restore the petrified to full health and humanity takes a potion made from mandrakes: the only kind of magical "plant" in Pottery said to sound-off in various "cries." The potions must be made from mature mandrakes: cries of the youngest only stun, whereas cries of older mandrakes are voiced so strongly that they kill people (II.92–3). When petrified by the basilisk, Hermione can't speak; but she clutches a paper in her hand. Harry spots and reads it, learning from her library research what they've been seeking (II.289). Later the mandrake potion awakens Hermione to full voice, movement, and political capacity. Political action and community depend on communication.

Inadvertently cursed by Voldemort with a capacity for Parseltongue, Harry can summon a perspectivist sort of "Sympathy for the Devil" in bidding the restroom waterworks to disclose the chute to the Chamber of Secrets (II.197, 300).[19] By this point, Harry knows what he's doing by talking in Parseltongue; and this holds also for many of his other magical acts—though not all. Being mistaken by students for the Heir of Slytherin has added to what Harry shares with Tom Riddle, which stokes the curiosity of Tom's diary projection. With communication mainly "a path through shared understanding," they speak more and more about each other (II.307–22).[20] This lets Harry defiantly declare his loyalty to Dumbledore; and that surprises Harry by bringing Fawkes, the Sorting Hat, and the Sword of Gryffindor to the rescue. Harry goes dark in resisting basilisk lunges by sound rather than sight, until Fawkes blinds the beast. Even Harry's deadly thrust with the Gryffindor sword is pretty much a stab in the dark to kill that giant worm. Harry doesn't plan on tears from Fawkes to overcome the basilisk poison in his arm, and Harry plunges the fang into the diary purely on impulse. Fawkes flying four people to safety from the Chamber is yet another magical gift. The pivotal action blends republican politics of loyalty and speaking with perfectionist politics of attunement and leaping.

The rescue roles of Fawkes and mandrakes also implicate two important kinds of Potter politics: again republicanism but this time populism as well. The phoenix is a ready emblem of republican revolution or populist restoration, depending on context. Its trajectory is a cycle of birth, growth, flame, ash, and rebirth.[21] Thus a republican take on curing petrification—possibly as ossification of institutions—is that a mandrake potion can renew through generational politics that call next generations (of man-dragons) to the frontlines of history. Arguably Dumbledore is practicing republican politics in sacrificing Harry as a young adult for revolting against tyranny, found-ing a new order, and reviving needed virtue-osities. Populist politics would instead locate in youths the initiative for overcoming ossified or oppres-sive elites, establishments, and such. In their uprisings, young adults can unfreeze societies and fit them for vigorous action. Are cries of the man-drakes figurally protests by the people in populist politics? Notice how the mandrakes soon get portrayed as teenagers, with the fifth Potter book pre-senting Harry's teenage rages and wild swings of emotion as a populist take on the people. Are we getting in the mandrake potion a distillation of the early adult power of Harry, Ron, and Hermione in the final Potter volume?

What does it take for Harry to slay the Slytherin basilisk? Figurally this is to ask what it might take for us to defeat—if not exactly end—the blood poli-tics of racism and fascism, since they seem rooted in our civilizational origins and threaded throughout our cultural institutions. Harry and his friends sum-mon the courage and wit to find and face the monster in its lair, at its source. They don't wait for others to be victimized one after another. Their teamwork requires lots of loyalty and articulate talk among themselves and with others. As always, their heroism attracts ample help and luck as well. Still it takes gathering information and attuning themselves to their situations as much as possible. Then, because the information can never be sufficient for foolproof plans, they must venture to go dark and leap into action when it feels right to do so.

NOTES

1. Tracy B. Strong, *Friedrich Nietzsche and the Politics of Transformation* (Berkeley: University of California Press, 1975); Mark E. Warren, *Nietzsche and Political Thought* (Cambridge, MA: MIT Press, 1991); Daniel Conway, *Nietzsche and the Political* (New York: Routledge, 1997).

2. See Joseph Schumpeter, *Capitalism, Socialism and Democracy* (New York: Harper and Row, 1942, 1950). Schumpeter's argument about creative destruction by capitalism is Marxian, although libertarian and Nietzschean capitalists invoke it too. A further reminder is that not all perfectionists are Darwinians, any more than all perfectionists are fascists.

3. See IV.117–44, 645; VI.28, 581, 620.

4. See Jan-Werner Müller, *What Is Populism?* (Philadelphia: University of Pennsylvania Press, 2016); Madeleine Albright with Bill Woodward, *Fascism* (New York: HarperCollins, 2018); Roger Eatwell and Matthew Goodwin, *National Populism* (New York: Penguin Random House, 2018); Barry Eichengreen, *The Populist Temptation* (New York: Oxford University Press, 2018); William A. Galston, *Anti-Pluralism* (New Haven: Yale University Press, 2018).

5. See Jim Collins, *Uncommon Cultures* (New York: Routledge, 1989).

6. J. K. Rowling as Robert Galbraith, *The Cuckoo's Calling* (New York: Little, Brown, 2013), 113.

7. J. K. Rowling as Robert Galbraith, *The Silkworm* (New York: Little, Brown, 2014), 24.

8. *Network*, directed by Sidney Lumet (1976; Burbank, CA: Warner Home Video, 2000), DVD.

9. On Harry acting out, see V.6–11, 31–35, 42–44, 65–66, 166–67, 217, 244–48, 261, 327–28, 341, 495–99, 531–37, 554–55, 591. The text hints that Harry might as well be suffering lovage effects of "hot-headedness and recklessness" (V.383). Only on occasion does he seem possessed by evil (V.468–75, 491). See Vandana Saxena, *The Subversive Harry Potter* (Jefferson, NC: McFarland, 2012). Also see Aristide R. Zolberg, "Moments of Madness," *Politics and Society* 2, no. 2 (Winter 1972): 183–207.

10. On active ignorance, see I.36; II.38; III.36; V.2, 545; VI.7, 258.

11. See Friedrich Nietzsche, "On Truth and Falsity in Their Extramoral Sense," *Essays on Metaphor*, ed. Warren Shibles (Whitewater, WI: Language Press, 1972), 1–13. Also see Gilles Deleuze, *Nietzsche and Philosophy*, trans. Hugh Tomlinson (New York: Columbia University Press, 1962, 1983), 47–72; Daniel Conway, *Nietzsche and the Political* (New York: Routledge, 1997), 103–14; Steven D. Hales and Rex Welshon, *Nietzsche's Perspectivism* (Urbana: University of Illinois Press, 2000).

12. See John S. Nelson, *Tropes of Politics* (Madison: University of Wisconsin Press, 1998); John S. Nelson, "Humanism, Materialism, and Epistemology: Rhetoric of Economics as Styles in Action," *Humanism Challenges Materialism in Economics and Economic History*, eds. Roderick Floud, Santhi Hejeebu, and David Mitch (Chicago: University of Chicago Press, 2017), 224–55.

13. See John S. Nelson, *Politics in Popular Movies* (Boulder: Paradigm, 2015), 55–104.

14. On kindness as benevolence and consideration see Cedric (IV.724), Dumbledore (IV.428; V.76, 832), Hagrid (I.86; III.98, 113; IV.179), Harry (II.13, 177–8), Hermione (V.76, 832, VII.198), Lily (VII.324), Lupin (III.92; IV.220–1), and Molly (I.93). Toward the end of the sixth film, Dumbledore tells Harry, "Just like your mother, you're unfailingly kind: a trait people never fail to undervalue, I'm afraid." *Harry Potter and the Half-Blood Prince*, directed by David Yates (2009; Burbank, CA: Warner Home Video, 2009), DVD.

15. On goods of their kinds, see III.13, 113; III.274; IV.327, 367.

16. On stereotyping in racism and specism, see I.78; II.29, 101; III.392; IV.53, 121–23, 434, 711; V.103, 170–71, 447–50; VI.208, 242, 616; VII.12, 241–42, 574. Hagrid does this too: I.52, 58.

17. On natural versus conventional, see Stanley Cavell, *The Claim of Reason* (New York: Oxford University Press, 1979).

18. See Roland Barthes, *Mythologies*, trans. Annette Lavers (New York: Farrar, Straus and Giroux, 1957, 1972), 109–59, on 125–7. Although I don't recommend

Barthes's Marxian conception of myth, his analyses of specific myths are often brilliant.

19. See Marshall Berman, "Sympathy for the Devil: Faust, the '60s and the Tragedy of Development," *American Review* (January 1974): 23–75.

20. I appropriate this definition of *communication* from colleague G. R. Boynton.

21. On political time cycling, see John S. Nelson, *Ironic Politics* (Chapel Hill: unpublished PhD Dissertation for the University of North Caroline Department of Political Science, 1976), 63–127.

Chapter 8

Friends and the Prisoner of Azkaban

The third Potter book is a fantasy thriller with a touch of time travel. In tone and detail, *Harry Potter and the Prisoner of Azkaban* is the last Potter book fully for children. Thus it begins and ends in wish-fulfillment. For the first time, Harry manages to study magic over the summer and even get a birthday card. Then he escapes the Dursleys early, the poor Weasleys win the lottery, and the scapegoated Hagrid becomes a Hogwarts professor. In the end, Hermione's time-turning gives Harry the family mentor he's craved—plus the confidence to cast a soul-saving patronus. In between, though, Harry and his friends face hosts of horrors. Supposedly to murder Harry, the notorious Sirius Black has just escaped the wizard prison. Harry keeps seeing the Grim that portends death. Soul-stealing dementors go from the prison to guarding Hogwarts School, but Harry can't even get there on the Hogwarts Express before they start attacking him instead. Harry and his friends even get a closet werewolf as their DADA teacher. Then the MOM sends an executioner for the hippogriff with whom Hagrid and Harry have gained strong rapport, but whom Draco has baited and lied into a capital offense.

As a genre, fantasy has affinities for romance but also power politics. This helps make the Potter series a prime arena for contests between the political styles of idealism and realism. By positions and implements, the wizarding sport of Quidditch epitomizes this. Neither idealism nor realism gets ideologized into a creed or a social science, and neither is a popular movement. But both have been practiced stylistically for thousands of years. As the names suggest, idealists stress bringing out the best in people and situations, while realists insist on facing and using the worst in order to get better results—if seldom better people. (Yes, this contrast is simple in the extreme; yet it'll do for starters.) The conventional inclination of fantasy, as of generic romance, is toward political idealism. When fantasy turns politically realist, however, let alone ironist or nihilist, we often call it "dark fantasy"—which is to say, "horror." As we're seeing, Potter books overflow with figures from horror as a popular genre; and so it features existentialist politics.

By Book 3, Harry's becoming a young adult. He faces rollercoaster moods and devastating events—especially endings. *Prisoner of Azkaban* uses these to focus a dialectic of idealism and realism for the whole series. It makes high standards handle harsh settings and awful disasters, yet it ends well through surprising reprieves. The Knight Bus appears out of the blue to rescue a stranded Harry from the Grim (Reaper, as we might say). The Minister of Magic and the Accidental Magical Reversal Department spare Harry grief from "blowing up" (inflating) Aunt Marge. On the Hogwarts Express, Remus Lupin awakens just in time to save Harry from "the Dementor's Kiss." Then the heroic trio learns that a therapy for horror is lots of chocolate!

And that's all before Harry and his friends even get back to Hogwarts. By year's end, they elude Snapean punishment while turning back the clock to free the hippogriff and Harry's godfather. They learn about real limits on powers for good, they find that flaws and misfortunes seem inevitable for ideals, and they continue to discover ways and whys to break even the best of rules. Politics of idealism and realism develop in the more adult books ahead, and they're plenty important before Book 3. But *Prisoner of Azkaban* is where they shift into higher gears. Accordingly the trio's rule-breaking in this book becomes more sophisticated and coherently political. This means opening further to perfectionist leaps and specifically existentialist devices. Chief among these is the magical Time-Turner, which shows Harry and Hermione how to learn from experience as realists propose, idealists imagine, and existentialists encourage.

IDEALISM

The main setting for the Potter series is Hogwarts Castle, home for the Hogwarts School. The name implies a realist (and perspectivist) facing of hard facts: encompassing the whole hog, warts and all. Even so, the entryway features the school's fundamental idealism. As Book 3 tells us for the first time, the castle frames its gateway with "winged boars" atop stone columns (III.87; IV.171). These flying pigs are appropriate symbols for education in magic, since "when pigs fly" is a commonplace of impossibility. Hogwarts is a magical place where the impossibly ideal happens safely and constructively, making it an ideal place *and* a place for idealism. To protest Umbridge bureaucratism, Weasley fireworks reinforce the figure with "winged piglets" (V.636). (The Dursleys appear insistently as "pigs" but *without* wings:

rampant consumerism and materialism make the Dursleys "piggish," as noted in connection with their conformism.[1])

If stories for children have default politics, they'd be idealist. That's the usual target of the cynical Rat's tales for children in *Pearls before Swine*, the comic strip by Stephan Pastis. To sidestep cynicism, Harry's idealism gains sophistication from Dumbledore's idealism as well as his realism, both serving liberal and republican politics. All this develops in the midst of a four-way struggle among the idealism of the school, the perfectionism of its focal hero, the realism of the MOM and Severus Snape, plus the perversity of Voldemort and his Death Eaters. This helps Potter idealism face and defend against dark arts of authoritarianism, bureaucratism, conformism, domination, elitism, fascism, and more.

In consequence, the series takes on idealism are decently complicated. Although the saga features the perfectionist politics of persistent excelling, it distrusts the eutopian idealism of fully perfected situations, let alone people. It respects the pure idealism of pursuing what's truly good and right, including impatience with opposing rules or people; but it worries that purity preempts attunement to other people and perspectives. Yet the saga warns graphically against the perverse idealism of power, profit, or purity—whether in blood, creed, culture, or country—with evils of fascist totalitarianism as continuing demonstrations. It insists on staunch toughness for the ironic idealism of self-disparaging activists, who stay measured in hopes and reserved in expectations but no less committed to ideals. Moreover it works to learn from the quixotic idealism of tilting at windmills, what they might symbolize, and how we might resist them.

A *u-topia*, such as Thomas More's, transliterates as a *no-place* in our reality—and thus an imaginary place, often used for critical reflection on recent actualities.[2] It's a device for ironical idealists to reconsider current arrangements. A *eu-topia*, such as Ernest Callenbach's *Ecotopia*, is also pronounced in English with a long *ū*. But it transliterates as a thoroughly *good-place*, and it's a form for true believers to specify their political dreams as societal blueprints.[3] Robert Frost wrote that "Nothing Gold Can Stay;" and Potter politics are too modest and practical to regard "perfected" situations, institutions, let alone systems as sustainable—or in fact, fully perfected.[4]

Book 2 shows Harry and Ron that what's ideal is impermanent. Blocked from King's Cross Platform 9¾, the two boys improvise a trip to Hogwarts in Arthur Weasley's flying car. Skimming the sky initially puts them figurally in heaven and politically in eutopia: a purely ideal, utterly good place. But only a paragraph later, the bloom is off the rose; then all too soon, the car is swooping down to earth—and into the Whomping Willow (II.71–2). Already the first book has told why the magical ideals of the Philosopher's Stone, for lengthening life and turning base metals to gold, still invites misuse that justifies Dumbledore in destroying it (I.295–7). Book 3 has Harry and Hermione save Buckbeak from the axe and Sirius from the dementors. Still these two fugitives must be sent into a seclusion all too similar to imprisonment, even while that means letting Wormtail go to resurrect Voldemort (III.413–15, 426–9). Similarly the Knight Bus gets introduced as miraculous and luxurious transportation. Lamp posts and road signs jump magically out of its speedy (and reckless) way. Yet its severe starts, stops, turns, tilts, and so on make passengers queasy and determined to use alternatives if at all possible (III.33–6; V.524–6).

The modern trouble with *eutopian idealism* has been its terrible talent for dystopia as the sort of dysfunctional place that results when a eutopian project goes awry.[5] In Book 3, the Time-Turner is a eutopian device that changes disaster into deliverance for Sirius and Buckbeak. Figurally this even turns back the calendar, not just the clock, by defeating the fascist perversions of family, leadership, loyalty, and strength as practiced by the Malfoys. Thus it rescues those as republican virtues enacted by Harry's godfather and the hippogriff. By Book 6, though, Sirius is dead, Buckbeak needs Hagrid's care, and every Time-Turner has been broken (III.115; VI.53, 231). Even the wondrous Room of Requirement is too good, too ideal to *stay* true; and its function as the Room of Hidden Things fuels its incineration (VII.706). In the Potter saga itself, without including movies about *Fantastic Beasts* or website extensions of what's in the original seven books, it's conceivable (if unlikely, given historical allusions) that Gellert Grindelwald is initially a eutopian idealist. If so, his project goes atrociously astray. Yet *neither* Dumbledore brother credits young Albus with fully good social intentions, let alone detailed political visions.

The Potter series makes better room for *pure idealism*, with several characters devoted sincerely yet self-critically to the pursuit of worthy ideals. Harry, Ron, and Hermione are pure idealists. So are Sirius and Lupin. None are *absolute idealists*: constitutionally incapable or opposed in principle to small accommodations for resistant realities.[6] Nor are any susceptible to the realist caricature of simply plunging ahead without significant reflection on means or ends. Instead pure idealists insist on keeping key moves compatible with major aims, with *both* in the plural so that no single goal overrides all others all the time. Pure idealism is self-sacrificing in that it can respect volunteering at awful personal cost to serve "the greater good," at least in dark times, as Harry and Hermione argue (VII.568). But it rejects sacrificing some sets of people to others for supposed improvements, thus diverging significantly from eutopian idealism. And it rejects lying to the public for its own good, as eutopians and some realists claim to do (VII.91).

Sirius and Lupin are pure idealists mainly in their fidelity to friends according to codes of honorable conduct. (In substance, they are republican idealists.) Regardless of personal risk, Sirius must defend his friends, the Potters, and his godson; Lupin must stand with Dumbledore. (As a character detector, Crookshanks approves Sirius and doesn't seem to reject Lupin.) Yet taking on further commitments causes the two terrible consternation. Lupin struggles with his ties to Tonks and baby Teddy, Sirius with his obligations to the Order of the Phoenix. Like the heroic trio, Hagrid is (arguably) a pure idealist who has little trouble standing with Dumbledore and many others at once. And whatever Hagrid's principles might be on political lies, he seems unable to lie persuasively to anybody in any event, although he can hold tenaciously to blatantly obvious falsehoods in order to keep faith with friends.

Knowingly or not, otherwise pure idealists can commit themselves to bad aims, foolish projects, or indefensible standards. The result is *perverse idealism*. Perhaps this is the dystopian danger when dementors overshadow the winged boars that guard the Hogwarts gates (III.87) or when death-eating Carrows take over from the Hogwarts teachers (VII.573–81). Candidates are the greater-good politics of Grindelwald and the pure-blood politics of Voldemort. Both claim merely to respect the "natural facts" of mage superiority over muggles and other fully sentient species, such as elves, giants, goblins, leprechauns, merpeople, vampires, and veela. Yet both pursue vicious campaigns to enforce mage superiority. And worse, it seems likely that the project in both cases becomes domination of everybody by the perverse leader, which counts not at all as any kind of idealism but rather as self-interest unto megalomania and power madness.

Looking to keep idealism alive, yet chastened short of purity (let alone perversity), can produce *ironic idealism*.[7] This gains or retains genuine ideals yet holds them at arm's length to keep commitments fundamentally critical rather than correctable only at the edges. Continuing attention to their own awful mistakes can teach ironic idealists humility, limits, and substantial tolerance for the (somewhat) conflicting ideals and projects of others. (Politically such others get respect as opponents rather than contempt as enemies.)

The Potter epitome of ironic idealism is Dumbledore. Of course, Dumbledore is the one who specifies and explains most of the political ideals that animate Potter politics. His reflective distance and turns on these ideals, which he does preach and pursue, help him do this. Hogwarts idealism and realism closely track Dumbledore's deeds and leadership. His playful, self-critical impulses help make the idealism in general as much ironic as pure, as the winged boars suggest. The irony opens Potter politics to appreciating realist perspectives and devices; yet Potter love for others and self-sacrifice for the greater good keep those politics respectably idealist for when the stakes are greatest in dark times.

At times, idealism can edge into folly, but more as a political tradition than as a political mistake. The modern symbol of this is Don Quixote tilting honorably, if oddly, at windmills; so we may talk about *quixotic idealism* too. Book 3 introduces this idealist in caricature as Sir Cadogan. He's the spirited little knight in a living portrait with a dappled pony, although he likes to race through other portraits on quests. He helps guide the heroic threesome to their first lesson in Divination, which seems to suit his noble-but-nutty idealism. Later we learn that the estimable Bill Weasley is a fan of this "mad" little knight (IV.616). Cadogan doesn't joust with windmills, but he does challenge people passing by, possibly to spur their senses of honor. As a comic character, Cadogan is brave, principled, and pugnacious—just overly so—and he talks like a pirate to boot. Cadogan volunteers to handle entry to Gryffindor rooms, after a Sirius break-in attempt leaves the Pink Lady's portrait in shreds. Typical of quixotic idealists, though, Cadogan's lack of common sense can be spectacular; and he admits Sirius with a password list in hand (III.268). Marching to different drummers, quixotic idealists seldom seem well-rhythmed for our realities or moralities; but remember the school song for Hogwarts. The hope is that the quixotic differences can afford us uncommon sense when we most need it in challenging times.

REALISM

Power is a primal aim of magic, and it's the primary focus of political realism. Realist power can be hard for coercion (military) *and* soft for cooptation or cooperation (diplomacy). Power is for winning, so that ends can justify means. Idealists often see realism as the main discipline of the dark arts. This helps explain the bad reputation in some quarters of Niccolò Machiavelli as the first modern realist among political theorists. (Machiavelli was republican too.) But Potter books join other recent works of fiction and film in associating dark arts more with perversions of perfectionism. Some Potter defenses against such dark arts are perfectionist, as the previous chapter explores. Some are idealist, especially in teaching resistance to misuses and temptations of power (IV.211–2). Yet many Potter defenses against dark arts are realist, particularly in countering power abuses and countenancing rule breaking.

In Potter politics, skeins of perfectionism get the most attention. But aspects of realism rival republicanism for second place. (Keep in mind that republicanism provides many of the ideals for Potter idealisms.) To explore realist politics, the Potter series deploys many types of characters, topics of analysis, and tropes of action. Together these offer extensive and insightful takes on political realism, so let's try to do them initial—if brief—justice.

Pottery treats political realism as a family of ethical styles in community-oriented action, to compare with idealism and other such families. Realism isn't attacking or abandoning ethics in general, although some critics argue to the contrary. Therefore the main characters recognized by political realists don't amount to a roster of villains. Only *enemies* qualify (at times) as evil, and Pottery is perspectivist enough to reserve that characterization for Voldemort, Death Eaters, dementors, Umbridge, and probably Grindelwald. Basilisks are enemies of spiders. Otherwise the Potter books use accusations of "enemy" to ironize claims of malice and villainy (IV.421–3; VII.645). Too little is said about such "dark creatures" as grindylows and red caps to declare them categorical enemies, and we learn that not even vampires or inferi should be seen simply as evils or enemies (VI.315–6, 460, 566). Potter books often cast dark creatures as *opponents* (who more or less know what they're doing in trying to stymie actors) or *obstacles* (who can't help but be in the way). Mage opponents in the second book range from Cornish pixies to acromantulas, but Aragog shows how the realist ambition can be to turn bystanders, opponents, even enemies into *allies* who collaborate short of friendship. Harry and Narcissa Malfoy ally in the last book.

For realists, the prime movers in politics are *actors*. The theatrical pun is apt, because realist doers should master arts of appearance (VI.328).[8] This is one respect in which apparating, as a magical art of disappearing here to appear immediately there, is a key part of Potter realism. It's also how transfiguration contributes to realist politics: this suggests strategies and tactics of misleading appearance, and it helps detect them too. Transfiguration adepts such as Dumbledore see through realist gambits like Riddle covering up his murder of Moaning Myrtle by framing Hagrid as the Heir of Slytherin (II.312). Realist actors are to be ambitious, audacious, bold, and confident (unto macho). Thus Harry misleads Ron into thinking he's swallowed Felix Felicis for luck to guarantee great goal-keeping, giving him the confidence to douse his fears of failure and act on his practiced talent (VI.293–9). Con games are common as realist devices, and confidence looms large in Potter accounts of action succeeding—or not (V.172, 368, 655; VII.392). Realists often chide idealists for conning themselves by failing to face hard facts; and realists tie idealism to femininity, possibly seeing Luna and Hermione as Potter idealists out of touch with realities. Until recently, most western politics have been sexist in assigning women to subordinate places or reviled roles. Potter politics seem to open all their places and roles to women. Before such a feminist move, however, realist politics treated women as masculinized by or for political action, mostly in male company (VII.116). Thus Ginny could count as a realist (VI.646–7; VII.116).

Advisors are major figures in political realism, where they counsel focal actors. Realist Machiavelli and idealist More use large parts of their best-known books for how to choose and listen to advisors (and how not) as well as how to choose and address advisees (and not). The perversely realist-republican politics of crime families, with codes of loyalty and silence, attend to advisors (*consigliari*) almost as much as bosses (*godfathers*). Harry gets his best advice from Dumbledore, but not enough of it; he gets most of his advice from Ron and Hermione, and it's usually good; but he most wants advice from his godfather, Sirius (IV.22). Still Harry excels in part by internalizing perspectives of all these figures. So he consults them as inner voices when deliberating, or just lets them flow into his impulses when leaping (IV.21–2; VII.705–23). With Priori Incantatum (IV.659–69) and the Resurrection Stone (VII.698–701), Harry taps shades of his parents and friends more for emotional support than specific information or strategic insight; but realist advisors provide all these. (That's why realist actors stay vigilant about advisors, who are positioned to manipulate the actors without their knowing it.) For advice, Harry also consults the Potions text of the Half-Blood Prince and the Marauder's Map (VI.447–9), as Ginny does the Riddle diary (III.309–10). This is why Arthur Weasley warns his daughter not to trust anything that can (seem to) think for itself when she can't see the brain which is guiding it (II.329).

Machiavelli's notorious text is *The Prince*, where the author auditions for advisor to the realist ruler of a principality. Hence the *prince* becomes the archetypal realist, inviting literary contrasts to the vampirical perfectionist Dracula as the Dark Prince, to the honorable republican Hamlet as the Sweet Prince, and so on.[9] Gryffindor passwords fit action motifs of the moment. For Harry's first entry, *Caput Draconis* as "head of the dragon" can evoke Godric Gryffindor as the brave knight St. George who slays a dragon (I.130). Figurally Harry becomes the slayer of Voldemort as the (head) dragon. In Harry's third year, Gryffindor passwords often evoke *The Prince* and Shakespeare's *Hamlet* (III.94, 230, 249, 295). By contrast, Dumbledore's passwords to the headmaster's office are whimsical, ironical, anti-realist, and oriented to sugary treats.[10]

Machiavelli's animal templates for princes include the commanding *lion* (Rufus Scrimgeour) and the cunning *fox* (Severus Snape). The fox is a clever trickster, which suits Snape as a *spy*, another archetype of realist politics. In trying to stop her sister Narcissa from seeking Snape's advice at Spinner's End, Bellatrix pauses on the way to kill a fox in the field, which is exactly what perverse perfectionists want to do with realist foxes (VI.19–20). After all, Snape repeatedly outfoxes Bellatrix and Voldemort, as she knows but can't prove to Voldemort's satisfaction. Of course, Snape does this anew at Spinner's End: a chilling name for what happens there. (And what are the political implications of *Fawkes* as a homonym for *fox*? Do they relate to naming Dumbledore's phoenix after Guy Fawkes?)

As a Hogwarts student, Severus Snape brands himself the *Half-Blood Prince*. Hermione interprets this more or less literally in terms of his mage mother and muggle father. The allusion to Machiavelli's realist prince and his off-shoots is clear, though, and the half-blood twist invites exploration. Is Snape a half-hearted realist? One who goes only half-way? One divided against himself? Is he half-realist and half-perfectionist? Half a Voldemort fan and half a Lily lover? A realist who limits wounds inflicted, blooding enemies only part-way: *Sectum Sempra* rather than *Avada Kedavra*? A likely candidate is that Snape spies as a double-agent: for Voldemort at first (VI.34, 545) then turned secretly to work for Dumbledore (IV.590–1; VII.684–7, 721, 741).

Realist politics get synopsized as spy-versus-spy, with the spy thriller as their popular home; and spy politics thread throughout the Potter saga.[11] The heroic trio spies repeatedly on Draco, and he returns the favor. By Book 6, both Harry and Draco operate as secret-agents (VI.382). In book 7, the trio mounts an undercover raid on Gringotts Bank. Yes, it runs into all kinds of trouble, requires tons of improvisation, and turns spectacularly public. But it begins covert.

Snape explains that his spying relies on skillful acting in the theatrical sense (VI.324–8). By cloaking himself in misleading appearances, Snape can conceal who he actually is and what he's truly doing. Thus spy movies are often called cloak-and-dagger films. As clothes, cloaks are cover-ups (II.26; VII.73); and Harry's *not* a realist fan of keeping truths from opponents, let alone publics (VI.344–6; VII.91). With Dumbledore's enablement and encouragement, though, Harry's cloak-and-wand work is well underway after his first Christmas at Hogwarts—when his gifts feature (what turns out to be) *the Invisibility Cloak* of Peverell invention and inheritance as a Deathly Hallow (I.201, 302). It's big enough for Harry, Ron, and Hermione to work covertly as a team by crowding (then crouching) under it. It keeps other beings from seeing their bodies, but not from touching, hearing, or smelling them. It's not a spell to camouflage them, for spells can wear off; and it's not a usual cloak of demiguise hair, which can wear out (VII. 410–1). Yes, magical maps and eyes can spot people under it; and dark detectors might register them too, for nothing realist is perfect (III.347, IV.322). Yet it's still said to be the one true Invisibility Cloak, least limited and most lasting. Consequently it's the most helpful of Harry's tools for breaking rules, followed closely by the Marauder's Map (IV.458).

Time and again, Harry uses the Marauder's Map in after-hours missions to disrupt the dark projects of others. The map was created by his father, James, and *his* friends Sirius Black, Remus Lupin, and Peter Pettigrew. It gets passed along to Harry by Fred and George Weasley for its identification of secret passages and especially its real-time tracking of true identities on the Hogwarts grounds (III.191–5). Ordinarily the map looks to be a blank parchment. To open and work it, the user pledges to do "no good" with it, echoing

Machiavelli's realist advice that the prince "must learn how not to be good."[12] To clear and close the map, the user taps it and declares that the mischief has been managed. The map lets Harry and his friends use the castle's hidden doors, halls, and tunnels—to mimic apparating even though it's disabled at Hogwarts (VI.387). Like any realist (or magical!) resource, the map can be used for ill, as it was at times by its makers. "Borrowed" from Harry by the younger Crouch, disguised as Mad-Eye Moody, the map even helps Barty murder his father. In Harry's hands, though, it's a major implement for good. There it shows the realist importance of manipulating and penetrating appearances. This offers an overall sense of any scene for action, to choose destinations and routes carefully then adjust paths as situations change. Up to a point, it also discloses true identities: of Scabbers the rat as Peter Pettigrew and of "Moody" as Crouch. But it doesn't disclose Crabbe and Goyle posing as Hogwarts girls, nor does it display the Room of Requirement or anybody in it. Realists must stay alert to everybody and everything having limits that might not be known in advance.

Apparating, too, can be crucial to spycraft; but Book 5 presents it even more as a take on political realism in general. (Technically a mage disapparates from here to apparate over there at the same instant, but Potter books also use *apparation* and even *apparition* to cover both as aspects of the same act. Mindful that ghosts are apparitions, leading in further directions, I'll write instead of apparating.) On entering adulthood, mages learn apparating as a milestone skill, akin to muggle driving (IV.66). At Hogwarts, apparating is taught by a visitor from the MOM. Wylie Twycross (ah, the puns) preaches three D's that cover realist acting as well as apparating. *Destination* specifies the aim, *Determination* mobilizes the will, and *Deliberation* assesses the means in moving through "nothingness" to the goal (VI.384–5). Especially smart is that deliberation reassesses the aim as well as the path in proceeding. This is how Hermione can reroute the trio away from Phoenix headquarters when Yaxley tags along in apparating from the MOM (VII.267–72). What makes this go, though, doesn't begin with a D but rather with a T. The action (the timeless transit to the goal) is gestural, figural, tropal. So the Twycross direction is to *Turn on the spot* in entering and navigating the nothingness, in order to appear at the distant destination. Of course, this twist makes the act magical and, arguably, perfectionist. Especially after we learn the three D's and a T, we readers can see these four terms appear over and over as the rest of the series narrates action by Harry and others.

What happens if any step is incomplete? Without a detailed sense of destination, you stay put. Often the focus is insufficient, and Hogwarts beginners don't even begin to disappear from their starting points. Without full and sustained will, you arrive in pieces or only in part.[13] Inexperienced apparators lack the confidence that comes with successful practice, or they lose the concentration needed to bring a whole body to the target place. Distraction is a great danger to would-be apparators. Ron learns this in leaving behind flesh from his upper arm as Hermione apparates him on the spur of the moment from their newly infiltrated safe house. Without decent deliberation along the way, apparators are too rushed and undiscerning to reach intended targets in the intended conditions. For realists, deliberation resists undue haste; and it enacts *pru-dence*, etymologically the *fore-sight* that senses well the ends *and* means. In Book 6, Harry tries to use the Marauder's Map to spy on Draco, in order to catch him out as a Death Eater (VI.388). But his destination is faulty, because he fails to recognize the meaning of Draco's absence from the map and because he doesn't focus instead on Crabbe and Goyle. Harry's determination is flawed, because it's intermittent rather than sustained, consistent, and concentrated. And Harry's deliberation is poor, because he doesn't take detailed, let alone reflective or self-critical, account of the information offered by the map. The three D's of apparating direct realist political action.

Not evoked by the three D's, though, are three perfectionist aspects of apparating, which also appear in political action by Harry and his friends. Turning on the spot is perfectionist in going figural. Moreover the turn into "nothingness" is said to be a turn into darkness. Hence apparating not only goes figural but also goes dark.[14] And the feeling is one of being squeezed down a narrow tube, with the "pressure" making an ordinary solid seem to surge through a pipe from one place to another (VI.58, 354–6, 554). It's as though bodies flow through a conduit from here to there. Thus apparating goes with the flow, to enact a perfectionist priority of fluidity. By perfectionist poetics, apparating is easy to conceive as leaping. Yet these further perspectives on apparating help clarify how perfectionist politics rev realist acting into leaping. As perfectionist legilimency (mood-reading) can be frustrated or defended against by perfectionist occlumency (mind-blocking), so apparating can be stopped by the anti-disapparation jinx (V.817).

For Machiavelli, the focal foe of any realist actor is the feminine dynamic of *Fortuna*, the disordering disposition in human affairs. Put colloquially, Lady Luck disrupts even the best-laid plans. Yet fortune in this sense arises from the ambitious action by many males who can't know each other beyond observable behavior, and thus find their interactions eventually unpredictable. Many realists follow Machiavelli in trying to counter fortune with information, intelligence, and audacity. Yet human limitations mean that fortune prevails in time.[15] The humility in seeing this can keep realism ready to minimize harms to people and costs to resources while winning, and it can turn realists away from "winning at any cost." This recognizes that winning comes and goes, while there are likely to be other battles ahead. Doing "whatever it takes" to win is often a lapse in realist politics, and the worst realist inclination can be an utter unwillingness to lose. This ties to the reluctance

of some realists to admit error or defeat, let alone apologize for it. The aim
is to project only strength and success, showing no weakness whatever. But
others are more skillful.

Through the Hogwarts course on Divination, the Potter saga explores
many perspectives on such fortune as a realist preoccupation. (Fortune as
foreshadowing for storytelling purposes also spotlights Sibyll Trelawney and
Firenze the centaur.) At Hogwarts, only prophecy (rather than mere prediction) seems to be taken seriously; and most regard it as surpassingly rare.
The dark tone of Divination methods and projections might simply register
that they're exercises in the occult, but it might also suit the saga's setting
in dark times. Most homework submissions from Harry and Ron, like most
Trelawney prognostications, feed her downbeat sensibility; and most seem
preposterous enough to garner grins and chuckles. Yet if we check out their
literal accuracy and figural acuity, we might be surprised at the many that
are (more or less) borne out. Are there subtle jokes here? On Harry and his
friends? On readers? On realists?

Similar ironies surface repeatedly in Potter books. After Ron polishes
school trophies and plaques all evening in Book 2, he can recall that one
for special services to the school had gone to a "Tom Riddle," whose name
is on the diary retrieved by Harry from Moaning Myrtle's restroom. When
Harry wonders about the reason for the award, Ron's mordant but unknowing joke is that maybe Riddle got celebrated for murdering the annoying
Myrtle (II.232). We learn later that this comes uncomfortably close to the
truth. After the Umbridge quill carves her "line" painfully into scars on the
back of Harry's hand, he gives it back to her collaborator, Scrimgeour, in
ironically rebuking the request that Harry lie to support him: "*I must not tell
lies*" (VI.347).

Wizard chess is a good Potter corrective for the theoretical temptation to
reduce political realism to strategy and tactics. Ron is good at wizard chess
in part because he has a purposeful sense of the big picture of pieces distrib-
uted on the board. He's also good because he develops the board's potential
through specific moves that prove clever at concealing his overall vision of
the unfolding game even as he executes his strategy. Surely we may regard
chess in these realist terms. But the wrinkles in wizard chess make it much
more like full-fledged realism in politics. In wizard chess, pieces claim
squares and take out other pieces by force, in combat. This seems to mean
that particular moves can fail—not only to produce victory in the long run but
even to advances pieces as directed in the short run. Resistance *can* be effective, piece by piece, move by move. Captures apparently can be defeated. As
a result, pieces can be reluctant to attempt particular moves; and the player
must persuade them to proceed as directed. Pieces see and hear for themselves what's happening in the game; and they sometimes object to orders,

argue back, or otherwise resist. Ron usually plays with his own pieces. In effect, they've trained in combat with him, learned the game with him, and come to share some of his perspectives. He can direct them better, because he can persuade them better, because they can trust him better (I.199). By realist standards, that Ron must play with different pieces on the way to the Philosopher's Stone makes his self-sacrifice all the more daring and his triumph all the more impressive (I.281–4).

For realists, politics are conflictual, contentious. Machiavelli portrays politics as arenas of force and fraud as well as fortune. To win, realists must face these and other truths (III.392). As the name says, realists prioritize realities, no matter how unwelcome or threatening. Realists chide idealists for failing to distinguish between dreams and realities (V.792). Idealists criticize realists for failing to appreciate principles (VI.375). But realists assess deeds by results. Realists question (and contrive) appearances; they distrust words, dreams, and ideals; they reach beyond books and texts (II.230, 297). Thus Snape departs from potions recipes in the textbook, and his annotations invite Harry to follow. Hermione remains fully a textualist. As in other ways, she's slower than Harry to open idealist politics to realist perspectives and resources. Like Snape, Voldemort reaches beyond books, and he flatters himself that he faces inconvenient truths. Yet as Dumbledore expects, Voldemort's arrogance is an ignorance that undoes him (VII.7, 709–11).

Realists must master attention, distraction, flattery, fear, and terror. They must bend and break rules. They must blackmail, conspire, entrap, frame, and manipulate. They must keep and steal secrets, take hostages, absorb and inflict pain, even go to war. The Potter saga includes all these. Some realists do whatever it takes to win this particular contest, but no more; others resort to force in facing hard facts or foes that must be fought now to preempt worse later. Both kinds of realists begin by respecting limits, and both stay wary of winning at *any* cost. This is because both expect more engagements down the road. Yet the danger for both is becoming unwilling to lose. Then there's no way to spot loyal opponents, honorable adversaries, or possible allies; then there's only upping the ante (by scorching the earth) as much as needed to prevail now and in the future. A time to worry is when the avowed realist says with a shrug that *winners write history*. Then realist ethics evaporate, leaving only *might makes right*. That's not realist, it's cynical; yet it's what's implied by the MOM's new fountain slogan: Magic Is Might (VII.241–2).

EXISTENTIALISM

Usually existentialism gets treated as a philosophy of life rather than a style of politics. Jean-Paul Sartre put this philosophy beautifully in the slogan that *existence precedes essence.* Existentialists are diverse; yet they agree that we humans make meanings in our lives as we live them, rather than enacting prior concepts or precepts that give our actions significance. Gaps or conflicts in our directives and accounts are unavoidable, because they arise analytically after the facts of our deeds. As products of finite imagination, information, and reason, they don't fully illuminate, can't completely limit, and shouldn't totally determine what we're doing and hence who we're becoming. Our practices exceed our categories and contraries, thank goodness.

Because humans aren't gods and can't attain complete knowledge or rigor, existentialists endorse "leaping" in logic or inference. They hold that heuristics, ideal types, models, stylized facts, and other "shortcuts" are unavoidable leaps. Even the most careful among us must make them. So we should embrace them as intelligently and responsibly as possible. We often learn that Harry makes such leaps of inference or insight. His dreams of detection, as we might call them, help with this.[16] Existentialists also would notice that Harry has dreams of desire (V.118, 179; VI.306). Yet Harry's dreams differ from the visions that link him telepathically with the Dark Lord. (Book 5 includes more than ten of these visions, and Book 7 features more than twenty.) The Potter saga presents its magical visions as perfectionist, not existentialist.

Existentialists also endorse leaping in judgment or action. Again human limitations mean that no reasoning can furnish grounds that fully guarantee good decisions or deeds. Always there are cracks and crevices, even caverns and canyons, to be leapt by anybody going on the ground, as we humans must. For existentialists, anybody who acts is liable to leap—including Harry and his friends. Perfectionists often agree with existentialists on this, but it's *not* what perfectionists mean by "leaping" to Just Do It. For existentialists, "leaping" entails choosing; it implicates the freedom of humans making themselves, their worlds, and their meanings. Even when we want them to, reasons (and experts and scientists) can't take away the (individual responsibility for) choosing that permeates our doing. Still existentialists mostly urge us to act after learning what suits our situations and reflecting as carefully as we can on what to do. By contrast, perfectionist leaping is acting on vital impulse—*not* on calculation, control, cultivation, learning, planning, reflection, research, tradition, or any other western ground. Sometimes Harry "leaps" both ways.

To stress that *becoming precedes being* is to appreciate humans as the temporal creatures, and existentialists treat humans as the bearers of time. *Prisoner of Azkaban* features this motif in its time-turning plot, and the film version develops the motif visually: picture Hermione bearing the Time-Turner as an hourglass charm on a chain around her neck, see the massive clock tower with its pendulum, and mark the seasons passing. While you're at it, notice the ties to Hogwarts hourglasses that track points for the House

Cup. *Order of the Phoenix* explores the Time Room in the Department of Mysteries, with myriad clocks, the bell jar that cycles from hummingbird to egg and back, plus the store of Time-Turners. Harry's crew and the Death Eaters wreak havoc in the Hall of Prophecy, shattering shelf upon shelf of dusty glass orbs that had preserved ghostly anticipations of events to come. The Time-Turners get destroyed. And Sirius succumbs to a Bellatrix curse in the Amphitheater of Life and Death. (The whole place is a Laboratory for Existentialist Experimentation.) Then the saga concludes with Harry increasingly concerned to deal wisely with *The Deathly Hallows.*

To regard humans (with their vaguely hourglass figures) as vessels of time is to feature doing, experiencing, and reflecting as distinctive of humans. Existentialists analyze these in the everyday "life worlds" of different civilizations, cultures, and individuals. (Environmentalists might extend these to different species as well.) Especially intriguing to existentialists are the "extreme experiences" that help configure our lives—including anxiety, boredom, death, desire, faith, fear, guilt, horror, joy, love, pain, and power. All appear amply in the Potter series. Thus existentialists often analyze cinema, drama, literature, or other arts to explore such aspects and responses for the human condition. Many Potter commentaries include existentialist projects.

The first book's obstacle course to the Philosopher's Stone (of alchemy and immortality) invites various angles of analysis interesting to existentialists. What might we make figurally of each challenge: a cerberus, a trapdoor, devil's snare, flying brooms for flying keys, a participant version of wizard chess, a mountain troll, a logic puzzle with potions and fires, plus the Mirror of Erised to reveal the Stone and the Dark Lord? What might be symbolized by the arrangements, the suppliers, the solutions, even the solvers? As some commentaries elaborate, these can be metonyms of stages in the mythic hero's journey to personal identity and community liberation. As others suggest, these can map the Hogwarts education under way for Harry and his friends. They also can foreshadow the theme park of experiences and exertions forthcoming for Harry and company. And of course, they can evoke defenses against the dark arts of the Dark Lord, who seeks Harry even more than the Stone. There are similar possibilities of meaning in the Triwizard tasks, the last book's odyssey of return to Hogwarts, indeed the entire saga of events. As perspectivists, some existentialists would plumb many such levels and networks of meaning. As personalists, other existentialists would assess the response-abilities of each character. And as *praxis* activists, who spot theory-in-practice and put theory-into-action, most existentialists would trace the styles and structures of everyday *and* exceptional endeavors by each character.

In practice, existentialists stress, we often embrace contraries, contradictories, dilemmas, and the like. Somehow we cohere what seems incompatible.

We don't always excel at this, and we shouldn't always try it, but we mustn't shy from it either. We mustn't let abstractions run the world. Therefore existentialists resist social and intellectual systems as overly homogeneous, as controlling and deadening. Existentialists typically endorse cracks and gaps as openings for air and light to enter, that we might breathe freely, see clearly, and reach beyond where we've been. Existentialists prize diversity as experimentation, and they celebrate experimentation as play.[17] Play keeps ideals and individuals flexible. It lowers stakes, relaxing the realist determination to win by any means necessary. It makes more room for fun and joy.

Enter the game of Quidditch. By positions, equipment, rules, and history, Quidditch is a composite of idealism and realism as interacting styles of play. Each side has idealist and realist aspects, so that the challenge is to coordinate the two rather than elevate one over the other. The sport is a competition for victory, and realist in this regard. Moreover it's full of strategy, tactics, and fouls—as players insistently bend and sometimes break the (nearly innumerable) rules. Yet there's a referee for calling fouls, enforcing rules, and encouraging fair play: idealist aspects all. The result is an existentialist stew that mages find supremely appetizing.[18] The name symbolism is not always subtle. Seekers, keepers, and golden snitches are (mostly) idealist in figural terms, whereas beaters, chasers, bats, and bludgers are (primarily) realist. Quaffles and hoops are more debatable, but they can fit too. The relations among idealist and realist elements can be telling.

The premier position is seeker. This player tries to capture the golden snitch, earning 150 points and ending the game no matter the score. Thus a seeker is a searcher, a quester. Usually a seeker is also a hero for winning (not just ending) the game, since the added points for catching the snitch almost always are enough to secure victory. Because the snitch is small and fast as it darts throughout a vast arena for broom flying, and because the arena is busy with other players and balls zipping around, a seeker must be a superb spotter too. Seekers identified by the series are among its leading figures. Gryffindor seekers include Harry, of course; and when Umbridge bans him, Ginny Weasley, though she prefers chaser. Earlier Gryffindor seekers include James Potter and Charlie Weasley. Regulus Black, the notorious RAB, was a seeker for Slytherin; and Draco buys his way into that position with his father's gift of the latest broomsticks. Cho Chang (Ravenclaw) and Cedric Diggory (Hufflepuff) are seekers who play against Harry. And even before he represents the Durmstrang Institute as Triwizard champion, Viktor Krum is famous as seeker for the Bulgarian team, runner-up for the World Quidditch Cup in *Goblet of Fire*. There's little that Slytherin can't corrupt on occasion, but seeker seems idealist by cast as well as task.[19]

The snitch's color is called "golden," which often evokes what's ideal. As a small ball, barely big enough to enclose a finger ring, the golden snitch has two delicate wings for flying; and these could call to mind the winged boars at the Hogwarts gates. *Snitch* is slang for *snatch*, which is what the seeker's to do with the little winged ball. As another idealistic touch, a Potter snitch has "flesh memory" to identify who catches it first, since disputes do happen. To *snitch* can be to *rat*, by betraying a wrong-doer to authorities; and by extension, to *snitch* is also to *spy*. Those are links to realism. But notice that the seeker spots and captures the (golden) snitch like a spy catches a "mole," a secret agent who's infiltrated the seeker's team or territory. Does such an outcome for spy-versus-spy suit idealism? Arguably Quidditch evokes aspects of the series plot.

Each side in Quidditch includes two beaters with bats to knock two heavy balls called bludgers away from teammates and toward opponents. This is the disruption and enforcement aspect of the game, and it's clearly realist in symbolism. When Harry joins Gryffindor's squad, its beaters are the Weasley twins, who emerge as the saga's main tricksters. Later they gamble with Ludo Bagman, famous beater for the Wimbourne Wasps then Minister for Magical Games and Sports. He passes them leprechaun (aka fake) gold, lies to everybody about paying up, and tries to rig the Triwizard Tournament to square his debts. This is not to say that realists need be dishonorable; but it's important to see that force, fraud, and risk (*fortuna*) are their métier.

If beaters are the first line of Quidditch defense, chasers are the front line of the offense. Three chasers advance the (one) quaffle by passing this ball among them as they race toward a three-hooped goal. Chasers for the other team try to intercept the quaffle and go the other way. Getting the quaffle through one of the hoops scores ten points. Films that pit spy versus spy, like thrillers in general, feature chase scenes. Play-by-play for Quidditch features chase scenes that alternate or entangle directions, except when the announcer is Lee Jordan or Luna Lovegood.

The hoops as rings or circles can symbolize wholes to encompass Quidditch complexity. As a ball for scoring for both sides, the quaffle has a name that might be pure whimsy or a funny sound while performing a realist function. But the quaffle can go both ways, so does it "waffle?" To *quaff* is to *drink* with enthusiasm and probably to *quench* thirst. Do players and fans imbibe it that way, and does it help satisfy a thirst for competition? The other player for each side is the keeper, who tries to repel shots on goal and deliver the quaffle to chasers bound for the other end of the arena. The keeper is the last line of a team's defense, with a good (or lucky) keeper highly important to winning. Harry's keepers for Gryffindor are Oliver Wood and Ron Weasley, while Rubeus Hagrid is Keeper of Keys and Grounds for Hogwarts School. By everyday definitions, *keepers* are *conservators* of significant things. Through selection ("this one's a keeper") and protection ("keeping it safe"), keepers are conservationists. As the staunchest defender of Albus

Dumbledore's regime at Hogwarts, Hagrid is an emblem of the conservative idealism in keeping.

As Quidditch symbolism might suggest, existentialism also implicates styles of political action, especially in dark times. Existentialists resist philosophical systems as exercises in the sterility and insufficiency of a modern rationality that claims to calculate the most effective and efficient means to given ends. Existentialists resist social systems as exercises in conformism. To systematize, they say, is to streamline by culling anything and anybody that goes against the grain. Hence social systems are hostile to humans as individuals. When forming, social systems might be resisted by hit-and-run disruptions that remind people of their personal powers to make meanings. Examples can include business boycotts, service denials, site occupations, and so on. Freeing Buckbeak and Sirius Black is crucial for those two individuals, yet it also could count as disrupting the Fudge-Malfoy moves toward an elitist (and at least figurally "demented") system of education for young mages in Britain. In practice, all this registers as existentialism in action.

But hit-and-run resistance has little prospect of undoing a social system locked into place and totalized, possibly for the foreseeable future. European existentialists faced such situations with Nazi domination in World War II. In response, their resistance went underground. When possible, the resisters collaborated with spies and armies from outside, working toward the overthrow of the increasingly totalitarian system. But the resisters also assisted dissenters on the run within tiny interstices not yet controlled by the system. (Of course, these dissenters included the resisters themselves.) This is how the resisters protected themselves from corruption by the consolidating system, yet it's also how they took responsibility for others as well as themselves.

In existentialist terms, this amounts to making and taking political stands.[20] A paradigm for this is the mythic Martin Luther, nailing his dissent to the church door then declaring, "Here I stand, I can do no other." To protect against depredations of the system, resisters withdraw from it into small communities of mutual aid and support that hold fast to principles routinely trashed by the society. In the Potter saga, Harry, Ron, and Hermione apparate secretly and unpredictably around Britain to elude Death Eaters and snatchers. Meanwhile the three are learning everything they can about the Voldemort regime, in hopes that they can someday join in an angle of attack with decent prospects of collapsing the system. This is similar to the modest network of people who contribute to *Potterwatch* as pirate radio. They hide (and apparently run when necessary) from the Voldemort regime and its operatives. Each of their broadcasts amounts to a symbolic raid on the death-eating system that seems relentless in pursuing the few, scattered holdouts. Yet the publicized defiance of *Potterwatch* heartens resisters, just as the heroic trio's ability to stay on the run boosts the morale of the *Potterwatch* people and the remnants of Dumbledore's Army at the Hogwarts School. From the first, Harry has explained to Neville the need at times to take a stand (I.218). And toward the saga's end, Neville explains to Harry how his own stand-taking against Umbridge and the MOM has inspired Hogwarts students (VII.574). Existentialism also involves kinds of practical action, and they prove important to Potter politics.

LEARNING THE TIME-TURNER

As a magical device, the Time-Turner enables Harry and Hermione to twist unfolding events toward better, even ideal directions—for the most part. Especially for our purposes, it positions the two friends to learn about *how to learn* from their political action and experience. Some lessons are realist, some are idealist, and some existentialist. Chapter 3 examines how the whole Hogwarts curriculum has students learn defenses-against-the-dark-arts as politics. The magical performance of Harry and Hermione in using the Time-Turner augments the school methods, especially for learning arts of political action from history and personal experience.

In figure, the Time-Turner is an hourglass (III.394). In one with sand or salt to measure time, gravity would trickle the grains slowly from the top chamber to the bottom. An hourglass works by inversion. Dumbledore tells Hermione to give it three turns, apparently to identify how far "back" in time she and Harry should go. Still three turns would mean turning it upside-down, first-top back up, then upside-down again. In outcomes, the two are to spin recent events upside-down. They change the book's plotlines for Buckbeak and Sirius from tragedy to comedy, or at least from execution to escape; and they invert the outcomes for Fudge and Snape from victory to defeat. Less happily, of course, Snape then exposes Lupin as a werewolf. All too soon, Sirius dies in an ambush foolishly catalyzed by Harry. And either way, Peter Pettigrew escapes to aid the Dark Lord; but Dumbledore does caution Harry that even this might turn out well (III.426–7).

In many tales of time travel to intervene in previous events, the travelers know the events only in outcome or outline. The interveners didn't participate initially in the events, so they must work from surviving evidence and accounts by others. There are many time-travel stories about preventing the assassination of President John F. Kennedy, and most of their interveners are new to Dallas in 1963. But before Harry and Hermione intervene, they participate—and recently too: hence the rule to steer clear of their earlier selves. To be sure, they know events only from their two perspectives, plus a little extra information from Dumbledore. Their intervention can't tap the extra perspectives and expert reflections sometimes available from accounts by historians or even reporters. How, then, do they act to overturn several bad results from the first time around?

They recall and share key details as needed to begin a course of mutual action and adjust it along the way. They begin with three priorities: to stay unseen while rescuing Buckbeak then Sirius. The plan is to intervene only twice, when the original actors aren't looking and won't see the interventions. Hermione and Harry already know key moves by key figures, so they sneak to the edges of the action (but just out of sight) to monitor it. Getting the hippogriff unchained and into the forest is harder than they expected, and the same goes for keeping him unseen until it's time to save Sirius too. Yet a bigger challenge turns out to be resisting apparent opportunities for minor repairs. Thus Harry would retrieve the Invisibility Cloak so that Snape can't use it to enter the Shrieking Shack; but Hermione knows to make the minimum changes needed, and talks him out of it. Then the biggest challenge is to spot impending deviations from the former script then improvise ways to prevent them. To feature this sort of complication, the film has the two throw pebbles to alert "themselves" just in time to make moves as before, when "they" are puzzled by the stones but do look and leave as needed.[21] The huge case in point is when dementors on the lakeshore are ready to "kiss" Sirius and Harry but get dispersed instead. Almost too late, Harry realizes that he must—and *can*—intervene by casting his patronus clear across the lake. As he says, he knew he could do it because he'd already done it, when mistaken for his father. Either kind of difficulty could derail the entire endeavor. It doesn't seem, though, that this second kind had dawned on the interveners; so they had to spot *and* fix it on their own in the midst of acting. What can these facets of time-turning teach us for learning personally about political action?

Almost everybody believes in learning from experience, especially politically; but there are different paradigms for doing so. Realists often follow Machiavelli's method by rehearsing historical anecdotes that illustrate rules of thumb for political action. (As a realist republican, Machiavelli could treat these precepts as "the lessons of history.") From the Bush invasion of Afghanistan, Machiavelli might retell early events to say, "Don't rely on mercenary militaries" or "Don't succumb to mission creep." From Dumbledore's duel with Grindelwald, Machiavelli—*and* Dumbledore—would enjoin Cornelius Fudge, "Face hard facts, and tackle the worst threats before they gain momentum." Machiavelli helps readers think through each case, and realists recommend engaging historiography in this way as vicarious experience to augment what actors can encounter firsthand.[22] Pithy, memorable precepts help actors recall such lessons and realize their relevance for new situations.[23]

Use of the Time-Turner as Dumbledore directs is a push to Harry and Hermione to think (back) through their last few hours of events in order to spot (and take) the steps that could save the lives of Buckbeak and Sirius Black. The second time around, they can see events as readers of history might, recognizing needs unmet and opportunities open for further action. There's no indication that Professor Binns ever teaches the History of Magic in this way, by putting students second-hand into action settings. His history isn't alive; it's cut and dried as impersonal facts to be memorized and regurgitated on tests. Notice that the two time-travelers do this thinking step by step, in the midst of their action rather than in advance of it. Realists regard advance analysis (many times over) as highly helpful for developing capacities of political judgment. Yet realists regard any plans that precede action as merely preliminary: as part of the actor's preparations for responding moment by moment to the peculiarities of present events as they happen. That's why the third D for apparation is Deliberation.

Dumbledore tells the two where Black is being held, and reminds Hermione that the law of time-turning is *not to be seen* by their other selves (III.393–4). He doesn't try to specify the steps to take. He doesn't know enough details, and he recognizes that the two must adjust to the events as they're unfolding again-but-with-adjustments. Of course, the time-travel perplexity is whether the initial events already included these interventions by the time-travelers. If Harry and Hermione aren't seen by "themselves" the first time around, and "additional" deeds must fit into the continuing framework of events, who (besides the three conspirators) is to say that anything has been altered? This is what stumps Fudge and maddens Snape after the time-turning is done. What each wanted was in his grasp, yet their hands turned out to be empty. How could that be?

Modern realists want historical learning and insist on intense preparation, but their sense of *Fortuna* and even the best-laid plans going awry implies the need to adjust on the fly. Every situation differs in small but potentially important ways from every other. Hence the lessons of history come in precepts that need specification by actors rather than in iron laws of history that could guarantee desired results from detailed plans followed in all particulars. Idealists are more categorical about events in history, more general about rules of occurrence, and more ambitious about blueprints for action. Like modern social scientists, idealists see types of events recurring. Therefore an instance of a type should respond reliably to specific kinds of intervention planned (scientifically) to improve it. This doesn't mean that idealists would join Professor Umbridge in teaching (political) action only through theories (historical generalizations) and plans (behavioral recipes). As in Potions, students would practice plans as safely as possible. (Umbridge wouldn't ban practice if she didn't fear students getting good at political action.)

Idealists would defend their paradigm of political learning as more general and reliable in application. This claim becomes plausible if we imagine an idealist science of action that could run through a type of event time and time again to get its rules right and its interventions refined. Then the Time-Turner would need to start events entirely anew each time. Actually it seems to enable the addition but not the subtraction of acts from one version to the next, fitting "new" acts into openings previously unnoticed by the returning actors. Do Unspeakables in the Department of Mystery try to use Time-Turners to repeat key (or maybe mundane?) events over and over to learn what mixture of moves can have the desired outcome? Fantasy time-loops can work this way, resetting the start of each loop as *Groundhog Day* (1993) does until Bill Murray's character can learn then do what's needed to gain the love of the woman he's come to love. That film's a romantic comedy, of course, and we shouldn't forget that other time-loops can be no-exit traps.[24] Typically there's lots of learning in both, but it's productive in some yet self-defeating in others. As an idealist, Lupin gives his DADA course for Harry a positively circular structure like this, to facilitate and test student learning. A culminating exam moves each student through an obstacle course of the year's dark creatures, each to be faced in something like its usual setting (III.318).

Existentialists would view the Time-Turner with a realist's sense of its power and danger yet with an idealist's bent for experimentation. The first time through the climactic events of Book 3, the heroic threesome resists the disciplinary regime of the MOM mainly by being out of place, repeatedly. They're in Hagrid's hut, the Whomping Willow's passage, the Shrieking Shack, and eventually the Forbidden Forest when it's against school rules and plans of various authorities, including teachers such as Lupin and Snape. And they're confronting the crazed Sirius Black too! Existentialists could view this resistance as virtually bound to fail, since it principally accepts the sites of action (and devices of power) imposed by their opponents. All the while, however, the three learn through their limited and manipulated participation how this nexus of discipline is contrived to work. The results are terrible, until we notice the learning.

The Time-Turner gets used to put this dawning knowledge to work for more effective resistance. It enables Hermione and Harry to spot the gaps, holes, or openings in the Ministry's incipiently authoritarian system, when extended to the Hogwarts campus. Dumbledore already has limited its penetration there. He's mostly kept Fudge and Lucius Malfoy of the governing board at arm's length. He's largely confined the Ministry's dementors to the edges of campus. He's brought Lupin to teach, supported Hagrid's defense of Buckbeak, nurtured the resisting threesome, and probably managed other moves beyond the view of us readers. He also starts Hermione and Harry into the existentialist project of making meaning and constructing history the second time around with the Time-Turner. It helps the two to take the initiative, inverting the hierarchy that had left them among the victims rather than the inventers of the history made at Hogwarts that afternoon and evening.

Historiography is the writing of history. Republicans write history to highlight its lessons for later generations. Realists write history to teach us its maxims for action now. Idealists write history to refine its forms for interpreting events and re-forming them. Existentialists emphasize that "writing" history is not just for the likes of Bathilda Bagshott or Rita Skeeter; even in dark times, it's for those who learn current systems and learn to resist them actively, appropriately. Spurred by Dumbledore, Hermione and Harry make bases for mutual support and protection on the edges of a disciplinary system. Then they act in careful raids, selective incursions, to turn some trains of events onto other tracks in hopes of sending the system off the rails—at least for some, at least for a time. Existentialists respect humans as the bearers of time, and the magical turners of time in this episode are Harry and Hermione. For them, learning from history is less about gleaning facts or rehearsing precepts after events than it's active learning within events, as we do them.

Action with the Time-Turner does not produce two time lines: one earlier and one later, or one effacing and replacing the other. Instead as a matter of history, it makes one plot, fitting events together in patterns of greater complexity. Or better, it complicates and discloses (more of) a field of action. Thus the magic of the Time-Turner fits realist or idealist politics less than existentialist politics. In all three modes, learning political action from history depends in part on spotting resemblances among events. But each mode does it differently. Realists assess the repetition, resonance, or rhyming of historical events of seemingly great similarity by parsing the potentially different results: first time as tragedy but second time as farce, for example. In such repetition, idealists recognize forms fulfilled and enduring, and these can be treated as time-loops for instructing and improving us or for enclosing and entrapping us. Existentialists see systemic loops inclined to encompass and corrupt us, yet still open at times to determined resistance and ingenious escape.[25] Turning time existentially with Hermione and Harry, we might learn and make history-in-action—spiraling outward, well beyond the grasps of Fudge and Snape.[26]

NOTES

1. Harry's aunt might be named for Petunia Pig, the cartoon character; and Hagrid gives Dudley a curly tail: see I.47, 59; II.4, 9; III.16, 29, 197; IV.28; V.12–13, 37, 85; VI.51; VII.31–32.

2. See Thomas More, *Utopia*, ed. Robert M. Adams (New York: Norton, 1992).

3. See Ernest Callenbach, *Ecotopia* (New York: Bantam, 1975). Also see Kim Stanley Robinson, *Pacific Edge* (New York: Tom Doherty Associates, 1990).

4. See Robert Frost, "Nothing Gold Can Stay," *The Poetry of Robert Frost*, ed. Edward Connery Lathem (New York: Henry Holt, 1969), 222–3.

5. See Judith N. Shklar, *After Utopia* (Princeton, NJ: Princeton University Press, 1957).

6. This pure idealism differs, therefore, from Max Weber's "ethic of ultimate ends" in "Politics as a Vocation," *From Max Weber*, eds. H. H. Gerth and C. Wright Mills (New York: Oxford University Press, 1946), 77–128.

7. See Isadore Traschen, "Pure and Ironic Idealism," *South Atlantic Quarterly* 59, no. 2 (Spring 1960): 163–70.

8. See *The Illusionist* (2006), *The Prestige* (2006), and *Death Defying Acts* (2007).

9. See John S. Nelson, *Popular Cinema as Political Theory* (New York: Palgrave Macmillan, 2013), 93–5.

10. See II.204; IV.557, 579; V.466; VI.182, 493. Also see VII.662.

11. Young Snape spies on the Evans sisters (VII.663–7); Petunia Evans Dursley on her neighbors (III.17); Rita Skeeter in her animagus beetle form on Hogwarts (IV.441–2, 576); and Harry on Draco (VI.149, 383). Barty Crouch Jr. spies for Voldemort on Hogwarts School (IV.688); Kingsley Shacklebolt and Arthur Weasley for the Order of the Phoenix on the MOM (V.95); Willy Widdershins for the MOM (V.366); Mundungus Fletcher for Dumbledore (V.370) on Knockturn Alley types; and Remus John Lupin for Dumbledore on werewolves (VI.334). In addition, Rubeus Hagrid, Madame Maxime, and Igor Karkaroff spy for their Triwizard champions on the dragons (IV.343); Dolores Umbridge is something of a spy who recruits others (V.252); Percy Weasley tries to get Ron Weasley to spy on Harry and Dumbledore (V.297); and Rosmerta gets imperiused, perhaps by Draco, to spy for the Death Eaters (VI.554).

12. Niccoló Machiavelli, *The Prince*, ed. and trans. Robert M. Adams (New York: Norton, 1992), 42.

13. Compare realist splinching to the realist stage magician who murders versions of himself in *The Prestige* (2006): see Nelson, *Popular Cinema as Political Theory*, 103–12.

14. See VI.58; VII.236, 267, 322, 365, 423, 524.

15. See Hanna Fenichel Pitkin, *Fortune Is a Woman* (Chicago: University of Chicago Press, 1984, 1999).

16. See I.130; III.265, 302; IV.489; VI.290. Such dreams of detection are prominent in Umberto Eco, *The Name of the Rose*, trans. William Weaver (New York: Harcourt Brace Jovanovich, 1980, 1983). Harry also dreams to refigure recent events: I.295; II.23; III.302; IV.192; V.9.

17. See Gary Snyder, "Lots of Play," *Left Out in the Rain* (San Francisco: North Point Press, 1986), 172.

18. See J. K. Rowling, *Quidditch through the Ages* (London: Bloomsbury, 2001).

19. The series adds little about other seekers it names: Harper (Slytherin), Higgs (Slytherin), and Summersby (Hufflepuff) at Hogwarts; and Aidan Lynch for the Irish

national team. Dobby describes needy mages who first encounter the Come and Go Room as "seekers" (V.386–7).

20. See John S. Nelson, *Tropes of Politics* (Madison: University of Wisconsin Press, 1998), 205–30.

21. Does Dumbledore orchestrate the melding of the two timelines? Of course, he tells his two students to use the Time-Turner to save two innocents. But does he act step by step to keep (at least) the rescue of Buckbeak happening? When the two need more time unseen to move Buckbeak into the forest, Dumbledore repeatedly delays officials and turns their attention elsewhere. When the executioner moves to search the forest, Dumbledore pokes gentle and effective fun at the thought that an abductor would do anything but fly away on the missing hippogriff. This might echo the first-book question of how amply Dumbledore might have arranged Hogwarts events to steer Harry safely to and through the final obstacle course. It's a further issue what such possibilities might imply for Pottery takes on political action.

22. On vicarious, virtual, and symbolic (or figural) experience in politics, see John S. Nelson and G. R. Boynton, *Video Rhetorics* (Urbana: University of Illinois Press, 1997), 195–232; John S. Nelson, *Politics in Popular Movies* (Boulder: Paradigm, 2015), 82–104.

23. On realist-republican precepts for political action, see John S. Nelson, "Prudence as Republican Politics in American Culture," *Prudence*, ed. Robert Hariman (University Park: Pennsylvania State University Press, 2003), 229–57.

24. Among time-loop movies, *Palm Springs* (2020) is another romantic comedy. The learning is also effective and the ending is also happy in *Source Code* (2011) as a science-fiction thriller plus *Edge of Tomorrow* (2014) as a sci-fi thriller and war film. The time-loops are traps in *Happy Death Day* (2017) and *Happy Death Day 2U* (2019), both slasher versions of horror.

25. On neo-noir plot loops as such existentialist history-in-action, with inflections toward realist, idealist, and perfectionist politics, see Nelson, *Political Theory as Popular Cinema*, 83–193.

26. This modifies the conservative tone of the postmodern spiral in William Butler Yeats, "The Second Coming," *The Collected Poems of W. B. Yeats* (New York: Macmillan, 1956), 184–85.

Chapter 9

Peoples and the Goblet of Fire

The fourth Potter book can be read to relaunch the Potter saga on larger stages in darker times. It parallels the first book in opening with a kind of murder mystery. Then it moves from an early song by the Sorting Hat and breakfast mail from delivery owls through a difficult obstacle course that brings Harry face-to-face with the Dark Lord. Like the first volume, the fourth is a quest for Harry as the epic hero; yet it's also the only series book with tropes of an epistolary novel. And as an adventure story, it features three extraordinary competitions: the Quidditch World Cup, the Triwizard Tournament, and the wizard duel between Harry Potter and a re-embodied Voldemort.

The book is long, and the scope is expansive. Character additions abound. In their initial appearances as major figures are Ludovic "Ludo" Bagman, Bartemius "Barty" Crouch (Senior and Junior), Fleur Delacour, Aberforth Dumbledore, Arabella Doreen Figg, Hogwarts Professor Wilhelmina Grubbly-Plank, Igor Karkaroff, Viktor Krum, Bellatrix Black Lestrange, Madame Olympe Maxime, Alastor "Mad-Eye" Moody, Nagini, Narcissa Malfoy, Rita Skeeter, and Winky. For the first time, Harry and his friends learn in detail about the Ministry of Magic, and they knowingly encounter Death Eaters. Harry learns about the Dark Mark, the Pensieve, Priori Incantatem, the Unforgivable Curses, and Veritaserum. The new DADA teacher is Barty Crouch Jr., impersonating Mad-Eye Moody. The new murder victims are Frank Bryce, Barty Crouch Sr., and Cedric Diggory. But by book's end, the big news *should* be that Voldemort is back, bodily and politically. Already, however, denial and cover-up are rampant in the Ministry and beyond.

Most major kinds of Potter politics surface significantly in this book, as in those to come. By far, though, this is the book with the most direct and detailed attention to nationalism as a set of political movements. Two other political movements pervade the Potter series without focal development in any particular book, so the consideration of nationalism provides a good context to articulate Potter takes on environmentalism and feminism as well. Movements typically work against what they experience as corrupt systems of society, which is why they emphasize styles of everyday action along with governmental policies. For all three movements, *Goblet of Fire* starts to show the heroic trio of Harry, Ron, and Hermione two political truths about such social systems, especially the corrupt systems that concern existentialists. One hard truth is that, when you're inside a corrupt system, it's hard to recognize it as corrupt or even as a system. The other is that, when you're inside a corrupt system, the corruption is inside you too. This is evident in several of Harry's magical moves at the end when traversing—and escaping—the hedge maze.

NATIONALISM

Through Book 3, the Potter series has treated Hogwarts as a boarding school with four "houses" that reach back a thousand years to the school's founders. House allegiance and spirit often seem more valid—and certainly more significant in the everyday lives of students—than school loyalty and spirit. (Recall that the school song is less a hymn to Hogwarts solidarity and pride than a satire of school sentimentality.) Book 4 shifts perspectives to spotlight the school as a whole. It contrasts Hogwarts as a British institution to the MOM and the *Daily Prophet*. It also has Hogwarts cooperate and compete internationally with two other European schools of magic: the Beauxbatons Academy and the Durmstrang Institute. This helps us see the Hogwarts Houses in a new light. Like factions, they often seem to fracture the school into antagonistic fragments. By the next book, the annual song of the Sorting Hat is a unity plea for a school riven by conflicts (V.209, 223; VI.163). These extend all the way to the Battle of Hogwarts, when Horace Slughorn as the head of Slytherin House finally stands fully with the school in following the lead of Minerva McGonagall to contest the violent takeover by Voldemort's forces. Hogwarts houses thus become metonyms of nationalist politics. This happens with Hogwarts as a whole in regard to Beauxbatons and Durmstrang. It arises with the MOM in negotiation with other countries, the sport of Quidditch in connection with its World Cup, the Triwizard Tournament, even Hagrid's skrewts. All help Book 4 explore several aspects of nationalism.

Nationalist politics are movements to premise a country's ruling arrangements on the shared beliefs and experiences that identify a distinct people. Most individuals are (taken to be) initiated into these beliefs and experiences beginning at birth, at *nativity*: hence the concepts of *nation* and *native*. (*Nationalism* sometimes gets used as a synonym for *racism*, as in recent talk of "white nationalism." Pottery instead treats mages, muggles, centaurs, and such as its "races," and not as nations.) Individuals not born into a nation can later become "naturalized" members, revealing that nations or peoples often get treated as given by a nature more basic than politics. Nationalism is generally taken to start with the French Revolution.[1] The notion is usually that nationality is a natural given from ethnic bloodlines; common languages, religions, or histories; even territorial traditions. Since none is exactly "natural," nationalists typically root them in the distant past. (As arguably "the first new nation," the United States sidesteps such troubles by grounding its nation in a shared creed evoked by its Declaration of Independence.[2]) From myth and history, many nationalists claim events and individuals as holidays and heroes, in celebrating them as sources of national liberation or self-rule. To bolster the sense of nationhood, some even create "relics" and "rituals" said to bless current ambitions with earlier sacrifices and victories.[3]

Nationalist politics usually start in resistance to exploitation and oppression that promote denigrating identities for dispossessed groups. (What does the Potter saga imply by focusing this on goblin rebellions as well as mage movements?) Nationalists try to turn the identities positive, encouraging group members to take pride in who they are and can become. Nationalists promote sharing the work of consolidating a group as a full-fledged community and empowering it to rule members' lives. To develop national identity, community, and power involves lots of boosterism and sometimes bloodshed. Sustained success seems to risk chauvinism, colonialism, nativism, racism, and xenophobia: in a phrase, fear and hatred of the (Cultural) Other. Notwithstanding idealist *and* realist talk of "national self-determination," notions of one nation per country (and vice versa) are seldom even approximated in practice—short of genocide or ethnic cleansing. Hence patriotism as allegiance to country is not exactly the same as nationalism.

The fourth book offers templates for nationalism. Earliest is the Quidditch World Cup. Harry and his friends travel by portkey to watch the Irish national team play the Bulgarian national team. The book seems to compare several ties, each ranging from strong to weak, good to bad, important to negligible. Harry and Ron have come to love the sport as a game of skills, strategies, and tactics. This might evoke a love of realist-and-idealist, rather than nationalist politics; and the book respects it. In stark contrast, many fans are rabid partisans of one team or the other. That's more like nationalism, and the book portrays it as readily going overboard. Still Harry and Ron cheer for Ireland but not with the full-hearted, full-throated passion of over-the-top fans. The book is much warmer about them as moderate partisans, open to appreciating the other team and its players too.

Hermione is like others in enjoying the competition as entertainment and the displays as spectacle. These include the national anthems, the veela and leprechaun mascots, the flags and hats, the rosettes and scarves, the rainbows and fireworks, the false gold and sexy dancing. They also include the attires and rites of fans as they camp out before and after the match: reminiscent of tailgating for an American football game. These are the kinds of paraphernalia and rituals that feed into and flow from nationalist politics. The book touts their color and energy; but it finds them fake, seductive, insubstantial, and ephemeral: not exactly an endorsement. As spectacle, nationalist politics often seem to need omniocular replay for full appreciation. Changing speeds, reversing directions, switching angles, diagramming moves, adding narration or commentary as desired: these might be perspectives that historical analysis and fictional rehearsal can provide. Yet perfectionists like Harry might do better immersed in the current flow of events (IV.106–7).

Ron joins the twins in idolizing the Bulgarian seeker Viktor Krum for his talent and style. Nations, like sports, cultivate stars, models, heroes, goddesses, and more. The book is favorable about Krum as a player and person. But it's less positive about Ron's inconstant hero worship, and it adds the animated figurine of Krum as a display item to satirize this (IV.93, 444). The Potter concern seems to be that nationalist celebration of founders, liberators, and fighters can become the ambivalent celebrity politics that loom large in populism, or even turn into fascism.

As memorable as any of those possible angles on nationalism, though, is the gathering's awful end in Death Eaters trashing campsites and terrorizing muggles. Such a rampage might present itself as a kind of lark, as though it's a rambunctious party turned vicious. Yet it's even more organized and sinister than that, evoking planned episodes of soccer hooliganism in Britain and beyond. But it also recalls Krystal Nacht in Germany, Ku Klux Klan marches in the United States, and other street violence meant to intimidate opponents and undermine governments. It certainly does confound the MOM under Cornelius Fudge (IV.145–54). Moreover the Dark Mark shows how ominous nationalist symbols and displays can be (IV.119, 141–3).

Book 4's shifts in perspective offer the Hogwarts Houses, and not just their Quidditch teams, as a second template for nationalist politics. Quidditch contests between houses do bring out some of the worst fervor and favoritism that Pottery implies to characterize nationalism too (V.574; VI.520). Yet house antagonisms reach far beyond overt competitions for the House Cup or the annual Quidditch championship at Hogwarts. A vivid example is the despicable treatment by Slytherin Snape of Gryffindor Granger when she's hit by a Slytherin curse that augments her already prominent front teeth (IV.300). Similarly Hufflepuffs shun Harry as a Gryffindor hog of Hufflepuff glory when Harry joins Cedric Diggory as a fourth Triwizard champion (IV.293). On the other hand, each house offers its members a nurturing sense of belonging and an empowering sense of community. Nations arguably do the same. (The ancient principle of western politics, going back at least to the Greeks, is that there's no significant inclusion without some exclusion.)

Even liberals concede that community ties are crucial for individual development and that many ties must form too early for young people to make well-informed choices of membership. Articulate nationalists of the last two centuries include lots of liberals, who think that choosing nations or countries should be an adult right. Even for adults, such a choice is widely agreed to be existential(ist), with reasons never entirely decisive, so that leaps are inevitable. Yet it's also clear that people need community ties to grow into good choosers, and that early nationality can influence any later choice among nations. Dumbledore promotes a liberal regime for Hogwarts, and he knows with Harry that the Sorting Hat respects house choices by students (VII.758). That is, the hat takes them into account but doesn't always defer to them. That's because it can detect aspects of who students are and what they think which exceed what they might "say" to the hat. When Dumbledore wonders aloud if Hogwarts sorts students at too early an age, he's doubting that even features formed at the front edge of adulthood can be sufficient for assigning houses (VII.680). Can nationality ever run "deeper" than culture and choice? Can birth ever decide it?

Hogwarts Houses highlight another peril of nationalist politics. Both are foundationalist. They generate pride and power from senses of continuity with their founders and foundations. These provide authority, direction, and inspiration for the community, which cultivates traditions to keep alive that heritage. As the Sorting Hat sings, Godric Gryffindor encourages members of his house to pursue republican politics of bravery and chivalry. Helga Hufflepuff urges hers to practice the democratic politics of equality and loyalty. Rowena Ravenclaw teaches hers to promote the liberal politics of intellect and learning. And Salazar Slytherin spurs his to perfect the realist politics of ambition and power. Yet fundamental troubles are hard to overcome. The Slytherin vision of perfection as the exclusive primacy of the pure in magical blood stains and terrorizes Hogwarts for the thousand years until Harry defeats Voldemort, *if* it ends then. Such racism is closely akin to the original sin of slavery that has bedeviled nationalism in the United States from its founding to the present. Even the advantageous diversity of Hogwarts founders and houses seems susceptible at times to antagonism unto schism. Whether England, (Northern) Ireland, Scotland, and Wales can stay a United Kingdom is likewise at least an intermittent (and possibly a continuing) question, largely due to the several nationalisms contending on this stage.

The Triwizard Tournament is a competition to encourage international cooperation. The international Olympics begun at the end of the nineteenth century is a likely model. With three participating schools, the implications for nationalism reinforce those of the Hogwarts houses. And further aspects of the tournament suggest additional dynamics of nationalist politics. Like the Olympics, Triwizard judging of competitor performances is often somewhat nationalist and sometimes outrageously so. Igor Karkaroff's abysmal scores for Harry are examples, sadly not much exaggerated from the "real life" Olympics. (Compare Snape deducting House Cup points from Gryffindor at almost every opportunity.) "Moody" tells Harry that cheating is traditional for Triwizard (and Olympic?) competitions (IV.343). Everybody knows that everybody does it. Thus would Crouch Jr. "welcome" Harry and his friends to the real(ist) world. Notice how the Potter series turns this into a more ideal(ist) politics of helping others and being helped yourself.

Of course, the notion of international cooperation is nearly intrinsic to nationalism. Key challenges of economy, ecology, culture, communication, and so on cross national boundaries and can have scant hope of adequate response without international and transnational politics becoming effective. Yet a downside of nationalism is how difficult it can make the needed collaborations. As it should, a magical Goblet of Fire selects a student to champion each school. To the surprise of everybody but unknown saboteurs, the Goblet then adds Harry as a fourth champion, although he's under-age. This is just the first of many complications that often have people angry, on the brink of withdrawing in protest, then trashing the rules for competing and judging. Cooperation among or across nations is often difficult because nationalism cultivates differences in allegiance and outlook, histories of antagonism and distrust, plus contrasts in experience and expectation.

The next notable event is the press opportunity for photographs and interviews with the champions. Book 4 boils this down to Rita Skeeter of the *Daily Prophet* using a closet and a Quick-Quotes Quill to turn a virtual abduction of Harry into exactly the story she thinks readers want, regardless of what Harry says. The satire of journalism has bite, but the larger point is that nationalist politics depend on press attention and promotion. The United States becomes the first nation of a modern kind in important part because it multiplies newspapers like mad—and soon follows them with all sorts of electronic media. Nationalist politics must "build" nations, which requires communication media that influence and nationalize individuals throughout a territory.

By this century, though, the same dynamics of communication (including transportation) reach past nations and states as the west has known them to globalize culture, economy, politics, and more. Globalization is not exactly the same as internationalization, which typically respects boundaries of nations and states as it increases transactions between them. In globalized actions, the main actors are seldom nations or states but instead corporations, nongovernmental organizations (NGOs), industries, bioregions (ecologies), universities, scientists or artists or educators or philanthropists, and others.

So far as I can see, nothing in the Potter saga spotlights globalization in a way similar to the Triwizard Tournament's focus on internationalization. On the other hand, the cultural and commercial success of the Potter books themselves can exemplify globalization.

Names imply that the Beauxbatons *Academy* and the Durmstrang *Institute* are "private" boarding schools (in the American sense), but Hogwarts School seems governmentally provided and thus "public." It seems free for any incipiently magical Brit, though there's no requirement to attend. The wide expansion of government-funded education free and usually required for all resident youngsters has been a major nationalizer in many countries. Like the media, the schools impart citizenship skills and information plus national identity and nationalist ideology. "Public" media and schools are crucial to developing national publics, and *Goblet of Fire* recognizes this.

There are glints of nationalist politics throughout the Triwizard tasks. The first is to take a magic egg from a mother dragon (IV.328). Colors of the dragons virtually repeat colors for the Hogwarts Houses, like national colors on flags, banners, clothes, and more (IV.326). Nationalist politics also involve defending the motherland and raiding others. The second task is to rescue a friend held hostage by merpeople deep in the dark lake. Nationalism presents itself as a kind of (generalized) friendship. Harry finds the hostages first, sees that any left by other competitors could drown, and sacrifices his competitive advantage to save Gabrielle Delacour as well as Ron. Nationalism portrays defense of the motherland as heroic sacrifice to defend compatriots. On the other hand, Harry is heroic here rather by the moral standards of individualism or internationalist humanism. The merpeople appreciate his "outstanding moral fiber," as do internationalists like Dumbledore, Madame Maxime, and Percy Weasly; Karkaroff, as a narrow nationalist, does not.

Next in the Triwizard calendar is the Yule Ball. It's not labeled as a competitive "task," even though arranging partners for the evening can seem that way. For Harry, it's daunting; and for Ron, disastrous. Coupling, marriage, family, and reproduction are paradigms of community in various kinds of political thinking, and nationalism is no exception. Much of the fourth book revolves around romance, given Harry's age group; and this fits the fact that nationalist politics come mainly from Romanticism as a nineteenth-century cultural movement centered in Europe. (Romanticism *is* an unusual take on romance.) Moreover the Yule Ball is a dance, with national politics especially attuned to community as a dance-like endeavor of "keeping together in time."[4]

Nationalist riffs on navigating the hedge maze can be too numerous to mention, but let's notice at least a few for this third Triwizard task. Overall a maze is an array of walls that divide people from one another or channel them together, as do nationalist politics. As hedges, walls in this maze can be seen through with considerable effort and passed through with enormous effort, which also evokes nicely the usual boundaries and barriers of nationalism. For Harry, the maze has many dead ends: Does this hold for nationalism in Potter politics? The maze establishes paths of migration for people; and it promotes competition among people, although it does allow for mutual aid and cooperation as exceptions (with Harry and Cedric). All this fits nationalism. In a loose sense, we might even say that the aim of nationalist competition is to claim the center of the international system. But it's not an equal contest, with champions entering through the same opening at different times, even though the Triwizard goal is to claim the centered cup first. It also turns out that "Moody" is "helping" Harry by hindering the competition. Is his surprise reward for winning this nationalist contest a deadly duel with a recently arisen superpower?

Among the many obstacles in the hedge maze is what seems to be the last of Hagrid's blast-ended skrewts. Without approval from the Department for the Regulation and Control of Magical Creatures, Hagrid crosses manticores and fire crabs. He creates a formidable critter for his classes in the Care of Magical Creatures and the Triwizard Tournament. As magical animals, these skrewts are so disagreeable and self-destructive that they satirize the politics of nationalism to the point of absurdity. For starters, they have no mouths. Republicans and populists, who construct "the people" to speak might argue by contrast that nations can't or don't speak for themselves. Leaders might try to speak for a nation, but it still moves forcefully on its own. Like nations, skrewts rely mostly on versions of force, not talk. All get massive and muscular to pull and push people around. All blast fire from (both) their ends. Early inspection leads Hagrid to guess that males have stingers and females have suckers. (He takes the suckers to be for blood: more vampirism?) But later, the remaining skrewts have both. Nationalist wars and insurrections sting and blast and burn to take blood from combatants and bystanders. Hagrid doesn't find food for skrewts; yet they grow large, strong, willful, and driven to attack any other skrewts. They seem to lack eyes and heads. They cover all but their undersides in thick, shiny, gray shells that repel magical spells. Yet skrewts are irritable and easily provoked. Harry sees them overpower efforts to control them, then drag would-be controllers behind, just as militant nations might drag their members to war. In the maze, Harry survives the skrewt by impulsively firing a spell at its underbelly even as it knocks and runs him over. The spell stops the skrewt for a moment, and Harry scrambles onward before it recovers (IV.625–6). To see nations as skrewts is *not* to get a pretty picture of nationalism.

To progress to the center of the maze, Harry needs to risk a riddle from a sphinx. (That this sphinx joins the head of a woman to the body of a lion is an intriguing twist on Gryffindor symbolism.) If the sphinx itself symbolizes nationalism, it evokes the Romantic idea of nations as rooted deeper in cultural and historical mysteries than modern rationality can fathom. As an icon of ancient Egypt, a sphinx can relate that way to western civilization. Egyptian theocracy forms long before the Greek polis, and remains a riddle of endurance for millennia prior to the Greeks. According to the fable formula, the sphinx offers Harry peaceful passage in exchange for the right answer to a riddle; but if Harry answers incorrectly, the sphinx will attack. These terms elicit from Harry the skill and trickery celebrated for the Greek Odysseus as "the man of many turns," for Harry realizes that a riddle too hard for him to solve still lets him stay silent and run away without an attack. Hence Harry can hear the riddle before he decides to risk an answer.

As the riddle breaks it into parts, the answer is what's revealing about nationalist politics. The first part invokes the realist politics of the *spy* as a dealer in secrets, lies, and disguise. The second supplies a middle letter of *d*, and the third a hesitant ending of *er*. What wouldn't Harry want to *kiss*? He sounds out the answer as *spider*, whereupon an acromantula drops down to go after Harry and Cedric. Again spells must be cast at the underbelly, this time together. Spiders are a political motif throughout Potter books. Harry lives with spiders in his cupboard. Hagrid keeps Aragog in a cupboard; later his offspring face Harry and Ron. Hogwarts spiders flee the basilisk. Snape is said to move like a spider, and Ron says that he fears spiders for the way they move. Voldemort's hand is spiderlike. Aberforth Dumbledore's grimy glasses reflect light like Aragog's blind, white eyes. Harry visualizes Horace Slughorn as a big spider with a huge web of patronage connections. After recruiting Slughorn, Harry and Albus Dumbledore confer in a Weasley broomstick shed, with spiders dropping all around. And so on and on. Spiders weave webs; they make connections, and those collect more connectors. With a large family that feels as though it has ties all over the place, Ron probably recoils from spiders also for symbolizing networks that threaten to entrap him. But regardless of Ron's psychology, the Potter books use spiders to suggest communities as networks of connections. And as the riddle of the sphinx can imply, "spyders" make good figures for the realist politics of community in national and international relations. For all the Romanticism in its symbolism of personal and communal identity, nationalism weaves its political webs with a realist sensibility. The Potter implication may well be that nationalism is a realist Romanticism and a Romantic realism: possibly a helpful insight.

Most movements are too diverse in principles and policies to ascribe much of a common creed for their different skeins. Nationalism makes this easy to see, since a key point of Scottish nationalism is its contrast to English, Irish, Welsh, or any other nationalism. Each nationalism is a celebration of the supposedly distinctive (if not always unique) virtues of its nation—mainly its culture and maybe its government. Every nationalism is so specific to its nation, by contrast with others, that only the American turn to focusing on creed rather than culture can make meaningful the oxymoronic possibility of a multicultural nationalism. A multicultural *country*? That's easy: most countries are multicultural. A multicultural *nation*? This is much harder, without melding the multiple cultures into one, and this parallels the challenge for Hogwarts School in trying to hold onto highly distinct houses that compete (rather than war) with each other. A "multicultural nationalism," however, would feature virtues of multiculturalism shared by diverse cultures; and the specification of those virtues seems likely to yield what we'd usually label as a "creed."

ENVIRONMENTALISM

Therefore most movements cohere principally in what they oppose. Nationalists of most stripes reject colonial or imperial rule by what they see as foreign powers. Environmentalists of most kinds attack unchecked *industrialism*. They see it as using modern science and technology to dominate and control *nature*. This natural *environment* is *the world apart from humans*, who take themselves as entitled to use it however they want. Yet their industrial uses destroy nature, as the ecological systems of planet Earth, *and* humanity—which depends on these environments. Some "greens," as environmentalists call themselves, trace efforts to subdue and destroy nature to the start of western civilization; others to the emergence of *homo sapiens*, even hominids. But all treat industrialization as revving any preexisting troubles to eventually unsustainable levels. Mass production means that people suffer the inverted values of materialism and consumerism, but next down the road, due to mass destruction of the environment, is civilizational collapse.[5]

Most ideologies of politics or economics develop green versions. Eco-conservatives try to conserve scarce resources and preserve wilderness. Eco-capitalists seek sustainable growth. Eco-liberals do the same or explore alternatives to growth or promote animal rights. To these projects, eco-socialists add expanding community deliberations to include externalities, listening to voices for other species, plus redistributing environmental helps and harms. Eco-anarchists experiment with voluntary cooperation as better for green responsibility than any government can be. Eco-authoritarians see green troubles as so urgent and resistant to needed coordination that only strongly centralized powers can reign in the self-interested individuals and institutions that otherwise will continue to trash the planet.

Recent movements show even greater variety, and *some* of their green projects are more radical. Eco-populists attempt to redress the distributive *injustice* of wilderness access, pollution imposition, and other green concerns. Eco-republicans promote public and private stewardship of the land, air, and water, especially in agriculture and (sub)urban development. Back-to-nature advocates mix primitivist, reactionist, romantic, and survivalist politics to live lightly on the land by reviving (or inventing?) earlier lifestyles: frontier, hermetic, Neolithic, Paleolithic, pastoral, and so on. Eco-feminists emphasize links between the western domination and control of nature on the one hand and the western domination and control of women on the other. Thus they see the two conjoined oppressions and exploitations taking terrible turns for the worse with modern industry, science, and technology.[6] In fact, a likely implication of most eco-feminism, like much environmentalism overall, is that decent action on troubles of industrialism and patriarchy—as rule by fathers in particular or men in general—must lead people beyond the modern West.[7]

For greens, a big liability of industrialism is its mechanistic mindset, which struggles to understand living systems that range from organisms to ecologies. Either modern sciences and technologies don't grasp systematicity at all or they only want linear, mechanical systems with fully independent and replaceable parts. Helpful as this perspective can be for many settings, it misses the strong, sensitive interdependence of ecosystems. Their organizations and operations are nonlinear; in mathematical senses, they are fractal and chaotic.[8] They flow and grow and tip abruptly from one phase to another; they reproduce and wither and die, or recover or relocate or mutate. (Movements do too.) Greens warn about the loss of biodiversity; the gross violation of rights for animals, plants, and even places; and the alteration of humans by new chemicals in their environments. Catastrophes in the making are argued to include rampant cancer, global climate change, overpopulation, pandemic, pollution, radioactive contamination, resource depletion, soil erosion, species extinction, and wilderness elimination. They also involve energy exhaustion, habitat destruction (coral reefs, icecaps, rainforests, tundra), medicine resistance, and rising sea levels. Yet the crucial challenge for greens is the pervasive interconnection of these troubles.

The only times that the Potter saga even hints literally at any of these green troubles is at the beginning of Book 6. Its second chapter starts by evoking Spinner's End as a rundown mill town, and this can amount to a quick nod at industrial decline. The weather is unseasonably cold and misty. Fudge says in the first chapter that this probably results from breeding by dementors who've defected to Voldemort. The collapse of the Brockdale Bridge from a "freak hurricane" likely traces instead to giant activity related to Voldemort. Talk about strange and destructive weather is as close as the series comes to addressing global climate change. Still it's telling that this is part of an inventory of troubles in our times that Fudge sees as interconnected (VI.1–14). Here is the key principle of environmental politics: as greens often say, "It's all connected."[9]

The two kinds of green politics that loom largest figurally in the Potter books are deep ecology and eco-feminism. Deep ecology demands respect for the "intrinsic value" of each kind, creature, and thing.[10] To borrow from Immanuel Kant's liberal morality, we could say that deep ecology aspires to treat every living thing (not just every human) as a member of the Kingdom of (Ultimate) Ends. No beings are (to be treated as) mere means; none have only "use value." This is what Draco Malfoy doesn't appreciate about blast-ended skrewts or anything else (IV.196). It involves acting toward individual creatures in terms of their kinds as well as their situations, in accordance with Rubeus Hagrid's perspectivism. Hagrid loves creatures in themselves, aside from their human or other uses; and he appreciates individual creatures in relation to their kinds. Turning on the spot to leap, apparating revs realism into perfectionism; similarly perspectivism revs Aristotelian taxonomy toward the deep ecology of intrinsic value. And just as Nietzschean perfectionism might leap beyond what is "human, all too human," Hagrid's ecological kind-ness may leave behind the arrogance of humanism.[11] Akin to Mother Earth or Mother Nature, Hagrid would teach an ethic of care for all creatures: the large, the small, and the monsters among them.

There are many kinds of creatures in the Potter series. Its inventive profusion of fantasy plants and animals comes with considerable elaboration on most species, and the prequel films focus on "Newt" Scamander as a magizoologist to provide further kinds and information.[12] We get a green view of Harry's world, because Newt collects creatures as nifflers collect treasures. The temptation is to say these magical plants are animated, the magical animals are sentient, and the magical sentients are anthropomorphized. Potter magic raises each a level, we might say. In our world, however, plants are more animated than we've often recognized. Animals are more intelligent and communicative than we've sometimes acknowledged. And humans are more diverse than we've often appreciated. Maybe it's better to say that Potter plants do more than (some of) ours, Potter animals seem more self-aware and sophisticated than (many of) ours, and Potter sentients symbolize that humans have greater variety and potential than we often realize.

We do better still to notice how Potter creatures cross and confound any such "levels," which in itself can be a green lesson for politics. Are magical plants such as devil's snare and venomous tentacula any less dangerous or even malevolent than magical animals like grindylows and basilisks (I.277–8; V.512, 580)? Are acromantulas, hippogriffs, and phoenixes "animals" or "sentients"? If we answer categorically, we might say "animals." Yet if we think of Aragog, Buckbeak, or Fawkes, we might say "sentients." Doesn't the Potter series contest any general elevation of mages over muggles, or vice versa, as well as any elevation of mages over centaurs, giants, goblins, house-elves, leprechauns, merpeople, veela, or others? It differentiates these in many directions, but it doesn't regiment the differences to imply a hierarchy for respect or rule. Radical greens argue likewise for ecocentric, rather than anthropocentric, biologies and polities. Interconnection and interaction claim attention more than a prime mover or a keystone species. Some greens spotlight "animal trials" in medieval Europe as giving all—or at least more—of God's creatures their rights through days in court: by having an advocate argue for the interests of locusts infesting a field, in order to get judicial authorization to drive them out.[13] Locusts too must eat, after all, and hence have claims for consideration. Buckbeak's trial for attacking Draco seems equally *pro forma*, but the form does acknowledge rights for Buckbeak (III.219–22, 290).

Potter magic even makes some implements into sentients. To say with Ollivander and others that "the wand chooses the wizard" is to acknowledge capacities of intelligence and self-direction sufficient for choice (I.85). The struggles of several mages with broken and temporary wands extend to the end of the series. The surprising action taken by Harry's wand emphasizes its sentience (VII.61, 83), as does his healing of it (VII.748). The horcruxes might be set aside as special cases of infusing Voldemort's sentience into magical objects. But it's clear from Arthur Weasley's warning against magical objects with unseen "brains" that others show sentience too (II.329). In fact, Arthur's own flying car could be said to develop "a mind of its own" in racing away into the Forbidden Forest (II.75, 279–80). It's specifically said to be "running wild," and some greens would applaud its escape from human control as the kind of "wilding" needed by much more of our world (IV.41). Of late, the "animism" prominent in fantasies with magic has become a significant resource for exploring green possibilities and perspectives.

If we recognize house-elves as an admiring Potter caricature of housewives, we can appreciate Hermione's campaign to liberate them from at least three angles. It examines the liberal condemnation of slavery. It explores the liberal and nationalist politics of liberating oppressed groups or peoples. Yet it also evokes the eco-feminist rejection of how arrogant humans, especially men, degrade and exploit other species. Then the eco-feminist "ethics of care" share much with the "land ethic" of Aldo Leopold.[14] Moreover the green injunctions to "think like a mountain" and "think like a carrot" help show in detail how ethics of care, whether green or feminist, rely on Hagrid's perspectivist politics of kind-ness.[15] Perhaps ironically, it's George Weasley who basically urges Hermione to think like house-elves before she acts further in their name (IV.239).

FEMINISM

Given a Rowling ambition to interest boys in reading, the Potter attention to Harry and Ron makes sense. Then Hermione, Ginny, and Luna become the key figures for feminist politics in the series.[16] From the nineteenth century on, feminists have come in waves, and a current map of feminist politics would resemble the great array of green politics. Most political ideologies and movements include feminist projects, while several forms of feminism even reach beyond the usual bounds of western politics. All oppose patriarchy and sexism for disadvantaging and often abusing some people simply on the basis of their sex (as biological) or gender (as cultural). Indeed many feminists see both as constructions rather than givens. All oppose keeping women from full participation in "public" life by confining them to "private" activity in the household. And contrary to most western politics, all feminists recognize that "the personal is the political." Hence they emphasize the politics of everyday life as much or more than the official politics of elections, governments, laws, and policies. The Potter series pursues these everyday concerns.[17]

Hermione opposes stereotyping women, especially by character and role (VII.293). It's arguable that the series as a whole does the same. The main kinds of exceptions would be some playful moments of humor (VII.120) and some accommodation of current realities to fit Harry's world of magic into our own, with its considerable sexism. For instance, the main households we see have stay-at-home mothers: Petunia Dursley, Molly Weasley, Mrs. Crouch, and Narcissa Malfoy. On the other hand, Hermione's mother and father are dentists. There are many witches in the Order of the Phoenix and Dumbledore's Army as quasi-military organizations for resisting Voldemort. Quidditch as the premier sport for mages is open to witches at every posi-tion—and gets them, including professionally (VII.115). When the heroic trio expands to six, as it does at times in the last three books, half of its members are female: Hermione plus Luna Lovegood and Ginny Weasley (as well as Neville Longbottom). Hogwarts School has four founders, two of them witches. When Dumbledore is temporarily gone from Hogwarts, his replacements as head are witches: Minerva McGonagall and (ugh!) Dolores Umbridge. Even Voldemort has a female shadow (or anima) in Nagini, a maledictus become a full-time snake. Hermione objects strongly to pronouns that presume unknown achievers to be males. Repeatedly she reprimands Harry for speaking as though the Half-Blood Prince must be male (VI.637), and she corrects Ron when he carelessly refers to the mysterious R.A.B., who took the locket horcrux, as "he" (VII.101).

As another matter of everyday life, feminists lambaste the degradation of women to "sex objects." This has its main satirical moment in the dis-parate reactions of Harry and Ron versus Hermione to the veela dancing as Bulgarian mascots at the World Quidditch Cup (IV.103–4). At the Burrow, Weasley women join Hermione in disgust at the males' responses to Fleur Delacour as Bill's part-veela fiancée (VI.90–2, 103–4). Eventually Harry does see the dancing veela as the seductive harpies they can be (IV.111); and readers get to see the Delacours as good people, the dazzling mother and daughters included. The saga presents lots of gentle stereotype-skewering and consciousness-raising of this sort. While Hermione enjoys a couple of cosmetic makeovers (IV.405, 414), there are many powerful women warriors at the Battle of Hogwarts.

Pottery also plays with basic (crude?) sexual symbolism. There is coy, quiet recognition that a wand is a figural penis and a cauldron is a figural womb. (And third in the Potter order of importance would be the flying broomstick: enough said.) If there's any doubt that readers are intended to notice these meanings, look at the ribald lyrics for a song by Celestina Warbeck, the favorite singer of Molly Weasley (VI.330). These are the two main implements for doing magic at Hogwarts, but doesn't the series attend more to wands than cauldrons? Again this might be expected in books more for boys. Yet cauldrons are mentioned in every book, and they appear earlier than wands. This is not only because getting to Diagon Alley for supplies takes Hagrid and Harry through the Leaky Cauldron (I.68), but also because Harry sees cauldrons of all sizes and many materials for sale well before he gets to Ollivander's to buy a wand (I.71). For Harry's first, second, fifth, and sixth years, his Hogwarts coursework focuses on Potions, with its focus in turn on cauldrons (I.136–7). For Harry, DADA is a dud under Quirrell, Lockhart, and Umbridge; whereas Harry's nemesis, Snape, makes Potions one miserably memorable class after another in Harry's first five years. Then the textbook annotated by the Half-Blood Prince turns Harry's last course on Potions into a lark under Slughorn, while Snape shifts to tormenting Harry in DADA. Percy Weasley's first post at the MOM negotiates standards for cauldron thickness (IV.56), and the last test in Harry's first year at Hogwarts covers self-stirring cauldrons (I.263). Most ominous is the huge stone cauldron in the graveyard for rebirthing Voldemort (IV.636–43).

Some feminists show impatience with women whose top priorities include mothering children and managing a household, especially one with a heteronormative nuclear family. The Potter series reads differently. Mothers are treated with respect and admiration in Potter books. Yes, there are mothers who go overboard in doting on some children at the expense of others—or even at the expense of the spoiled ones: Dudley Dursley's mother and Regulus Black's come to mind. But even they seem appreciated for the love and self-sacrifice, however unwise, which go to their favored offspring. It's unclear whether that holds for Eileen Prince, the mother of Severus Snape. It definitely doesn't for Fridwulfa, the giantess mother of Hagrid; but her lack of maternal effort is excused as natural for her species (IV.427–8). In addition to the home-based mothers mentioned, the series seems to esteem the mothers of Susan Bones; Maisie, Ellie, and Alfred Cattermole; the Dumbledore brothers and sister; Seamus Finnigan; Frank

Longbottom; Neville Longbottom; Luna Lovegood; Teddy Lupin; Harry Potter; Albus, James, and Lily Potter; Tom Riddle; Nymphadora Tonks; Rose and Hugo Granger Weasley; and Victoire Weasley. The affection for mothers extends to Hagrid, who might be the main mother figure in the series: for Harry Potter and another magical creature (VII.145). Is this a feminist twist? Harry does get a third mother in Molly Weasley (IV.714). Even Dobby tries to (over)mother Harry.

This brings us to house-elves as housewives. Surely Winky continues to care for the two Bartys when Mrs. Crouch has died. But the case for this per-spective is far larger—taking in the loves, loyalties, powers, prides, responsi-bilities, and skills of house-elves *and* housewives. The possible identification plays both ways, as satire often does. It slams the virtual enslavement of many housewives, even as it chides the feminists or other critics who find no genuine virtues or joys in mothering and homemaking. In this context, Hermione's campaign to free house-elves—who mostly feel enriched and exalted rather than enslaved and degraded in their self-sacrificing care for others—dramatizes real tensions between movements to liberate women and the women meant to benefit. Hermione fails to recognize how unusual Dobby *might* be as a free elf. Still her direct-action devices are familiar from many movements, and Potter books have gentle fun with the mismatches to house-elf and housewife situations. Winky's misery and decline is much less a laughing matter (IV.383, 537; V.385). Hermione is right to insist on personal kindness for Kreacher too, yet she doesn't achieve all that much sense of his perspectives (V.832; VII.198).

Hermione's campaign to liberate house-elves raises questions of whether it's defensible or even conceivable for individuals and peoples to enslave themselves "voluntarily." Her work also provokes informative arguments over whether and how it can be permissible, desirable, or even possible to free others. However necessary help might also be, must people still liber-ate themselves? The political symbolism in house-elves wearing pillowcases when enslaved is not hard to parse. Beyond leaving that behind, however, what's the political symbolism in a gift of clothing as the house-elf ticket or consignment to freedom? What might it mean that Hermione seemingly for-gets that the gift must come from the head of the house to be liberating? And what are the implications of the fact that house-elves do magic different and sometimes more powerful than do the wizards and witches who command them? In the end, though, perhaps Hermione's feminist politicking—on her own and with others, including Harry—should be seen in terms of the last two glimpses of Kreacher: leading house-elves in the defense of Hogwarts against the forces of Voldemort (VII.734–5) and imagined by Harry as bringing him a sandwich (VII.749).

TRAVERSING THE HEDGE MAZE

The third task for the Triwizard Cup is a hedge maze. This labyrinth includes many tests of skill, character, and invention. First champion to touch the hidden Cup wins. It's yet another obstacle course for Harry—but with a concealed, sinister difference. When the four contestants prepare to enter the maze, none knows that it functions as a corrupt system.

It's a system, more than a task. It enfolds then encloses the champions in a regime of competitions for personal, institutional, and national distinction that permeates their cultures, economies, societies, polities, even psychologies. Arthur Weasley doesn't seem to like the mage system a whole lot, and he apologizes for it at the Quidditch World Cup; yet (he knows) he still participates in it (I.79). For their time in the hedge maze, and even the Triwizard Tournament, this regime would configure what the four young mages experience, how they act, even who they are. Thus the hedge maze is an emblem of the Triwizard Tournament, which is a metonym of the competitors' school lives, which is a minor-league version of the magical society that these four mages are entering—certainly in Europe and possibly worldwide. The regimes are nested, with each a figure of the others and networked to feed into the others. Each level's activities validate and reproduce themselves, but they also serve the self-similar activities on the other levels. This is how the hedge maze is (in itself) a nonlinear system *and* simultaneously is the school system in symbol and the societal system in miniature.

Harry's version of the tournament is configured so that the mage who completes the maze and grasps the Triwizard Cup wins not only the third task but the tournament overall. In turn, the winner of a Triwizard Tournament can expect enduring celebration that resounds throughout the magical society and its history. Proclaims the fourth film's Dumbledore to everybody assembled for the opening banquet, "Eternal glory: that is what awaits the student who wins the Triwizard Tournament."[18] The book includes impressive prize money too (IV.187–8). Many students seem wary of the Triwizard dangers, but they're already so much parts of the magical society that most are attracted to the Triwizard riches and acclaim.

Does this just systematize the perfectionist excelling that earlier chapters spot in Harry's political action? No. For one thing, Harry's sort of perfectionism is personal and anti-system, overlapping existentialism in this respect. For another, Harry's perfectionism is individual and anti-competitive, even anti-comparative. Inheritance has left Harry uninterested in accumulating more money, and he keeps learning to rely on self-assessments more than the congratulations or criticisms from others. Harry seldom, if ever, seeks celebrity or glory. Rarely does he *fantasize* about it, and then briefly. Even with winning the Triwizard Cup in prospect, I count only three instances, all shallow and quick (IV.192, 256–7, 264). Instead the maze competition for money, glory, and superiority much more readily epitomizes capitalist, conformist, conservative, liberal, republican, and some socialist systems. The claim is not that interests in wealth, fame, or esteem must corrupt; it's simply that these concerns don't characterize Harry's politics of perfectionism. (Along with racism, power mania, and death terror, these do pervert Voldemort's perfectionism.) The suggestion here is simply that, like the Triwizard Tournament and mage society in Europe, the hedge maze works as a system of competition for glory, wealth, and superiority.

As a system, it's corrupt several times over. Some obstacles play more to Harry's recent experiences than to those of others: the riddle of the sphinx, the acromantula, and arguably the blast-ended skrewt. To insure that Harry wins, "Moody" patrols outside the maze to intervene covertly. He stupefies Fleur and induces Krum to attack Cedric, leading Harry to stupefy Krum. Worse, "Moody" turns the cup into a portkey for apparating Harry to a graveyard for the planned rebirth of Voldemort and death of Harry, thus corrupting the purpose of the competition. Worst, the super-high stakes of this last leg of a once-in-a-lifetime contest for wealth and "eternal glory" can corrupt the conduct and character of the contestants. Is it *designed* to corrupt some, at least to tempt them? After all, only contestants are supposed to be able to see what's happening in the maze. ("Moody" cheats to watch.) And Fudge shows how easy it can be for officials to ignore any unwelcome account of maze events. Indeed the book hints strongly that cut-throat conduct is a danger, even a likelihood (IV.187–8). The film is more explicit, with Dumbledore taking the competitors aside for a final caution before they enter the labyrinth: "In the maze, you'll find no dragons or creatures of the deep. Instead you'll face something even more challenging. You see, people *change* in the maze. Oh, find the cup if you can; but be very wary: you could just lose yourselves along the way."

From inside, systems can be hard to see as such; and corruption can be difficult to detect. But systems encompass and permeate their participants, so that systemic corruption is inside the people inside the systems. When you're in a corrupt system, it's in you. With the cup in sight, even Harry and Cedric feel strong, systemic inclinations to go for it, regardless of their previous virtues (IV.631–5). Yet they communicate first, talking themselves past the temptations and into reaching the cup together. Still the system is corrupt, it turns their teamwork against them, and it delivers them to a fatal ambush beyond Hogwarts and the hedge maze.

That the hedge maze condenses the larger society symbolically as a system is also shown by the particular obstacles and Harry's magical performances in response. Harry prepares for the maze by working specifically on four spells (IV.608). The shield charm seems difficult. Harry's struggles with it link to later success by the Weasley twins with shield cloaks, hats, and gloves

(VI.119). Harry doesn't pause to try it in the maze, and this might be a smart move. In a corrupt system, many people simply can't shield themselves reliably against most depredations. Hence they (must?) turn to more active, even aggressive counter-measures for protection.

Harry uses the reductor curse only twice in the maze. Harry succeeds in making a hole in the hedge to stun the imperiused Viktor and stop his attack on Cedric. In a corrupt system, some specific, concentrated obstacles to good action can be destroyed, at least in small part and for a short time. But Harry fails in trying to destroy or disperse the golden mist that turns him upside-down. Like a mist, a corrupt system is worst for us when it's all around and through us. Then it's too diffuse and enveloping to blast out of the way. (Those more active, aggressive counter-measures don't work.) In running into the mist, Harry is seeking and facing the threat. When it inverts him, Harry soon responds by going dark. To escape, he closes his eyes to shut out the disorienting sights. Then he focuses on stepping (blindly) out of the mist, walking (carefully) as though he were upright (IV.624).

In this connection, it's telling that another move Harry's learned for the maze is the four-point spell. That Harry would face several dead-ends in the maze is what could be expected of an enclosing system—and all the more of a corrupt one. Especially in dealing with cul-de-sacs, the compass spell enables Harry to get oriented, by pointing his wand due north then redoing his route. The spell helps him with going forward-or-back and left-or-right. Yet he's not anticipated a need to navigate up-and-down. Should we say that Harry must learn to play three-dimensional chess? In the maze, he could be said to rely more effectively on inversion than any other move.

We might say that a corrupt system uses inversion a lot too. As with Harry in the mist of the maze, it can throw us for a loop. A corrupt system is in us and of us. Hence it's attuned to our weaknesses, strengths, plans, and preparations. Particularly at crunch time, it can be counted on to surprise us. But in general and almost by definition, a corrupt system is structured to frustrate attempts at resistance. Preparing for the maze as his third task, Harry masters the impediment curse for repelling attacks; and the maze gives him urgent reasons to cast it time and again. Yet it seldom stymies maze attackers, because they're armored to deflect such spells.

As Harry enters it, the maze is darkening at dusk. So he might start to go dark, but soon lights the tip of his wand with *Lumos!* This lets him spot the skrewt and avoid it at first. Calling further on his previous experience, Harry calmly faces an apparent dementor in the maze—and ridicules it away as a boggart. A corrupt system can mobilize our fears against us, so calm and good cheer can keep our responses smart and sustained. Seen from inside, a corrupt system is a menacing riddler. This makes the sphinx a figure for the whole maze, and its resonance, in turn, for the griffin of Gryffindor House signals again the nesting of (corrupt) systems constructed by and for the Triwizard Tournament in Harry's time. Again his experienced composure is crucial to subduing any fight-or-flight impulses, as he figures out what to do (hear the riddle first) then what to say (in answer to the riddle). As already explained, many of Harry's earlier experiences converge on the correct answer in this case: "a spider." Of course, webs spun by spiders, and all the more by giant spiders, make good figures for the vast, sticky networks of corrupt systems.

Were Harry hearing only the gist of the riddle, taking its climactic question to be which creature is Harry *least* willing to kiss, he might leap to "dementor." On careful reflection, the full riddle and maze, with the boggart, might still correct him. Therefore the composure to listen, think, and respond carefully can be all the more important for a perfectionist in facing a corrupt system. Here Harry's attunement to the situation helps by preempting any impulsive leaps.

In the next instant, though, Harry needs that impulse power when an acromantula appears and attacks Cedric. Impediment and stunning charms only turn the spider's attention to Harry. Grabbed by the spider, Harry has the inspiration to cast the disarming spell at it. This makes Harry fall from its clutches, as though he were a wand expelled from a wizard's hand. From the ground, Harry and Cedric then stun the spider from below, aiming their spells at its underbelly. Harry had fallen into doing this earlier, when he'd failed to sidestep the armored skrewt a second time. Then his spells bounced away from its back and sides, it knocked and ran him over, so he desperately cast the impediment spell at its unprotected underside. This stopped the skrewt long enough for Harry to scramble up and away. As strongly armored as they might be, even corrupt systems have soft spots; and the best resistance often comes from below. Subverting the system often requires inverting it or the resisters. But let's not miss that Harry and Cedric only get as far as they do in the maze because they aid and support each other at key moments. Then the cup's corruption into a portkey inverts their victory and perverts their cooperation to serve Voldemort.

NOTES

1. See Ernest Gellner, *Nations and Nationalism* (Ithaca, NY: Cornell University Press, 1983, 2008); Homi K. Bhabha, ed., *Nation and Narration* (New York: Routledge, 1990); E. J. Hobsbawm, *Nations and Nationalism since 1780* (Cambridge: Cambridge University Press, 1990).

2. See Seymour Martin Lipset, *The First New Nation* (New York: Norton, 1973, 1979).

3. See Eric Hobsbawm and Terence Ranger, *The Invention of Tradition* (Cambridge: Cambridge University Press, 1984).

4. See William H. McNeill, *Keeping Together in Time* (Cambridge, MA: Harvard University Press, 1995).

5. See Jared Diamond, *Collapse* (New York: Viking, 2005); Naomi Oreskes and Erik M. Conway, *The Collapse of Western Civilization* (New York: Columbia University Press, 2014).

6. See Carolyn Merchant, *The Death of Nature* (New York: Harper and Row, 1980).

7. See Carolyn Merchant, *Radical Ecology* (New York: Routledge, 1992).

8. See James Gleick, *Chaos* (New York: Viking Press, 1987); N. Katherine Hayles, ed., *Chaos and Order* (Chicago: University of Chicago Press, 1991). For a linear take on the interdependence of ecosystems, see Aldo Leopold, "The Round River," *A Sand County Almanac* (New York: Ballantine, 1949 1953, 1966), 188–202. Also see John S. Nelson, *Politics in Popular Movies* (Boulder: Paradigm, 2015), 31–54.

9. A well-known version of this insistence of interconnectedness is the Gaia Hypothesis that conceives the Earth as a living organism. See James Lovelock, *Gaia* (Oxford: Oxford University Press, fourth edition, 2000).

10. See Bill Devall and George Sessions, *Deep Ecology* (Salt Lake City: Peregrine Smith Books, 1985); Arne Naess, *Ecology, Community, and Lifestyle* (Cambridge: Cambridge University Press, 1989); Warwick Fox, *A Theory of General Ethics* (Cambridge: MA, MIT Press, 2006).

11. See David W. Ehrenfeld, *The Arrogance of Humanism* (Oxford: Oxford University Press, 1978, 1981).

12. See J. K. Rowling as Newt Scamander, *Fantastic Beasts and Where to Find Them* (New York: Scholastic Press, 2001). Also see *Fantastic Beasts and Where to Find Them* (2016) and *Fantastic Beasts: The Crimes of Grindelwald* (2019). And see J. K. Rowling, *Fantastic Beasts and Where to Find Them: The Original Screenplay* (New York: Scholastic Press, 2016); J. K. Rowling, *Fantastic Beasts—The Crimes of Grindelwald* (New York: Scholastic Press, 2018).

13. See Luc Ferry, *The New Ecological Order*, trans. Carol Volk (Chicago: University of Chicago Press, 1992, 1995).

14. See Carolyn Merchant, *Earthcare* (New York: Routledge, 1995); Aldo Leopold, "The Land Ethic," *A Sand County Almanac,* 237–64.

15. See Aldo Leopold, "Thinking Like a Mountain," *A Sand County Almanac,* 137–41; Michael Pollan, "Green Thumb," *Second Nature* New York: Dell, 1991), 139–59.

16. See Christopher E. Bell, ed., *Hermione Granger Saves the World* (Jefferson, NC: McFarland, 2012).

17. See Elizabeth E. Heilman, "Blue Wizards and Pink Witches: Representations of Gender Identity and Power," *Harry Potter's World*, ed. Elizabeth E. Heilman (New York: RoutledgeFalmer, 2003), 221–39; Ximena Gallardo-C. and C. Jason Smith, "Cinderfella: J. K. Rowling's Wily Web of Gender," *Reading Harry Potter*, ed. Giselle Liza Anatol (Westport, CT: Praeger, 2003), 191–205; Leslee Friedman, "Militant Literacy: Hermione Granger, Rita Skeeter, Dolores Umbridge, and the (Mis)use of Text," *Reading Harry Potter Again*, ed. Giselle Liza Anatol (Santa Barbara, CA: ABC-CLIO, 2009), 91–108.

18. *Harry Potter and the Goblet of Fire*, directed by Mike Newell (2006; Burbank, CA: Warner Home Video, 2006), DVD.

Chapter 10

Institutions and the Order
of the Phoenix

The fifth Potter book plumbs the mystery of the unidentified weapon. It tells the tragedy of the courageous and impetuous Sirius Black. It offers horror stories of the monstrous Dolores Umbridge. And it relates adventures that prepare Dumbledore's Army for a final confrontation with Voldemort in the last book's Battle of Hogwarts. It even makes room for Hagrid's tale of finding giants in the mountains—and bringing one back to Hogwarts' dark and forbidden forest.

The unidentified weapon turns out to dwell in the Department of Mysteries within the Ministry of Magic (MOM). Under Cornelius Fudge, the Ministry is becoming an authoritarian regime. When Umbridge as Fudge's assistant takes over the Hogwarts School, decree by decree, she does something similar by pushing it toward bureaucracy. To resist these power grabs, as well as their distraction from the machinations of the Dark Lord and his Death Eaters, Dumbledore and Harry activate distinctively republican institutions of orders and armies. Harry's mercurial resentment and anger as a teenager mimic the passions for a popular uprising, and the DA helps bring down the Umbridge regime. This frees Harry and his friends to rescue Sirius, yet Death Eaters trick and trap them. Then Black's sense of honor brings him to Harry's rescue but Black's own death. Let's focus accordingly on Potter politics of authoritarianism, bureaucratism, and republicanism. Then let's see how such politics construct their histories with contrasting media and principles.

AUTHORITARIANISM

Many political theorists say that the first modern ideology of politics is liberalism, but a different answer deserves respect. Instead liberalism arises partly in reaction to authoritarianism. Thomas Hobbes (1588–1679) as the primary architect of authoritarianism precedes John Locke (1632–1704) as a proto-liberal. Locke implicitly adapts much of Hobbes on politics while trying to limit the tyrannical potential of modern governmental authority as Hobbes articulated it.

Again let's define *ideologies* more or less literally as *logics of ideas*. Modern ideologies of politics are initially inventions of the European Enlightenment; and they often take themselves to be modern sciences of society, with society treated as a complex of ideas. That's why we can conceive these political ideologies as networks of concepts and claims about the construction of communities. It's also why we can characterize ideologies in our everyday practices as families or styles of figures or tropes. And it's why we can spot current social sciences of psychology and political science as stemming from liberalism, sociology from socialism, economics from capitalism, and so on for other disciplines or fields.

Most modern ideologies of politics can be seen as attempts to scientize (systematize) key features of the republican politics that loom large in classical antiquity and medieval feudalism, as well as the code of honor, friendship, loyalty, responsibility, and such that characterizes the heroic trio of Harry, Ron, and Hermione. Hannah Arendt argued that the Roman republicans invented authority; and as the name says, that's the project central to authoritarianism as an ideology. It sees law-and-order as the reason for government, which must centralize power to end a republican penchant for feud-alism or other drives to disorder in the streets. To justify this, Hobbes propounded a Euclidean geometry of politics as a Newtonian science of bodies in motion. The pyramid of Authority can eradicate the chaotic an-archism of continual war in a State of Nature without modern government. Locke sketched an empiricist science of human experience to show how authority and order limited by political representation of citizens can still provide for peace, property, prosperity, and progress. Both Hobbes and Locke treated authorities as author-izing social acts, through writing societal laws. In Latin, *legere* is *to read*; and *legislation* makes rules public, readable, and predictable for the citizens. Tyrants practice martial law as *dictators*, whose ever-changeable *oral* words are "law."

Of course, *the* authority figure for the Hogwarts School and especially the heroic trio is Albus Dumbledore. Clearly he's not absolute as an authority, even institutionally, because the Minister of Magic and the twelve governors of Hogwarts are "over" him as School Headmaster. Likewise he is higher in the Hogwarts pyramid than the teachers, staff, students, and house-elves—in descending order. Chains, ladders, or pyramids of authority are hi(gh)er-archies. We can parse authority structures in terms of who takes orders about what from whom (going down) or who reports on what to whom (going up).

Paramilitary command structures are authority arrangements with commands flowing down and information rising up. But Cornelius Fudge is not an absolute authority either, because he cannot simply order the expulsion of Harry from Hogwarts or even keep himself in office after the events of book five. His authority is limited by the Wizengamot in the first instance and possibly by public (mage) opinion in the second. And limited or not, authority can be *in*formal, coming from charisma, credibility, or trust.

Ideological authoritarians seek to centralize formal authority, so that there is a clear locus of power and responsibility: "The buck stops here," as the sign said on Harry S Truman's desk. Somebody must have the last word to avoid endless contention. With early authoritarians such as Hobbes, however, the authority of the modern state should—indeed could—be absolute only in (merely) formal terms. Neither technologically nor politically could the early authoritarians conceive power that's absolute in practice. Total control, as we might now term it, was neither their concrete ambition nor their abstract thought. They were not even proto-totalitarians.

From time to time, coordination challenges for communities become so severe, so much matters of life and death, that people who ordinarily abhor strong authorities come to think them needed. In recent decades, some anti-terrorists have argued for authoritarian governments to save civilization from nihilism. Rufus Scrimgeour seems to defend his authoritarian moves as required to resist the fascist totalitarianism of Voldemort and the Death Eaters. Dreads of nuclear annihilation and environmental collapse have informed similar cases for authoritarian moments in politics. Some former communist states seem to see their authoritarianism as what's required to develop advantages of capitalism without risking the social order that a strong man (or party) can direct. Even more often, worries about social chaos or enemy advantage from incorrigible sectarian or tribal conflicts have led anti-authoritarian countries to help preserve authoritarian regimes that can suppress strife and maintain alliances in other countries of concern.

Modern tyrants seek government structures that regiment all subordinate activities. Thus governmental (rather than ideological) authoritarians lately *claim* to dedicate government to law-and-order, yet they actually work to put themselves as rulers *above* any law that could keep them from imposing whatever order they want. Governmental authoritarians pursue for themselves a "state of exception" to the regular making and enforcing of law.[1] Often they cite, produce, or at least proclaim crises, emergencies, terrible troubles, indeed "dark times" that could justify—nay, necessitate—their otherwise outrageous deeds or powers. No matter how peaceful, all protesters become "anarchists," "insurrectionists," or "revolutionaries." No matter how civil, all dissenters, and even reporters become "enemies of the state." Denounce and threaten them. Then send in the troops or, better, the secret police to "crack down" on them. It's good if they can be silenced or subdued; but if not, then provoke them to acts that can be portrayed as violence, for that stokes the fears of disorder which advance the law-and-order agenda for governmental authoritarians.[2]

Fudge takes some steps in this direction, but his is mainly a MOM reluctant to admit and correct mistakes. Fudge knows better, but still scapegoats Stan Shunpike as a Death Eater. Fudge ought to know better, yet he actively ignores evidence of Voldemort's return. The main danger with Fudge is his refusal to face the crisis that Voldemort portends. Rather than use this actual emergency to gain extraordinary powers, he tries to wish it away by sidelining then defaming his Voldemort experts in Dumbledore and Harry—while manipulating the Ministry and the media to gaslight magical Britain.

On the other hand, authoritarian regimes can be surprisingly ramshackle in structure and operation. Not all authoritarian oppression starts at the top. In the name of would-be autocrats, some subordinates take initiatives to prevent or punish resistance. Others go further to provoke disorder as a pretext for policing the people 24/7. Some promote scapegoating, hostage-taking, torture, or assassination by thugs who nominally act for public or private militias to shield them from legal or moral accountability. In our world, authoritarian governments do all these things.

In Potter politics, authoritarian personalities use government positions to inflict outrages anonymously and covertly. They act from personal loyalty to a ruler (such as Fudge) or personal fervor for a fading social order (of blood privilege). Thus Umbridge has dementors attack Harry in Little Whinging (V.7–19, 746–7). It seems unlikely that Umbridge knows of Harry's prowess with the patronus charm, so her plan seems to be that a dementor's kiss would suck out Harry's soul and stop his resistance to the Fudge regime. (Or maybe she wants him murdered?) When Harry survives through underage magic, Umbridge tries to expel him from Hogwarts and strip him of his wand. Frustrated momentarily by Dumbledore's alert use of Ministry rules, she seems to work with Fudge to rig a Wizengamot trial to the same end: discrediting, disheartening, and disempowering Harry—and by extension, Dumbledore. Again Dumbledore's preparations and improvisations prevail (V.137–51). That the menace comes more directly from Umbridge than Fudge exemplifies how authoritarianism often operates, especially when it's in the making.

Bartemius Crouch Sr. seems more authoritarian in personality and procedure than does Fudge. Crouch is more fanatical about social order; and he muscles Sirius Black into Azkaban without any trial, no matter how rigged. The Voldemort threat was sincerely seen by Crouch and many other mages as so severe that he could grab and corrupt the powers of prosecutor, judge, and jury without objection in an exceptional, emergency situation. When

Voldemort disappeared just afterward, Crouch's sincerity did save something of a career for him in government. After all, he didn't invent or provoke the slaughter of muggles blamed on Black or of mages traced to Voldemort. Still Crouch's authoritarian moment did derail his ambition to be Minister of Magic.

Like the senior Crouch, Rufus Scrimgeour seems to be another sincere and honorable—if categorically mistaken—authoritarian. Like Fudge, Scrimgeour knows better but still imprisons Stan Shunpike as a Death Eater, despite Harry's pleas. For Scrimgeour's authoritarian regime, but not for Stan, there's poetic justice in Stan's incarceration resulting in him later collaborating as a Death Eater. (If inadvertently, a prison can train criminals, all too much like Hogwarts can educate magicians.) In our world, it's been all too easy to spot authoritarian wannabes who try to hide actual crises and cover up awful mistakes with vast fabrics of falsehood, yet who also provoke and pretend to face other emergencies for purposes of putting themselves above the law.

Authoritarian moves are many, and authoritarian figures can be diverse. The same goes for authoritarian institutions. As a prison, Azkaban is a likely example. What might its guards or escapes tell us about authoritarianism? (Do keep in mind, though, that dementors eventually support the fascist totalitarianism of Voldemort and the Death Eaters.) Weasley careers in the MOM could indicate that the MOM degenerates from authori*tative* to authori*tarian* as Book 2 moves toward Book 7. MOM offices and facilities, their spatial arrangements, kinds of communications, and modes of transportation can show features of authori-tative or authori-tarian politics. Surely St. Mungo's and Hogwarts School seem different, don't they?

Michel Foucault treated prisons as paradigms of the "discipline and punishment" in our everyday lives from Victorian times to the present. The Carrows bring these to Hogwarts in the last book; but even earlier, regimes of authority and authoritarianism are relevant to academic disciplines at Hogwarts, academic disciplines in universities, or diverse martial-arts disciplines. Often these disciplines are self-regimentations, sometimes involving self-inflicted punishments such as guilt feelings. Often they include authoritative surveillance of behavior, or internalizing it as self-monitoring.[3] Typically, as Foucault and many others maintain, authoritarianism turns trust in authorities like Dumbledore or Sprout into fear of authorities like Snape or Scrimgeour.

To justify modern government as a formally absolute authority that might be modified in practice, both Hobbes and Locke contrasted its law, order, peace, and such to the an-archistic condition without government. Hobbes saw it as chaotic, Locke as tribal, and both as feud-al. The Hobbes portrait is the more dire—and notorious: a continual "war of all against all" with "life solitary, poor, nasty, brutish, and short." It's a life-and-death struggle to become King of the Mountain, where no one can win for long or stay safe, let alone get ahead. Even autocracy must be better! Many later theorists of politics argue for modern, "sovereign" government by contrasting their specific takes on it with their distinctive versions of a "State of Nature" as a setting that lacks any effective, centralized, unto absolutized authority enforced through what Max Weber called a territorial monopoly on the legitimate means of violence.

Does this State of Nature seem familiar? Isn't it the situation of the giants as visited by Rubeus Hagrid on behalf of Dumbledore? Pottery wizards take the giants to lack civilization, more than government; but momentary as he might be, the Gurg of the giants is that kind of an authoritarian ruler we term a "gang leader" or an "alpha male." To analyze such authoritarianism, consider the political symbolism of Dumbledore's gifts for the Gurg, why most giants side with Voldemort, what Hagrid's neglectful but possibly charismatic mother implies about giants, and how the civilizing of Grawp proceeds. Yet Rowling begins *Harry Potter* on politics with rules in place rather than their free-for-all absence. So her gigantic State of Nature is less a condition of anarchism than one of unstable, semi-formal authoritarianism. Let's analyze it accordingly.

BUREAUCRATISM

If we see bureaucracy merely and loosely as administration, to apply rules and policies, or even make them, we can find it in ancient China and Egypt. But the word is newer, because the specific thing is a nineteenth-century invention of Otto von Bismarck. It's soon emulated by Grover Cleveland and Woodrow Wilson, and it's been promoted most vigorously in the United States by twentieth-century Progressives such as Theodore Roosevelt. Bureaucracy rationalizes administration (as authority structure) through the (social-) scientific design of offices (bureaus) for maximum efficiency and effectiveness. The work is to be run with time-and-motion studies, cost-benefit analyses, strategic plans, outside audits, and so on. The citizens, clients, and customers are to be processed as cases, files, and numbers, not as people. The officials (bureaucrats) are to be experts in each area of assignment (authority). They are to be apolitical professionals, neither partisan nor prejudiced by personal traits and ties. Their appointment and performance are to be assessed solely by (scientific measures of) merit. Ideally bureaucracies are organizations that function as computers at the service of their society. This is the ideology behind America's Civil Service. But bureaucracy is not just for government; it's prominent in business and culture too.

Its defenders-in-principle are many, but its detractors-in-practice have made *bureaucracy* into a bad word. Sociology texts used to define *bureaucracy* as *the most efficient and effective mode of organization for a large-scale collective endeavor.* Long before Trumpian populists started sniping at "the deep state," though, Franz Kafka and other existentialists worried about bureaucracy as a "totalizing institution"—nightmarishly totalitarian or disciplinary. Rather than clarify rules and responsibilities for clients *or* bureaucrats, the specialization, proceduralism, record-keeping, and assessment mania can often jargonize, mystify, and misdirect bureaucracies. They become impenetrable mazes of cubicles, forms, run-arounds, turf wars, absurdly complicated rules and arbitrary rulings, red tape, secrecy, spying, and petty perquisites. Hence the reputation (but not the prominence) of bureaucracy has plummeted over the past century.

The (Laurence J.) Peter Principle explains that bureaucrats *might* advance by something like merit, but rise to their levels of *in*competence and stick there, making bureaucracies inept. The Nelson Principle is that a single-minded focus on efficiency is inefficient. The diffusion of responsibility is so pervasive that Arendt described *bureaucracy* as "rule by nobody," devolving into anarchism. The Nelson Experience of bureaucrats often subverting rules which they inflict on their clients and competitors, clarifies how bureaucracies often turn into feud-al fiefdoms of antagonistic authoritarians. For Arendt, the epitome of bureaucracy was Adolf Eichmann as an unfeeling technocrat, without monstrous motives or later remorse, who streamlined the murder of millions. For J. K. Rowling, by comparison, the embodiment of bureaucracy becomes Dolores Umbridge; and the bureaucratization of Hogwarts is a huge horror faced by Harry in Book 5.

Umbridge is not exactly authoritarian *or* totalitarian but specifically bureaucratic. She usually abides punctiliously by institutional rules, even when she'd prefer not to; but she also delights in using rules to punish resisters and using her connections to get rules changed more or less as she wants. On occasion, adherence to rules puts her a step behind the brilliant legalism of Albus Dumbledore, the fierce courage of Minerva McGonagall, even the disruptive genius of the Weasley twins; but she usually prevails. Faced with an inconvenient rule, any full-fledged authoritarian redoes it on the spot, while a true totalitarian junks rules *or* commands by having subordinates figure out which aspects of the leader's example to follow (or likewise with mortal peril, which not). Umbridge incurs a few momentary defeats, but these ironically reinforce the overall legitimacy of her moves; and she soon gets the MOM to issue more decrees (*not* laws) to close any loopholes that resisters have identified. Yes, Umbridge breaks rules (and worse) in setting dementors on Harry and his cousin in Little Whinging; and yes, she is eager to use the Cruciatus Curse on Harry and his friends. But these are exceptions that show her *usual* bureaucratic deference to rules. Then *occasional* overriding of rules is a perk exercised by many bureaucrats, whereas authoritarians and totalitarians trash rules continually in their own cases. Consider not only members of the Inquisitorial Squad but also several of the Hogwarts prefects.

Bureaucratese can resemble secret code, and bureaucratic discretion in interpreting this gobbledygook can help it work that way. But mostly the language of bureaucrats is notorious for boiler-plate piety, technical complexity, studied vaguery, and stilted impenetrability. (How am I doing?) The Hogwarts speech by Umbridge is a case in point, taking the likes of Hermione and McGonagall to get the gist of it. Or assess the weird words and emotional tones of "owls" to Harry from Mafalda Hopkirk in the Improper Use of Magic Office. What do they say about (politics in) the MOM under Cornelius Fudge? How do those memos compare to the Umbridge remarks on teaching or to the language in *Daily Prophet* articles by Rita Skeeter? And speaking of memoranda, what do their devices of circulation among offices say about the MoM as a governmental institution by contrast with Hogwarts as an educational institution?

In bureaucracies, information is power. Therefore individual bureaus or bureaucrats collect, intercept, hoard, but also analyze lots and lots of data. Then they use it for blackmail, extortion, bureaucratese, plausible deniability, and just jerking people around. Accordingly Hannah Arendt treated bureaucrats as spies, as secret agents like James Bond, who steal secrets from other bureaus and experts while sabotaging competitors to gain information advantages. This is why Umbridge creates an Inquisitorial Squad of informers and investigators. Can the inventors of Extendable Ears then surprise us as effective foes of the Umbridge bureaucracy?

Clever individuals can sometimes turn bureaucratic rules against particular bureaucrats and rulings, at least momentarily and on matters of relatively small import to the bureaucrats. So to watch Umbridge get stymied temporarily might prompt us to ask about Hermione. She arrives at Hogwarts with an undue deference to rules, from the perspectives of Ron and Harry at any rate. They help her unlearn this, but was she bound in the beginning for bureaucracy? Notice that Percy Weasley seems to have stayed a long time like the newly arrived Hermione: self-righteous about seeing that he and others abide by almost all rules and respect almost all bureaucratic superiors—almost regardless of circumstances. As a prefect, Hermione stops the Weasley twins from experimenting on unsuspecting first-years, as against school rules. But she lets the twins sell elements for skiving snackboxes after developing them by experimenting (only) on the twins themselves. She hates these sales, but cannot find in good faith that they violate school rules (V.368). How much is this like Umbridge accepting Dumbledore's right as Hogwarts Headmaster, even under her new rules, to decide that Sibyll Trelawney may still reside at

Hogwarts when no longer teaching for the school? At the time, Umbridge accepts that Dumbledore is acting within the rules. But she threatens with ill grace that the rules can be changed. (Instead she replaces Dumbledore as head of Hogwarts.) The bureaucratic Umbridge does not want to publicly weaken the rules, not only because she fancies herself a rule-abider but mainly because she seems to be making most rules and using them to her advantage. She would rather not diminish their legitimacy and thus her power. Hermione, on the other hand, still thinks that it's seldom justifiable to break rules, especially as a prefect in a good regime. *The Cursed Child* suggests that Hermione's savvy and self-control help make her (a markedly non-bureaucratic) Minister of Magic in later life.[4] As McGonagall joins Hermione in explaining to Harry, he needs to control himself and keep his temper in the face of Umbridge provocations. Indeed a nice irony is that this eventually starts to happen.

Still what's most impressive (and instructive) about Umbridge is her bureaucratic style of self-presentation and everyday action. A focus on bureaucratic style and defenses against it is crucial to our lives, rife with bureaucracies; and it helps make *The Order of the Phoenix* one of the best Potter books. As the boogey-woman of bureaucracy, Umbridge is a striking invention. Stephen King has enthused that "the gently smiling Dolores Umbridge, with her girlish voice, toadlike face, and clutching, stubby fingers, is the greatest make-believe villain to come along since Hannibal Lecter."[5] The villainy of Umbridge eventually serves Voldemort as a fascist, a perverse perfectionist. But she acts more in her own interest than his, and she does not become a Death Eater. Eichmann appalled Arendt for the "banality," the mundane superficiality, of his "evil."[6] Yet the all-too-familiar evils of Umbridge may be more unsettling. Her weaponization of rules, her girlishly aggressive use of manners, her puritanical condemnation of difference and dissent, her garish mix of the cute and the cruel, her terrifying sense of grievance and greatness, her simpering hostility: the Umbridge style is a vivid, provocative take on bureaucratic politics.

Caretaker Argus Filch is a discipline-and-punish authoritarian, and it's telling that he's eager for the punitive bureaucratism of Umbridge. Anticipating "her" Educational Decrees in spirit, if not in letter, Filch's door bans hundreds of student items and activities. His filing cards and cabinets detail records of every student punished; her teacher evaluations get meticulously specified and filed with the MOM. She uses her office to make students carve "lines" into their hands, whereas his office clanks with medieval implements of imprisonment and torture. In function and architecture, the MOM divides its labor into little departments that often struggle to collaborate—or defend themselves against each other. Even the Department of Mysteries is bureaucratized, with prophecy orbs filed in neat but dusty rows for retrievals seldom

(if ever) to come—and with awful punishments lurking throughout its laby-
rinthine halls and chambers.

Analyzed "rationally," in the modern sense of the most efficient and effective means to given ends, any bureaucratic failure is a reason to bureaucratize more. Indeed the ambition of bureaucracy is *control*, by *regulating* and
monitoring a sphere of behavior *completely*. This is why totalitarian regimes
bureaucratize left and right, up and down. It is also why the rationalizing
and streamlining meant to serve our societies often disempower or even
infantilize us as clients. Like fanaticism for efficiency, mania for control can
defeat itself. Under Umbridge at Hogwarts, Educational Decrees proliferate,
as do rulings from the High Inquisitor. Yet prohibiting student groups drives
Dumbledore's Army underground, making it hard to track and boosting its
esprit de corps. Depriving Harry and the twins of Quidditch gives them more
time and energy for the DA. Banning *The Quibbler* interview with Harry soon
has everybody knowing it. Trying to cow Harry spurs more students to speak
up, at least in the short term. Taking powers from teachers empowers them
to run the new Headmistress ragged when troubles sprout around the school.

Bureaucracy as rationalized organization aspires to an automaticity
that keeps personal connection and political bias from affecting results.
Bureaucracies are not exactly depoliticized, yet they usually promote professional rather than partisan agendas. In bureaucracies, fairness and merit mean
standardized tests and point systems to assess diverse individuals for various
jobs: It's not *who* you know, it's *what* you know. OWLs and NEWTs link
Hogwarts education to careers, and they help measure the success of teachers. (At least, these exams are "practical," as well as quill-and-parchment,
exercises.) Sometimes this ideology of impersonal merit can correct for
stereotypes or inherited advantages; but sometimes it can hide unwelcome
agendas; and especially on auto-pilot, it can approximate one-size-fits-all to
spread stupidity or disaster. Managed bureaucratically by the MOM, the Floo
Network is an obvious candidate for policing by Umbridge to control outside
links with Hogwarts. Ponder the debacle, however, when Arthur Weasley
has the MOM link the Burrow to the Dursley house via the Floo Network.
To stop teachers from fanning student rebellion, Educational Degree Number
Twenty-Six bans them from imparting information beyond course subjects.
But strictly construed, this prohibits teachers from rebuking misbehavior, as
Lee Jordan is quick to say—and suffer in consequence.

Campaigning as a populist in 1972, presidential candidate George Wallace
attacked the arrogance and power of "pointy-headed" intellectuals and
bureaucrats. In 2016, Donald Trump vowed similarly to "drain the swamp"
of special-interest lobbyists and deep-state bureaucrats. Thus there is poetic
justice in the Weasley twins bedeviling Umbridge with a "portable swamp"
to challenge her bureaucratic regime at Hogwarts. Harry and other students

must reign in their populist passions and teenage hormones to prepare effectively for resistance to Umbridge rule. As a nascently republican institution, Dumbledore's Army helps handfuls of them develop the discipline and other skills for rebelling successfully. Harry gains particularly in self-discipline. The (republican) revolution or (populist) uprising of the DA enjoys lots of help and luck—as Harry repeatedly insists to hold also for the surprising success he has known in action. To see bureaucratic inclinations toward elitism and tyranny is to realize why opponents might turn to populist uprisings or republican revolutions. But can these suffice to defeat the totalitarianism pursued by Voldemort and the Death Eaters? What other resources might there be? Tune in to the last two Potter books to see what Rowling can show us . . . .

REPUBLICANISM

By *republicanism*, with a small, lower-case *r*, let us refer to the politics that distinguish republics and their supporters. In the ancient world, republics were to combine the best aspects of the other three legitimate forms of rule: monarchy, aristocracy, and democracy. And in the modern world, from the European Renaissance and the Reformation to the present, republicans developed this ambition into such principles as federalism, free press, and separation of powers into legislative, executive, and judicial branches of government. Modern republicans oppose illegitimate forms of rule such as theocracy, timocracy (crowd rule), oligarchy, plutocracy, and tyranny. Current "republicans" of Britain and the European continent oppose monarchies and aristocracies, no matter how diminished to merest figureheads. America's Republican Party is no more, and these days often much less, politically republican than its Democratic Party; while the claim to be "democratic" has now become standard for republicans and many, many others.

Most republicans condemn hosts of vices such as arrogance, complacency, cowardice, factionalism, greed, impulsivity, irresponsibility, selfishness, and treachery. These contrast with republican virtues, led by liberty as community independence of corruption-from-within and domination-from-without. Other republican virtues include ambition for glory and heroism, courage, decorum, duty, energy, honor, justice, loyalty, magnanimity, prudence, and respect. As such lists might suggest, *virtue*'s linguistic roots imply *manly* (unto *masculinist* or *patriarchal*) commitments, although recent republicans have been trying to undo this bias. Perverse kinds of republican politics can be found in crime families and gangs. Related flaws of republicanism have long been recognized as inclinations to militarism, expansionism, and imperialism. Latter-day republicans have been trying to get past those troubles too.

Republics locate political freedom for their citizens within public spaces for speech and action. *Citizens* are *denizens* (residents and members) of a *city*. There they construct, defend, and otherwise attend to the common-wealth. For this, citizens (or their tribunes) come together (con-vene) to make and carry out laws, policies, or the like (conventions or rules). They do so in a place available to all city members. So the *res publica* is the *thing that is public*, the *public space* (as Hannah Arendt termed it), or simply the *public*. And what is *public* is what is *of the populus*, what is *of or among the people*. The republican tradition explores how shared speech and action produce and sustain peoples. (Nationalisms typically are offshoots of republicanism.) Thus spatial and functional publics—the agoras and arenas and amphitheaters and commonplaces and forums and interests and media and publications and so on—are what situate, receive, assess, and re-member the shared speech and action of citizens.

The republican tradition turns on contrasts and connections between private realms and public spaces. As members of a commonwealth, citizens address their shared concerns through speech and action in the common places which Romans called *forums* and the commonplaces of rhetoric, which Greeks called *topoi* or *topics*. Sustaining these devices across many meetings and issues, citizens can maintain the *public* as the shared place for the words and deeds that most fully make them a community. Public speech and action by citizens emerge from households, farms, businesses, academies, and other private realms. But personal speech and action attain shared, political reality in public. There citizens together become free in saying and doing what they judge best about the natural, rational, willful, and other elements that affect human affairs.

As a political tradition, republicanism proper began in ancient Rome. It arose from the sites of politics and disciplines of rhetoric generated in Greece. Thus we do well to appreciate it as the republican-rhetorical tradition. In Rome, it could be regarded as a successful experiment in appropriating the principles and practices of political life from their place of invention in the small Greek *polis*, in order to fit them for an increasingly cosmopolitan society. The Romans needed politics suited to larger and more diverse memberships; and for a fair time, the republic as their new form of rule met that need. Later it notoriously gave way to an even larger and more ramshackle empire. Far from ending the public tradition of freedom, however, the later imperialism, decadence, and collapse of Rome mainly set the stage for medieval arrangements that adapted republicanism into codes of chivalry and solemn oaths of loyalty as the European patchwork of medieval feudalism loosely "under" (or continually contesting) the Holy Roman Empire. Then the Renaissance revived and began to modernize classical republicanism even as the Reformation unraveled the Holy Roman Empire. Eventually the

Enlightenment enlarged and ideologized republicanism into authoritarianism, liberalism, socialism, conservatism, and so on. Still modern republicanism inspired revolutions in America and France. It turned into modern takes on political prudence. And by the end of the twentieth century, it had resurfaced as a "communitarian" movement in liberal and social democracies. Thus it has proved far more enduring as a modern dream of political virtue, talent, and participation than it initially showed itself to be as a Roman invention. It supplies many elements of political idealism in our times.

As a kind of politics, republicanism celebrates virtuous deeds. It improves through developing rhetoric as the first systematic study and practice of speech-in-action-in-public. As a discipline, rhetoric is the first "political science." It cultivates pru-dence (fore-sight) in action, it analyzes words and deeds into tropes and gestures, and it promotes virtues as styles of living. Early republican politics respect property as propriety, through honor codes of proper conduct, rather than privatizing property as a liberal-capitalist sovereignty of persons over particular goods. In other words, republican owners need to defer to community standards in having and using personal property, whereas liberal individuals and corporations may do almost anything they want with their own private property—except hurt other persons.

Republicanism puts immense emphasis on cultivating good character in public action. For republicans, your character is behavioral, as *who* you are for others in public, not an inner conscience or a psychological structure. (The Greek-rhetorical word for such character is *ethos*.) Republics typically promote public education for virtues in conduct both personal and political. Republican virtues especially prepare people for the slings and arrows of vigorous interaction. Confidence, decency, daring, discipline, objectivity, perseverance, resourcefulness, sympathy, and toughness loom large. Altogether, republican character bears a considerable resemblance to the calm stoicism celebrated by Rudyard Kipling in "If." Republican virtues inform and limit our individual freedoms—a major advantage for republicans over libertarians whose sense of freedom need not extend beyond militant license and self-assertion. Republican politics pride themselves on ceremony, ritual, and tradition.

Republicans know that principles inspirit whole polities. That is why republicans focus on foundings and constitutions, for these endow polities with first principles that delineate the publics of a polity, leading us to call this distinctive network of principles its constitution—in a sense larger than any document which might become its legal focus and share that name. These foundations inform but do not fix the political trajectories of republican regimes. Furthermore republicans expect practices gradually to diverge from their definitive beginnings, and so they prize public education as a vital remembrance of the words, deeds, characters, and virtues that created the

polity. This accounts for a keen republican interest in political myths and traditions—which liberals confuse with ideologies, tolerate as lore, or dismiss as
superstition. To repair eventual divergence and resist corruption or takeover,
republican politics also make room for revolution, either as a return (revolv-
ing) to first principles or a creation of a new constitution.

The republican tradition is so foundational for politics in the twenty-first
century that many elements of current politics bear the Latinate (or Greek-
rooted) names that mark them as legacies of ancient or modern republicanism. A bare but helpful beginning could be: authority, avenue (and venue),
common sense, communication, community, conservatory, conspiracy,
constitution, conviction, cultivation, education, family (tribe and generation), (lessons of) history, institution, judgment, justice, law, leader, liberty,
lodge, mentor, militia or military, monument, myth (as symbolic story),
office and official, order (as a guardian organization), persuasion, power (as
cooperation), precept or principle, prudence, public, respect, revenge, revolution, responsibility, tradition (as augmentation), trust, vice, vigilance (against
abuses of power), virtue, and so on.

Several medieval ingredients of wizarding culture in Pottery have republican resonance. Book 2 introduces the wizard duel, for example; and it gets
enacted many times after the face-off between Harry and Draco Malfoy.
The wizard duel is a martial contest, sometimes to the death. Even more
fundamentally, though, it's a republican institution of honor similar to the
showdown in popular westerns. Republicans more or less invent *institutions*
as *stitches in* space, time, and people. These provide fabrics or templates to
civilize humanity by stabilizing interactions and "clothing" them to suit the
community's conventions of conduct. At least four of the main institutions in
Book 5 are distinctly republican: Hogwarts School, the Order of the Phoenix,
Dumbledore's Army, and the family—from the Blacks to the Weasleys.

Loosely superintended by the MOM, the Hogwarts School offers something akin to a public education for young witches and wizards in Britain.
Its take on education is fundamentally republican, for it links theory as in-
principle learning from books and lectures with practice as disciplinary demonstrations and recurrent exercises that cultivate mental and physical skills as
second nature. Is the MOM itself republican? That's less clear, partly because
the Potter books don't explain much about its connections with Britain's
witches and wizards. Still Book 5 shows that the MOM includes some republican branching of political powers. The *Daily Prophet* epitomizes "the press"
as "the fourth estate," and *The Quibbler* is that offshoot of "public journalism," which we call a "populist tabloid." The Wizengamot works as a somewhat independent "judiciary" in trying Harry for unjustified underage use of
magic then acquitting him despite the desire of the Minister of Magic and
some other higher "executives" to get Harry expelled from Hogwarts. The

Department of Magical Law Enforcement and many other parts of the MOM also qualify as "executive" departments. Yes, the Ministry leans authoritarian under Cornelius Fudge and likely even more under Rufus Scrimgeour as Ministers of Magic; while the Death Eaters turn the MOM into a totalitarian regime for Lord Voldemort through the imperiused Pius Thicknesse as Minister of Magic. But republics can be conquered or corrupted.

The Order of the Phoenix resists these developments. An *order* is a distinctly republican device of vigilance against abuses of power. Orders can be similar to small, secret militias, with members pledging life and limb to defend a community's liberty or an institution's integrity. The secrecy protects against early detection and defeat. Often it keeps an order akin to a *conspiracy*, from Latin for *with-breath* because its work proceeds more or less in whispers off-stage or behind closed doors. A second edition of the Order of the Phoenix springs into action to resist the return to power of Voldemort's fascists. The Order's leader, Albus Dumbledore, has a phoenix as his pet and his patronus. This mythic bird has great strength and healing powers, as Book 2 says of Fawkes, Dumbledore's pet; and these are premier aspects of "the body politic" sought by republicans. The life cycle of the phoenix gets invoked as a beautiful symbol of republican time. The bird grows impressively, eventually declines into decrepitude that ends in self-immolating fire, yet rises anew: reborn from the ashes to fly and sing again.

Dumbledore's Army is itself a republican order, especially for education in the dark arts of magic as martial arts. Eventually it becomes a militia for rebellion against the Umbridge and Snape regimes at Hogwarts. Led by generals, propelled by privates, and cultivating martial arts for war, intimidation, or deterrence, full-fledged militaries likewise link to politics of republics. In this family of institutions, as in republics overall, reciprocal loyalty binds the leaders and the led. The leaders offer general knowledge, big-picture vision, energy, judgment, and education for followers; the led empower leaders by supplying local knowledge, personal responsibility, deference, and vigilance against abuses of power. This is why Hermione and Harry can judge Marietta Edgecombe to deserve defacing for betraying the DA. It's also why Fawkes arrives in the Chamber of Secrets to reward Harry's loyalty to Dumbledore.

Ancient Greece and Rome treated families as prime institutions of political community. The demes in Athens and the tribes in Rome functioned as extended families, which became the basis for political participation. Book 5 extends Book 4 attention to the Weasley family. Most of their personal names pay homage to British legend and royalty, but most of their deeds (as what the fascist Malfoys call "pure-blood traitors") are pro-muggle and amply republican. Book 5 compares the Weasleys to the Blacks, who are elitist or even fascist for the most part. The notable exceptions are Sirius Black, his cousin Andromeda Black Tonks, and her daughter Nymphadora Tonks.

But Regulus Arcturus Black, brother of Sirius, and their other two cousins Bellatrix Black Lestrange and Narcissa Black Malfoy follow Voldemort to the end—or almost. (As usual, the name symbolism can be fun and clarifying.) Books 4 and 5 contrast the elitist and foreboding house of the Blacks with the ramshackle but welcoming Burrow of the Weasleys. (The last book shows the Malfoys in a mansion with white peacocks on the grounds.) We do well to compare the Black family tapestry to the Weasley family clock, the Black location in the big city to the Weasley setting in a countryside village, even the Black house-elves to the Weasley garden gnomes. The Blacks "honor" favorite house-elves by mounting their shrunken heads on the walls, arguably a fascist defilement of republican busts, statues, trophies, or other monumental history that seems almost as perverse as Voldemort's horcruxes. And when Harry surveys the Great Hall with the Battle of Hogwarts done, he sees families reunited (VII.735–6).

Republicans and perfectionists pay more respectful, specific attention to political styles than do other kinds of politics. Although republicanism is prominent in Potter institutions and principles, unsurprisingly it's even more evident in the Potter words and deeds of everyday life. This holds, too, for the magical creatures and devices in Pottery. If flying brooms are figurally perfectionist in their implicit politics, the 3Ds of apparating as taught to Hogwarts fifth-years by Wilkie Twycross are realist republican, largely in the Machiavellian manner of the Marauder's Map earlier on the Potter scene. A clear sense of destination (and destiny) is a republican ideal. Determination as commitment, grit, or will is evident in republican courage and perseverance. For apparating, deliberation is careful attention to detail during action, which is the realist bent that republicanism takes public. Yet deliberation is also one of the three main kinds of (ancient) rhetoric for public life: epideictic speech praises or blames, forensic oratory argues cases, then deliberative rhetoric discusses and decides what to do. (The key to apparating, though, seems to be "turning on the spot"—with *turns* as *tropes* crucial to the perfectionism of Potter magic.)

The sense of destinies opening along different paths for different (sets of) people is a prominent outlook among classical republicans, especially, but more than a bit among modern republicans too. (Postmodern republicans, such as Hannah Arendt, are another matter.) Not exactly a democratic device, the Gryffindor-republican Sorting Hat respects (but also produces) different classes of students. Yet Dumbledore wants Harry to recognize in his own experience that the Sorting Hat takes personal choices into account in assigning students to the Hogwarts Houses that cultivate their talents. Potter destiny, in other words, is not deterministic. Rather it is republican, prizing the flexibility of individual freedom required for personal responsibility. (Dumbledore's regime at Hogwarts seems to go even further, turning away from the militarist discipline of the Durmstrang Institute to make room for the individual freedom of self-making in public action *and* in private life that seems to be promoted by Dumbledore's liberalism.)

Talk of destiny takes us into the territory of prophecy. This hovers ominously over the Divination course that Sibyll Trelawney unwillingly cedes to Firenze, the centaur; and from this book forward, her initial prophecy troubles but steers the whole series. In Potter politics, details often matter immensely. As Dumbledore explains in detail, Voldemort lacks key particulars of Sibyll's prophecy about the Dark Lord marking his nemesis. Moreover Dumbledore is at pains for Harry to see why it matters that, even though Harry becomes the Chosen One prophesied to stand in Voldemort's way, this results from Voldemort's choices rather than Sibyll's prophecy. Dumbledore tells how these choices may have been mistakes, so that Voldemort is *not* destined to defeat and kill Harry. Harry's virtues of republican courage and Christian love *can* prevail, if *he* makes good choices at turning points in what can be the Potter, rather than the Riddle, saga.

To make good choices, Book 5 shows, Harry needs to master his hormonal impulses, teenage anger, and repeated provocations. Then he can act with republican prudence. At the book's start, Harry epitomizes "the people" as constructed by populism more than republicanism. Populists spur people to be fed up with elite exploitation and disrespect. When we get "as mad as hell," maybe we *really* "won't take this anymore," as "the Mad Prophet of the Airways" proclaims in *Network* (1976).[7] Maybe we'll "rise up" to resist and overthrow our oppressors. But as with "the people," Harry's anger surges, subsides, surges, and seeps away. Initially his righteous passion is interspersed with simmering resentment and sullen self-pity. To stand long-term against the Umbridge-Fudge regime at Hogwarts, Harry needs to learn prudent preparation for resistance with others. To rise up and revolt, these collaborators need republican devices of conspiracy, cooperation, discipline, drill, and more. That's where the Order of the Phoenix, Dumbledore's Army, and the like contribute. Then overcoming the Inquisitorial Squad, sidelining Umbridge, and flying to save Sirius in the Department of Mysteries become possible; and the shootout at the MOM seasons six of the DA for surviving the Battle of Hogwarts that climaxes the series.

The idealistic, impulsive Sirius also has trouble with prudent choices; and he bridles at authority, even Dumbledore's. Sometimes he's self-sacrificing and heroic; sometimes he's easily manipulated by Snape taunts. But occasionally he's simply foolish, and eventually this gets him killed. In republican terms, Sirius acts as a responsible godparent in returning to keep an eye on Harry at Hogwarts. Ironically he acts as a self-sacrificing hero in staying so long undercover at home, even though he craves direct action against the Death Eaters. And of course, he's foolish to romp as Padfoot along with Harry going to catch the Hogwarts Express on Platform 9¾.

When Sirius donates the unplottable Black House as headquarters for the Order, Molly Weasley directs something like a war against its deterioration from Kreacher's neglect and its infestation by boggarts, doxies, puffskeins, and worse. Sly jokes abound. *Doxies* is from the Dutch and German for *little dolls*, but we might trace it back further to the ancient Greek *doxa* for mere (popular) *opinion* by contrast with rigorous (expert, philosophical) *truth*. The elitist Black House has been infested with public opinion because Kreacher as the fascist house-elf has been unwilling to disturb the abode as his mistress left it. Does it get cleansed of popular opinion by the Order of the Phoenix because such quasi-military institutions defend republics against inner corruption as well as outer domination? Why do doxies resemble thuggish fairies, and why do they infest drawing-room curtains? What is suggested by the twins' interest in doxy poison for use in Skiving Snackboxes to liberate students from class? And what of other cleansing targets?

Upstairs in the Black House is Buckbeak, the hippogriff who flew Sirius to safety at the third book's end. Joining an eagle and a horse redoubles the hippogriff as a (Roman) republican figure who demands the (shows of) respect crucial to republican codes of honor. And let's not neglect Buckbeak helping Harry and Hermione to liberate Sirius from dementors in that earlier volume. Is it figurally republican for Sirius to feed Buckbeak on rats, like Scabbers? The mafia's warped code of honor and loyalty is called *omerta* (*silence*) because, in American parlance, the worst thing that mafiosi can do is to *rat* on the crime family by telling its business to outsiders such as legitimate authorities. A sad sign of Percy's debasement is his letter urging Ron to help Umbridge by ratting on Harry. Marietta's boils say "SNITCH," but they could as well say "RAT."

Among the magical creatures that Rubeus Hagrid introduces to Hogwarts students in Book 5 are bowtruckles. As "tree guardians," they enact for wand trees, especially, the same republican stewardship of responsible care that Hagrid extends to a vast array of creatures. He has cultivated the largest herd of thestrals as invisible, intimidating, but tame transportation for long distances to and from Hogwarts Castle, as well as the short carriage ride from Hogsmeade. With her cultivation of diverse plants, Professor Pomona Sprout comes closer to the specifically agrarian republicanism associated in America with farming and Thomas Jefferson. But Hagrid, in his semi-survivalist hut on the edge of the wild, Forbidden Forest, is the heroic trio's go-to guy. Harry, Ron, and Hermione return time and again to Hagrid for friendship, information, perspective, and outside-the-city virtue that republican politics know they can need for when politics inside the city (here, the castle) get corrupted or overridden. Hagrid is their source for the natural virtue and rural wisdom that can complement the castle's big-city sophistication.

MONUMENTALIZING THE HISTORY OF MAGIC

In Book 5, the climax of the climax is the shootout in the MOM. It moves from deep in the Department of Mysteries to the atrium on the main floor. Stunned by the death of his godfather, Sirius Black, Harry still runs after the killer. Following Bellatrix Lestrange to the main hall, Harry ducks behind the Fountain of Magical Brethren to cast curses at her. The retaliations shatter parts of the fountain statues. Then his scar erupts in pain as a hooded figure in black materializes ahead, to taunt and murder Harry. But Voldemort's killing curse bounces off the fountain's golden wizard, animated by Dumbledore to protect Harry. Next the fight is joined by other fountain figures, magicked to "life" by Dumbledore *and* Voldemort. Their brief duel makes the atrium a killing zone, if only for the statues. Soon the Death Eaters escape, but not before the floo-using Fudge arrives to see that the Dark Lord really has returned (V.807–17).

The fountain has been a monument to the history of magic as many mages imagine it. Its golden figures look larger and more virtuous than life. All gaze up in adoration at the towering wizard and the shorter witch, both of such stylized nobility and beauty as to seem vacant when Harry looks again. Harry knows that even admiration from a centaur and a goblin is unrealistic; but he sees the house-elf's servility as creepy, not false (V.127, 156). In the Fudge regime, these fountain figures are specist, sexist, self-congratulatory propaganda pieces for mage (and wizard) superiority in magical Britain. Dumbledore's animation turns them into self-sacrificing heroes, which is what a virtuous republic would want them to be. But already Harry is seeing that public monuments and other memorials are ventures in political mythmaking. (Remember nationalists who sometimes fabricate relics?) Seldom are public commemorations simply good or bad as art, right or wrong as history, uniting or dividing as politics. In general, they can be true *and* false, constructive *and* destructive, loved *and* reviled, depending on perspectives.

When Death Eaters dominate, the Ministry atrium is ruled by a black stone monument to that regime's racism. A huge wizard and a huge witch loom over vast thrones carved with small, massed, naked figures that deform and defame muggles (VII.241–2). Not much ambiguity there, admittedly—or much contrast with the monumental symbolism of authoritarian and totalitarian regimes in our world. But what Soviet Communists loved about super-sized statues of Stalin and Lenin in Balkan squares is largely what many Bulgarians, Romanians, and Serbians hated. Nor is such symbolism missing from liberal and social democracies. Ask Native American Indians about Mount Rushmore and statues of Andrew Jackson, descendants of slaves about Confederate flags and monuments, or Africans about statues of

Leopold II and Cecil Rhodes. In one country after another, statues rise and fall, monuments gleam then go to ruin—soon or after centuries.[8]

Controversies over enduring commemorations are nearly inevitable, or part of the work is undone. To claim some singular significance for all parts of a polity is silly for monuments and for histories. What's *the* meaning? For whom, when, where? At best, a memorial introduces people to several perspectives, while advancing its principal views with trenchant symbolism. But the more preachy and heavy-handed it becomes, the less happy—let alone educational—it proves for many people to experience. This isn't how republics have seen monumentalizing the lessons of history, but it could become so. It's an advantage of "abstract," "geometrical" figures in monuments. Pro or con, a gigantic general atop a massive horse raised high on an imposing pedestal is not readily excused from celebrating its soldier, war, and cause. When people think otherwise, it typically attracts pigeons, graffiti, or toppling.[9] When water sculptures, beacons in the night, or ascending steps invite reflection on historical deeds and events, the politics can be more open and welcoming. Much the same holds for diversifying the commemorations in their purposes and politics. Atrocity reminders such as Holocaust museums and bombing memorials are lamentations more than celebrations. Even with its heroic statue of the Potters, isn't the old Potter house in Godric's Hollow overall melancholy for marking the murders there (VII.323–4)? Similar are disaster sites marked for visitors to ponder. Halls of fame enable diverse groups and institutions to commemorate and educate from many angles. (Halls of shame can help too.)

Potter books acknowledge many kinds of memorials and approaches to them. There are republican busts that use three-dimensional heads and shoulders to portray the public characters that publics construct and recall (V.281; VI.527; VII.420, 620). The halls and stairs of Hogwarts feature a multitude of commemorations. They include the living portraits as well as the statues and the suits of armor (III.195; IV.171, 728; VI.195, 527) which McGonagall animates to defend the castle against Voldemort's minions (VII.602). Otherwise the statuary at Hogwarts seems more whimsical than republican; or perhaps it offers lessons in folly by commemorating Gregory the Swarmy (I.155; V.659), Boris the Bewildered (IV.431, 459), Lachlan the Lanky (V.271), and Wilfred the Wistful (V.281) as well as Rowena Ravenclaw (VII.620). Similarly a castle tapestry portrays "Barnabas the Barmy's foolish attempt to train trolls for the ballet" (V.389). Perhaps in this spirit, a piece of the portable swamp invented by the Weasley twins is kept as a memorial in its Hogwarts hallway (V.675–7, 848). Likewise the castle features gargoyles (II.204, 244; V.467; VII.619–20). They fit the founding of Hogwarts in the middle ages, and they suit the form of the Potter series as dark fantasy. Yet they also serve the series' wry takes on public statuary. The series even treats trophies as irritants or perversions as much as awards (I.159; II.118, 241; VI.504).[10]

Emphasis on such public memorials surges with Book 5's republican resistance to Fudge authoritarianism and Umbridge bureaucratism. Rough equivalents for the other politics also get attention. *Memo* is short for *memorandum*; and as a vehicle for organizational memory or communication, the memo characterizes bureaucracies. Harry learns from Arthur Weasley that the MOM used to rely on owls to circulate its interdepartmental memos, but now minimizes the mess by magicking them into paper airplanes that transport themselves to designated receivers (V.129–30). *Decree* stems from *dēcernere*, a Latin word for *decide*, which hints with its *dē-* that the decision get removed from its initial site.[11] Thus authoritarians don't need to negotiate or deliberate with anybody else; instead they decide and authorize their decisions as authoritative decrees for others to obey. Before widespread literacy, medieval kings had town criers proclaim decrees aloud to the realm's subjects. The fifth film memorably makes Argus Filch climb a rickety ladder to "post" the Ministry's "Educational Decrees" on the foyer walls just outside the Great Hall. The film animates front pages of the *Daily Prophet* too. In Book 5, students read decrees in the *Daily Prophet* or on their dormitory notice boards (V.351). The more authoritarian a ruler or regime, the less say others get as to the meanings of decrees. That Dumbledore and others effectively contest some of Umbridge's initial interpretations of Ministry decrees is, as already detailed, a sign that she's more a bureaucrat than an authoritarian.

In myriad ways, the Potter saga helps us recognize that our politics make their histories in many media and genres: plaster busts, bronze statues, and stone monuments among them. Some commemorations like Filibuster's and Weasleys' fireworks are less enduring. These days, we even memorialize with documentaries and video games. The key point is that we do histories—as we do politics—with diverse purposes, principles, and people. Never should we be surprised at monumental controversies, and seldom should we begrudge monumental disagreements. Isn't that a reliable lesson of history—and Pottery?

NOTES

1. See Giorgio Agamben, *State of Exception*, trans. Kevin Attell (Chicago: University of Chicago Press, 2005).

2. See Timothy Snyder, *On Tyranny* (New York: Penguin Random House, 2017); Timothy Snyder, *The Road to Unfreedom* (New York: Penguin Random House, 2018); Anne Applebaum, *Twilight of Democracy* (New York: Penguin Random House, 2020).

3. See John S. Nelson, *Tropes of Politics* (Madison: University of Wisconsin Press, 1998), 34–46.

4. See Jack Thorne (script with story by J. K. Rowling, John Tiffany, and Jack Thorne), *The Cursed Child* (New York: Scholastic Press, 2016).

5. Stephen King, "Review of *Harry Potter and the Order of the Phoenix*," *Entertainment Weekly* (July 11, 2003): http://www.ew.com/ew/static/pdf/2007/03/stephenking.pdf.

6. See Hannah Arendt, *Eichmann in Jerusalem* (New York: Viking Press, 1963, 1964).

7. *Network*, directed by Sidney Lumet (1976; Burbank, CA: Warner Home Video, 2000), DVD.

8. Thanks to Professor J. Gordon for suggesting a detailed discussion of public monuments.

9. Or such statues provoke poems. See Carl Sandburg, "Ready to Kill," *Chicago Poems* (New York: Henry Holt, 1916), http://carl-sandburg.com/ready_to_kill.htm; W. H. Auden, "Marginalia," *Collected Poems*, ed. Edward Mendelson (New York: Random House, 1976), 589–602; Billy Collins, "Statues in the Park," *New Yorker* 81, no. 21 (July 25, 2005): 76–77.

10. See the third chapter for Pottery books of biography and history, which often function as public commemorations. Other Potter candidates for public monuments are headstones and statues to mark graves (VII.325, 328). Still other possibilities seem less public, making them more memorabilia than memorials: bequests, diaries, family tapestries (V.111), horcruxes, moving photographs (I.96, 103), speaking photographs (V.117, 174), and personal paintings (e.g., Luna's ceiling).

11. See John Ayto, *Dictionary of Word Origins* (New York: Little, Brown, 1990), 175.

Chapter 11

Patrons and the Half-Blood Prince

The sixth Potter book reviews the troubles brewing for Harry and his friends, especially Dumbledore. Harry and Dumbledore resist efforts by an increasingly corrupt Ministry of Magic (MOM) to coopt them. Harry helps Dumbledore recruit Horace Slughorn back to Hogwarts as its Potions professor. And Snape's old potions text helps Harry augment his repertoire for political action, while getting lucky in love, Quidditch, and learning about Voldemort. None of this is enough to forestall the danger to Dumbledore. Death Eaters invade Hogwarts, Snape kills the headmaster, and the funeral for Dumbledore resolves the heroic threesome to act—as soon as they can figure out what to do.

All the politics in previous Potter books operate in this one, and its title character would have us discussing Machiavellian realism here if we hadn't already addressed its Potter treatment in connection with Book 3. Book 6 uses Slughorn to show downsides of the patronist politics that Dumbledore practices to better effect. The patron motif is prominent throughout the Potter books, where it's crucial to the overarching plot. Still the Rowling treatment of patronism is especially good to read as a contribution to recent theories of politics, which mostly neglect it. Book 6 also puts us in a good position to articulate the liberal politics in Dumbledore's direction of Hogwarts School. And since Hogwarts as we know it is an institution that combines Dumbledore innovations with thousand-year-old traditions, the occasion has come for assessing some of the diverse kinds of conservative politics that also are at issue these days.

Half-Blood Prince turns on promises made, lapsed, and kept. Promises are commitments for conduct. To make, bend, break, or abide by promises resembles the politics of rules, except that promises are largely voluntary, self-made, and self-enforced. This is why Harry's *not* a big promise-breaker:

he (mostly) agrees with the promises he makes, and he takes his honor to be at stake in fulfilling them. The cases of Draco, Snape, and Dumbledore can be more complicated. Toward book's end, all these cases converge in Dumbledore's death on the tower; and together they clarify politics important in the Potter books.

PATRONISM

The Potter series focuses on politics as dark arts and defenses against them in our dark times. Arguably its key contributions emerge most vividly in its overall takes and telling details for magical characters, creatures, devices, and institutions. Thus it explores current variants of perfectionist politics—good, bad, or otherwise—along with lots of other politics as well. Still its overall approach is not something we readily recognize in politics of excellence. Nor is it an aspect of our everyday politics analyzed all that much in political theory. Fortunately it was set to music by the Beatles in *Sgt. Pepper's Lonely Heart's Club Band*. There Ringo Starr sings "With a Little Help from My Friends," as John Lennon and Paul McCartney urge him on by interjecting questions and comments. It might be mere coincidence that the Potter novels are flecked with quick evocations of "beetles" in disparate contexts. Yet it's no accident that Potter books have Albus Dumbledore explain repeatedly how the old, neglected magic of love shields Harry from Lord Voldemort. Neither is it inadvertent that Dumbledore persistently celebrates Harry's keen capacity for personal responsibility and self-sacrificing love. The Potter books connect this love to republican politics of friendship and loyalty as well as Christian politics of joy, remorse, and forgiveness. As with Hannah Arendt's work, there also are significant skeins of existentialism in the Potter politics of heroic, selfless humanity for facing dark times and extreme experiences. But mostly, the Potter saga uses neglected terms of patronism to develop its stress on "Help!"

Like *dark, eye, spot,* and *turn, help* is one of the key words in the Potter series. It's worth noting again that an Aeschylus epigraph from *The Libation Bearers* concludes the saga, and that it ends with a "call" for dark, "underground" powers to "send help" to "the children." Already by Book 2, Dumbledore is saying and showing that help will come to those at Hogwarts who ask for it. In accounting for his superhuman success in surviving dark arts from infancy onward, Harry tells anyone who will listen that he's had far more help and luck than skill. Each book is an obstacle course in Harry's odyssey, and he gets help at almost every turn. Patronism is politics of help.

A patron is someone who helps from a position of power and a motive of investment. The help can come as advice, connection, encouragement, information, money, protection, rescue, or other resources. The position of power puts the helper's standing and resources qualitatively above the recipient's in some crucial respects, usually permanent yet sometimes temporary. The motive of investment often supports the success of others as a good in itself, but always expects a further yield of resources for the helper, even if that is small in comparison to the resources invested. This return on investment makes patronism a reciprocal relationship; and the investment dynamic sometimes gets the people helped classified as "clients," although we often do better to recognize the junior or otherwise lower parties as the patron's protégés. In both directions, patronist politics cultivate continuing connections and exchanges of assistance.

Although widely practiced, patronist politics seldom get much recent attention from the academy, save in connection with social networking. They have never focused a movement, let alone been ideologized into a putative social science. Yet as a style, patronism is prominent in the Potter books and our everyday lives. Some of its best aspects appear early in the first book, and the series amplifies them markedly through *The Deathly Hallows*. Some of its worst features are examined in Book 6 on *The Half-Blood Prince*. This introduces Horace Slughorn as an inveterate patron of a mutual-advancement network. It compares him to Albus Dumbledore as a tireless orchestrator of resistance to fascism in the wizarding world. And it lets us see how the Death Eaters who follow Voldemort form a cult or gang, but *not* a mutual-advancement network. There are five kinds of patronism pertinent to Pottery and us. Two stay partial, marginal, and in the background. The other three stand out in the Potter brew of stylistic politics.

One is *patriarchy* as rule by fathers or males. This is the arch-enemy of feminist politics, as addressed earlier. In a nutshell, the Potter books might contest and decenter patriarchy; but they don't displace it altogether. Nor are they probably intended to, because that could disrupt the narrative focus on Harry Potter; and it could disconnect the Potter world too much from our own for the series to address its diverse range of troubles in our dark times. Our world remains highly patriarchal, so Harry's must be at least peripherally so. Most of its top, powerful figures are male; most of their roles are familiar from our own patriarchies; and most of the female roles are familiar from ours too. In the early 1700s, for example, Dilys Derwent headed Hogwarts; yet she had distinguished herself first as a healer at St. Mungo's Hospital for Magical Maladies and Injuries. Yes, St. Mungo's has male healers; but healing is much more a female focus. Severus Snape is Dumbledore's go-to guy for daunting injuries; yet Madam Pomfrey is the Hogwarts nurse for regular healthcare, and Hermione Granger heals for the heroic trio in the last book.

A second form of patronist politics is *patronage* in the style of Renaissance princes and popes, Enlightenment autocrats and nobles, or later business tycoons and cultural institutions. Then the patron supports various adventurers, artists, builders, causes, charities, composers, inquiries, and more. The usual goal is for patrons to shine brighter due to the glories of their beneficence and the accomplishments of its recipients. In the hindsight of history, some clients surely outshine their patrons; but collecting a sparkling array of recipients often beams much brighter in the moment. Some of these patrons want enrichment, entertainment, stimulation, or moral improvement too. Similar in key respects are the patronage systems of government by city bosses like the first Mayor Daley of Chicago and the notorious Mayor Tweed of New York. Americans have come to define such patronage as corrupt reliance on personal connections and kickbacks. Yet the U.S. Postal Service long ran effectively as a patronage system where the local representative to the U.S. Congress had a key voice in appointing mail carriers and clerks, then could be held accountable by voters for the cost and quality of postal service in the district.

The only Potter figure who even comes close to this sense of patronage is Dumbledore. As the Hogwarts Headmaster, his staffing of the school doesn't seek a strict alignment of skills with positions in the meritocratic modes of liberalism, let alone bureaucratism. Nor is it only a republican exercise in judging character as a personal complex of virtues and vices, even though this seems to loom large in some of the hires Dumbledore makes (Hagrid) or refuses (Riddle). Dumbledore employs also to gain political resources or keep them from foes: Slughorn, Snape, and Trelawney are examples. Loosely speaking, Dumbledore might be regarded as this kind of patron for his staff or even for (some of) his students. Yet he doesn't seek to bask in their glow of attainment, and his cultivation of continuing connections with many of them stems far more from personal regard and political exigency. In fact, Dumbledore is more like a patron saint.

Help from a "patron saint," a "guardian angel" in the figural sense of someone powerful who looks out protectively for someone else, is the crucial kind of patronism in the Potter series. Always a man of many motives for any course of action, Albus Dumbledore nonetheless acts in important part as Harry's guardian angel in passing along his father's Invisibility Cloak in Book 1. In Book 2, Dumbledore's phoenix makes good on his pledge to help Hogwarts students, especially those most loyal to him. In Book 3, Dumbledore repeatedly helps the heroic trio with the timing central to their successful action in turning a tragedy into a thriller. As he later explains, Dumbledore takes care in Books 4 and 5 to stay (or at least seem) distant from Harry *in order to protect* him from Voldemort. Yet a careful review of the events can reveal Dumbledore just offstage. There he often contrives to aid Harry covertly or even overtly—but without looking him directly in the eye, which would have provided the reassuring respect that Harry still craves. By Book 6, Harry gets taken directly under

Dumbledore's wing. This helps Harry learn what he needs to know for defying and eventually defeating Voldemort. The same goes for Book 7's bequest by Dumbledore of key items to the heroic trio. By the series climax, and in the best tradition of guardian angels, the "Dumbledore" at "King's Cross Station" who helps Harry figure out how to proceed has been incorporated into who Harry is and what he can do.

This "Dumbledore" is almost literally an angel on call to help Harry. Moreover a further version of Dumbledore as a guardian angel joins the gallery of predecessors on call in the head's office to help with Hogwarts School. In life, too, Dumbledore is something of a patron saint to many, and Elphias Doge eulogizes Dumbledore as a helper for diverse friends. This is similar to the Sirius Black sense of his commitment as godfather for Harry. It's even how Harry is seen—by friends *and* foes—to stand out in standing up for others. Dobby hails Harry as the heroic defender of other magical creatures, as well as Dobby's personal liberator. Griphook allows, as a goblin who distrusts wizards, that Harry's deeds distinguish him. Even in sneering at Harry as "Saint Potter" for befriending mudbloods and muggles, Draco Malfoy acknowledges Harry as their patron, their helper. This is the role of patron saints, who are on call for protection in distinct conditions or endeavors: St. Christopher for travelers, St. Francis (of Assisi) for animals, St. Joan (of Arc) for soldiers, St. Teresa (of Calcutta) for missionaries, and St. Jude for children.

The patronus charm is the most prominent spell in the Potter series. Most powerfully, it projects a glowing, ghostly creature unique to the caster. Such a patronus is "corporeal," but some are non-corporeal. A corporeal patronus erupts from a wand and moves as directed by the wielder. With exceptional skill, a patronus can be cast great distances as though apparating; and it can "talk" to deliver messages, as in the last book with Kingsley Shacklebolt's lynx then Arthur Weasley's weasel. A patronus is indispensable for warding away dementors, making it invaluable for resisting their attacks and for dispersing defenses by authoritarian or totalitarian figures. Thus a patronus is, as the name says, quite a "helper."

The kind of creature can change with a major change in the caster's character; but this is rare, and the new patronus stays distinctive for its caster. Hence every corporeal patronus can be used to help characterize its mage. Harry Potter's patronus becomes a stag like that of James, his dead father. Severus Snape's patronus changes to a doe like that of his murdered love, Lily Evans Potter. When Dora Tonks comes to love the werewolf Remus John Lupin, her patronus changes to a huge wolf. Ron Weasley's patronus is a terrier, Hermione Granger's an otter. Luna Lovegood casts a hare, and Ginny Weasley a horse (but only in the movies); while the weakly magical Neville Longbottom casts only a non-corporeal patronus. Aberforth Dumbledore casts a goat, and Albus Dumbledore a phoenix. Minerva McGonagall casts a cat that looks as though it's wearing eyeglasses, while Dolores Umbridge projects a long-haired cat. In the DA, Seamus Finnigan casts a fox, Ernie Macmillan a boar, and Cho Chang a swan. The obvious comparison for a corporeal patronus is a spirit animal: another mythical-magical helper in times of need.

The patronus figure matters immensely to a key event in Book 3 and three further events in Book 7. The reason that a patronus can repel dementors is that they feed on the human misery induced by draining away all happiness and hope. A patronus must be powered by a spirit so overflowing with joy that, projected toward dementors, it begins to undo their constitutive despair and causes them to retreat. When Harry uses the Resurrection Stone as he walks in the forest to face death from Voldemort, he gets such joy from the reappearance of his dead parents and dearest friends. Their words ease his doubts and fears, while their smiles fill him with love and joy. All this shields Harry from the damning despair of the dementors in the way as he moves courageously to his doom. To conjure his patronus in the face of dementors, Lupin tells Harry to summon something akin to such joy, by focusing on the happiest memory he can. Such intense concentration seems crucial to most strong magic; and it's generated *not* by trying hard, which gets in the way, but by Just Doing It—Fully Feeling It, Truly Meaning It.

The challenge that this poses to young mages-in-the-making is daunt-ing. They usually have to think through spells rather than performing them instinctively. Harry's facility for this joyful, loving focus produces his corpo-real patronus early and potently, and this helps identify him as a prodigy in defenses against the dark arts. Likewise his early difficulty in loathing fully (or at least hating truly) seems to limit his gifts for the darkest arts. He resists the Unforgivable Curses surprisingly well, but he struggles to inflict them effectively. Bellatrix Lestrange jeers at him for this during the shootout in Book 5, taunting that his Cruciatus Curse for her couldn't work, because he didn't really mean to torture her, even though she'd just killed his godfather. But by the time he uses that curse effectively on Amycus Carrow in Book 7, Harry says and shows that he's learned what Bellatrix was talking about. That Harry can slice Draco grievously with Snape's Sectum Sempra Curse in Book 6 hints at the hugely hateful impulse that spurs it.

In dark fantasy, such horrors are the stuff of secular Halloween, when children "Trick or Treat." By religious tradition, Hallowe'en is All Hallows' Eve, commemorated on the evening of October 31, before All Saints' Day on November 1. George Weasley's lame but game joke in the last book coaches us to recognize that, as what are hallowed, hallows are "holies" are saints. And saints are patrons are helpers. As some wizards surmise, "The Tale of Three Brothers" can suggest that the Deathly Hallows are Death's Helpers.

Yet the irony of history is that the Elder Wand turns power into death, the Resurrection Stone spurs the living to join the dead, and only the Invisibility Cloak protects wearers from death as advertised.

The historical items seem to have been invented by the three Peverell brothers, long-ago inhabitants of Godric's Hollow. Holding all three of the hallows makes a mage into "the master of death," an ambition pursued avidly by Gellert Grindelwald and Albus Dumbledore in their younger days. Despite his desperation to "conquer death," Voldemort never learns the myth; and Dumbledore thinks that a disregard of tales for children or other inferiors would have kept Voldemort from the hallows path. Instead he takes the horcrux route of murdering others in order to magic parts of his soul into so many objects as to seem invulnerable to a final demise. The choice between hallows and horcruxes frames the series culmination in its concluding book.

As an adult, Dumbledore takes the Elder Wand from Grindelwald, but uses it without flaunting it. He locates the Invisibility Cloak, yet returns that to Harry as the only living descendant of its creator, Ignotus Peverell. Dumbledore has learned not to trust himself with ultimate power. When seeking Voldemort's horcruxes, however, Dumbledore discovers the Resurrection Stone in the Peverell ring, ironically handed down by Voldemort's family but unrecognized by him. Dumbledore's sense of guilt for the death of his sister Ariana momentarily rekindles his greed for power over death. Apparently he forgets that the ring is a Voldemort horcrux, and it inflicts a mortal curse that's killing Dumbledore torturously from his wand hand inward. This is why a surprised Dumbledore can be disarmed by Draco, and it's why the killing curse from Snape can be a mercy ordered by Dumbledore weeks earlier. Harry's heroism is magnified by his decision to walk Dumbledore's humbler path. He turns away from the lure of mastering death through the three hallows, and he searches instead for the horcruxes that keep Voldemort from death. The trio seeks, spots, and destroys horcruxes one after another; and eventually Harry can end what remains of Voldemort. Then he hides the Resurrection Stone, does what he can to end the power of the Elder Wand, and keeps only his personal inheritance of the Invisibility Cloak—always the best of the helpers for Harry.

Arguably Halloween is *the* Harry Potter holiday. Hogwarts celebrates it elaborately in Harry's first four years there. But once that fourth feast is done, the Goblet of Fire selects the Triwizard champions, with Harry an impossibly and dangerously underage fourth. And with the series turning ever darker and more adult from that book onward, no further note is taken of such celebrations. And even earlier, the Potter series shows us the darkness of Halloween, its anticipation of helpers notwithstanding. Voldemort murdered Harry's parents, orphaning him on the Halloween after his first birthday. Nearly Headless Nick, the Gryffindor ghost, died on Halloween in 1492, making All

Hallows' Eve into his annual deathday. As helpers themselves, the heroic trio supports Nick by attending his 500th deathday commemoration rather than the Hogwarts feast. This gruesome experience is instructive, but the trio fails to get Nick included in the Headless Hunt. On the previous Halloween, Ginny Weasley gets possessed by Tom Riddle's diary horcrux. She heralds the Heir of Slytherin's return with a message in blood and an attack on Mrs. Norris. The initial Hogsmeade outing for Harry's class at Hogwarts falls on his third Halloween there, but he (likely alone) lacks guardian permission to make the trip. That night, Sirius Black slashes the portrait of the Pink Lady in trying to get at Peter Pettigrew, hiding as Scabbers in the Gryffindor dormitory. The ensuing upset positions Harry to hear as accepted fact the awful falsehood that Sirius as Harry's godfather had betrayed his parents to Voldemort, murdered many himself, then escaped from Azkahan Prison to finish off Harry.

But already help is at hand, as silver linings emerge from these dark events. Harry and Nick become friends. Harry saves Ginny later in the Chamber of Secrets, and their connection advances. Fred and George Weasley take aside the stranded Harry, to give him the Marauder's Map so that he need never miss another Hogsmeade trip. Harry even gets the chance that day to speak with Lupin about the terror of dementors, and a friendship for those two starts to form. Soon Sirius turns out, after all, to be the true helper for Harry that a godfather hopes to become. Godparents, guardian angels, and patron saints epitomize this third brand of patronist politics, promoted by the Potter series as personal or institutional help so we need not manage all alone.

A fourth kind, patrónism with the Latin accent, is the least important for Potter politics, even though it might get the most attention in political science. Patrónism has been recognized formally and informally as widespread in the "Latin" countries of Central and South America. There the patrón is a taken to be a benign, competent father-figure who decides major questions for all in his community. So members take any matter of community import to the patrón for a ruling, and many take a personal issue of special significance to the patrón for advice. Often the patrón is responsible for effecting such a ruling, but often by directing the deeds of others more than by the patrón's action in itself. There can be a female patróna instead of a male patrón, yet the implication of masculine authority (from macho power to old-man wisdom) often remains. Plainly this can make such patrónism a version of authoritative unto authoritarian politics. Still an atmosphere lingers of help-from-on-high—more than commands-from-above.

A patrón is not a government position so much as a government substitute—at least for a modern government that claims to monopolize authority and legitimate violence in a specific territory. Inside or outside a modern government, a patrón is an unofficial boss whose reach is limited. Thus patrónism as a kind of politics can seem to devalue the apparatus of parties and governments in ways similar to the leadership principle for fascist politics and the charismatic cults constructed for totalitarian leaders. Yet Mussolini in Italy and Hitler in Germany swept away the contrasts between community and personal matters that demarcate a patrón's power. Their "advice" became decisive across the board. Even though Juan and Eva Perón also have been treated as patrónists, their tours as populist champions in Argentina surely started down a totalitarian road. Likewise Voldemort might start as something of a patrón for the Death Eaters, but totalitarian control of Britain and beyond seems to be his ambition. And Dumbledore may get consulted on issues outside his authority for Hogwarts School or the Order of the Phoenix, because he has friends and colleagues far and wide. But these aren't exactly clients or protégés, he takes care to limit his spheres of power, his suggestions remain advice, and his ambitions become anti-totalitarian. Overall the Latin sort of patrónism is not a big part of Potter politics.

By contrast, a fifth variant of patronist politics is a focal concern of *The Half-Blood Prince* and a noticeable ingredient in other Potter books. Like the second version, it's sometimes called "patronage." Yet a patron saint or guardian angel as a helper-on-high features dimensions and dynamics of hierarchy that are mostly missing from Horace Slughorn as a patron in Book 6, so we need another name for his kind of helper. Slughorn is an initial or symbolic boss rather than a top commander. Think of him as the hub of a wheel more than the pinnacle of a pyramid, but he's not a centralizer either. Instead he's a networker, a nexus. In *The Tipping Point* by Malcolm Gladwell, Slughorn could count as a "connector."[1] Yet his Slug Club also can be said to educate his protégés in connecting, so that his work gets augmented by many others in many directions. The Potter books present him as a spider who weaves an extensive web. Even so, we do better to recognize the model of the Weasley broomstick shed, where Dumbledore and Harry talk just after recruiting Slughorn back to Hogwarts. That tiny space is filled with tangles of webs from busy spiders large and small. (Such spiders are horrifying to Ron in part because they evoke his vast web of family ties and attainments for measuring success and earning respect.) These webs of connection are continually being remade by multiple connectors who strengthen some links, let others dangle or detach, and add new ones. As nearly relentless networking, this version of patronist politics could be called patroning. The gerund is meant to evoke an ongoing activity that advances its participants by making themselves into more patrons with further links.

The Half-Blood Prince is especially systematic in presenting four dynamics as crucial for such mutual-advancement networking. First is talent-scouting. Slughorn takes care to observe, sometimes interview, and collect lots of information on Hogwarts students. He taps gossip and social interaction for this, extending his antennae to the wizard world beyond Hogwarts as well.

By accounts like Dumbledore's and Molly Weasley's, what makes Slughorn extraordinary as a networker is his eye for diverse abilities and connections. Of course, he's not acutely attuned to all signs, and he's not known for selecting late-bloomers. But he still identifies future celebrities and stars or potential leaders and networkers before their talents and ties gain general attention. He spots Ginny Weasley on the Hogwarts Express from her spectacular bat-bogey hex.

Slughorn is expert, though not extraordinary, in collecting, connecting, and promoting the talent he spots. Dumbledore explains to Harry how Slughorn will try to recruit him—with flattering invitations, intriguing companions, increasing standing and visibility, advantageous opportunities, and other elite resources. These are par for the collector's course; and since many are elitist appeals, we can recognize that some already have been tried unsuccessfully on Harry by Draco and others. Dumbledore presumably senses that Harry might instinctively resist such moves, so putting Harry on alert is meant to diminish his usual distaste and defenses. After all, Dumbledore wants Slughorn's gambits to succeed with Harry.

Slughorn's connecting is right out of the Gladwell playbook. He holds luncheons and throws parties. He includes people who are disparate but distinguished (or on their ways to distinction). He introduces them in terms of overlapping interests and possibilities for mutual projects or favors. He keeps in frequent contact with others in his network, celebrates their successes to each other, and displays his personal connections to them with a good mixture of pride and fondness. He offers advice and introductions when asked, he volunteers these too, yet his tone is friendly and collegial more than personally authoritative or judgmental. In all this, Slughorn shows a strong sense of "political correctness." Accordingly it's not surprising that his bearing leavens self-confidence and self-satisfaction with some self-effacement.

To promote his protégés after they leave Hogwarts, Slughorn mainly offers connections and recommendations. If he were decently prominent in wizarding politics, business, healing, or some other sphere outside education, he would have additional resources to offer. But at Hogwarts, he's been well-placed to balance the educational resources he can contribute with the little treats and opportunities that come back to him from the network partners he assists in advancing. In a mutual-advancement network, such reciprocity seldom takes the form of an explicit trade in the moment. Participants provide help as needed and when they can, with the general sense that advancing the network by helping its people as possible is the thing to do.

These networks-in-process extend up and down, inward and outward, slant and so on. Yes, Slughorn has high standing at Hogwarts as a professor. Yet he not only cultivates protégés from promising beginners but also reaches out to students and others whose social (or political or professional) standing already exceeds Slughorn's own. In other words, he links "upward" as well as "downward." Slughorn recruits mainstreams, backwaters, even countercurrents—expanding his networks "outward" as well as "inward." This serves his somewhat delusional sense that he's free of prejudice against mages who aren't (don't claim to be) "pure in blood." But mainly, it enables Slughorn to advance as many of his connections as possible in his larger network of networks. Slughorn's personal payoffs are the perquisites of a prospering network: creature comforts, occasional treats and shows of respect, special opportunities, pleasures of socializing, but particularly pride and preening in the glow of his linked luminaries. Slughorn is truly talented as a wizard, an educator, and a networker. He's a minor-leaguer compared to Dumbledore, of course, and largely content with that. Slughorn's perks are more modest than great political power, bright social positions, big bank accounts, or high historical regard. These rewards still differentiate him from a patron saint or guardian angel; and neither are those other figures deeply into the pleasures of networking in particular, *nearly* for its own sake.

Patroning involves favors and friendships more than authorizations or justifications. It taps authority at times, as when Slughorn expects invitations to be accepted or adjourns the Slug Club for the evening; and it justifies most kinds of contacts as keeping up connections. Mainly, however, patroning dispenses with authorizations and justifications by asking and citing favors. (This feature gets perverted when crime or gang bosses use the language of favors to soft-pedal commands or sidestep liability for extortions.) Patroning often benefits from diffuse feelings of elitist inclusion and naughtiness plus little signals of insider recognition—such as winks, nods, secret handshakes, or special tattoos. These feelings are evident in Slughorn's memory of the Slug Club back in the days of Tom Riddle. Treating a mutual-advancement network as a club can accentuate these dynamics, while "good manners" and energetic charm are effective too. Slughorn demonstrates these devices and more.

LIBERALISM

Among modern ideologies, variants of liberalism arguably are best attuned to treating politics as dark arts. For liberals, politics are activities in government, by government, or with respect to government. Unlike republicans, liberals equate "public" with "government." Thus liberal politics feature "public" negotiation or other endeavors to produce laws and policies, "public" enforcement of laws and policies, plus the electioneering, lobbying, petitioning, and other "private" action to influence who's in government and what it does. Such "government" starts as the modern state of authoritarians: it is full and enforced authority within a territory, except that liberals regard as legitimate only the states that *respect the human, individual rights* of their citizens and *represent the interests* of those citizens. Without these safeguards, states are too likely to lapse into tyrannies or other illegitimate forms. Liberal societies need the peace, order, and prosperity made possible by centralizing power in authoritative states that monopolize the legitimate means of violence. Yet liberal individuals can't be free and self-fulfilling unless there are limits on government power and "public" action. The limits must protect a sizable private realm for personal endeavors of many and diverse kinds.

As the name implies, liberalism celebrates liberty above all. Like republicans, liberals contrast liberty with foreign domination of the community (from outside) and with tyrannical domination of the community (from inside). Yet like authoritarians, liberals accept the need for government law-enforcement (coercion) to provide for pursuing prosperity. Therefore a further priority of liberals is to limit government by citizen rights and direct it by citizen representation. Liberals even see personal freedom as crucial to keeping a modern community free from foreign domination. For liberals, nevertheless, politics as arts of government are coercive, dark arts.

For republicans, politics as public actions are "positive," since people fulfill themselves mainly in public, acting with other citizens on common issues. For liberals, politics as actions in, by, or toward government are "negative," since people fulfill themselves mainly in private, freely doing and associating as they wish on what they wish. For republicans, politics liberate, because action in public is the substance of freedom. For liberals, politics coerce, because public action involves government, government enforces, and coercion is the antithesis of freedom. So government and politics begin as "necessary evils," at least initially for ideological liberalism.

To learn much about government and politics, let alone participate in them, could be similar to the self-sacrifice that republicans seek from "reluctant leaders." These can be trusted with power and won't abuse it, because they don't crave it in the first place. Liberals distrust individuals eager for command and coercion. Moreover they worry that such power gradually corrupts those who wield it. Republicans see power as cooperation that helps us to do together what we couldn't alone. For the republican-rhetorical tradition, power is persuasion rather than coercion. Liberals see power as leverage that forces others to do what they otherwise wouldn't.

Hence liberals often respect ambition in private endeavors more than ambition in public, aka governmental, affairs. For most of us as private citizens, informed voting is enough. Who wants to govern or police or lobby—ugh! evils all!—when we could pursue personal passions of art, business, family, farming, money, sport, worship, and whatever? (People committed to public service, that's who, whether republicans, socialists, or others.) Harry's fourth year of DADA treats the darkest arts (such as the Unforgivable Curses) as evils necessary to learn *about* in detail—if defenses against them are to succeed. Liberals such as Albus Dumbledore insist on this, even as they concede that at least a few of us private citizens need to be as skilled at the dark arts as Dora Tonks, Mad-Eye Moody, or Kingsley Shacklebolt, if not Dumbledore himself.

In much the same way that lots of republican words and elements remain in our politics, the "western liberal-democracies," as we call many current countries, are legatees of liberalism. Its ideas are familiar in our ordinary ways of talking about politics in everyday life, our media, even our political sciences. So it can be plausible to array versions of these liberal politics on a spectrum from Left to Right. Left-liberals favor active states that see citizen rights as expansive and citizen welfare as the public interest, whether met by public policies or private enterprises. Right-liberals favor fairly inactive states that focus on national security, domestic tranquility, and crisis aid. Not only do liberal regimes develop many possibilities between these poles, but liberals use new technologies (especially of communication) to reconceive the limiting cases and to stretch them further apart. Thus "welfare-state liberals" resemble "democratic socialists" of late, while "classical, minimal-state liberals" unto libertarians call themselves "conservatives."

Akin to liberalism as a political ideology is the economic ideology of capitalism, which arguably becomes economics as a social science. For both, personal freedom depends on *private property*, as almost complete control over what's owned, and on *free markets*, where owners trade without government interference (save for small taxes). *Capital* is a good rented from an owner for limited use. The user pays an arranged return on this investment, enabling accumulation of capital by the owner. Ideally the user gains more than the cost, the rent, which exceeds any loss in the good's value from its use, so both borrower and lender profit. Medieval Christianity had banned renting money, aka "charging interest," as sinful "usury." But capitalism systematizes the unrestricted circulation of money and other goods in an economy as *free trade*, claiming it to be crucial to productivity and prosperity. By our times, "neo-liberals" strive to globalize free markets in most goods. (Some populists, socialists, and traditionalist conservatives resist this.)

The Potter books don't delve far into political economy, as it long was called. Gringotts Bank is prominent in Pottery; but if it lends, we don't learn about that. Instead we see its vaults storing goods. Harry gives (not lends) his Triwizard winnings to the Weasley twins for a joke shop. They'd tried to capitalize on their savings by bets with Ludo Bagman; but he'd reneged, as he did with goblins too. As a form of risk-taking, capitalist lending (investing, rent-seeking) gets compared by critics to gambling. Still the cautious goblins who run Gringotts might steer clear of money-lending because their sense is that wizards are bad risks. Bill Weasley learns in working for Gringotts that, regardless of any contract, goblins don't take goblin-made goods to become private property for wizards to trade or bequeath among themselves. In effect, mages may only rent (not buy) such objects, which should revert to goblins when wizard buyers die. Of course, wizards do what they can to keep these "purchases," which goblins seldom get back. If capitalism operates in Pottery, it's only among wizards—and doesn't involve "their" bank.

The Weasley family is where aspects of Potter economy surface most clearly. In addition to Bill Weasley as a curse-breaker in Egypt for Gringotts Bank, Arthur, Percy, and the twins are employed in roles familiar from a neoliberal world order. Fred and George epitomize capitalist entrepreneurs and inventors in launching Weasleys' Wizard Wheezes as a small business meant to grow rapidly. Percy's first post in the MOM is in the Department of International Magical Cooperation, where he refines International Magical Trading Standards for cauldrons. This is the kind of cross-governmental agreement that enables diverse countries to collaborate in the liberal regulation of (largely) free trade. While policing the Misuse of Muggle Artifacts in the Ministry Department of Magical Law Enforcement, Arthur is lobbied repeatedly to reverse a British ban on flying carpets. This exemplifies government regulation of the domestic economy. In the residual patriarchy of magical Britain at the turn of the century, Molly's economic role is "homemaker." (It's unclear that Ginny is inclined likewise.) Through the age-old symbolism of dragons as hoarders of treasure in general and gold in particular, even Charlie as a government-employed handler of those dangerous creatures has economic links. First names identify these lower-middle-class Weasleys nonetheless as British royalty, yet their neoliberal occupations are politically telling too. (As usual, as he mostly dreads, Ron proves exceptional in both respects.)

Other close kin to ideological liberalism include many liberation movements, although some *can* be closer to republicanism or socialism. Many animal liberationists are eco-liberals, many in the women's liberation movement are liberal feminists, and some national liberation fronts include liberals. Hermione's Society for the Promotion of Elfish Welfare (SPEW) sounds vaguely socialist in stressing welfare. Inspired by Dobby's pride as "a free elf," though, her campaign to knit "clothes" for elves spurs Ron's more liberal language about the House-Elf Liberation Front. Hermione's insistence on equal rights and respect for women is clearly liberal. The series even gives a liberal spin to its takes on nationalism, by coupling them with accounts of the *free press*. In Books 4 and 5, Potter portraits of the *Daily Prophet* as a newspaper and *The Quibbler* as a tabloid range from jocular to acidic. Yet their liberal roles in constructing "the wizarding nation" in Britain are shown by the authoritarian and totalitarian moves in Books 6 and 7 to commandeer or squelch those media of information and opinion. With the Order of the Phoenix dispersed in the last book, the resistance to Voldemort resorts to *Potterwatch* as a "pirate radio" broadcast for at least a little light in the darkest times. Its liberal conviction that free expression of truths and free debate of political views can be great liberators recalls Radio Free Europe and *samizdat* as devices for resisting post–World War II oppression in the Communist Bloc.

From its Anglo beginning with John Locke, the liberal project of individual freedom has led into vexed questions of principle and practice. Among the philosophical concerns is how we can commit ourselves in good faith to completing courses of action. Once committed, how do we retain the freedom that validates our faith? How do the promises and contracts central to liberalism as political economy bind free individuals without undoing their freedom? Pottery enchantments and prophecies can raise this issue, but its most poignant appearance in Potter books is also the most urgent for early liberals. *Can* slavery be justified? For liberals, the test is whether an individual *can* choose freely to become a slave, stay indentured, or otherwise trade away all freedom for any (other) good. Locke contended that this is conceptually incoherent: it's nonsense, impossible to attain, and abominable to attempt. A chooser can't genuinely choose to live without choice. Critics rejoin that liberal cases of this sort (like some defenses of capitalism) implicitly depend on implausible dichotomies between choice and coercion, freedom and force.

House-elves are the Potter vehicles for posing such questions. Dobby is desperate to be liberated, and relishes his identity as a free elf. But others embrace their servitude. Thus Winky experiences her "liberation" as the crushing punishment of excommunication that it was meant to be. She is desperate to return to the usual happiness of house-elves serving their masters. (Is Kreacher a more complicated case?) Can "happiness" in slavery be authentic? Even if so, could it justify the choice to become or remain a slave? Harry has strong reasons to realize that Dobby wants freedom. But the Hogwarts house-elves show Hermione repeatedly that their choice is not Dobby's, nor is it Hermione's to make for them. Yet how can a true defender of individual (liberal) freedom simply accept, let alone benefit from, enslaving others? Does Hermione go too far in trying to trick house-elves into liberation, in the Enlightenment conviction that living free means learning to love freedom? Should the one counter-case of Winky weigh heavily against liberal principles, especially when Dobby's case supports them? This problematic is liberal.

Liberalism promotes individualism: expressive (free-speech rights), possessive (private-property rights), and progressive (self-development rights). Some liberals are "methodological individualists" who claim that the only adequate explanations are in terms of individuals. Then talk of classes, races, groups, or institutions at best abbreviates specifics about particular human beings. Some liberals are even "ontological individualists" who say that only individuals really exist. Armies and firms and nations and such somehow aren't exactly there; only the individual humans who comprise them are fully or basically real. Brits speak thus, using plural pronouns and verbs for collective nouns; whereas Americans mainly use singular pronouns and verbs for collective nouns like *army*, *government*, or *school*. Brits favor, "Today the army [soldiers] train, tomorrow they invade." Americans say instead, "Today the army trains, tomorrow it invades."

As "moral individualists," some liberals reject concepts of "collective guilt" and "group rights." Hence some oppose affirmative action, group reparations, minority representation, and so forth as fascist or at least unjust. Yet liberals respect rights of peoples when constituted as countries, and some echo Woodrow Wilson on "the right of national self-determination." This nationalist ideal, like the notion of a nation-state, allocates a government to each culture. Of course, actual states govern several (swatches of) cultures, ethnicities, nations, or peoples, sharing these with other countries. Many liberals now accept this, adding it to global markets as foundations for a "liberal international order." An increasing portion of liberals even embrace "multiculturalism" as a celebration of group identities that revs liberal "toleration" into a cultivation of "diversity" and "inclusion." Nonetheless liberals want all individuals to enjoy full equality before the law, effective representation in the government, and the maximum freedom extendable to everyone.

Enter Albus Dumbledore as Hogwarts Headmaster. His school regime is recognizably liberal in its due process, humane discipline, and dedication to the individual development of every student. As a leading scholar, with research into the uses of dragon's blood recognized even on his chocolate-frog card, Dumbledore is a notable practitioner of liberal enlightenment. As a brilliant youth of modest background, he rises high through the individual talents touted by liberals; yet he also learns the individual limits needed to sidestep most evils of government. Mainly, though, Dumbledore epitomizes liberalism as a style of political action that strives for rationality and consistency from everyday conditions to the darkest of times. He enacts many tropes of liberal politics: civil communication, rigorous inquiry, individual dignity, and more.

Dumbledore hopes to treat people who disagree with him as "opponents," who remain within and for the community, rather than as "enemies" outside and against it. He doesn't treat Fudge, Scrimgeour, or even Umbridge as though they were Grindelwald, Voldemort, or Death Eaters. Still he spots and resists those genuine enemies with great skill. He wants Hogwarts open to all eleven-year-olds with magical potential, whether born of muggles, mixed families, or magical parents. He rethinks Hogwarts traditions, since he wants good reasons for action and he doesn't count, "We've always done it that way." Hence he's widely recognized as a "progressive," which explains much of what Umbridge says at the year-opening feast. These days, "progressive" is what liberals call themselves when they fear that "liberal" will be taken to mean "spendthrift," "sentimental," or "arrogant." In the best liberal mode, Dumbledore is strikingly reflective and self-critical. Yet he proves all the more decisive and effective for this, contrary to caricatures of liberals as hesitant to act. Likewise Dumbledore combines strategic planning for policy with tactical intelligence for administration plus fast footwork on the spot, when unanticipated events intervene. Take his brilliant responses to Fudge and Umbridge all the way through Book 5, even as he keeps a clear and vigorous eye turned to Voldemort.

As a liberal, Dumbledore wants the political community to provide choices (freedoms) and chances (opportunities). He gives Hagrid, Harry, Ron, Draco, Sibyll, Firenze, and no doubt others second chances, third tries, fourth attempts, and more. Dumbledore reminds Harry how the Sorting Hat takes student choices into account, and he works hard to explain to Harry how even the truest of prophecies leave room for choices. Notwithstanding his manipulative, if far-seeing strategies, Dumbledore takes great care to respect Harry as a chooser. Harry's choice in the final book between pursuing hallows and destroying horcruxes to overcome Voldemort is a vivid example. But it's only one among many throughout the series, arguably starting with the crucial decision posed for Harry by the Mirror of Erised. As a liberal, Dumbledore turns away from sheer causes and supposed determinants like elitist birth, fascist blood, traditionalist fate, republican destiny, or realist fortune. Not determinism but development is Dumbledore's path for Harry as an individual, however successful or happy or heroic Harry might become.

CONSERVATISM

For several decades, "conservatism" has become a label for a large grab-bag of political views. Some are systematized into ideologies, although they differ strikingly from each other. Some are practiced as anti-ideological styles of "preserving the past," "muddling through," or "accommodating change as necessary." Some romanticize early liberalism, crony capitalism, or contested cultural traditions. Yet these miscellaneous impulses often make common cause, and the resulting "conservative movement" has come to occasional prominence in several countries, including Great Britain and the United States. Long before it emerged in *any* ideological form, though, conservatism was a temperament of caution, nostalgia, and distrust of modernization. Doubts about modern, means-ends rationality ran so deep in this early conservatism that it only became a full logic of ideas in reluctant self-defense. Reacting against the French Revolution, as an anti-traditionalist travesty that evoked such modern ideologies as socialism and liberalism, Edmund Burke in Britain and Joseph De Maistre in France argued deeply different cases against those modes of reasoning. In doing so, they more or less made a mood into two logics of ideas.

Indeed De Maistre's logic seems more a *reactionism* that would reconstruct an idealized past than a *conservatism* that would retain what's defensible in the present. Burke's theory gives principles for recognizing what can and should be conserved, what can and should be adjusted, and how to do so. If there has been general agreement among self-identified conservatives as to what should be conserved above all, it probably is (law and social) *order*. Most conservatives imagine order as hierarchy, making it easy to tell why many can seem authoritarian at times. Yet many conservatives conceive order as bodily and organic, seeing institutions and societies as limbs, organs, and organisms. (Authoritarians and liberals imagine institutions as machines; republicans treat them as fabrics, cloths, or clothes made as stitches in space and time; socialists vary; while populists typically distrust or oppose institutions as incipient bureaucracies.)

As with De Maistre, though, a difficulty is that conserving of any kind is a low priority for many so-called conservatives. It would be hard to find a more misleading name in recent politics, at least for ideologies, movements, and styles. The label carries a warm glow for many people: reminding them fondly of who we've been, whence we've come, or what we've hoped. Thus calling a cause or policy "conservative" can be a good rhetorical gambit. But several kinds of "conservatism" seek change far more radical (basic, reaching the roots) than do most brands of liberalism or socialism. Then the conservative appeal of holding fast to who we are and what we have amounts to political bait-and-switch, for audiences or even advocates.

"Conservative" is an intelligible label for those who want to conserve earlier liberalisms, possibly all the way back to the "classical liberalism" attributed to Locke or American founders. This also includes the "neo-conservatives," who see domestic tranquility and social order as far more imperiled needs than do the "bleeding-heart liberals" whom they scold. And it includes "new right" campaigns against economic regulation, cultural libertinism and permissiveness, as well as the welfare state. All these we could examine as liberalism, more than conservatism; but they don't surface significantly in the Potter series. Nor do the Potter books attend directly to the libertarianism of utterly minimal government, a radical kind of politics that often resembles anarchism more than liberalism, let alone conservatism. Likewise the objectivism of Ayn Rand acolytes, who sometimes claim to be conservatives, is a heroic or perfectionist kind of capitalism, which departs radically from any practices in history . . . and doesn't appear either in Pottery.

Arguably the kinds or aspects of "conservatism" most suited to the name are the politics that cling to threatened cultures or institutions, trying to "conserve" them by keeping them vital for coming generations. Such *cultural conservatism* has been a powerful part of "the conservative movement" in several countries of late. It's also an important project in fascist, nationalist, and populist politics, which often accredit themselves as continuations of identities, institutions, and traditions that reach back many centuries. Historical studies sometimes agree with these claims of cultural ancestry, but often debunk them as recent inventions. What often matters politically, however, is the meaning that such myths (true or false) can provide for present conditions and possibilities. In this way, cultural conservatism can loom large in our politics. And it can lurk quietly in our comedies, where happy endings often restore comfortable orders nearly lost. The epilogue to the Potter saga ends thus with Hogwarts School restored for the next generation.

When the "conservative" effort is to hide from changes that already have happened and plainly cannot be called back, a better term might be "delusional politics." To cling desperately and blindly to an empty bag, while pretending that the cat must still be in it, is sad at best but often dangerous. By the fifth Potter volume, Cornelius Fudge has become such a head-in-the-sand conservative. And his desperation to keep people turned away from the true situation becomes increasingly dangerous to Hogwarts, the MOM, and more.

Still there can be honor and wisdom in clinging to an established order, *almost* without regard to its structure or content, when the practical alternative seems to be blood in the streets. Thus revolutionary upheaval usually appalls conservatives, because it seems naïve about likely results but also because it seems bound to be bloody beyond any redeeming gains. This is why conservatives embrace *law and order* in principle, policy, and style. It makes most conservatives big on *duty* too. Rufus Scrimgeour is a formidable but tragic example. As Minister of Magic in Book 6, he hectors Harry, Ron, Hermione, even presumably Dumbledore on the duty to stand with the Ministry in dark times. When Harry objects that scapegoating Stan Shunpike gives the lie to any pretense of defending law, Scrimgeour suggests, with most conservatives, that crisis makes order more important. In our dark times, such situations become so familiar that liberals and socialists often criticize self-identified conservatives as authoritarian lions who merely pose as democratic badgers. (Recall the animal comparisons for Scrimgeour and Hufflepuff House?) But Snape would say that Harry, as an incorrigible rule-breaker, has no right to this complaint.

Like De Maistre, some "conservatives" would return (impossibly) to romanticized pasts. Most *aristocratic* and *traditionalist* conservatives celebrate nobilities, institutions, and ways of life eclipsed long ago by modern values and endeavors. Our world has moved on from these older arrangements in part because there has been plenty of reason to denigrate them. This includes the modern refusal to respect the traditionalist's "it's long been done that way" as any kind of reason. (Authoritarians encounter a version of this trouble in the modern rejection as a reason of "because I said so.") Modern individuals plausibly take such "arguments" as implicit threats rather than persuasive reasons. Thus conservatives have needed to generate modern reasons to justify their preservation, let alone their restoration, projects. That is why Burke and De Maistre can be read as trying to ideologize conservatism (or reactionism), despite their indictments of the technical rationality central to modern political ideologies. And rationally, if bringing back defunct aristocracies or traditions is unrealistic, how about adapting them to recent sensibilities, needs, and technologies? Few conservativisms try to detail such adjustments and defend them, but those we can respect. How about learning from older ways? Much the same goes for such "conservative" lessons, specified and justified.

Actually this is where some classicist and medievalist fantasy comes into the picture as political theory. Its ample popularity suggests current curiosity for early theocracies, empires, and republics or for feudal courts, hordes, and monasteries. Even the "escapist" satisfaction of such curiosity is bound to make connections with present challenges and responses, and many fantasies have bigger political ambitions. For example, various conservatives see property as a key concern for politics; yet only those partial to liberalism and capitalism treat private property as sovereign ownership. Fantasies that feature ancient myths or medieval institutions often pay careful attention to other, non-individualist takes on property as imagined from earlier times or contrasting creatures. The goblin conception of property is a Potter case in point.

As fantasy in medieval dress and setting, Pottery gestures at times toward traditionalist conservatisms. We *might* look at the four houses of Hogwarts that way: conserving institutions from the middle ages. That these houses can be readily recognized as republican lodges would not stand in the way, since many medieval devices are largely republican. Yet let's not miss the forest for a tree or two. Politically Harry's world is our world, even after he goes to Hogwarts. As Arthur Weasley seems to recognize, even the magic in Harry's world has rough equivalents in our electricity, surgery, and such (III.250: IV.548). Especially with Voldemort and the Death Eaters, Harry's world isn't exactly classical, medieval, or even modern: already it's racing past those periods.

Beyond the urgent need to conserve order, conservatisms worthy of the name usually emphasize seven further themes. Individual humans are imperfect and will remain so. The main seats of rationality and wisdom in this world are enduring societies and institutions, *not* modern individuals. Social institutions should mediate between individuals and governments, to protect them from each other. Societies and institutions endure as healthy organisms that keep human individuals from lawlessness (anomie), loneliness (alienation), meaninglessness (absurdity), and powerlessness (vulnerability). Through institutions like families and schools, societies should shape dutiful people who respect elders, established powers, and social rules—but not overly. Rational plans to remake societies and institutions are recipes for tragedy or atrocity. So conduct should be "pragmatic," to conserve what it can and adjust what it must.

We do well to appreciate how the Potter brand of perfection*ism* that Harry exemplifies need not conflict with a conservative insistence on human imperfection. Neither Harry nor his author even flirts with the (sometime modern) ambition for personal or societal "perfection" as the elimination of flaws, sins, or mistakes. Most conservatives scoff at the (e)utopian projects of (some versions of) other modern ideologies as impossible and perverse. The impossibility is in principle, but the perversity is in practice. The French Revolutionary dream of liberty, equality, and fraternity to end the *ancien régime* culminates in the Reign of Terror rather than a republic. The Marxist project of a communist condition where the modern, coercive state "withers away" is foolish in theory and appalling in the Soviet gulag. The German Nazi myth of a "New Aryan Race" to rule "the Third Reich" for a thousand years ends quickly in World War II and the Final Solution. Even the liberal efforts to "make the world safe for democracy" with a "war to end all wars" and campaigns to "democratize" all countries or "globalize" all markets can strike many conservatives (and others) as hubris in ambition and catastrophe in consequence. And then there are the environmental travesties induced by the industrialization embraced by most modern ideologists, conservatives included. Actually, for these reasons and more, lots of liberals, socialists, and others have come to share such conservative skepticism about humanity.

The Potter series rehearses this recent history of human folly in vivid terms, which many a conservative could endorse. In response, though, it offers Potter perfectionism as a turn away from conformism and fascism, especially. It would have us recognize conformism as enforced mediocrity, and deplore fascism as a perversion of the defensible perfectionisms we often need. The Potter saga has Harry pursue "perfection" in ways comparable to the American attempt to constitute "a more perfect union." To be sure, some literalist grammarians try to rule out talk of increasing *perfection*, by degrees or otherwise, on the ground that anything truly "perfect" can't be improved. But this should strike us as small-minded conformism that Harry and his friends learn to leap beyond. Potter perfectionism learns from Emersonian,

Nietzschean, *and* Christian versions. Harry's aspirations to excel impel him toward good rather than glory, love more than genius, and sacrifices more than superpowers. He stays humble, loyal, and loving by learning from other people and other politics. In the Potter books, as we are seeing, he learns especially from republican, liberal, feminist, and environmental practices.

Harry and company show impressive respect for the wisdom and authority of Hogwarts School, although Harry shows even more for Dumbledore as his mentor and patron. The most impressive evidence in both cases includes Harry's kinds and reasons for departing from their direction, as well as his crunch-time faith in the school and its headmaster. For all its students, teachers, and staff, Hogwarts operates as what some conservatives call a mediating institution. It repeatedly protects its individuals from most direct manipulation by the government, even as it helps them in accommodating aspects of government action when they would prefer not to. The Potter series focuses sufficiently on Dumbledore himself doing this for others that it could be easy to miss how he's often operating in an institutional tradition in this respect. Surely that's suggested by the counsels kept and errands done by the "living portraits" of prior heads. In at least a loose way, such "portraits" contribute touches of organic symbolism to Hogwarts, St. Mungo's, and other Pottery institutions. They even evoke how institutions, as enduring across generations, can know more and think better than most (modern) individuals on their own.

The Potter reliance on impulse and improvisation for most of Harry's best successes is perfectionist more than conservative. But both kinds of politics oppose the modern domination of strategic rationality, and both expect even the most carefully calculated of plans to miscarry more than not. (This is one of the many ways in which Dumbledore, the great liberal planner and orchestrator of Hogwarts, is exceptional.) Conservatives at least can approve the insistent collapse of one plan after another, even when the heroic trio tries to act as rationally as possible. Rather than rely on societal intelligence or institutional wisdom, though, the trio turns sketchy plans from Dumbledore into choices and improvisations that prove mostly good enough.

KEEPING THE MAGICAL PROMISE

On the day that Dumbledore dies, he hopes to find a horcrux made and hidden by Tom Riddle, aka Lord Voldemort. All year, Dumbledore and Harry have been using the Pensieve to review memories of Voldemort's past. Dumbledore has collected these, save for the one that Harry promises to get from Horace Slughorn. When Felix Felicis makes Harry lucky enough to fulfill that promise, the memory specifies Dumbledore's guess that Voldemort has been secreting his soul in magical containers—probably six beyond his own body. One horcrux was the Riddle diary, already slain by Harry in the Chamber of Secrets. A second was the Peverell ring, found and destroyed by Dumbledore, although his attempt to use its Resurrection Stone has inflicted a fatal curse on the headmaster that Snape could only slow, not undo. Dumbledore infers that a third horcrux is probably the Slytherin locket, which has been an heirloom in the Gaunt family of Voldemort's descent on his mother's side. He thinks that it's hidden in a cave discovered by the young Riddle, and he thinks that its magical defenses will be daunting. Harry can help recover the locket, but he must promise to obey Dumbledore completely on their trip.

It's a tough go, and Harry has to help a desperately weakened headmaster back to a castle now menaced by a Dark Mark over the Astronomy tower. On the ramparts, Dumbledore orders Harry to fetch Snape. But a noise alerts Dumbledore to have Harry hide. Draco bursts from the door to the staircase with a disarming charm for Dumbledore, who's immobilized Harry only an instant before the Elder Wand flies from the old wizard's hand and off the roof. As a new Death Eater, apparently in place of his imprisoned father, Draco has pledged or been commanded to kill Dumbledore. Apparently on pain of death, Draco has been trying all year. A cursed necklace and poisoned mead have misfired. Yet now his repair of the vanishing cabinet in the Room of Hidden Things has let other Death Eaters into the castle, to support his assault on Dumbledore. Draco crows that Dumbledore is at his mercy; Dumbledore calmly says that it's the other way around. Unseen off to the side, Harry's arrested in word and deed.

While the other Death Eaters fight their way past some of Dumbledore's Army and the Order of the Phoenix, Dumbledore talks Draco down. Other Death Eaters arrive on the ramparts to demand that Draco proceed. But Snape arrives; and Dumbledore begs Snape to do what he's promised, in order to spare Dumbledore some indignity and pain in his inevitable death. Snape casts the killing curse, and Dumbledore falls from the ramparts. To the amazement of Bellatrix Lestrange, Snape had earlier made the unbreakable vow to her sister, Narcissa Malfoy, to kill Dumbledore if Draco were to falter and fail to manage it. Snape has fulfilled that promise too. (These wrenching complications help make Snape into the tragic hero of the Potter series.)

Promises, promises everywhere! What, exactly, are they? What are their political roles, especially in this fatal confrontation? How do promises compare to loose equivalents like oaths, pledges, vows, compacts, contracts, and other commitments? Brief answers to such questions can help us explore how Potter magic can change promises, and with what political implications.

Promises are easy examples of speech refining raw bodily motions into specific actions, politically or otherwise. In the twentieth century, in fact, ordinary language philosophy says that promises are cases of speech *as* action: speech by itself, without gesture. Thus promises are said to be "performatives." To say the (right, relevant) words, to yourself or others, is to do the deed; it's to make the promise.[2] Okay, but this admits of adjustments in several directions. Even the uttered words that *are* promises wouldn't (even couldn't) be so without contexts or forms of life that link earlier and later acts-with-gestures to the words' meanings.[3] Therefore "performatives" in the philosophers' sense aren't cases of speech doing all the work but rather of moving bodies staying in the background. Second, as philosophers are quick to emphasize, the vocal or written (as well as gestural) delivery of the words matters to their meanings and deeds. This extends the scope of "performance" at issue, matching it better to the politics presented here as republican, existentialist, and perfectionist. The style of speaking inflects the (political) action. And third, *all* kinds of "speech acts" are performatives in that the literal meanings of their words turn out to be residually and prospectively figural, so that they must be performed in ways that include the listeners, readers, viewers, or other interactors in achieving shared understandings. Promises, like laws and other rules, usually seem especially reliant on careful wording and (confinement to) literal meaning—or other meaning fully sharable with any other parties such as a promise's recipients, witnesses, or enforcers.[4] Even then, their figurality remains, as debates about "the spirit versus the letter" of the law testify. Because all language is tropal, is "fossil poetry," all language is "performative." And because all action is tropal, all deeds are performances.[5]

As we've been seeing, Potter magic helps spotlight this; and Potter promises contribute. They show the figurality—the turning—in making, bending, breaking, and otherwise performing commitments, whether to ourselves or others. The Snape vow takes the form of a magical ritual. It's a ceremony with a promiser, a recipient, and a spell-caster. Does the spell-casting guarantee fulfillment of the promise? Not if the situation for performance fails to occur. But if it does, is the spell a physical cause, a biological drive, or psychological compulsion to perform as vowed? No, Ron says that it's a penalty imposed magically upon failure to perform as vowed: violators die (VI.325–6). The magic isn't puppeteering but punishment, not inducement but enforcement. This is almost as though a state were to monitor Snape's compliance with a contract and, when surveillance shows any violation, executes him summarily: no argument, no appeal, no waiting.

In republican terms, but without Potter magic, the Snape vow is a solemn oath: not just a serious or sincere but a ceremonial promise. It's a specifically public act. Bellatrix as the spell-caster is a stand-in for public witnesses to the oral promise. Instead of conclusive governmental (or magical) assessments and automatic consequences, the scene would have public observation, judgment, maybe action—in addition to whatever the promiser and the recipient do. In a public, participation by diverse individuals means that none of these elements need be consensual. Yet they can be authoritative. The unbreakable vow gives to public authority the initially authoritarian twist of the modern state as a formally absolute sovereign: a full and final decider and enforcer. (Remember that liberalism, socialism, and conservatism as modern ideologies move to limit that power in principle and in practice.) Or worse, the unbreakable vow eradicates public authority in favor of fascist solidarity in following the leader. Action imitates what the Dark Lord would do.

Imagine that the "public" is other Death Eaters. Clearly there are disagreements among them about whether Snape is abiding by whatever commitments he's made in becoming a Death Eater. He's viewed and treated differently from one Death Eater to the next. But as *the* leader, Voldemort's views matter the most by far—*so* far that we might not agree to the premise that the Death Eaters form a public. Nevertheless Death Eaters such as Bellatrix, Igor, Quirinus, and Lucius differ in their support and respect for Snape. Unsurprisingly the same is true for (commitments of) Snape as a colleague in the Order of the Phoenix. There Dumbledore is the (republican) founder and authority when disputes need to be resolved. Voldemort, however, is the (fascist) dictator or dominator of the Death Eaters. In a genuine public, without an absolutized authority or idolized exemplar, third-party witnesses for a solemn promise can (help) make good on it, adjust it, waive it, and so on. Simple talk of "enforcement" fits only the police action of a modern state, the terrifying surveillance of a totalitarian regime, or the conformist impositions of a mob, which often signals worse public trouble than a broken promise. By implication, the unbreakable vow is authoritarian unto totalitarian. It fits Death Eaters but not Hogwarts students or Dumbledore's friends, who embrace individual freedom in ways more liberal (or conservative or socialist). In fact, it's fair to see liberal politics as largely a texture of promises, compacts, contracts, and such.

(The blood pact between Dumbledore and Grindelwald in *Fantastic Beasts* differs from the unbreakable vow in that the promise is two-way, made by both parties to each other rather than by only one to the other. It's sealed by sharing and storing their blood in a magical vial. Yet, typically, there are no third parties, no extra spell-casters, no "public" witnesses. Still there's something of a ceremony to the performance of the magic, underscoring the solemnity and stakes of the mutual promises. As with the unbreakable vow, magic monitors compliance and punishes violation. Similarly it functions like governmental enforcement unto totalitarian surveillance and control. Of course, the blood politics mark such a magical pact as racist and fascist in symbol.)

Dumbledore seeks promises from Harry in private (one-on-one) and without any magical force. Dumbledore has to remind Harry repeatedly to keep pursuing the Slughorn memory until he succeeds. This doesn't seem to surprise Dumbledore. He's a teacher, prodding to help Harry learn about obligations and priorities. Hermione keeps telling Harry that persuasion is the only way to part Slughorn from his memory, and Dumbledore works to persuade Harry to fulfill his commitment to retrieve the memory. Persuasion seldom operates by purest logic, so the appeals rely on Harry's good faith plus his senses of honor, shame, and guilt. But these arise in relation to Dumbledore as the recipient of Harry's promise. There's no larger public involved (at least until Harry tells his best friends about it). Here Dumbledore engages Harry in a liberal practice of promising. When Harry persuades Slughorn, it's likewise by reminding him of commitments to Lily, Harry's mother, and how these have become obligations to her son. It's also by showing the life-or-death priority for Harry. (The future of mages under Voldemort doesn't seem a focal consideration for Slughorn.) By limiting the act to the recipient and the promiser, these liberal politics make the commitment and fulfillment in promising as fully free or voluntary as possible. Does Harry want the extra push of something like "public" pressure from Hermione and Ron?

In building on months of Slughorn reminders for Harry, Dumbledore does the same when he requires that Harry promise unquestioning, unhesitating obedience for the cave trip. In this case, Dumbledore has Harry pledge his compliance repeatedly before they actually depart. This adds to Dumbledore's choice of words and tone of voice in communicating the stakes. It also reminds Harry of his previous need to be reminded time and again to pursue his promise to get the Slughorn memory. Whatever guilt, honor, and learning this summons will have to suffice, because Harry won't have a chance to add further "encouragement" from his friends. Keeping an eye on educating Harry as a moral individual, who chooses to make good on promises even when it's agonizingly hard, Dumbledore again proceeds to keep Harry's commitment private in order that it be given and performed as freely as possible. Dumbledore thinks that Harry is ready for this challenge, and he is. Dumbledore helps by explaining as much as he can, while the two are pushed to the brink (and over for a moment or two) in defeating the defenses for the locket.

Back on the Hogwarts tower, though, the situation is different; and Dumbledore sees it. Harry doesn't know enough about what's happening to recognize good priorities for action, let alone the reasons for them. (In Harry's limbo of King's Cross Station, "Dumbledore" confesses later that he didn't think Harry could handle this knowledge.) Dumbledore anticipates plausibly that Harry's love, loyalty, and honor are on the verge of propelling him into the tower action. If there'd been time for a promise from Harry, and there probably wasn't, Dumbledore recognizes that such a commitment wouldn't come or, even if it did, wouldn't hold from Harry. Rather than seek a promise to stay silent and out of the way, Dumbledore simply freezes Harry in place and voice. (No one needs to worry about restoring Harry to action afterward, because Dumbledore's spell lapses with his death; and even then, Harry seems stunned for a further moment.)

Modern liberals, conservatives, and socialists all admit the likelihood and legitimacy of exceptional times for governments to sidestep usual delibera-tion or other limits on action. Then temporarily authoritarian moves might be in order to create, preserve, or restore social order. On the tower, this is figurally what Dumbledore takes himself to do with Harry. Most ideologies of politics seek measures to abbreviate these moments of crisis, these "states of exception."[6] In a nutshell, the project is to tame the relevant authoritarian devices while holding them in reserve for emergencies. Anarchists doubt that this can be done, they see state imposition of order as death to individual freedom, and they seek social arrangements to accomplish voluntarily what states enforce.[7] Harry gets caught in the "binding magical contract" con-nected with the Goblet of Fire. This rules him even though he doesn't apply and doesn't even qualify to compete in the Triwizard Tournament. He's (magically? institutionally? socially?) forced to do so. This is what anar-chists expect as the awful, oppressive result from conjuring modern states into operation.

Patronism sometimes operates with explicit promises, as when it involves membership in (private) clubs. But more often, it works with implicit prom-ises that invoke flexible, informal commitments that can be fulfilled in many ways by most members of the advancement network. This puts a premium on (modes of) performance, on doing things in style. Think of Slughorn's responses to the stylish perquisites provided by Tom Riddle and others. It's easier to imagine anarchists happier with promises of the second kind, and it's plausible to see some anarchism *as* such patronism without the authority fig-ure (the patron) at its hub. After all, the loosely socialist anarchism of mutual aid and support fundamentally *is* an informal unto semi-formal network of individuals collaborating for survival and advancement.

NOTES

1. See Malcolm Gladwell, *The Tipping Point* (Boston: Little, Brown, 2000, 2002), 30–59.

2. See J. L. Austin, *How to Do Thing with Words*, ed. J. O. Urmson (New York: Oxford University Press, 1962); John R. Searle, *Speech Acts* (New York: Cambridge University Press, 1969). After starting with Austin, Searle, and company, the interest in politics of promises in Pottery turns this discussion away from the concerns and technical terms of ordinary language philosophy; so the "performatives" here aren't

exactly "performative utterances" in Austin's or Searle's senses, since they're not talking about political styles.

3. See Ludwig Wittgenstein, *Philosophical Investigations*, trans. G. E. M. Anscombe (New York: Macmillan, third edition, 1958).

4. See Friedrich Waismann, *How I See Philosophy*, ed. Rom Harré (New York: St. Martin's Press, 1968); John R. Searle, "Literal Meaning," *Erkenntnis* 13, no. 1 (July 1978): 207–24.

5. See John S. Nelson, *Tropes of Politics* (Madison: University of Wisconsin Press, 1998).

6. See Giorgio Agamben, *State of Exception*, trans. Kevin Attell (Chicago: University of Chicago Press, 2005).

7. See Robert Paul Wolff, *In Defense of Anarchism* (New York: Harper and Row, 1970); April Carter, *The Political Theory of Anarchism* (New York: Harper and Row, 1971); Ursula K. Le Guin, *The Dispossessed* (New York: Avon, 1974); David Miller, *Anarchism* (London: J. M. Dent and Sons, 1984); James C. Scott, *Two Cheers for Anarchism* (Princeton, NJ: Princeton University Press, 2010).

Chapter 12

Fools and the Deathly Hallows

Book 7 relates the odyssey of Harry, Ron, and Hermione in traveling a long and weary way back to Hogwarts, barely in time to battle successfully for its soul. Along the way, their obstacles, decisions, and lessons are many. Harry must choose between acquiring hallows to make him the Master of Death and killing horcruxes that must die to make Voldemort vulnerable (VII.429–32). Ron must choose between protecting his ego and protecting his friends. And Hermione must choose between self-righteousness and forgiveness. Each chooses well in the end. Harry's even able to take advantage of the three hallows—although one after another, wisely, rather than all at once. Luna Lovegood says that lost things always come back in the end (V.862–4; cf. III.427–8). This turns out to hold for (most of) Harry's friends—and Hogwarts too.

The odyssey encounters several totalitarian devices and situations of the regime, which the Dark Lord largely controls from behind the scenes. We do well, accordingly, to consider how the Potter saga differentiates totalitarian arrangements from authoritarian politics—then relates them. The second half of the Potter saga increases details about the Ministry of Magic and public services to suggest that mages in Britain are like muggles in Britain in dealing with what political theorists term a welfare state. This kind of government is shared by polities with diverse ideologies these days, but its historical association is strongest with socialism. Thus we should examine the Potter strains of socialist politics before we're done. Then this chapter turns with decently detailed attention to J. K. Rowling's versions of traditional folly as kinds of what we can call chaotic anarchism. Unlike the libertarian or mutual-aid-and-support species, chaotic practices of anarchism don't aspire to stand on their own as forms of community. Rather they try mainly to resist any form of domination—while sparking laughs, smiles, good humor, and hope.

As chapter 5 explains, Pottery develops its politics of totalitarianism in general and fascism in particular through horror figures strongly linked with vampires. Potter books abound in snakes and worms, bats and rats, basilisks and dementors. The politics of vampires often turn on how to disable or kill them. Several conventions inform this, and individual stories use these tropes in telling ways. The Potter saga presents Voldemort as its totalitarian leader and fascist-in-chief. And because Voldemort is vampirical, we do well to close by assessing the politics in how this last book ends each perversely perfectionist piece of the Dark Lord, horcrux by horcrux.

TOTALITARIANISM

As the name is meant to imply, totalitarianism involves aspirations and technologies for the complete control and regimentation of whole societies. The absolutism of the concept limits it to serving as (what Max Weber called) an "ideal type," for clarifying realities by exaggerating at least some of their aspects. In practice, totalitarianisms are approximate, partial, or "failed," because their technologies are never quite extreme enough to make good on their aspirations for total control over entire populations. But the claim is that regimes worthy of the name come all too close to perfecting their domination over all inhabitants—and that all too many regimes are worthy of the name. Until the French Revolution's Reign of Terror, on the eve of the nineteenth century, republicans opposed kings as actual or potential tyrants—and took tyranny to be the worst kind of community because it can be pervaded by fear of what tyrants and their enforcers are likely to do if they come to feel crossed in any number of specific ways.

Liberals and many socialists took up this opposition to kings—then added a Hobbesian horror of anarchism as an absence of any (hierarchical) order. Advocating modern government, these ideologists held that anarchism, as the absence of community, must be the worst possible condition. But the Reign of Terror, as a glimpse of how terror could be systematized, disclosed a deeper circle for Political Hell on Earth. As the nineteenth century generated the twentieth, modern, large-scale, representative democracies began to promote "government of the people, by the people, for the people." This vision of democracies started to supplement or supplant the republican ideal of mixed, stable government as Political Heaven on Earth. After World War I, unfortunately, democracy found an extreme contrast in conditions emerging that can be even worse than sustained disorder—because their totalized dominion through terror seemingly need have no end. Compliance is effectively total; opposition is next-to-impossible.

Some early treatments of totalitarian regimes regarded their devices as irresistible, at least in combination with each other. The suggestion was that totalitarian control cannot be forestalled for long, let alone defeated from within. A totalitarian regime might be woefully inefficient yet sustain its abuse of humanity indefinitely. Only an outside event or intervention could make a totalitarian system of control collapse or even falter. By now, we know better. Eastern Europe has become a site of lapsed totalitarianism with the dissolution of the Soviet Union and its Communist Bloc. Internal resistance could be erratic and squelched repeatedly without disappearing altogether. Whether it would have succeeded on its own we can't know for sure, because there were many (if often modest) attempts to help from "outside." Yet the internal declines in morale and escalations in morbidity seemed to triumph eventually, albeit temporarily in some cases. In theoretical terms, this is because "totalitarianism" must remain aspirational: complete control of any institution, let alone society, is not a human possibility.

In a Cold War world of democratic ideals, perhaps more than practices, totalitarianism, however incomplete, becomes the supreme political horror. Familiar examples include Adolf Hitler's Nazi regime in Germany and Benito Mussolini's Fascist regime in Italy plus Communist regimes of V. I. Lenin and Josef Stalin in the Soviet Union, Mao-Tse-Tung in China, (Josip Broz) Tito in Yugoslavia, Nicolae Ceaușescu in Romania, Enver Hoxha in Albania, the Kims in North Korea, and the Castros in Cuba. This list is not exhaustive; and there are other awful regimes in the past hundred years, though some get analyzed as authoritarian. (More on that in a moment.)

Accordingly a major project of political theory and mythmaking in the twentieth century was to come to terms with totalitarianism as either "a novel form of government" or not exactly a form of government at all. This takes us into the seventh and culminating book in the Potter saga. As an exercise in political theory, it resembles accounts of totalitarian regimes by Yevgeny Zamiatin in *We*, George Orwell in *1984*, Hannah Arendt in *The Origins of Totalitarianism*, and Arthur Koestler in *Darkness at Noon*.[1] All explore the radical departures of totalitarian regimes from the public politics cultivated by western civilization. All trace the psychological and social dynamics of regime bosses, minions, and resisters. The big difference is Rowling's interest in defenses against authoritarian unto totalitarian devices of intimidation, confusion, and control.

As the examples imply, totalitarianism can cover ideological extremes, because content is strictly subordinate to control. Totalitarians can engineer huge, sudden changes in "political principles" and "factual realities," because those are merely frauds of momentary convenience to controllers. To keep compliant, the dominated populace must practice what Orwell called "doublethink." People must believe fervently in the fabrications of the day but stay ready as needed to convert overnight to believing with equal fervor in virtual opposites. Arendt saw this as simultaneous "gullibility and cynicism." In Pottery, the cult version is possession, of Ginny Weasley by the Riddle diary or of Nagini by Voldemort. This fully cancels another's awareness in order to control that being in body and mind. The country version can be the imperius curse. Death Eater Corban Yaxley maintains this spell over Pius Thicknesse as Minister of Magic. It overwhelms any impulse to resist direction, mainly by imposing a diffuse but disabling feeling of well-being. Thus puppeteered by Yaxley, the Thicknesse regime hides the subversion of the Ministry and pacifies (most of) the populace into accepting Voldemort's covert rule.

Totalitarian movements and regimes arguably arise from sources all too evident in the nineteenth century, but totalitarianisms in practice and theory are inventions of the twentieth. The sources include nativism and nationalism, imperialism and colonialism, racism and slavery, bureaucratism and eugenics, ideology and propaganda, plus electrification of communications. The inventions that help distinguish truly totalitarian arrangements are even more numerous.

One is a decentering of modern government, in one or more of three ways. Totalitarian leaders, movements, and parties—*not* governments—are the primary sites of power. There is no sovereignty of the government. A state "apparatus" remains, but it's pushed to the side and dominated by the others. The Soviet state matters, but Stalin and the Communist Party matter much more; a German government endures, but Hitler and the Nazi Party trump and direct them. In *Deathly Hallows*, the MOM operates after its subversion; but Voldemort and the Death Eaters are the main powers in magical Britain.

Second, a society has no central "authority," not exactly. Instead of authoritative rulers at a regime's center to issue laws (commands, decrees, regulations) for people to obey, there are totalitarian leaders for people to follow. Contents count for laws and the like, but contents limit the control and the controllers, as well as their puppets, servants, or victims. Follow the leaders is less about meaningful deeds than momentary behavior and future identity: Do what we do, not what we say—to be who we're becoming, not who we've been. To imitate leaders in living as specimens of "the new Aryan Race" or as embodiments of "the new Soviet Man" can leave a regime lots of wiggle room for interpreting conduct and for trotting out erratic examples. As Book 7 begins, look at how even the Death Eaters at the Malfoy's table struggle to "read" Voldemort's gestures, so as to stay in his graces—evil, but graces nonetheless. Regime-wide, totalitarian pseudo-directives can be easy to interpret arbitrarily and alter unexpectedly. This compounds the atmosphere of terror that can make the populace more and more malleable.

Totalitarian regimes are more like cults than cultures, let alone institutionalized states. And as cult figures, totalitarian leaders are more symbol than substance. Third, therefore, the power "center" of a totalitarian regime can be empty, vacant, occupied by no actual person. It can be filled as ably by a puppet or a poster. In the 1984 film of Orwell's *1984*, Big Brother is simply a stylized picture on a poster; and Arendt's take on the structure of totalitarian regimes as onions leaves their centers empty. Such a form of concentric spheres or circles displaces the (ruler's) pinnacle of authority and twists the authoritative pyramid in weird ways. Power is no longer height in hierarchies. The vertical yields to the horizontal, turning power into proximity to centers that don't exactly exist. (It's ironic and telling that democracies claim this form too.[2]) Bureaucracies suit totalitarianism for their run-arounds; responsibility is deferred indefinitely. The imperius curse has pacified Pius Thicknesse to the point of disappearance: at the center of "his" Ministry, nobody's home. And if Yaxley's pulling the strings, Voldemort lurks behind a further curtain. Yet for years, Voldemort has stayed a mysterious if suffusing cultural presence (IV.527; VII.443). Where *is* he, *what* is he, and what's he *doing*? Harry and Dumbledore want to know so they can stop him. Such curiosity can be heroic, because it can get you murdered. But what if you just want to stay in sync with the Dark Lord, instead of learning more than is good for you? Must you be in the inner circle of Death Eaters sitting around the Malfoy dining table?

This complication is not easy to see in the Voldemort case, because he stays outside the official government, and there's no official recognition of him or the Death Eaters. This locates the subverted Ministry part-way between its increasingly authoritarian version under Rufus Scrimgeour and its incipiently totalitarian edition—featuring Voldemort eventually? Sidelined by Voldemort already? This arrangement evokes Vichy France—nominally ruled by Marshal Pétain during World War II but really dominated by Adolf Hitler from Nazi Germany. Yet the politics in Book 7 have more to tell us about the hybrid regimes that lately seem to meld authoritarian governments, which ordinarily rely on devices of fear and command, with some totalitarian devices of terror and control. Military-led regimes in Asia and South America have often worked this way, while "authoritarian populisms" (China, Turkey, and Argentina) on those continents have too. Europe (Russia and Hungary) has added itself. Thus Book 7 explores the distinctively totalitarian devices developed these days even by authoritarian regimes. Liberal democrats need to know what their enemies are doing, how, and why.

Pottery provides introductions to such totalitarian devices. Voldemort's Death Eaters resemble Hitler's Brownshirts as the paramilitary arm of his Nazi movement scheming to create a totalitarian regime in Germany. With Krystal Nacht and other provocations, they spur a reign of terror. (Movie scenes from Book 7 show the dark contrails of flying Death Eaters as they wreak similar havoc.) This kind of bloody anarchism can make a populace desperate for iron-handed (unto total) order. Death squads in Central and South America keep this terrifying sense of disorder prevalent by "disappearing people" almost daily and arbitrarily. Of course, at least some "disappearances" are not so arbitrary; and some leave bodies behind. Voldemort himself murders Harry's parents and Amelia Bones, Head of the Department of Magical Law Enforcement. We have to wonder if Nagini disappeared Bathilda Bagshott, because of how this Voldemort horcrux ingests Charity Burbage, Hogwarts Professor of Muggle Studies, just after Harry, Ron, and Hermione have fled. Book 7 has snatchers disappear not only resisting wizards but also random muggles. And even earlier, Voldemort and the Death Eaters vanish such individuals as Bertha Jorkins and Barty Crouch Sr.

Rigged trials just for show demoralize and terrify people too. Such a "show trial" is what Harry's Wizengamot hearing for underage-magic was meant to be, before Dumbledore's careful preparations and deft stagecraft derail the scheme of Umbridge and Fudge. Fudge's Ministry is not totalitarian, however, or it would have prevented the Dumbledore appearance and the Potter acquittal. And especially it would have publicized the fully fake trial throughout the land: this is a key contrast between corrupt "justice" that railroads a victim to prison and totalitarian "justice" that stages a confession, conviction, and execution in order to exterminate a community parasite.

Like historical regimes rife with totalitarian devices, the Voldemort operation hides itself behind false legalities (more decrees) and imperiused officials (first Barty Crouch Sr., later Pius Thickness, and unnamed others). It manipulates and persecutes scapegoats (Stan Shunpike). It takes hostages (Luna Lovegood). It savages children: mages in the making at Hogwarts under the Carrows but also muggles, seemingly for appalling amusement (VII.439, 573). Does Voldemort's Ministry follow European totalitarianisms in killing or exiling whole classes? At the least, the Voldemort version drives "muggle-borns" and other potential opponents into hiding. Does the Voldemort regime seek to oppress, enslave, or eradicate whole races and species? Mixed bloods must defer to pure bloods; muggles must become merest servants; and (momentary alliances notwithstanding) it's hard to see why giants, goblins, merpeople, and more wouldn't become (even more) endangered. Equivalents in our world include genocide and ethnic cleansing.

Totalitarian devices include media control, with Death Eaters commandeering the *Daily Prophet* then dictating to *The Quibbler*. Histories and sciences get perverted. Thus Rita Skeeter's one-sided sensationalism in *The Life and Lies of Albus Dumbledore* serves the Voldemort march to ultimate power, and DADA becomes drill in dark arts—practiced as punishment for students. The project is what Arendt named "systematic mendacity," for replacing realities with fabrics of falsehood that cow and terrorize the populace while staying susceptible to change at the drop of a hat. This atomizes and demoralizes people into masses, breaking down any constructive ties or capacities for resistance. Relentless propaganda and ideology mobilize these masses willy-nilly, since keeping them in motion but going nowhere likewise disables and debases people. Systematic deception through Big Lie techniques practices the (German Nazi) principle that the larger the lie, the easier it is for dominated masses to swallow—and the harder it becomes for outsiders to believe horrifying (true) reports about what's happening "over there." The news is too outrageous to be better than exaggerations at worst, when usually they're understatements instead.

On the run from Voldemort and Death Eaters, the heroic three apparate all over Britain, but know that they're going nowhere. Ron, especially, but the others too become demoralized. Yet their friendship prevents sustained isolation and massification. Unless we count Azkaban Prison, Pottery doesn't include the most extreme and effective device for isolation, terror, and control. Concentration camps strip inmates of legal standing, moral concern, then biological being. Still Pottery does acknowledge major elements of the camps and the terrorized societies that they epitomize. Totalitarian extremes of surveillance, entrapment, and torture by secret police get enacted by the Death Eaters. Criminalizing even the most private dissent (Orwell's "crimethink") and reshaping language (Orwell's "newspeak") as a basic maker of reality both lurk in the curse on the name "Voldemort," so that its merest utterance brings Death Eaters to nab the defiant (or forgetful) speaker. Regime schools for youths and reeducation camps for resisters are further tools for the total reshaping of a society, with Hogwarts under Snape and the Carrows to serve as both. Leaving no room at all for free thought, let alone action, is how a totalitarian arrangement can seem to stumble onward indefinitely, no matter how ramshackle or disheveled it might become. Authoritarian regimes use such totalitarian devices to endure.

Totalitarian regimes also use these devices to last and expand without limit. But even more, at least as an ideal type, they use devices of terror and control to catapult totalitarians beyond mere humanity (IV.15). As Orwell wrote, they pursue this less by purifying bloodlines, breeding super-races, or propounding divine creeds than by dominating and debasing actual people. Orwell visualized this as "a boot stamping on a human face—forever."[3] With Draco newly a Death Eater, he "stamped, hard, on Harry's face" (VI.154). Thus totalitarianism is not just sadism as a delight in inflicting pain, but something more like nihilism as a fanaticism of destruction. As Hagrid tells a Three Broomsticks gathering, "when a wizard goes over ter the Dark Side, there's nothin' and no one that matters to 'em anymore" (III.207). As Harry learns from the diary's piece of Tom Riddle toward the end of Book 2, neither ideological creeds nor biological and cultural vendettas count any more for Voldemort. Thus Dumbledore tells Harry that Voldemort has moved "beyond 'usual evil'" (VII.103). This is what totalitarian movements and regimes (try to) do on a scale far beyond human individuals.

Totalitarianism has been claimed to move beyond political evil as western civilization is able to know or combat it. The same claim has been lodged against terrorism even when it's not systematized into a regime. As Political Hell on Earth, these end western civilization figurally in a bonfire—or more literally, a fiendfyre. Rowling takes care to encourage our recognition of the Room of Requirement as an emblem of the west. In thousands of pages written over a decade, the only time she comes close to repeating her prose word for word is in evoking this magical place. In its manifestation as the Room of Hidden Things, she likens it to a large cathedral with high windows and to a city with towering walls that store many forbidden and forgotten things (VI.526; VII.627). The west is the civilization that melds the political city of Greece and Rome to the religious cathedral of Christianity. Just as western civilization encompasses many aspects and activities, this Hogwarts room has many powers, uses, and names: also the Come and Go Room, the Unknowable Room, the Unplottable Room, and possibly more. Of course, Hogwarts School and Castle can themselves evoke western civilization in the widely articulated symbolism of the Grand (or Overlook) Hotel; the Gleaming City, Ramshackle Mansion, or Haunted House on a Hill; the Great Arcology or Library; the Immense Skyscraper; even the Tower of Babel.[4] And when the terrifying forces of Voldemort's fascist totalitarianism assail the castle in the climactic Battle of Hogwarts, the Room of Hidden Things gets incinerated in a holocaust of fiendfyre. Crabbe as the firebug gets consumed. But Harry throws a broomstick to Ron, who picks up Hermione then Goyle. Harry barely manages to fly himself and Draco to safety before the amazing room seals itself off. Western civilization has been for us a Realm of Requirement. But its own totalitarian politics can be its death, igniting the awful flames of Political Hell on Earth. (Should we keep in mind the spectacular flames of the phoenix that symbolizes Albus Dumbledore?)

Rowling devotes hundreds of pages in the final Potter book to considering the political moves and devices for effective resistance. Her resisting characters, institutions, and practices draw from republican, perfectionist, and existentialist politics. Many of the moves and devices have clear inspirations in fairly recent history: *Potterwatch* as a pirate radio station, at least a few subverters inside inner circles, and some assassinations of central figures. (For that's what the trio's destruction of horcruxes involves: killing Tom Riddle, piece by mythic piece.) Other moves and devices invite more imaginative contemplation of their possible politics: What does each of the three Deathly Hallows imply, and how do they work together in defending against totalitarian arts? How can realist spying or trickery help in the face of totalitarian surveillance? How can alliances be forged even momentarily among oppressed populations with long, strong reasons for mutual distrust, as in the case of Voldemort enemies among wizards and goblins? Why might the liberation from Gringotts of an enslaved and tortured dragon be significant in itself for undoing Voldemort's regime—which is to ask, what contra-totalitarian politics might it symbolize? And more generally, once Voldemort has been killed and his regime undone, why reconstruct Hogwarts School to include all four of the traditional houses—given that the home of the dark arts for a thousand years plainly has been Slytherin House, which at one point is said to suit future politicians especially? Plenty of issues for political thought and action arise in the Potter saga on the dark arts and defenses against them.

SOCIALISM

Concern for equality, community, and need distinguish socialist politics from liberalism, which instead features freedom, law, and merit. These are good places to start in appreciating socialism, because it often shares so much with liberal politics and capitalist economics that it's plausible to treat socialism in general as becoming the main counter-culture of liberal-capitalist societies. Socialism criticizes liberalism and capitalism not so much by rejecting them outright as by relativizing and historizing them. It literally puts them in their historical places, usually accepting them as (passing) stages in the modern enlightenment of humanity, development of equality, and progress toward better and better community. Some socialists offer their visions of good societies as culminations of modern civilization. (And some dystopians have depicted actual impositions of these visions as going awry to produce dark times in totalitarian regimes.)

Socialist politics take diverse paths that spring from sources scattered around the globe. Attempts to fuse several species of socialism into effective movements typically lapse short of lasting success. Labor movements are the signal exceptions. Arguably as influential, though, are efforts to ideologize skeins of self-identified "socialism" into quasi-scientific platforms for political analysis and action. At least in umbrella terms, instances can include communalisms, Marxisms, democratic socialisms, and some liberation theologies. Marxists aren't the only ones who develop their socialist ideas as principles of political economy, and this complicates many comparisons because it matters whether we find socialist contrasts in liberalism or in capitalism.

Yet it's fair to see mutual convergence in the paths of liberal and socialist polities as well as in capitalist and socialist economies. Early socialists generally rejected liberal government as class rule that keeps capitalists or corporate managers in control, while denying most humans the dignity, development, and power of participation in community affairs. Recent socialists often celebrate representative democracies, while insisting that free and fair elections must give equal voice and full participation to all citizens, regardless of social standing or economic class. Early socialists often condemned free trade as concealed coercion, and fair profit as unconcealed exploitation, while favoring expert planning and administrative pricing. Current socialists fear hidebound bureaucracies, fantasy plans, and distorting prices. Lately capitalists have promoted nimble bureaucracies, strategic plans, and informally fixed prices. Now socialists scramble to embrace markets, while explaining how decent government regulation is needed to free them of corporate corruption and domination.

In short, it's easy to hype differences between socialist and liberal regimes, by presenting as philosophical contrasts what practices make into mixed pictures. Liberal capitalists lambaste socialists for nationalizing industries such as education, energy production, and healthcare. Yet some socialist regimes don't; others do, but only in partial ways for a few sectors; while quiet collaborations of corporations and interest groups with government agencies sometimes mimic nationalization in liberal-capitalist regimes. Socialists condemn liberal-capitalist countries for having no government programs to meet basic human needs. But liberal welfare states do have such programs, and they've become the rule rather than the exception. Moreover some of those liberal-capitalist countries treat private institutions, tax laws, economic measures, and so on as ways to address basic needs. Telling contrasts of socialist to liberal politics come in practical terms, which vary from one country to another, seldom in lockstep with overall labels or philosophies.

Especially as ideologies, socialism and liberalism share the modern kind of government apparent in the MOM. Yes, its specific mechanisms are often unclear. Ministry terms of office seem indefinite, not fixed. Elections appear only as Hermione's idea for selecting Harry to lead Dumbledore's Army. And the one clear implication about Ministry officers is that the Minister of Magic can have considerable say about every lower post. Still the diffuse Potter sense is that the Ministry responds to citizen (mage) opinion—until subversion of the Ministry by the Dark Lord and his minions. By form and activity, the Ministry is a welfare state. So it's responsible for international relations (including liaisons with muggle governments), domestic tranquility, and crisis response. But it also provides routinely, in at least some important ways, for the basic needs and well-being of community members. Myriad appointments are arranged by the Ministry. It issues acts, decrees, guidelines, and international treaties. As Percy Weasley might say, the Ministry makes many rules—even more than his twin brothers could break.

Just to evoke schematically how detailed Rowling's take on the modern state becomes, permit me to inventory the Ministry's "levels," both administratively and architecturally. After a first-level entrance from the street or the Floo Network, officials and visitors get screened near a spectacular atrium. Then they access lifts, apparently near offices of the Minister of Magic and the Support Staff. Magical Maintenance also operates from this floor, which eventually houses the Hogwarts High Inquisitor, the Office of Misinformation, and the Muggle-born Registration Commission. Level two is for the Department of Magical Law Enforcement. It encompasses the Auror Office, the Council of Magical Law, the Improper Use of Magic Office, the Magical Law Enforcement Squad (including Hit Wizards), the Misuse of Muggle Artifacts Office, the Office for the Detection and Confiscation of Counterfeit Defensive Spells and Protective Objects, the Registry of Proscribed Charmable Objects, the Wizengamot, and Wizengamot Administration Services. Lodged somewhere on this level, presumably, are Ministry Interrogators and staff who superintend Azkaban Prison. Even so, there are seven more levels and divisions to go.

The third houses the Department of Magical Accidents and Catastrophes. It offers the Department of Magical Catastrophes, the Accidental Magic Reversal Department, Obliviators, and the Committee on Experimental Charms. The fourth level is for the Department for the Regulation and Control of Magical Creatures. It has divisions for Beasts, Beings, and Spirits; and it provides the Goblin Liaison Office, the Pest Advisory Bureau, and the Committee for the Disposal of Dangerous Creatures. The Department of International Magical Cooperation is on level five; and it includes the International Magical Trading Standards Body, the International Magical Office of Law, and British delegates to the International Confederation of Wizards. On level six is the Department of Magical Transportation, with the Floo Network Authority, Broom Regulatory Control, the Portkey Office, and the Apparation Test Center. (Does the Knight Bus also get an office here?) The seventh level is for the Department of Magical Games and Sports, with the British and Irish Quidditch League Headquarters, the Official Gobstones Club, and the Ludicrous Patents Office. Level eight houses the Unspeakables of the Department of Mysteries, sectioned into the Brain Room, the Amphitheater of Life and Death, the Love Room, the Time Room, the Hall of Prophecy, and (by implication) the Astrology Room. Courtrooms for the Wizengamot begin on level nine; but there also seem to be older, deeper ones on a tenth level.

These offices indicate the functions performed by a modern government of, by, and for mages. If they put us in mind of democratic socialism, let's add five institutions unto industries superintended, yet not run directly, by the MOM: incarceration and punishment at an Azkaban Prison staffed by dementors rather than mages; education by the Hogwarts School; transportation by the Hogwarts Express and the Knight Bus; plus healthcare from St. Mungo's Hospital for Magical Maladies and Injuries. Like the National Health Service in Britain, does St. Mungo's count as "socialized medicine?" Azkaban appears to be a public prison rather than a private one with a government contract. And so on. Should these five be seen as nationalized industries? For contrast, there are plenty of private, nongovernmental businesses: Gringotts Bank, several publications, the Leaky Cauldron and other taverns, along with the many shops in Diagon Alley, Knockturn Alley, and Hogsmeade. When Fudge and Scrimgeour as Ministers of Magic pressure the *Daily Prophet* to vilify Harry and Dumbledore, still the press is not exactly government-run, as it becomes under the Thicknesse regime. Other signs of an ample "private sector" would be that Potter property is "private" in the liberal and capitalist sense of complete owner control, at least in principle. The property is not "personal" as some socialists wish, with owner uses respected only aside from waste or misuse that might deprive the community of the property's value. (But here again, inheritance and eminent domain provisions in many liberal-capitalist countries can shrink the theoretical distance between private and personal property.) Just as some recent socialisms make lots of (private) room for markets, these versions promote vast realms of "civil society" as private places for individual freedom and personal fulfillment.

Beyond the character of government, therefore, we may spot socialist politics in styles of action by Potter individuals and institutions. A standard stylistic contrast is that liberal modes of conduct are keenly competitive, whereas socialist modes are markedly cooperative. This can surface in institutional arrangements. Free markets and private banks are often seen as liberal-capitalist constructions, even in socialist countries where many are now mainstays. Producer cooperatives and professional associations are often seen as distinctively socialist devices, even in liberal-capitalist countries. Yet these don't avoid working as "special-interest lobbies," even in socialist countries. Similarly evolutionists who debated the importance of competition versus cooperation now see the two as mutually defining and advancing, more or less as two sides of the same coin. This is apparent in the dynamics of personnel and strategy for the Gryffindor Quidditch team, in the details of points won and lost for the House Cup at Hogwarts, and in the multidimensional interactions of champions and schools during the Triwizard Tournament.

Most socialists do want personal development to feature participation in the community affairs that western civilization calls politics. For many socialists, though, politics are even more oriented to society than to government. (As a name, *socialism* virtually says as much.) Thus our everyday associating *is* politicking, even when it's not electioneering, lobbying, or other activity related to government. That's because everyday associating helps make our communities what they are. Our political action at all levels *can* be positive and personally ennobling rather than negative and necessarily corrupting. This includes governing. One after another, the Quidditch captains for Gryffindor struggle with temptations to unjustly favor friends, fault teammates, or win at any cost. Neither Oliver Wood, Angelina Johnson, nor Harry himself represses all these impulses. So Pottery pays homage to the liberal concern that power corrupts. Yet each captain does resist the temptations successfully for the most part, each gains skills and grows better as a result, while each captains (as well as competes) with a fierce joy that could make the captaincy a lasting thrill. This is what socialists want (and work) for people to get from everyday politics in their societies, as from taking positive parts in more specialized affairs of their governments.

Other stylistic tropes of socialism in daily conduct echo contrasting principles for Potter politics. In action as in justice, liberals (Hermione?) stress rules and procedures, while socialists (Ron?) go straight to attaining outcomes and conditions. Like anarchists (Weasley twins?) who disdain government in favor of informal, personal assistance, socialists (Arthur Weasley?) direct personal as well as governmental action toward mutual aid and support of citizens. Still these anarchists would distinguish their sociality from a socialist appreciation of solidarity, which an anarchist would take to go too far. Of course, mutual aid and support fits the Potter emphasis on (at least) a little help from friends. But patronist help begins vertically, because it arises in hierarchical contexts of patron and client (or protégé). Networks for advantage or survival can become less exclusively up-and-down; yet they're developed to take wider advantage of high status or other power, so some verticality lingers. Socialist and anarchist help is meant instead to begin and end horizontally, with social class and standing eliminated (or sidelined) in favor of egalitarian networking. Strictly speaking, the Slug Club is patronal more than cooperative. By contrast, the heroic trio of Harry, Ron, and Hermione is cooperative through and through, although their collaboration (as heroic) often seems more specifically republican than socialist.

ANARCHISM

From the first book forward, Potter politics feature resisting oppression; and this is the spirit that animates all kinds of anarchism. Some oppression, such as conformism, is informal. Some, like fascism, ranges from semi-formal to formal. And some, especially authoritarianism, is fully formal. To resist various oppressions, Harry and his friends break rules, harass rulers, and stymie power-plays. Eventually they even overthrow a government, although they aren't acting as anarchists in fighting Death Eaters, killing Voldemort, and unseating Pius Thicknesse as Minister of Magic. Rather than make Kingsley Shacklebolt into the new Minister, anarchists would go further. They would oppose, overthrow, or even prevent any and every government of a modern, sovereign kind. This is because anarchists agree with liberals that government is intrinsically coercive and thus evil; but anarchists disagree that any government is necessary for community security, tranquility, or crisis management. States simply shrink personal freedom.

Ideological anarchists come mainly in two kinds. A rationalist insistence on individual autonomy and unenforced agreements yields a *self-reliance anarchism*. A voluntarist priority of mutual aid and support characterizes a *communal anarchism*. There is seldom much difference these days between self-reliance anarchism, construed loosely, and the libertarian politics easy to see proclaimed (if harder to see practiced) in the United States. The self-reliance anarchists typically try to show how they can sustain not-exactly-governmental ways to address problems like pandemics, pollutants, and weapons; while the libertarians often attempt to show how they can minimize so much the tiny gestures toward governing needed to meet such challenges that next-to-no-government is really there. Similarly socialism and communal anarchism can seem to meet, at least in aspiration, with Marxian projects of socialism working for the modern state to wither away once class conflicts over scarce resources yield to affluent fraternity and sorority. But none of these ideological kinds of anarchism (or its near neighbors) are in the Potter series.

Instead the tale of Hagrid and the giants evokes what William Butler Yeats called "mere anarchy." This is sheer savagery, disorder, and destruction. It's an authoritarian, Hobbesian take on anarchism as Political Hell on Earth. It's a State of Nature as a war of all against all, a worst possible condition for humanity. The absence of modern government means the absence of any civilization. The "vicious nature" attributed to Pottery giants makes their lot even worse. Save for Dumbledore and Hagrid, wizards see giants as savages incapable of collective survival, let alone progress. A harsher condemnation of anarchism is hard to imagine, yet Pottery doesn't leave it there. Consider Dumbledore's gifts for the Gurg, the changing giant chieftain. Sans civilization, giants can't even keep fires going, so the first gift is a branch of everlasting fire. In continual warring, what could be more useful than an indestructible battle helmet? (Crafted by goblins, of course.) For harsh conditions, savages are bound to lack durable, protective fabrics. So the third gift is a huge stretch of dragon hide. Could fire, armor, and clothes kindle civility? Maybe not alone; but with Grawp, familial love and republican responsibility go still further.

The kind of anarchism developed in the Potter series is the resistance to oppression and hierarchical order practiced as the politics of folly. So far, this gets little attention from political theorists, if more from historians, sociologists, and satirists.[5] The Potter series is full of laughter and humor, making it for most people a great pleasure to read. Yes, some of the humor is bitter or black, but much more is clever or wry, while at least a little is truly joyful. And yes, there's a great need for comic relief when book after Potter book faces troubles of fascism, nationalism, racism, sexism, slavery, terrorism, totalitarianism, and war (IV.733). On the whole, however, the Potter humor is ironizing or satirizing as well as comedic. This serves well the Potter focus on dark arts in dark times, with no dark arts more prominent in the Potter saga than those of folly.

As a tradition of political action, folly amounts to a *chaotic anarchism*. This is not *chaos* in the ancient Greek sense of primal disorder, the Hobbes sense of barbarism, or the Yeats sense of bloody conflict. It's nearer the mathematical sense of nonlinear systems as "chaotic" because they feature tipping points between qualitatively contrasting phases or conditions that can't be specified before being experienced. (Examples are the states of matter as solid, liquid, gas, and plasma.) In political terms, it's chaos as disruption, distortion, or fluidity—friendly or hostile, momentary or lasting. Its instigators are "agents of chaos," or "tricksters," as kinds of "fools."[6]

Folly as a practice of politics traces to the Greek dramatists and the Roman satirists. It's a thriving tradition in medieval and modern Europe, its recent cultural reach is global, and the resonance with trickster myths makes it richer still. Many fools are "natural born." But some are "artificial," even official, including itinerant entertainers and court jesters. Festivals of Fools turn institutions or societies upside-down. The lowliest monk can be paraded as a faux pope or bishop, the humblest peasant can be feted as king for a day, while all in the monastery or village can run riot in libertine revelry. The indulgence of Mardi Gras can introduce the abstinence of Lent, and the early but false onset of spring can occasion the human pranks of April Fools' Day. This extends to the Trick-or-Treat tradition for pretend superheroes and celebrities, unto ghosts and goblins, on *the* Harry Potter holiday of Halloween. Scary tales of lost ships and souls feed legends of a literal skeleton crew on the mythic Ship of Fools. Whether sighted at sea or near a port, this ghost boat presages disaster. Bringing doom and damnation wherever it goes, a ship of fools sails the globe to claim more sailors. Karkaroff's Durmstrang crew comes to Hogwarts for the Triwizard Tournament in a ghostly derelict that resembles a "resurrected wreck." This ship of fools rises in the moonlight from the castle's "dark lake." And what doom does it bring?

As folly, Potter resistance to doom and domination forms many *versions*. The Latin root says *turns*, as does the Greek root for *tropes*. And the chaotic anarchism of folly is a repertoire of political turns: aversion, adversion, conversion, diversion, inversion, perversion, reversion, or subversion, for starters. (Introversion and extraversion may be psychological more than political.)

The Marauder's Map and the Invisibility Cloak repeatedly help Harry avert Argus Filch, Mrs. Norris, or Severus Snape. To make something adverse is to turn it against another, making it a trouble for that adversary. (This dynamic makes it easy to see how folly can be regarded as formidable politics in opposition to almost anybody or anything.) Harry's signature disarming charm not only separates enemies from their wands but also turns around attacks, causing them to rebound against attackers. The curse that kills Voldemort comes from him, but Harry turns it around. Such jujitsu is key to a trickster's repertoire, turning adversary strengths against them.

To make something into its converse is to turn it against itself, and to convert someone is to turn around a belief or commitment. In Book 5, Hermione gets the Rita Skeeter interview of Harry into *The Quibbler* to convert critics and doubters into Potter supporters. To divert is to turn in another, second direction—redirecting action, attention, or other resources elsewhere. Harry sparks a small explosion to divert Snape's class, so that Hermione can steal ingredients for polyjuice potion in Book 2. In Book 7, he deploys a decoy detonator from Weasleys' Wizard Wheezes to divert Umbridge's department, so that he can sneak into her office at the MOM. In Book 2, Nearly Headless Nick coaches Peeves the Poltergeist to crash a Hogwarts vanishing cabinet onto the floor over Filch's office, to divert Filch from his plan to punish Harry. This breaks the cabinet, letting the Weasley twins pervert it into a prison for Montague of Slytherin in Book 5. Fixing this cabinet in Book 7, so it can revert to its original use as transportation, Draco Malfoy then perverts it into an opening for Death Eaters to attack Dumbledore. To revert is literally to turn again, typically back into what something was before. And perversion, as literally through-turning, admits the capacity of folly-as-turning to trash or sideline proper applications in favor of different and (all-too-often) dastardly uses.

To subvert is to turn under or over, more or less as tilling a field turns under the soil or revolting overturns the government. With Dumbledore dead, Death Eaters eventually subvert the Scrimgeour regime. Yet Harry and friends overturn the Thicknesse government that results, just as they earlier subvert the Umbridge rule as Head of Hogwarts. To invert is to turn upside-down. So the DA subversion of the Umbridge regime follows the foolish inversion of her rule, when student pranks run her ragged and undo her authority. Overdone, ironical deference by teachers compounds those dynamics. All told, these political turns of folly fill Potter books with knowing smiles, outright laughter, and effective action.

Another way to appreciate the politics of folly in *Harry Potter* is to analyze its profusion of fools. The Potter books include more kinds of fools, distinct in character and deed, than we can inventory here. Partly this is because we share cultures where we've had good reasons to recognize many sorts of fools and practices of folly. A beginning typology might be helpful (table 12.1).

Even when one of these general categories comes from me, its components usually spring from our everyday language. Thus "inflated fool" collects

Table 12.1   Folly as Chaotic Anarchism

Kind of Fools	Synonyms and Subtypes	Key Characteristics
Natural-born fool	Natural fool, moron, and dolt	Deformed in mind or body
Traumatized fool	Deeply damaged in confidence	Deformed by disaster
Prudential fool	Bungler or bad judge in key cases	Poor performer and prone to error
Tragic fool	Opposite of a tragic hero	Terrible actor and prone to disaster
Christian fool	Sinner, human, and fallen	Succumbs to temptations
Damn fool	Mischief maker, and bad influence	Ill-willed misjudgment and tempter
Simple fool	Simpleton, rube, and yokel	Deprived in wit or culture
Inflated fool	Buffoon, blowhard, and narcissist	Smugly exceeding his abilities
Professional fool	Artificial fool, clown, and comedian	Witty, acrobatic, and independent
Kept fool	Court jester, domestic fool, and stooge	Ridiculous and dependent performer
Sacrificial fool	Scapegoat, sacrificial lamb, and cat's paw	Symbolic victim to appease
Holy fool	Martyr, mystic, saint, and visionary	Fool for God, blessed, and imbued
Wise fool	Cowboy poet and front-porch philosopher	Seeming fool but sage judge
Fool for love	Love sick, enamored, and enchanted	Heels-over-head infatuation
Fortunate fool	Incredibly lucky individual	Preternaturally good results
Foolish idealist	Eiron, hopeless romantic, and noble fool	Unrealistic, imprudent goals
Foolish realist	Pessimist, depressive, and cynic	Unduly realistic and manipulative
Foolish sophisticate	Dandy, aesthete, and trickster	Unduly devoted to appearances
Foolish idiot	Naïf, hick, innocent, and purely private	Unsophisticated and other-worldly
Satirical fool	Caricaturist, ironist, and folly buster	Debunker and enemy of pretense
Ironical fool	Sophisticated mark, and self-victimizer	Unknowing self-underminer
Nobody's fool	Shrewd, independent, and self-possessed	Humble critic of self and others
Everybody's fool	Dupe, patsy, and pawn	Butt of many manipulators

Source: Table developed by author.

under one banner such ordinary-language synonyms in American English as "buffoon" and "blowhard." Likewise "dandies," "aesthetes," and "tricksters" can all be seen as "foolish sophisticates." And so forth: our languages, like our lives, seem at times to be full of fools. We humans may manifest several sorts of foolishness at once, let alone over different occasions; and a Potter character can enact more than one kind of folly. We have come a long way from the medieval duality between natural and artificial fools.

As exercises in horror and humor, Potter books include fools of many kinds. From start to finish, Harry himself is a sacrificial fool, a scapegoat—as well as a holy fool, complete with visions. Hagrid gets scapegoated twice when implausibly fingered as the Heir of Slytherin. Introduced in Book 3 as a natural-born fool, Stan Shunpike gets scapegoated as a Death Eater by Scrimgeour in Book 6. Much of that book lampoons Ron Weasley as a fool for love. Peeves the Poltergeist enlivens the Hogwarts School as a court jester. He dresses in cap, bells, orange bowtie like a clown, plus the blatantly mismatched fool's clothes called motley. As a stooge of the Dark Lord, Peter Pettigrew (Wormtail) is a different kind of kept fool. Filch, the Hogwarts caretaker, comes across as a simple fool, too preoccupied with pet peeves to focus on the key points. Sir Cadogan, the portrait knight who doubles Don Quixote, is a noble fool. To Harry, Nearly Headless Nick confesses that he's been a coward and a prudential fool. Albus Dumbledore surely qualifies by Book 6 as a wise fool in confessing his own mistakes to Harry. But Dumbledore, Cornelius Fudge, Gilderoy Lockhart, and Horace Slughorn also are dandies or aesthetes, with fancy clothes and exotic tastes. Most Potter fools appear in amusing ways; and most of their follies help disrupt dark schemes, even if by accident or boomerang.

Neville Longbottom, Harry's near-double, begins at Hogwarts as a traumatized fool who's greatly impaired in memory, confidence, and coordination. (Like Dora Tonks, Neville is good for laughs as a klutz, surely a close cousin of fools.) At times, Fudge as Minister of Magic comes across as an inflated fool, a buffoon, a blowhard; but mainly he's a tragic fool who helps induce the disaster of Voldemort's slyly triumphant return by misjudging the crucial questions of the moment. As a double agent, Snape turns out to be a talented trickster; and his ultimate trick is to sacrifice his life to defeat Voldemort without the Dark Lord even starting to see Snape as the sacrificial doe, er lamb, he proceeds to be.[7] Lucius Malfoy and possibly Quirinus Quirrell seem to be sophisticated marks of Voldemort: his ironical fools. Slughorn and Hepzibah Smith much earlier become sophisticated marks of Tom Riddle as a master manipulator. Not exactly a Death Eater, but still a bureaucratic and racist contributor to Voldemort's return, Umbridge is a damn fool. Corrupt, ill-willed, shrewd, yet misjudging disastrously in the end, she eventually finds herself out of her league in evil.

Winky the house-elf might be a foolish idiot—a purely private naïf who stays innocent of public issues and machinations—although her nominal master mistakes her for a simpleton. As house-elves, Winky, Hokey, Dobby, even Kreacher are more or less legally classified as kept fools, because they at least begin (enslaved) as domestic servants. As a free elf, Dobby joins Lily Potter as a sacrificial fool in martyring himself to protect and support Harry as a liberator. And in a lighter vein, Dobby's socks evoke the many wizards foolishly ignorant of muggle styles who wear what cries out for labeling as the motley garb of many official fools (e.g., jesters).

Definitely odd, and thought daft by many, Luna Lovegood repeatedly reveals herself to be a wise fool—though in ways that diverge somewhat from Dumbledore's. Luna's campaign against wrackspurts plus her opposition to Fudge for torturing goblins and recruiting a private army of heliopaths clamor for recognition as quixotic folly—stressing her similarities with Sir Cadogan. Don Quixote champions a feudal (republican) code of chivalry (honor) and nobility (responsibility) by "tilting at windmills," which he sees as villainous knights. The impossibility and misperception in such a quest makes him a fool, of course; but the wisdom of his folly lurks in the fact that windmills are harbingers of the modern, industrial development that he knows to undo the virtues of his traditions, turning them into mere values for cost-benefit calculations. So he's not exactly deceived symbolically or politically. Hence Luna is wise to warn against the experts in the *Daily Prophet* and the MOM, who can cloud the increasing signs that Voldemort is back. However looney *The Quibbler* conspiracy theories about Fudge, Luna, and her father do sense figurally where the Minister's power and pure-blood trips could take him.

Harry needs a long time and a lot of experience to learn how to listen intelligently to Luna, but he's starting to "get" her by the conclusion of Book 5. He's starting to understand that (even why) people take things from her (and him)—and why those things "always come back," how they *do* "turn up" in the end. Much better at the literal than the figural, Hermione needs even longer than Harry to esteem Luna. But we readers not only can enjoy Luna's folly as whimsy or Sir Cadogan's as farce, we also can respect their follies as forms of quixotic action that fit chaotic anarchism. Both disrupt the dark uses of dark arts by dark forces in dark times.

The same can be said of the Weasley twins. In Book 1, Fred and George instinctively pummel snowballs at the back of Quirrell's turban, where lurks the revenant of Voldemort. In Book 2, the twins satirize classmate fears that Harry is the Heir of Slytherin by parading him as though he's their cult figure. In Book 3, these two "borrow" their father's flying car to rescue Harry from imprisonment by the Dursleys; thereafter they give Harry the Marauder's Map to anoint him as their heir in foolish mischief. Book 4 begins with Ton-Tongue Toffee left at the Dursleys' house by the twins to retaliate for Dudley bullying Harry, and it ends with Harry contributing his Triwizard galleons to Fred and George for developing a joke shop. In Book 5, the twins and their jokester buddy Lee Jordan join Harry as banes of the Umbridge reign at Hogwarts—where they pervert her decrees, subvert her enforcers, and swamp her oppressive order. Before he dies defending Hogwarts in Book 7, Fred uses broad silliness and black humor as "Rapier" on *Potterwatch*, which resists Voldemort with news and solidarity. Certainly from the standpoint of overbearing order, Fred and George are agents of chaos.

But it's in Books 5 and 6 that the twins shine brightest, as they invent magical powders, gags, and devices for the joke shop. As an emporium for pets, potions, pranks, tricks, fakes, fireworks, diversions, and illusions, Weasleys' Wizard Wheezes is one version of a fool's paradise. In turning professional as fools, the twins expand defenses against Death Eaters and their dark arts in service to the Dark Lord. To be sure, Draco using Peruvian Instant Darkness Powder to hide Death Eaters at Hogwarts joins Snape ironically cursing away George's ear as two among many demonstrations for Harry and his friends that life can make fools of us all. Still the shield hats, gloves, and cloaks created by the twins are not alone in appropriation as defenses against dark arts. The chaotic anarchism of the twins works small wonders, at least.

Aspects of the twins' folly appear in their father, Arthur Weasley. He is, as the colloquial phrase has it, "a fool for" muggles (II.51). He loves to tinker with the electrical and mechanical devices of muggles that often mimic his own magic (II.30–43, 66; IV.45). He shows real talent for magically enhancing muggle devices such as the flying car and motorcycle. And he could be said to tinker unintentionally, even foolishly with muggle words (II.47; IV.43, 46; V.133). Like other wizards, he gets muggle words "just a bit" wrong—in ways that comment humorously and insightfully on the intended thing or person. Thus the senior Crouch insistently refers to Percy Weasley as "Weatherby," which fits a careerist who changes views to whichever way the wind is blowing. This trope is *malapropism*. It's a comedian's tool, and Rowling uses it in every Potter book but the first and last. Some cases are debatable, and at least one is more visual than verbal, but I count forty overall. Some come, unsurprisingly, from muggles mistaking wizard words. In Book 5, Vernon Dursley's panicked riff on *dementors* is rollicking but also shrewdly revealing (V.32–8). Even when Arthur doesn't intend it, he displays a penchant for play that his twin sons turn toward chaotic anarchism. Are these three Weasleys a paean to British senses of humor?

On the other hand, J. K. Rowling takes care to show how such chaotic kinds of folly can be dangerous too. Just as dark arts have all kinds of uses, and defenses against dark arts feature dark arts themselves, devices of folly have diverse uses, their disruptions can be disastrous, and effective preventions or responses can involve disrupting any noxious disruptions. This holds all the more because agents of chaos can prank with little regard for the permanent, disproportionate damage they can do. Ron Weasley tells how his dad hit the ceiling when the twins tried to trick young Ron into an unbreakable vow, for it would have left him liable to die. Isn't Hermione right to rebuke the twins for experimenting with magical candies and the like on unknowing first-years? Aren't the twins perverse to tempt Dudley with Ton-Tongue Toffee? Sometimes their empathy is, shall we say, incomplete. Less often, there is more than a hint of evil in their motives. This might be why Rowling has Harry liken the look of Gellert Grindelwald as "a merry thief" to the faces of Fred and George as tricksters (VII.283). Snape's memories show Harry this evil also in some pranks by James Potter and Sirius Black as teens.

Even so, agents of chaos and other chaotic anarchists of folly have legitimate, important, if complicated places in our politics. Resisting oppression often requires rule-breakers who act at times with humor and joy—to complement some careful judgment and grim determination. To become heroic, Harry, Ron, and Hermione must learn to break some rules, at Hogwarts and beyond. Likewise the three must learn when to *leap before you look*. This is a playful principle of folly as chaotic anarchism, and the Weasley twins practice it amply. The sober principle of prudence, of course, is to look before you leap—or even to look so you needn't leap. But the trouble for those who would resist dark times is that looking strongly discourages leaping. This is why chaotic anarchism can be indispensable politically, but it's also why that counts as folly.

The Potter books repeatedly portray the twins as kindred spirits of Peeves, the Hogwarts Poltergeist. As another agent of chaos, Peeves is surely the figure easiest to recognize as a fool. The Pottermore account of how Peeves came to haunt Hogwarts also implies why this notorious prankster can't be expelled—as long as the castle houses a school for witches and wizards. For he is said to embody and enact the disruptive spirit of generation after generation of Hogwarts students. Peeves has a "malicious" face, presumably because his pranks are mostly malicious. He afflicts the afflicted as well as the comfortable. Peeves annoys, humiliates, or torments with words. He tries to get students into trouble with Filch or teachers. As a bodily being, he blocks paths in emergencies, throws chairs, drops busts and vases onto heads, tosses pots and pans in a kitchen full of elves, even tries to strangle a student with tinsel. (But maybe Ron exaggerates.) Most of this can be comical because Rowling coaches us to take it lightly; in literal, flat-footed terms, it's often cruel—and motivated only, as Peeves proudly declares, to double the trouble.

The Peeves version of folly might be the most radical and telling of all. Certainly it's not good through-and-through, yet even the Peeves kind of chaotic anarchism can be constructive. The obvious case, almost book-long, is the poltergeist's campaign to disrupt the life and regime of Dolores

Umbridge at Hogwarts. From the first tome onward, though, Peeves proves to be a helpful agent, notwithstanding the dangers he poses almost continually to people at Hogwarts. Harassment by Peeves is what drives the initial foursome of Harry, Ron, Hermione, and Neville down a third-floor corridor and into the locked room where Fluffy the Cerberus guards the trap door that leads to the Philosopher's Stone. This is so productive that we readers might wonder if Dumbledore puts Peeves up to it, just as Nick encourages Peeves's mischief in order to spring Harry from Filch's office. To all students, Peeves provides continual training in the constant vigilance preached by Mad-Eye Moody. From keeping eyes and ears attuned to where Peeves might be, the saga shows Harry in particular acquiring a second-nature sensitivity to otherwise unpredictable disruptions. This heightened alertness helps make Harry a superb "spotter" in almost every respect. Appreciating this, may we say that chaotic anarchism strikes again?

The Potter books overflow with fools and follies. Surely this is to entertain readers and counter dark moods from dark times. Yet Potter attention to politics of folly comes from their repertoire for effective resistance to oppression as well as depression. The Potter appreciation of folly as an arsenal of turns against domination and doom can enrich our resources for action.

KILLING THE RIDDLE HORCRUXES

Like a conventional serial killer, Voldemort could be said to collect *trophies* (same root as *tropes*) to commemorate his conquests. "Ordinary" serial killers keep body parts or treasures from their murder victims. At the orphanage, Tom Riddle's "keepsakes" come from the children whom he terrorizes. But the adult mage moves beyond this, regarding later victims to rank so far beneath him that souvenirs from murdered muggles won't suffice. Instead he stores the severed pieces of his soul, magically derived from some of his murders, in artifacts of symbolic value to him. Each is a *horcrux*, and it holds some of Tom Riddle's basic being. Then Voldemort hides most of these objects to defend himself from dying.

Because a horcrux is a horror creature, the word's sound is superb; and it's compounded of provocative figures. The first syllable can evoke a period of time (*hora* for *hour*). It also can mean *dirty* or *hairy*. And it can suggest hair standing on end in an adrenaline rush of terror, with *horrore* for *bristling* and *horripilation* for *hairs erect from gooseflesh*—as a bodily reaction to ghost stories or nearby sharks (predators).[8] The second syllable names a *cross* as a *crossroad* or *pivot*; a *crucifix* as a device of torture and murder or an icon of divinity and sacrifice; plus a *crux* as what's important, necessary, even crucial. Put 'em together, and what've we got? A scary but crucial time: the witching hour? The gist, heart, or essence of horror, terror, torture, and death? What's at once holy and horrifying, awesome and awful? Making, facing, and killing a horcrux can bring all these (and more) into the picture. The horcrux is a condensation symbol of Pottery as dark fantasy and Potter magic as dark arts.

As *the* Eater of Death, Voldemort partitions his soul this way to escape or conquer death. Why he doesn't (even try to?) conjure the Philosopher's Stone (or steal Flamel's) *before* making horcruxes is unclear. Dumbledore infers that the Dark Lord never hears of the Deathly Hallows (or deigns to respect a children's myth). Still Voldemort seeks in effect to become the Master of Death, as would one who controls all three of the Peverell inventions at once. Dividing his soul into many parts could remind us of a master vampire transforming into masses of rats, hordes of bats, even clouds of mist. It's a bit reminiscent of a master vampire making vampire "drones" to extend his senses, control their communications, and direct their bodies over great distances. A Riddle horcrux somehow retains some of Riddle's powers, including legilimency and possession, plus much of his ill will. Yet they don't communicate with one another or even Voldemort, who doesn't sense the abduction or destruction of his horcruxes when they're out of his sight. (To protect them further, he's taken sinister care to hide most of them far beyond his oversight.) In loosely vampirical terms, nonetheless, the vessels selected by Voldemort and the ways these horcruxes are killed by Harry and his friends stand to tell us useful things about Potter politics.

Imposing slivers of Riddle's soul on objects seems not to eradicate any previous magic in them, but overlays and might twist it. This matters because all Voldemort's horcruxes are made from magical objects. Voldemort favors totems of Hogwarts founders. To use founder artifacts is to claim his legacy from those founders, assert his superiority over them, and perhaps murder them symbolically. Associations of each founder and artifact with distinctive politics underscores that most politics can have perfectionist variants and most can be perverted. (The corruptions usually aren't perfectionist.) Does killing the soul in a horcrux end its earlier magic? This might depend on the prior magic and the mode of "murder" for the horcrux. The Resurrection Stone still works for Harry after Dumbledore kills the Peverell ring as a horcrux, but maybe that's because the ring was the horcrux and the stone was merely set in it (VII.698–701).

It's hard to know further, because we learn of magical powers only for the other founder artifacts that don't get horcruxed by Voldemort. A mage must possess all three Peverell Hallows to become the Master of Death, and all seven Voldemort horcruxes must be killed to make the Dark Lord mortal. It might have mattered immensely if Voldemort had been able to horcrux an artifact from every Hogwarts founder, but the Gryffindor Sorting Hat and

Sword stay under the protection of the school and its head. Ironically they bring death to the Riddle snake (basilisk) and the Voldemort snake (Nagini). Moreover killing the basilisk puts its venom into the sword, turning it into the weapon that destroys the horcruxed ring, locket, and snake. A further irony is that Harry *might* be taken as a horcrux made from a Gryffindor legacy. But Voldemort doesn't recognize that he's made Harry into a horcrux (VII.709). Hence Voldemort doesn't know that he's divided his soul into eight parts rather than a lucky (stable?) seven.

Nor does Voldemort realize that any horcrux ironically renders the maker's soul *more* vulnerable, because the part of the soul in the horcrux is destroyed when the horcrux is killed. What remains in the original body seems to become more vulnerable and less viable with each ensuing horcrux. The pathetic remnant crying on the floor in "King's Cross Station," with that serving as Harry's crossroad between life and death, is a vivid figure for the little that's left of Voldemort's soul when his own deflected curse kills him (VII.705–23). Hermione explains to Ron that damages to the horcrux container of a soul fragment damage that fragment too. Yet a whole soul survives when its body gets grievously injured or even dies (VII.104). Or maybe Voldemort had encountered this principle but didn't fully believe it and thought that the lucky number seven could protect him from its consequences.

Dumbledore professes surprise that the Riddle horcruxes are *weapons*. They're hard to find and kill, plus they're actively hostile and harmful to mages near them. (Vampire drones are independently dangerous to humans nearby.) Like a psychic vampire, the Riddle diary possesses Ginny, drains her life energy for itself, and prepares to strike at Harry (VI.500). Similarly the Slytherin locket sucks hope and energy from its wearers, then it tries to strangle Harry (VII.370). Possessed by Voldemort, Nagini tries to crush and *bite* Harry (VII.346)—after its poison almost kills Arthur Weasley (V.488) but before it does kill Severus Snape (VII.656). At Dumbledore's command on the tower, he's euthanized by Snape, after a curse of the Peverell ring incautiously used is killing the old wizard from the wand hand inward (VI.503; VII.683). The sentience and powers of the Riddle horcruxes make killing them much more like slaying drone vampires than any foe of Voldemort might wish. (Even when they're dead, there's still the master left to kill.)

I call these the Riddle horcruxes because they start with Tom and they function as riddles. Their *possible* existence is to be known only to Voldemort, although Slughorn has a memory that puts him in danger from Death Eaters—as an unknowing Sibyll Trelawney has been too. Lucius Malfoy doesn't realize the risk in getting the diary back to Hogwarts, where it spurs Dumbledore to investigate. The hiding spots for other horcruxes are supposed to be unknowable by anybody but Voldemort. Yet Dumbledore, joined by

Harry, could unravel each of those riddles once the importance of personal significance to Voldemort for the choice of objects and sites is inferred.

Hunters must trace vampires to their lairs, coffins, or ancestral grounds. The politics are often republican, with a small set of intrepid adventurers—a "band of brothers"—joining forces to seek, face, and stake the perversely perfectionist beast. In discovering and daring the horcrux cave, Dumbledore and Harry as a duo take a step in that direction. Yet they're still master and apprentice, mentor and mentee, which is more about republican leadership, followership, and education than community. When Harry, Ron, and Hermione resume the horcrux quest, after Dumbledore's death, they meld republican adventuring with existentialist stand-taking. This happens with vampire hunters who must find and kill the monster while a secret police of death-eating drones try to track, trap, and eliminate the would-be slayers. These are the politics in the general pattern; but each horcrux has distinctive properties, and its slaying gets a special spin.

The Riddle diary had lurked for many years undetected in the Malfoy compartment for darkest objects. It probably would have been the hardest for the horcrux hunters to imagine, let alone find, except that Lucius disastrously flaunts it under Dumbledore's nose. Does fidelity to Voldemort as the Heir of Slytherin lead Lucius to plant the diary on Ginny Weasley? Is this act one of malevolent mischief-making? Dumbledore mentions these probabilities (VI.508). Also lurking in details are the too-smart-for-its-own-good revenge politics of a Voldemort disciple. Lucius is past irritation at Arthur Weasley's efforts to confiscate dark objects from the Malfoys and to clip the wings of likely Death Eaters. Why not thwart Arthur, upend Dumbledore's school, and frame a Weasley for it in one fell swoop?[9] After all, Riddle tried to frame Hagrid and Aragog for the basilisk murder of Myrtle, which Riddle had orchestrated as Slytherin's heir.

Harry confronts the horcrux diary twice without quite knowing what it is. Both times, the diary's version of Riddle has four main aims: parade the maker's genius, spread misinformation, learn about Harry, and return to killing Voldemort's foes. At first, Harry engages the diary in its charming but disturbing mode as social media. The Riddle in the diary flatters Harry, feeds him a misleading vision of earlier events, yet alarms him with such magic. At the climax, Harry sees the diary destroying Ginny, defaming Dumbledore, and summoning the basilisk to murder Harry. This Riddle proudly identifies himself as Voldemort, denigrates Dumbledore, volunteers that his pure-blood politics are cynical, and taunts Harry as merely lucky to have survived until now. In the classic mode of a villain crowing too much on the verge of victory, Riddle goads Harry into speaking up—not for himself, but for Dumbledore. That brings Fawkes to the rescue with the Gryffindor sword in the Sorting Hat, the healing tears, and the final flight home. Harry merely has to display his republican courage and virtue-osity in sacrificing himself to slay the basilisk, then perform his perfectionist, impulsive leap in stabbing a venomous basilisk fang into the diary. Thus Harry connects with the republican empowerment of Dumbledore and Fawkes through a republican profession loyalty to the headmaster. By contrast, he fights the fascist disinformation of Riddle's social-media campaign with a largely liberal, procedural investigation of the murder of Myrtle and the framing of Hagrid. And he combats the perversely perfectionist horcrux in the Chamber of Secrets with a preternatural attunement to that strange situation and an impulse to just-do the perfect thing. Already Harry is coordinating republican, liberal, and perfectionist politics as his saga suggests on the whole—yet always with at least a little help from his friends.

Dumbledore finds the Peverell ring in searching the old Gaunt hut (VII.503–4). Spotting that the inset might be the Resurrection Stone, Dumbledore apparently leaps to its use for calling his sister or parents back from the dead (VII.680, 713–6). As a Riddle horcrux, the ring defends itself with a killing curse that Snape manages to slow but not cure (VII.681). Perfectionist leaps can be disastrous, so we should resist romanticizing them. Later Dumbledore recognizes that the goblin magic of Gryffindor's blade takes in only what strengthens it. Like Hermione, he deduces that the sword now has basilisk venom, which killed the Riddle diary (VII.304). So Dumbledore uses the sword to destroy the ring. Gryffindor republicanism is being "perfected," we might say. Killing the horcrux ring is a tale of liberal detection and logic, perfectionist leaping and debacle, more liberal inference, then a somewhat "perfected" republicanism. Good politics meld again.

Pensieve immersions in replayed memories contribute mightily to figuring out the Riddle plans and principles for horcruxes. (It's equally crucial for Harry learning the tragedy of Snape's heroism.) Memory is a key concern of politics in republics. As we've been seeing, myths and monuments tell public stories to keep alive the community's glorious and inglorious moments as lessons of history.[10] Gilderoy Lockhart abuses and incipiently subverts these republican politics of public memory with his stolen adventures and awards, as well as his obliviation spells. Mages are using those spells on muggles (to conceal dragons, accidents, misdeeds, and more) in keeping the two communities separate; and this is a backhanded demonstration of republican politics.

Lockhart and Dumbledore do lots of legwork to collect the memories of others. Most of the interview subjects are unsung, and Lockhart tries to keep them that way. The interviews are mostly in the liberal mode of detective investigations. Likewise the Pensieve as private storage for personal thoughts and experiences also becomes a vehicle for liberal politics. But these are all uses, rather than properties, of the Pensieve. As chapter 6 notes, entering the Pensieve is for Harry a perfectionist exercise in going dark. But what mainly stands out about this medium is its 3D performances by contrast with merely verbal histories or the glinting images of many aging memories. Putting Pensieve users into the midst of these performances helps with the inferences that Dumbledore and Harry seek on personal motives and responses. Republican pageantry and drama show an appreciation of such performance, while cultural rites and rituals demonstrate its importance to perfectionist politics. Even a secondhand memory of orphans traumatized in a cave is vivid enough to evoke the secret site of the Slytherin locket—or at least its replacement.

Locating and killing the horcrux locket becomes by far the most convoluted of horcrux accounts. Here its long roster of obstructions, impersonations, thieves, house-elves, and other helpers must defer to the locket's dramatic destruction by Ron. He returns from self-inflicted exile in the nick of time to save Harry from the Slytherin locket and fetch the Gryffindor sword. From this and perhaps the diary's aggressive self-defense, Harry intuits that *Ron* should kill the locket. In Parseltongue, Harry bids it to open. Ron stands by, sword in hand. Sensing Harry's hero-worship, the diary Riddle had focused its abuse on Dumbledore. But the locket strikes at Ron's sense of guilt and failure in relation to family and friends. It freezes him, and only Harry's urgent encouragement to "Do it!" moves Ron to strike back and destroy the horcrux (VII.373–8). One implication is that Ron has been all too republican in his quest for glory and admiration by others. The glassy windows of lockets show families, lovers, and closest friends: often figures of republican politics. This horcrux opens to reveal staring eyes that project hateful, distorted images of Ron in company he loves and dreads. Like the gaze of the basilisk, this arrests Ron. To act, he needs to let go of ambitions for glory and public acclaim to Just Do It. Once he does, this awful moment seems to prove as therapeutic for him as stabbing the diary has for Harry.

At Malfoy Manor, with his own life and others on the line, Harry spots panic by Bellatrix at her thought that the Sword of Gryffindor has been stolen from her Gringotts vault. He leaps to the likelihood that a Voldemort horcrux is stored there, and his Pensieve work leads him to think that it must be the magical cup of Helga Hufflepuff. Two narrow escapes and a heart-wrenching fatality later, the heroic trio tries a desperate plan to steal that horcrux from the bank. The plan derails from the start; but one improvisation after another by Harry or Hermione gets the trio into the vault, out of it with the cup, and onto a blind dragon who instinctively flies itself and them to the lake country in the north. Having Harry free the dragon and ally with its primal perfectionist magic is a telling twist. Another is leaving the goblin sword with Griphook, whose alliance with the three young mages ends the instant he fulfills it technically, if not before. Realist politics can make strange bedfellows. They also can be slippery and surprising, if less than the alternatives.

The cup's destruction is mainly a platform to display more of Ron's growing talents. He recalls the deadly venom of the basilisk fangs left in the Chamber of Secrets—plus how to enter from Myrtle's restroom. To open the pipe as before, Ron mimics Harry's use of Parseltongue in opening the locket. Ron and Hermione get some fangs, and he has her stab the cup (VII.622–3). Enough said. But why not more? A narrator might cite pacing. An analyst might observe that poisoning the first three horcruxes already shows this to turn Voldemort's snaky perfectionism against him. A feminist might wonder why Hermione doesn't get equal time and treatment. Is she too idealized for a horcrux attack to be telling? Is her kill too decisive and speedy to let the horcrux get started? Would even a quick account eclipse Ron's moment to shine?

As events accelerate into the Battle of Hogwarts, the cup's story overlaps the diadem's. Again there are riddles. How can Harry seek something if he doesn't know what or where it might be? Does the phoenix or the flame come first? Who can help Harry find the lost diadem of Ravenclaw if it hasn't been seen in living memory? Eventually Harry recalls that he *has* seen the diadem, in the Room of Hidden Things; but he just didn't realize what it was. That his effort with Ron and Hermione to retrieve it gets disrupted by Draco, Crabbe, and Goyle seems right in political terms. That the disruption results in Crabbe's Fiendfyre destroying the diadem is hard to interpret apart from incinerating the Room of Hidden Things as an emblem of distinctively western civilization. That's what the death-eating fascism and totalitarianism enacted by the three sons and their fathers would do: topple the towers, trash the spires, and burn the remnants. How is even a horcrux to withstand that? But containment is required; so somehow the magical room does it, and the castle endures.

Harry is the accidental horcrux, unrecognized by its maker; therefore many things get reversed. Voldemort arranges a horrendous hostage situation to challenge Harry's honor and call *him* out of hiding. With Harry helped to muster the courage *not* to resist, Voldemort's killing curse slays the piece of his own soul somehow lodged in Harry, yet gives Harry the choice to go on living. But Harry could not *know* this in advance; and his willing sacrifice of self to save his friends at the battle magically protects them from Voldemort, as Lily's loving sacrifice of herself for Harry deflected Voldemort's earlier curse. Then Harry was left with only the lightning scar, while Voldemort's own spell had blasted him toward a death prevented only by his horcruxes. So Voldemort's maledictions against Harry's supporters start to weaken and go awry, although the Dark Lord doesn't yet notice the new pattern. The magic of (Christian) love and (republican) friendship strikes anew, and again Voldemort's perverse perfectionism of pure will is heedless.

Once more with help, including from a momentarily allied Narcissa Malfoy, Harry hides his survival. He plays dead until his (more democratic) double in Neville Longbottom shows the courage and loyalty that brings *him* the promised help at Hogwarts—again in the form of the Sorting Hat and Gryffindor sword. Abused by Voldemort, Neville suffers but perseveres. He takes the sword that comes to him and decapitates Nagini. This destruction of the last horcrux clears the way for Harry to duel the Dark Lord fully unto death, and the two face off.

Holding the upper hand, even though Voldemort holds the Elder Wand, it's Harry's turn to talk, even taunt. Presumably the wand already knows what Voldemort doesn't—until Harry's account: events over the last year and more have made Harry the wand's "master," its proper wielder. Human and wand sentience aren't the same, of course, but I can't help wondering if the review helps make sure that the wand as well as we readers share Harry's sense of the situation. This would reinforce the Potter importance of speech for political action. Giving Voldemort the information might even move him belatedly to remorse, as Harry suggests but doesn't expect. Yet it also rattles Voldemort at the decisive instant. His killing curse rebounds from Harry's disarming charm, and the Dark Lord dies. Meanwhile the Elder Wand spins skyward and falls into Harry's hand. Again Harry's signature defense wins the day by stymying one of the darkest arts. And again, this is partly because defense can become offense too.

NOTES

1. See Yevgeny Zamiatin, *We*, trans. Gregory Zilboorg (New York: Dutton, 1924); George Orwell, "1984," *Orwell's Nineteen Eighty-Four*, ed. Irving Howe (New York: Harcourt Brace Jovanovich, 1963, 1982), 3–205; Hannah Arendt, *The Origins of Totalitarianism* (New York: Harcourt Brace Jovanovich, 1951, fourth edition, 1973); Arthur Koestler, *Darkness at Noon*, trans. Daphne Hardy (New York: Macmillan, 1963). Also see Carl J. Friedrich and Zbigniew K. Brezezinski, *Totalitarian Dictatorship and Autocracy* (New York: Praeger, 1956); Milovan Djilas, *The New Class* (New York: Praeger, 1957); Irving Howe, ed., *1984 Revisited* (New York: Harper and Row, 1983).

2. See John S. Nelson, "Toltechs, Aztechs, and the Art of the Possible: Parenthetic Comments on the Political Through Language and Aesthetics," *Polity* 8, no. 1 (Fall 1975): 80–116; John S. Nelson, "Orwell's Political Myths and Ours," *The Orwellian Moment*, eds. Robert L. Savage, James E. Combs, and Dan D. Nimmo (Fayetteville: University of Arkansas Press, 1989), 11–44.

3. Orwell, "1984," 175–78.

4. See Jim Collins, *Uncommon Cultures* (New York: Routledge, 1989). It's telling to compare the Room of Hidden Things in Hogwarts Castle, where Voldemort

stashes the lost diadem of Ravenclaw, with Voldemort's cave for securing the Slytherin Locket (VI.547). The cave is an instructive emblem of totalitarianism.

5. Especially see Anton C. Zijderveld, *Reality in a Looking-Glass* (London: Routledge and Kegan Paul, 1982). Also see Sandra Billington, *A Social History of the Fool* (New York: St. Martin's Press, 1984); Beatrice K. Otto, *Fools Are Everywhere* (Chicago: University of Chicago Press, 2001).

6. See Norman Spinrad, *Agent of Chaos* (New York: Popular Library, 1967); Laurie R. King, *To Play the Fool* (New York: Bantam, 1995); Laurie R. King, *Folly* (New York: Bantam, 2001); James Lee Burke, *Feast Day of Fools* (New York: Pocket, 2011). Also see Barbara Swain, *Fools and Folly during the Middle Ages and the Renaissance* (New York: Columbia University Press, 1932); Enid Welsford, *The Fool* (Garden City, NY: Doubleday, 1936, 1961); Susan Kuhlman, *Knave, Fool, and Genius* (Chapel Hill: University of North Carolina Press, 1973); Paul V. A. Williams, ed., *The Fool and the Trickster* (Totowa, NJ: Rowman and Littlefield, 1979); John Southworth and Joan Southworth, *Fools and Jesters at the English Court* (Stroud, UK: Sutton, 1998).

7. See Lorrie Kim, *Snape* (Pekin, IL: Story Spring Publishing, 2016).

8. See Ron Rosenbaum, "Gooseflesh: The Strange Turn toward Horror," *Harper's Magazine* 259, no. 1552 (September 1979): 86–92.

9. Compare how Swooping Evil does its thing as a *Fantastic Beast* who helps Newt Scamander in the films of that name.

10. See Hannah Arendt, *The Human Condition* (Chicago: University of Chicago Press, 1958), 50–58.

Conclusion

Political Action in Dark Times

Harry Potter is a form of political education and political theory, but it's also a form of political action.[1] Our times often impose and suffer chronic troubles for political action. Most people don't know or care much about official politics in the high places of government or the low places of lobbies and elections. Most of us do know and care a great deal about politics in our everyday lives—but not about links among them, labels for them, or relations to what usually get termed "politics." Most of us also know and care considerably about popular cultures, even though we differ individually in the forms and topics that attract us. Often these popular cultures can provide good meeting places for our personal and official politics. By tapping enjoyment for the Potter saga to clarify all these connections, the book at hand aspires in its own small way to a kind of political action. Especially it strives to encourage us Potter readers to act politically—by showing how we've been cultivating our capacities for political action in many places and ways.

As dark fantasy, *Harry Potter* is political horror; and horror as a popular genre insistently faces evils.[2] Dark times portend all too many evils, and sensing them can stop us in our tracks or turn us aside from political action. Political evils can *arrest* us, as chapter 7 evokes the basilisk to explain.[3] In Harry's situations, as in ours, official politics can be dominated by lying, gaslighting, and systematic mendacity. Politicians can revel in demonizing people, assassinating characters, and trashing any institutions that get in the way. Then the official rules are only for us underlings, and resisters had better learn how to protect one another before trying to do more. Yet in Harry's situations, as in ours, everyday politics can resonate with similar troubles. This is how we Potter readers can come to admire Harry, Ron, and Hermione for their courage to plunge into political action on every level. It's how we can respect Harry and his friends for waiting and holding out at times for better conditions to act. And it's why we can learn from their substantial array of principles, plans and moves. But mostly, it's why we can learn from their impulses to Just Do It. Thus the present project is to suggest how reading *Harry Potter* can help attune us in diverse ways to leaping beyond at least some of our formidable obstacles—and into good action.

COMING OF AGE

To say what's obvious to Potter readers, the magic is far from all that matters politically in the Potter series. It's the focus of the book at hand because the dark arts and defenses against them are so instructively, so provocatively takes on *our* politics. Yet the non-magical in Pottery is also hugely important to politics for Harry and us. This includes labors of love and friendship, tests of antagonism and tolerance, and challenges of learning and forgiving. Even overall, the Potter series is susceptible to appreciation from angles other than fantasy and horror. Already its tropes of detection, epic, action-adventure, and thriller genres have been noted in specific contexts. But it's often acknowledged that the saga's main setting and many other recurrent conventions could make it a boarding-school story—with a strongly British bent rather than an American one. And this points to a more encompassing form of the Potter series as a whole. This is a popular genre with even greater relevance for various ventures of political action in our dark times.

The Potter saga is also a coming-of-age account. Step by step, it narrates the maturation of the title character. As the journey to adulthood of a mythic hero for our times, its details seem more familiar in archetype than stereotype. For Britain and America early in this century, to be orphaned at age one is exceptional rather than normal, although "broken homes" are not as rare as we might like. Boarding-school educations aren't standard, and they seldom happen without warning. Few children are celebrities, and fewer still wouldn't know it if they were. Children do fantasize about secret parents or superpowers; yet this usually dissipates with adolescence, which is when these become clear realities for Harry. And so on. Nevertheless Harry's developmental challenges and responses are readily recognizable by most of us non-magical individuals. That's because Harry and his friends face social situations, educational regimes, cultural entanglements, and initiation rites instructively similar to ours.

Harry enters Hogwarts School when he's just starting to learn about Voldemort and has never even heard of Death Eaters. In fact, Harry doesn't begin to learn about Death Eaters until *Goblet of Fire*, when the Potter books are restarting on more adult levels, half-way through the whole saga (IV.142–3). Thereafter he finds in small moments of frisson that he's been brushing against them—even in the strictest organizational and philosophical sense—for much of his life since starting at Hogwarts. In at least a loose sense, though, Death Eaters operate on occasion in most of our everyday lives. Maybe Dursley outrages against Harry count instead as caricatures for comic effect. But Uncle Vernon still strikes me as a candidate in Harry's life, while Dudley treats Harry in much the same way as does Draco Malfoy, eventually an official Death Eater. It matters, too, that both young men might be somewhat repentant and reformed by the saga's end. Voldemort is the extreme rarity whom Harry rightly regards as beyond all possible redemption.

Potter books take us through many kinds of situations, everyday as well as extraordinary. To disclose the varied politics in these settings is to provide diverse perspectives on the aspects of elitism, racism, sexism, specism, and such that surface in headline news *and* in daily events. Dark times intensify these troubles but don't originate them. If some liberals and conservatives are correct to insist that humans are fallen and sinful by nature, this can be no surprise. Even if we don't launch our politics from such a bleak generalization, do we doubt that there is reason to say (with several colleagues) that *some* people are "no damn good?" Aside from individuals, moreover, existentialists show how social systems try to sustain themselves, usually are effective at it, and often feature some of their worst dynamics in doing so. We do well to learn with Harry and his friends how to resist the devices of such "Death Eaters," whether persons or systems.

In the preceding pages, we've been exploring how this is true in political terms. As we grow into adulthood in electronic societies, most of us acquire early senses of enemies, friends, party identifications, and political institutions from our families. To be sure, Harry inherits these more structurally than socially from his deceased parents. He doesn't develop initial support for their political outlooks and projects from extended experiences of associating with them or being indoctrinated by them. Still personal loyalty and honor draw him toward defending their causes and deeds as he learns their histories in episodes encountered all too erratically. Significantly for us, Harry also learns to reconsider those initial commitments. He makes them better informed, more reflective, as well as better attuned to his developing self and unfolding circumstances. In short, he makes his politics much more his own and, we may hope, much better for us all. This is one of the biggest reasons for advancing educations all the way to, and often through, college.

TEACHING OF POLITICS

Many students come to college knowing Harry and his world.[4] Potter books, especially, teach politics astonishing in range, detail, and relevance. Better still, the books foreground most of their politics. They rely on several sorts of symbolism, but the political meanings are bold. They spring readily from names, lines of plot and dialogue, plus configurations of characters, creatures, inventions, and institutions. Potter allusions to our histories and headlines are readily accessible. Seldom are Potter politics elusively subtextual. Mostly they are provocative and responsive to the challenges of our times, specifically as we engage these in our everyday lives.

The Potter attention to politics of great reach and currency is highly unusual in books for children, tweens, and teens. Therefore the Potter novels can be terrific for introducing college students to theories of politics. Some university courses approach political theories as debates over philosophical concepts and questions. Or they present political theories as contests among modern ideologies such as liberalism, conservatism, socialism, and fascism. Often these courses also extend to politics better seen as postmodern movements like environmentalism, feminism, nationalism, and populism. As we've seen, the Potter books encompass these and more. Potter figures face ethical challenges and community issues persistent in political philosophy. Potter scenes feature deeds, devices, and ideas from political ideologies and movements. And Potter settings excel at diverse styles of political action in everyday life.

Like learning, teaching is a practice of rhetoric, and a cardinal principle of rhetoric is to start with the audience. In teaching, this means to craft lessons in terms of student experiences, interests, and perspectives. College students are like many other citizens in seldom having much reflective involvement in the official politics of governments, elections, and policies that occupy political science. Citizen and student experiences usually focus on the politics of everyday life in families, schools, sports, businesses, and other cultural institutions. Nonetheless students usually enter early college courses on politics with awareness of headline events and issues of the times, even if it comes these days from internet browsing and social media more than TV viewing or newspaper reading. So the challenge for a college introduction to political theories and practices can be how to address this situation. Fortunately the new century has brought a new resource.

I've been learning Potter politics by teaching them to college students. So I've read the Potter books time and time again, always finding in them more than before. Likewise I've read many good commentaries on them. But especially, I've discussed them with students: assessing deeds and devices, debating connections, then proposing implications. Of course, we've drawn on other treatments of politics too. These explain, extend, and reflect on what we read in *Harry Potter*. We've related Potter politics to theories by Plato and Aristotle, Niccolò Machiavelli and Thomas Hobbes, John Locke and Jean-Jacques Rousseau, Karl Marx and Friedrich Nietzsche, Max Weber and

Hannah Arendt.[5] Their canonical works help us see how Potter inventions can breathe life into bloodless arguments or even how they can add insight into politics for our times.

Teaching political theory with *Harry Potter* is similar to assigning literary classics by the likes of Albert Camus, Fyodor Dostoevsky, William Shakespeare, Aleksandr Solzhenitsyn, Mark Twain, or Robert Penn Warren. To be sure, cautions to American students can be helpful: don't learn British spelling, British grammar (treating collective nouns as plurals), or Rowling's prose style (adverb use); and do remember that Potter books are for children, tweens, and teens. Still the literary strengths of the Potter novels are many. The plots are intellectually taut and vivid. The integration of seven novels into an overall story arc is impressive, and the uses of popular genres are ingenious. The characters are diverse, complicated, and mythically resonant while inventive. The creatures, institutions, and settings are colorful as well as clever. The language is sly and fun. The action scenes are engaging, often thrilling. The philosophizing builds from elementary to sophisticated, but seldom seems preachy.[6] The motivations are plausibly mixed, dense, and instructive. These link to politics that stretch from momentous affairs of state to humble encounters of everyday life. And the key virtue of *Harry Potter* is that its politics feature issues important for personal action and political theory in facing our own times as dark and difficult.

Moreover *Harry Potter* offers several advantages over adult classics when introducing political theory. Most college students have read the Potter books at least once before, and most have seen the Potter movies too. Only a handful in each of my courses had not read the books, and those students had no trouble participating fully and effectively. If students don't enjoy the Potter novels or films, they don't sign up. Yet many who do enroll are fervent Potter fans, and they often enrich the political analysis with Potter information that surpasses the teacher's. The ready accessibility of Potter politics plus the previous familiarity of students with Potter plots, settings, and characters equip classes to join the professor for adventurous inquiries into the particulars, patterns, and implications of Rowling's takes on our dark times. The teacher and a couple of textbooks help with links to ideologies, movements, and other politics; then everyone in each course considers together how the Potter novels enact and extend such political theories.

Students who engage *Harry Potter* for its political theory learn to read for symbolism and story as well as tenet and argument. This holds too for using epics, plays, poems, histories, and other novels (or movies) in theorizing politics. Because the explanatory insights and persuasive powers of political theories owe much to their figures of language and narrative, this emphasis can shine in introducing the political theory. It also has the advantage of calling on reading skills that students already have been cultivating for participating in popular cultures. Then it shows how to turn similar moves of invention and interpretation toward doing and distilling politics. This holds for whole courses on Potter politics, but quick Potter examples help in other courses too. Many students recall Pottery well enough to learn from Potter illustrations of current points.

Experiments in teaching the Potter books show that they can introduce these aspects of political theory in exciting ways. Here I've tried to evoke how. This covers the ample capacity of Pottery to illustrate recent isms, perplexities, and principles of politics. It also explores Potter books for what they can teach us as theorists of politics. Classics of literature can complement canons of political theory, histories of politics, analyses of institutions, surveys of individuals, and myriad other sources of political learning. So can concerted engagement with *Harry Potter*, which many readers already know and love. Casual readers might not spot Potter implications for accounts of our politics, but together these form a map of political theory for our dark times. For Harry and his friends, including us readers: There Be Dragons—and telling politics to learn!

FANTASIES OF POWER

The Potter series stands out because it foregrounds most of its politics, yet it has several ways of doing this. Most obvious is the Potter concern with its fantasy government of mages and other magical creatures in Britain. This parallels and communicates with a fictional version of the actual British government. A fantasy series accessible to children that attends in detail to official arenas of politics is highly unusual. This goes double for a children's fantasy literature where the institutional details are decently realistic. Potter politics are instructively comparable to *current* governments, laws, lobbies, policies, newspapers, international relations, and the like.[7]

Tied particularly to its interest in magic, the popular genre of fantasy is fascinated by power. Practitioners and theorists of politics in the modern west share this preoccupation. Yet obvious, specific allusions to governmental officials or occurrences from recent history are *not* conventional in fantasy for children, tweens, or teens. In the Potter series, Rowling pays homage to the *Earthsea Cycle* by Ursula K. Le Guin, which explores power and responsibility in relation to psychosexual and cultural politics of maturation then further aging by males and females. Le Guin's *Annals of the Western Shore* can offer political theories of community and power, but no more than the *Earthsea Cycle* does it reference recent people and events in the politics of our world. Nor does it address different ideologies, movements, philosophies, or styles of politics in detail. *The Twilight Saga* by Stephenie Meyer is clever at airbrushing vampire romances. With subtextual politics of chastity and anti-abortion, it offers a Mormon version of perfectionism. Still that saga invokes few recognizable figures or species from American or other politics. Rick Riordan's several series (re)locate Greek, Egyptian, Roman, or Norse figures and settings into American popular cultures as experienced by kids of late. But his books to date ignore official, or otherwise overt, kinds and levels of politics.

Those contrasts to Rowling on Potter come from American rather than British authors. Might British children be ready sooner than American kids to engage politics self-consciously, even systematically? Aiming younger than Meyer and more for boys, Darren Shan (Darren O'Shaughnessy) is strikingly smart in telling the troubles and attractions of perfectionist politics in the vampire mode of Friedrich Nietzsche. His *Saga of Darren Shan* occasionally *might* come closer to governmental traumas, yet it stays distant from any kind of headline politics. Of course, the usual British comparisons for Rowling are C. S. Lewis and J. R. R. Tolkien. Earlier than Rowling, Lewis and Tolkien continued a British tradition of fantasy that spans children and adults—a tradition often invoked when taking stock of the Potter enterprise. *The Chronicles of Narnia* sends a family's four children to a country manor to escape the London bombardment in World War II. Soon they move to a magical kingdom where adventures await them as princes and princesses. But only a few words about the war were enough topical politics for Lewis, who focused his tales instead on Christians facing personal, social, or soulful difficulties.

Tolkien's epic is a more complicated case. Its echoes of World Wars I and II are strong at times—for readers already attuned to those terrifying conflicts. Yet Tolkien's allusions mostly stay oblique and enfolded in the battles that fill fantasies of sword and sorcery. Young readers, who know little of the World Wars, are unlikely to make these connections. In the Tolkien books, Saruman's use of his mesmerizing voice can call Adolf Hitler's to mind. But again, it's a tie completed only by some older and better-informed readers. Peter Jackson films of the Tolkien books don't push this political link, in part because Christopher Lee's sonorous, sinister bass as Saruman is octaves away from Hitler's higher pitch and hectoring delivery. Nor do Jackson's endings for *The Return of the King* feature Tolkien's apparent condemnation of the industrial development and pollution of postwar England in "The Scouring of the Shire." Yes, the films are vivid and detailed in presenting Tolkien's eloquent environmental politics: aghast at Saruman's dirty industrialization and his war on trees, then elated at his defeat by the Ents. And the films give decent ideas of the sparse institutional and historical politics readily available in *The Lord of the Rings*. (*The Hobbit* is less topically political.) Yet on the whole, we may say that

Tolkien's books engage some political details, but not many and not in much complexity.

The Tolkien saga of recognizing, resisting, and destroying the Lord of the Rings invites our reflections on power in general and from a standpoint of totalitarian domination. Its moral, mythic, philosophical, and psychological aspects are highly developed by the Tolkien books. By contrast, breaking the spell of the Elder Wand of power eventually craved by Lord Voldemort is a much smaller part of the Potter series. Indeed this is a skein slight enough to leave somewhat uncertain in the end. The Tolkien Ring of Power melts away in a moment within the molten lava of Mount Doom, whereas the Rowling Elder Wand of power might molder away ever so slowly in Dumbledore's tomb. Decentering the fantasy preoccupation with totalizing power enables the Potter series to address those somewhat abstract, philosophical concerns in detail while giving sustained attention to many other important aspects of politics. This is another way of saying that lots of politics (and kinds of power) matter greatly for Harry and his friends, including us.

CAPACITIES OF ACTION

Plainly I can hardly say enough in praise and appreciation of the Potter saga, especially its treatments of politics. Let me accredit this pervasive enthusiasm by admitting to two mild disappointments with the ending. First the epilogue seems to restore the Hogwarts of Harry's youth, by the time that Harry and his friends have children ready for school. Haven't events in the series almost necessitated some major changes? Shouldn't the epilogue at least acknowledge this possibility, even if sidestepping any specifications? Second the epilogue seems to evoke a Harry Potter who's almost entirely the teen who survived Voldemort and temptations to become the Master of Death or at least the wielder of the Elder Wand. Don't get me wrong: the Harry of the epilogue seems heroic, compassionate, and prudent—which is to say, admirable and maybe awesome. Yet he doesn't seem much seasoned by nineteen years of further experience, although we've learned from Harry's time at Hogwarts that he's highly adept at learning along the way. An exception is parental patience, but we may hope that Harry's been learning political patience too. It can be crucial for sustaining political action, and it typically comes coupled with a sense of irony that Harry seldom shows. The epilogue could be more heartening if it hinted at this.

A comparison to Tolkien's myth-making for politics might help clarify the first thought. Written more expressly for children than was *The Lord of the Rings*, Tolkien's *Hobbit* bears the subtitle *There and Back Again*. This is said by some to be apt because *The Hobbit* is a children's tale, and children need the reassurance of a good world restored after some trouble. True as this might be of many stories for many children, it disserves even those children for *all* their stories to conserve a good order. These days, their worlds will change somewhat, with restoration not always possible or desirable. Starting to help children face this in constructive ways can help. In teaching *Harry Potter*, for example, there's much to learn by pondering why a restored Hogwarts seems simply to reestablish Slytherin House. Isn't its racism too perverse and ingrained? Isn't its institutional disloyalty too blatant? Isn't its political trajectory too disastrous? Could any Slytherin exceptions justify the costs? Defenses for Slytherin House are also supported by the saga, of course. But even an epilogue sentence or two on its reform (or resistance to that) might keep the saga's conclusion from seeming reflexively conservative without reason.

A more specific defense of Tolkien's subtitle is that Bilbo's trek to the Lonely Mountain and return to the Shire do not change him in the major, developmental ways that characterize the modern novel as an adult genre. Not so for Bilbo, though, or for Harry. Yes, both these heroes are archetypal in Joseph Campbell's sense.[8] Yet this doesn't mean that the archetype of the hero has no trajectory of development. It's a principal purpose of the hero's journey. With Bilbo on the verge of his grand adventures, Peter Jackson's movie version of Gandalf explains, "You'll have a tale or two to tell of your own when you come back." An anxious Bilbo hazards, "You *do* promise that I *will* come back?" "No," replies Gandalf, "and if you do, you'll *not* be the same."[9] Since Harry changes markedly, how about his friends? And the larger community? Even after the Battle of Hogwarts and torching the Room of Hidden Things, would Hogwarts School come back essentially unchanged? Luna anticipates the saga's epilogue when she says that lost things return in the end. Yet the epilogue could still acknowledge how changed they might be.

A big share of the magic in *Harry Potter* is its energy for political action. Participation in politics only in order to realize specific ends is ripe for frustration by failures, complications, and learning that successes seldom satisfy fully or for long. As Max Weber maintained, "Politics is a strong and slow boring of hard boards. It takes both passion and perspective."[10] When times are darkest, politics can demand a hope beyond hope that leaps past conclusive reasons to surrender. When times are more normal, "Death Eaters" still lurk; and resistance requires persistence. As to systems that normalize themselves, dissenters who last long times often advise patience. They report that the more things stay the same, the more they change when eventually they do. In the meantime, a sense of joy in performing politics can help keep us going—can fuel our patience.

This is patience in the usual sense of keeping our perspectives and capacities of (political) judgment intact and attuned to the settings (more than ourselves), while waiting for apt moments to act. Undue patience is no virtue; yet needed patience can be scarce, and a virtue of the Potter books is their appreciation of this. Lately we've had many reasons to remind ourselves of Martin Luther King Jr.'s beautiful vision that "the arc of the moral universe is long, but it bends toward justice." The Potter saga gives Harry, Hermione, and Ron lots of opportunity to learn the long game. Thus sustaining patience is a major challenge when they're apparating around Britain to escape Death Eaters and snatchers. Yet patience seldom comes easily, if at all, to teenagers. On the run for months, the three students struggle to stay together in a micro-community that they need for mutual responsibility and support. Harry's no Hamlet (VII.502). Hermione and Ron don't often dither in indecision, either. Moreover they do wait with appropriate patience while Harry feels his way through the fateful choice between seeking hallows and horcruxes. All three have good reasons to bide their time in the (political) wilderness. But they do crave action, and their patience is too often in short supply. Eventually risk-taking does get them snatched and delivered to Death Eaters. What saves them begins with the irony of events when Wormtail's silver arm probably hesitates to kill Harry because he'd earlier shown mercy to Peter Pettigrew.

What generates appropriate patience in political action? Self-discipline and good humor help with patience, to be sure, and the full saga shows these developing in Harry and his friends. Nonetheless patience also gains greatly from a rich sense of irony.[11] This is the other aspect of political development that could be more evident in the heroic threesome and especially Harry. Irony isn't the same as sarcasm, which simply inverts or reverses literal meanings, usually in an edgy tone of voice. Nor does irony need to be bitter or condemnatory, as popular usages might imply. Irony is more complicated. Like Potter magic, irony recovers and redoes our figures. As a figure of speech, experience, or action, irony loosens and plays with literal meanings. This lets us hint at further implications and responses for those words, events, or deeds.[12]

As a device for plots and politics, irony of events abounds in the Potter books. When Professor Binns as an immaterial ghost rejects rumors of a Chamber of Secrets because history must address only "solid . . . fact," it's an irony of events (II.152). It's an irony of events that using horcruxes to become superhuman and immortal leaves Voldemort subhuman and ghostly, when Lily's love for Harry turns the Dark Lord's killing curse back on him (VI.497). And it's an irony of events for Harry to ignore a parting gift from his godfather, only to learn after the death of Sirius that the two-way mirror could've enabled safe communication to keep Sirius alive and others unharmed (V.523). Engaging such events almost has to give Harry some sense of irony.

Even by the epilogue, though, Harry shows little sign that he's developing capacities of irony for speech and action. Verbal and behavioral irony help hearten Ron and others who listen to *Potterwatch* broadcasts from Lee Jordan and Fred Weasley in particular. And such irony is a feature of Weasley folly overall. On their own, though, Harry, Ron, and Hermione don't manage much irony when eluding Death Eaters in the last book—or otherwise, for that matter. It'd be good to find resources of irony developing by our last looks at Harry, especially, and his friends.

Irony can help with self-examination, toleration, and other political virtues promoted by the Potter series. Especially it can nurture patience, and together they can sustain political action in dark times. A greater sense of irony might've given Harry the political capacity to cope more patiently with the visit by Aunt Marge early in book three. Weber's political plea for patience and persistence can come to mind when we read that "Aunt Marge's voice seemed to be boring into [Harry] like one of Uncle Vernon's drills" (III.28). This is one among many instances when Harry's political capacities for effective action could've been enhanced with more patience and thus more irony. Harry's political genius is to Just Do It. Yet a more ironical sensibility could help him attune his impulses to his situations. Harry's character certainly doesn't showcase this capacity for irony in the series epilogue; but politically, I like to imagine an adult Harry who's a little less earnest and at least a tad more ironical. With every reading, I hope more and more for glimpses of such a Harry, with a greater repertoire of refiguration available to him—if only as an example to us. Political action springs from many sources, but patience and irony can help keep it flowing effectively.

NOTES

1. This conclusion benefits from suggestions by Anna Lorien Nelson and Professor J. Gordon.

2. See John S. Nelson, *Politics in Popular Movies* (Boulder: Paradigm, 2015), 24–30; John S. Nelson, "Horror, Crisis, and Control: Tales of Facing Evils," *The Politics of Horror*, ed. Damien K. Picariello (New York: Palgrave Macmillan, 2020), 17–31.

3. I adapt this sense of *arrest* from Roland Barthes, *Mythologies*, ed. and trans. Annette Lavers (New York: Farrar, Straus and Giroux, 1957, 1972), 109–159, on 125.

4. See Valerie Estelle Frankel, ed., *Teaching with Harry Potter* (Jefferson, NC: McFarland, 2013).

5. Classical and literary connections, too, are prominent in Pottery: see Richard A. Spencer, *Harry Potter and the Classical World* (Jefferson, NC: McFarland, 2015); Beatrice Groves, *Literary Allusion in Harry Potter* (New York: Routledge, 2017).

6. See David Baggett and Shawn E. Klein, eds., *Harry Potter and Philosophy* (Chicago: Open Court, 2004); William Irwin and Gregory Bassham, eds., *The Ultimate Harry Potter and Philosophy* (New York: Wiley, 2010); Patrick McCauley, *Into the Pensieve* (Atglen, PA: Shiffer, 2015).

7. Even *His Dark Materials* by Philip Pullman has a Victorian setting. Moreover it focuses on religion and politics in "the Magisterium"—a take on the Roman Catholic Church as ruling an imaginary Britain, not a "Ministry of Magic" in communication with a British Prime Minister. See Philip Pullman, *The Golden Compass* (New York: Ballantine, 1995); Philip Pullman, *The Subtle Knife* (New York: Ballantine, 1997); Philip Pullman, *The Amber Spyglass* (New York: Ballantine, 1999).

8. See Joseph Campbell, *The Hero with a Thousand Faces* (New York: World, 1949).

9. *The Hobbit: An Unexpected Journey* (2012).

10. Max Weber, "Politics as a Vocation," *From Max Weber*, eds. H. H. Gerth and C. Wright Mills (New York: Oxford University Press, 1946), 77–128, on 128.

11. See John H. Schaar, "Power and Purity," *American Review* no. 19 (January 1974): 152–79.

12. See Søren Kierkegaard, *The Concept of Irony*, trans. Lee M. Capel (Bloomington: Indiana University Press, 1965); D. C. Muecke, *The Compass of Irony* (London: Methuen, 1969); Wayne C. Booth, *A Rhetoric of Irony* (Chicago: University of Chicago Press, 1974); Richard Rorty, *Contingency, Irony, and Solidarity* (Cambridge: Cambridge University Press, 1989).

Bibliography

Adatto, Kiku. 1993. *Picture Perfect* (New York: Random House).

Agamben, Giorgio. 2005. *State of Exception*, trans. Kevin Attell (Chicago: University of Chicago Press).

Albright, Madeleine, with Bill Woodward. 2018. *Fascism* (New York: HarperCollins).

Anatol, Giselle Liza, ed. 2003. *Reading Harry Potter* (Westport, CT: Praeger).

_____, ed. 2009. *Reading Harry Potter Again* (Santa Barbara: ABC-CLIO).

Anelli, Melissa. 2008. *Harry, A History* (New York: Simon and Schuster).

Applebaum, Anne. 2020. *Twilight of Democracy* (New York: Penguin Random House).

Arendt, Hannah. 1958. *The Human Condition* (Chicago: University of Chicago Press).

_____. 1963. *On Revolution* (New York: Viking, 1963).

_____. 1964. *Eichmann in Jerusalem* (New York: Viking Press).

_____. 1968. *Between Past and Future* (New York: Viking, 1963).

_____. 1968. *Men in Dark Times* (New York: Harcourt, Brace and World).

_____. 1971. "Thinking and Moral Considerations," *Social Research* 38, no. 3 (Autumn): 417–46.

_____. 1972. *Crises of the Republic* (New York: Harcourt Brace Jovanovich).

_____. 1973. *The Origins of Totalitarianism* (New York: Harcourt Brace Jovanovich).

Auden, W. H. 1976. *Collected Poems*, ed. Edward Mendelson (New York: Random House).

Auerbach, Nina. 1995. *Our Vampires, Ourselves* (Chicago: University of Chicago Press).

Austin, J. L. 1962. *How to Do Thing with Words*, ed. J. O. Urmson (New York: Oxford University Press).

Ayto, John. 1990. *Dictionary of Word Origins* (New York: Little, Brown).

Baggett, David, and Shawn E. Klein, eds. 2004. *Harry Potter and Philosophy* (Chicago: Open Court).

Barratt, Bethany. 2012. *The Politics of Harry Potter* (New York: Palgrave Macmillan).

Barthes, Roland.1972. *Mythologies*, trans. Annette Lavers (New York: Farrar, Straus and Giroux).

Baum, L. Frank. 1899. *The Wizard of Oz* (New York: HarperCollins).

Bear, Greg. 1990. *Heads* (New York: Tom Doherty Associates).

_____. 1997. *Slant* (New York: Tom Doherty Associates).

Beinhart, Larry. 1993. *American Hero* (New York: Ballantine).

Bell, Christopher E., ed. 2012. *Hermione Granger Saves the World* (Jefferson, NC: McFarland).

_____, ed. 2016. *From Here to Hogwarts* (Jefferson, NC: McFarland).

_____, ed. 2016. *Wizards vs. Muggles* (Jefferson, NC: McFarland).

Berman, Marshall. 1974. "Sympathy for the Devil: Faust, the '60s and the Tragedy of Development," *American Review* (January): 23–75.

Berra, Yogi, with Tom Horton. 1989. *It Ain't Over ...* (New York: Harper and Row).

Berry, Wendell. 1985. *Collected Poems, 1957–1982* (San Francisco: North Point Press, 1985).

Bhabha, Homi K., ed. 1990. *Nation and Narration* (New York: Routledge).

Billington, Sandra. 1984. *A Social History of the Fool* (New York: St. Martin's Press).

Booth, Wayne C. 1974. *A Rhetoric of Irony* (Chicago: University of Chicago Press).

Brake, Mark. 2017. *Science of Harry Potter* (New York: Racehorse Publishing).

Brenner, Lisa, ed. 2015. *Playing Harry Potter* (Jefferson, NC: McFarland).

Brown, Norman O. 1973. *Closing Time* (New York: Random House).

Burke, James Lee. 2011. *Feast Day of Fools* (New York: Pocket).

Callenbach, Ernest. 1975. *Ecotopia* (New York: Bantam).

Campbell, Joseph. 1949. *The Hero with a Thousand Faces* (New York: World).

Canovan, Margaret. 1981. *Populism* (New York: Harcourt Brace Jovanovich).

Carter, April. 1971. *The Political Theory of Anarchism* (New York: Harper and Row).

Cavell, Stanley. 1979. *The Claim of Reason* (New York: Oxford University Press).

_____. 1990. *Conditions Handsome and Unhandsome* (Chicago: University of Chicago Press).

_____. 2004. *Cities of Words* (Cambridge, MA: Harvard University Press).

Collins, Billy. 2005. "Statues in the Park," *New Yorker* 81, no. 21 (July 25): 76–77.

Collins, Jim. 1989. *Uncommon Cultures* (New York: Routledge).

Conway, Daniel. 1997. *Nietzsche and the Political* (New York: Routledge).

Crile, George. 2003. *Charlie Wilson's War* (New York: Grove Press).

Cuarón, Alfonso, dir. *Harry Potter and the Prisoner of Azkaban*. 2004; Burbank, CA: Warner Home Video, 2004, DVD.

Deleuze, Gilles. 1983. *Nietzsche and Philosophy*, trans. Hugh Tomlinson (New York: Columbia University Press).

Derrida, Jacques. 1974. Derrida, *Of Grammatology*, trans. Gayatri Chakravorty Spivak (Baltimore: Johns Hopkins University Press).

_____. 1978. *Spurs* (Chicago: University of Chicago Press).

Devall, Bill, and George Sessions. 1985. *Deep Ecology* (Salt Lake City: Peregrine Smith Books).

Diamond, Jared. 2005. *Collapse* (New York: Viking).

Dick, Philip K. 1980. *The Golden Man*, ed. Mark Hurst (New York: Berkley).

Djilas, Milovan. 1957. *The New Class* (New York: Praeger).

Eatwell, Roger, and Matthew Goodwin. 2018. *National Populism* (New York: Penguin Random House).

Eco, Umberto. 1983. *The Name of the Rose*, trans. William Weaver (New York: Harcourt Brace Jovanovich).

Edelman, Murray. 1988. *Constructing the Political Spectacle* (Chicago: University of Chicago Press).

Ehrenfeld, David W. 1981. *The Arrogance of Humanism* (Oxford: Oxford University Press).

Eichengreen, Barry. 2018. *The Populist Temptation* (New York: Oxford University Press).

Emerson, Ralph Waldo. 1983. *Essays and Lectures*, ed. Joel Porte (New York: Library of America).

Erikson, Erik H. 1958. *Young Man Luther* (New York: Norton).

———. 1969. *Gandhi's Truth* (New York: Norton).

Ferry, Luc. 1995. *The New Ecological Order*, trans. Carol Volk (Chicago: University of Chicago Press).

Firestone, Amanda, and Leisa A. Clark, eds. 2018. *Harry Potter and Convergence Culture* (Jefferson, NC: McFarland).

Flathman, Richard E. 1976. *The Practice of Rights* (New York: Cambridge University Press).

Foucault, Michel. 1970. *The Order of Things* (New York: Random House).

———. 1972. *The Archaeology of Knowledge* and *The Discourse on Language*, trans. A. M. Sheridan Smith (New York: Random House).

Fox, Warwick. 2006. *A Theory of General Ethics* (Cambridge: MA, MIT Press).

Frankel, Valerie Estelle. 2012. *Harry Potter, Still Recruiting* (Hamden, CT: Zossima Press).

———, ed. 2013. *Teaching with Harry Potter* (Jefferson, NC: McFarland).

———. 2019. *Fan Phenomena: Harry Potter* (Chicago: University of Chicago Press).

Friedman, Leslee. 2009. "Militant Literacy: Hermione Granger, Rita Skeeter, Dolores Umbridge, and the (Mis)use of Text," *Reading Harry Potter Again*, ed. Giselle Liza Anatol (Santa Barbara, CA: ABC-CLIO), 91–108.

Friedrich, Carl J., and Zbigniew K. Brezezinski. 1956. *Totalitarian Dictatorship and Autocracy* (New York: Praeger).

Frost, Robert. 1969. *The Poetry of Robert Frost*, ed. Edward Connery Lathem (New York: Henry Holt).

Gallardo-C., Ximena, and C. Jason Smith. 2003. "Cinderfella: J. K. Rowling's Wily Web of Gender," *Reading Harry Potter*, ed. Giselle Liza Anatol (Westport, CT: Praeger), 191–205.

Galston, William A. 2018. *Anti-Pluralism* (New Haven: Yale University Press).

Geertz, Clifford. 1964. "Ideology as a Cultural System," *Ideology and Discontent*, ed. David Apter (New York: Free Press), 47–76.

Gellner, Ernest. 2008. *Nations and Nationalism* (Ithaca, NY: Cornell University Press).

Gellner, Ernest, and Ghiţa Ionescu, eds. 1969. *Populism* (New York: Macmillan).

Gierzynski, Anthony, with Kathryn Eddy. 2013. *Harry Potter and the Millennials* (Baltimore: Johns Hopkins University Press).

Gladwell, Malcolm. 2002. *The Tipping Point* (Boston: Little, Brown).

Gleick, James. 1987. *Chaos* (New York: Viking Press).

Gramsci, Antonio. 2000. *The Antonio Gramsci Reader*, ed. David Forgacs (New York: New York University Press).

Granger, John. 2007. *Unlocking Harry Potter* (Wayne, PA: Zossima Press).

_____. 2009. *Harry Potter's Bookshelf* (New York: Berkley Books).

Gray, J. Glenn. 1977. "The Winds of Thought," *Social Research* 44, no. 1 (Spring 1977): 44–62.

Groom, Winston. 1986. *Forrest Gump* (New York: Simon and Schuster).

Groves, Beatrice. 2017. *Literary Allusion in Harry Potter* (New York: Routledge).

Gunnell, John G. 1968. *Political Philosophy and Time* (Middletown, CT: Wesleyan University Press).

_____. 1979. *Political Theory* (Cambridge, MA: Winthrop, 1979).

_____. 1986. *Between Philosophy and Politics* (Amherst: University of Massachusetts Press).

_____. 1993. *The Descent of Political Theory* (Chicago: University of Chicago Press).

_____. 1998. *The Orders of Discourse* (Lanham, MD: Rowman and Littlefield).

Gupta, Suman. 2009. *Re-Reading Harry Potter* (New York: Palgrave Macmillan).

Hales, Steven D., and Rex Welshon. 2000. *Nietzsche's Perspectivism* (Urbana: University of Illinois Press).

Hallett, Cynthia, and Peggy J. Huey, eds. 2012. *J. K. Rowling* (New York: Palgrave Macmillan).

Hariman, Robert. 1995. *Political Style* (Chicago: University of Chicago Press).

Hayles, N. Katherine, ed. 1991. *Chaos and Order* (Chicago: University of Chicago Press).

Heidegger, Martin. 1962. *Being and Time*, trans. John Macquarrie and Edward Robinson (New York: Harper and Row).

Heilbroner, Robert L. 1975. *An Inquiry into the Human Prospect* (New York: Norton).

Heilman, Elizabeth E. 2003. "Blue Wizards and Pink Witches: Representations of Gender Identity and Power," *Harry Potter's World*, ed. Elizabeth E. Heilman (New York: RoutledgeFalmer), 221–39.

Heilman, Elizabeth E. ed., 2003. *Harry Potter's World* (New York: RoutledgeFalmer).

Heller, Joseph. 1966. *Something Happened* (New York: Simon and Schuster).

Hobbes, Thomas. 1968. *Leviathan*, ed. C. B. Macpherson (New York: Penguin).

Hobsbawm, E. J. 1990. *Nations and Nationalism since 1780* (Cambridge: Cambridge University Press).

Hobsbawm, Eric, and Terence Ranger. 1984. *The Invention of Tradition* (Cambridge: Cambridge University Press).

Howe, Irving, ed., 1983. *1984 Revisited* (New York: Harper and Row).

Irwin, William, and Gregory Bassham, eds. 2010. *The Ultimate Harry Potter and Philosophy* (New York: Wiley).

Jacobs, Jane. 2004. *Dark Age Ahead* (New York: Random House).

Kellogg, Jean. 1975. *Dark Prophets of Hope* (Chicago: Loyola University Press).

Kierkegaard, Søren. 1965. *The Concept of Irony*, trans. Lee M. Capel (Bloomington: Indiana University Press).

Kim, Lorrie. 2016. *Snape* (Pekin, IL: Story Spring Publishing).

King, Laurie R. 1995. *To Play the Fool* (New York: Bantam).

―――. 2001. *Folly* (New York: Bantam).

King, Stephen. 2003. "Review of *Harry Potter and the Order of the Phoenix*," *Entertainment Weekly* (July 11, 2003): http://www.ew.com/ew/static/pdf/2007/03/stephenking.pdf.

Koestler, Arthur. 1963. *Darkness at Noon*, trans. Daphne Hardy (New York: Macmillan).

Kolbert, Elizabeth. 2014. *The Sixth Extinction* (New York: Henry Holt).

Kuhlmank, Susan. 1973. *Knave, Fool, and Genius* (Chapel Hill: University of North Carolina Press).

Le Guin, Ursula K. 1974. *The Dispossessed* (New York: Avon).

Leopold, Aldo. 1966. *A Sand County Almanac* (New York: Ballantine).

Lévi-Strauss, Claude. 1978. *Myth and Meaning* (New York: Schocken Books).

Lewis, C. S. 1955. *Surprised by Joy* (New York: Harcourt, Brace).

Lipset, Seymour Martin. 1979. *The First New Nation* (New York: Norton).

Littlefield, Henry M. n.d. "*The Wizard of Oz*," http://www.amphigory.com/oz.htm.

Louch, A. R. 1966. *Explanation and Human Action* (Berkeley: University of California Press).

Lovelock, James. 2000. *Gaia* (Oxford: Oxford University Press).

Lumet, Sidney, dir. *Network*, (1976; Burbank, CA: Warner Home Video, 2000), DVD.

Machiavelli, Niccoló. 1992. *The Prince*, ed. and trans. Robert M. Adams (New York: Norton).

Manlove, Colin. 2010. *The Order of Harry Potter* (Hamden, CT: Winged Lion Press).

Marx, Karl. 1977. *Selected Writings*, ed. David McLellan (New York: Oxford University Press).

McCauley, Patrick. 2015. *Into the Pensieve* (Atglen, PA: Shiffer).

McIntyre, Alasdair. 1984. *After Virtue* (Notre Dame, IN: University of Notre Dame Press).

―――. 1988. *Whose Justice? Which Rationality?* (Notre Dame, IN: University of Notre Dame Press).

McNeill, William H. 1995. *Keeping Together in Time* (Cambridge, MA: Harvard University Press).

Merchant, Carolyn. 1980. *The Death of Nature* (New York: Harper and Row).

―――. 1992. *Radical Ecology* (New York: Routledge).

―――. 1995. *Earthcare* (New York: Routledge).

Mill, John Stuart.1975. *On Liberty*, ed. David Spitz (New York: Norton).

Miller, David. 1984. *Anarchism* (London: J. M. Dent and Sons).

Mitzman, Arthur. 1969. *The Iron Cage* (New York: Grosset and Dunlap).

More, Thomas. 1992. *Utopia*, ed. Robert M. Adams (New York: Norton).

Muecke, D. C. 1969. *The Compass of Irony* (London: Methuen).

Mulholland, Neil. 2006. *The Psychology of Harry Potter* (Dallas: BenBella Books).

Müller, Jan-Werner. 2016. *What Is Populism?* (Philadelphia: University of Pennsylvania Press).

Naess, Arne. 1989. *Ecology, Community, and Lifestyle* (Cambridge: Cambridge University Press).

Nasaw, Jonathan. 1996. *The World on Blood* (New York, Penguin).

Nelson, John S. 1975. "Toltechs, Aztechs, and the Art of the Possible: Parenthetic Comments on the Political Through Language and Aesthetics," *Polity* 8, no. 1 (Fall): 80–116.

_____. 1976. *Ironic Politics* (Chapel Hill: unpublished PhD Dissertation for the University of North Caroline Department of Political Science).

_____. 1977. "The Ideological Connection: Or, Smuggling in the Goods, Parts I-II," *Theory and Society* 4, nos. 3-4 (Fall-Winter): 421–48 and 573–90.

_____. 1983. "Political Theory as Political Rhetoric," What Should Political Theory Be Now? ed. John S. Nelson (Albany: State University of New York Press), 169–240.

_____, ed. 1983. *What Should Political Theory Be Now?* (Albany: State University of New York Press).

_____, ed. 1986. *Tradition, Interpretation, and Science* (Albany: State University of New York Press).

_____. 1989. "Orwell's Political Myths and Ours," *The Orwellian Moment*, eds. Robert L. Savage, James E. Combs, and Dan D. Nimmo (Fayetteville: University of Arkansas Press), 11–44.

_____. 1998. *Tropes of Politics* (Madison: University of Wisconsin Press).

_____. 2003. "Prudence as Republican Politics in American Popular Culture," *Prudence*, ed. Robert Hariman (University Park: Pennsylvania State University Press), 229–57.

_____. 2013. *Popular Cinema as Political Theory* (New York: Palgrave Macmillan).

_____. 2015. *Politics in Popular Movies* (Boulder: Paradigm).

_____. 2017. "Humanism, Materialism, and Epistemology: Rhetoric of Economics as Styles in Action," *Humanism Challenges Materialism in Economics and Economic History*, eds. Roderick Floud, Santhi Hejeebu, and David Mitch (Chicago: University of Chicago Press), 224–55.

_____. 2018. *Cowboy Politics* (Lanham, MD: Lexington Books).

_____. 2020. "Horror, Crisis, and Control: Tales of Facing Evils," *The Politics of Horror*, ed. Damien K. Picariello (New York: Palgrave Macmillan,), 17–31.

Nelson, John S., and G. R. Boynton. 1997. *Video Rhetorics* (Urbana: University of Illinois Press).

Nelson, John S., and Barbara J. Hill. 1986. "Facing the Holocaust: Robert Arneson's Ceramic Myth of Postmodern Catastrophe," *Human Rights/Human Wrongs* eds. Robert Hobbs and Fredrick Woodard (Seattle: University of Washington Press), 189–209.

Nelson, John S., Allan Megill, and D. N. McCloskey, eds. 1987. *The Rhetoric of the Human Sciences* (Madison: University of Wisconsin Press).

Nelson, John S., and Anna Lorien Nelson, "Institutions in Feminist and Republican Science Fiction," *Legal Forum* 22, no. 4 (1998): 641–53.

Newell, Mike, dir. *Harry Potter and the Goblet of Fire*. 2005; Burbank, CA: Warner Home Video, 2006, DVD.

Nexon, Daniel H., and Iver B. Neumann, eds. 2006. *Harry Potter and International Relations* (Lanham, MD: Rowman and Littlefield).

Nichols, John. 1974. *The Milagro Beanfield War* (New York: Ballantine).

Nietzsche, Friedrich. 1956. *The Birth of Tragedy* and *The Genealogy of Morals*, trans. Francis Golffing (Garden City, NY: Doubleday).

———. 1967. *The Will to Power*, ed. Walter Kaufmann, ed. and trans. Walter Kaufman and R. J. Hollingdale (New York: Random House).

———. 1972. "On Truth and Falsity in Their Extramoral Sense," *Essays on Metaphor*, ed. Warren Shibles (Whitewater, WI: Language Press), 1–13.

———. 1979. *Friedrich Nietzsche on Rhetoric and Language*, ed. and trans. Sander L. Gilman, Carole Blair, and David J. Parent (New York: Oxford University Press).

———. 1982. *On the Advantage and Disadvantage of History for Life* trans. Peter Preuss (Indianapolis: Hackett).

Nolan, Christopher, dir. *The Dark Knight*. 2008; Burbank, CA: Warner Home Video, 2008, DVD.

Oakeshott, Michael. 1962. *Rationalism in Politics* (London: Methuen).

Oreskes, Naomi, and Erik M. Conway. 2014. *The Collapse of Western Civilization* (New York: Columbia University Press).

Orwell, George. 1946. *Animal Farm* (New York: New American Library).

———. 1982. "1984," *Orwell's Nineteen Eighty-Four*, ed. Irving Howe (New York: Harcourt Brace Jovanovich), 3–205.

Otto, Beatrice K. 2001. *Fools Are Everywhere* (Chicago: University of Chicago Press).

Palahniuk, Chuck. 1996. *Fight Club* (New York: Henry Holt).

Pettit, Philip. 2008. *Made with Words* (Princeton, NJ: Princeton University Press).

Phillips, Derek L. 1975. *Wittgenstein and Scientific Knowledge* (New York: Basic Books).

Pitkin, Hanna Fenichel. 1972. *Wittgenstein and Justice* (Berkeley: University of California Press).

———. 1999. *Fortune Is a Woman* (Chicago: University of Chicago Press).

Pollan, Michael. 1991. *Second Nature* New York: Dell).

———. 2013. *Cooked* (New York: Penguin).

Priest, Christopher. 1995. *The Prestige* (New York: Tom Doherty Associates).

Prinzi, Travis. 2008. *Harry Potter & Imagination* (Hamden, CT: Winged Lion Press).

———, ed. 2009. *Hog's Head Conversations* (Hamden, CT: Winged Lion Press).

Pullman, Philip. 1995. *The Golden Compass* (New York: Ballantine).

———. 1997. *The Subtle Knife* (New York: Ballantine).

———. 1999. *The Amber Spyglass* (New York: Ballantine).

Reagin, Nancy R., ed. 2011. *Harry Potter and History* (New York: Wiley).

Rice, Anne. 1976. *Interview with the Vampire* (New York: Ballantine).

Rickels, Laurence A. 1999. *The Vampire Lectures* (Minneapolis: University of Minnesota Press).

Robinson, Kim Stanley. 1990. *Pacific Edge* (New York: Tom Doherty Associates).

Rorty, Richard. 1989. *Contingency, Irony, and Solidarity* (Cambridge: Cambridge University Press).

————. 1998. *Achieving Our Country* (Cambridge, MA: Harvard University Press).

Rosenbaum, Ron. 1979. "Gooseflesh: The Strange Turn toward Horror," *Harper's Magazine* 259, no. 1552 (September): 86–92.

Ross, Alex. 2019. "The Eternal Return: Why Thinkers of Every Political Persuasion Keep Finding Inspiration in Nietzsche," *New Yorker* 95, no. 31 (October 14): 34–9.

Rowling, J. K. 1997. *Harry Potter and the Sorcerer's Stone* (New York: Scholastic Press).

————. 1999. *Harry Potter and the Chamber of Secrets* (New York: Scholastic Press).

————. 1999. *Harry Potter and the Prisoner of Azkaban* (New York: Scholastic Press).

————. 2000. *Harry Potter and the Goblet of Fire* (New York: Scholastic Press).

———— as Newt Scamander. 2001. *Fantastic Beasts and Where to Find Them* (New York: Scholastic Press).

————. 2001. *Quidditch through the Ages* (London: Bloomsbury).

————. 2003. *Harry Potter and the Order of the Phoenix* (New York: Scholastic Press).

————. 2005. *Harry Potter and the Half-Blood Prince* (New York: Scholastic Press).

————. 2007. *Harry Potter and the Deathly Hallows* (New York: Scholastic Press).

————. 2007. Rowling, *The Tales of Beedle the Bard* (New York: Scholastic Press).

————. 2012. *The Casual Vacancy* (New York: Little, Brown).

———— as Robert Galbraith. 2013. *The Cuckoo's Calling* (New York: Little, Brown).

———— as Robert Galbraith. 2014. *The Silkworm* (New York: Little, Brown).

————. 2016. *Fantastic Beasts and Where to Find Them: The Original Screenplay* (New York: Scholastic Press).

————. 2018. *Fantastic Beasts — The Crimes of Grindelwald* (New York: Scholastic Press).

Rushing, Janice Hocker, and Thomas S. Frentz. 1995. *Projecting the Shadow* (Chicago: University of Chicago Press).

Sagan, Carl. 1985. *Contact* (New York: Pocket).

Sandburg, Carl. 1916. *Chicago Poems* (New York: Henry Holt).

Saxena, Vandana. 2012. *The Subversive Harry Potter* (Jefferson, NC: McFarland).

Schaar, John H. 1974. "Power and Purity," *American Review* no. 19 (January): 152–79.

Schumpeter, Joseph. 1950. *Capitalism, Socialism and Democracy* (New York: Harper and Row).

Scott, James C. 20120. *Two Cheers for Anarchism* (Princeton, NJ: Princeton University Press).

Searle, John R. 1969. *Speech Acts* (New York: Cambridge University Press).

_____. 1978. "Literal Meaning," *Erkenntnis* 13, no. 1 (July): 207–24.

Shklar, Judith N. 1957. *After Utopia* (Princeton, NJ: Princeton University Press).

_____. 1977 "Rethinking the Past," *Social Research* 44, no. 1 (Spring): 80–90.

Sims, Jean, ed. 2012. *The Sociology of Harry Potter* (Hamden, CT: Zossima Press).

Snyder, Gary. 1986. *Left Out in the Rain* (San Francisco: North Point Press).

Snyder, Timothy. 2017. *On Tyranny* (New York: Penguin Random House).

_____. 2018. *The Road to Unfreedom* (New York: Penguin Random House).

Southworth, John, and Joan Southworth. 1998. *Fools and Jesters at the English Court* (Stroud, UK: Sutton).

Spencer, Richard A. 2015. *Harry Potter and the Classical World* (Jefferson, NC: McFarland).

Spinrad, Norman. 1967. *Agent of Chaos* (New York: Popular Library).

Spragens, Thomas A. 1973. *The Politics of Motion* (Lexington: University of Kentucky Press).

Stambaugh, Joan. 1972. *Nietzsche's Thought of Eternal Return* (Baltimore: Johns Hopkins University Press).

Stavrianos, L. S. 1976. *The Promise of the Coming Dark Age* (San Francisco: W. H. Freeman).

Straub, Peter. 1979. *Ghost Story* (New York: Simon and Schuster).

Strong, Tracy B. 1975. *Friedrich Nietzsche and the Politics of Transformation* (Berkeley: University of California Press).

Swain, Barbara. 1932. *Fools and Folly during the Middle Ages and the Renaissance* (New York: Columbia University Press).

Thorne, Jack, script; with story by J. K. Rowling, John Tiffany, and Jack Thorne. 2016. *Cursed Child: Parts I and II* (New York: Scholastic Press).

Traschen, Isadore. 1960. "Pure and Ironic Idealism," *South Atlantic Quarterly* 59, no. 2 (Spring): 163–70.

Vacca, Roberto, 1973. *The Coming Dark Age*, trans. J. S. Whale (Garden City, NY: Doubleday).

Waismann, Friedrich. 1968. *How I See Philosophy*, ed. Rom Harré (New York: St. Martin's Press).

Walzer, Michael. 1983. *Spheres of Justice* (New York: Basic Books).

Warren, Mark E. 1988. *Nietzsche and Political Thought* (Cambridge, MA: MIT Press).

Warrren, Robert Penn. 1953 *All the King's Men* (New York: Random House).

Weber, Max. 1946. *From Max Weber*, eds. and trans. H. H. Gerth and C. Wright Mills (New York: Oxford University Press).

_____. 1968. *On Charisma and Institution Building*, ed. S. N. Eisenstadt (Chicago: University of Chicago Press).

Welsford, Enid. 1961. *The Fool* (Garden City, NY: Doubleday).

Whited, Lana A., ed. 2004. *The Ivory Tower and Harry Potter* (Columbia: University of Missouri Press).

Williams, Paul V. A., ed. 1979. *The Fool and the Trickster* (Totowa, NJ: Rowman and Littlefield).

Winch, Peter. 1958. *The Idea of a Social Science, and Its Relation to Philosophy* (New York: Humanities Press).

Wittgenstein, Ludwig. 1958. *Philosophical Investigations*, trans. G. E. M. Anscombe (New York: Macmillan).

Wolff, Robert Paul. 1970. *In Defense of Anarchism* (New York: Harper and Row).

Wolosky, Shira. 2010. *The Riddles of* Harry Potter (New York: Palgrave Macmillan).

Yates, David, dir. *Harry Potter and the Half-Blood Prince*. 2009; Burbank, CA: Warner Home Video, 2009, DVD.

Yeats, William Butler. 1956. *The Collected Poems of W. B. Yeats* (New York: Macmillan).

Zamiatin, Yevgeny. 1924. *We*, trans. Gregory Zilboorg (New York: Dutton).

Zijderveld, Anton C. 1982. *Reality in a Looking-Glass* (London: Routledge and Kegan Paul).

Zolberg, Aristide R. 1972. "Moments of Madness," *Politics and Society* 2, no. 2 (Winter): 183–207.

Index

PEOPLE

Arendt, Hannah, 32, 40n3, 68, 104, 192, 197–99, 202, 206, 214, 243–46, 275
Aristotle, 114n17, 274

Barratt, Bethany, 6
Barthes, Roland, 142n18, 281n3
Baum, L. Frank, 7
Beatles, 39, 69n2, 214
Berry, Wendell, 59
Brown, Norman O., 24
Burke, Edmund, 230–32
Bush, George W., 17, 162

Camus, Albert, 275
Cavell, Stanley, 50, 57, 61, 89, 96–97, 108

Darwin, Charles, 66–68, 119, 140n2
Derrida, Jacques, 108
Dostoevsky, Fyodor, 275

Emerson, Ralph Waldo, 50, 57, 61, 89, 96–97, 118, 130, 132, 233
Erikson, Erik, 110

Flathman, Richard, 108

Foucault, Michel, 108, 195
Frost, Robert, 106, 145

Gandhi, Mahatma, 110
Geertz, Clifford, 40n3
Gladwell, Malcolm, 221–22
Gramsci, Antonio, 40n3
Gunnell, John G, 2, 108

Hegel, G. W. F., 109
Heidegger, Martin, 108
Hitler, Adolf, 5, 19, 29, 72, 118–21, 221, 243–45, 277
Hobbes, Thomas, 108–9, 114n17, 192–95, 242, 254–55, 274

Jefferson, Thomas, 208

Kafka, Franz, 197
Kant, Immanuel, 180
Kierkegaard, Søren, 104
King, Martin Luther, Jr., 280
King, Stephen, 1, 15, 199
Kipling, Rudyard, 203
Koestler, Arthur, 243

L'Amour, Louis, 1
Leopold, Aldo, 181
Lewis, C. S., 277

293

POLITY

POTTERY

About the Author

John S. Nelson professes political theory and communication at the University of Iowa. He has written *Video Rhetorics* (1997), *Tropes of Politics* (1998), *Popular Cinema as Political Theory* (2013), *Politics in Popular Movies* (2015), and *Cowboy Politics* (2018). Also, he has edited three books on political theory and epistemology; *Poroi*, an ejournal on rhetoric in culture, inquiry, and politics; and book series on New Practices of Inquiry (Chicago) and Rhetoric of the Human Sciences (Wisconsin).